1001

HOUSEHOLD
QUESTIONS ANSWERED

1001

HOUSEHOLD
QUESTIONS ANSWERED

HAMLYN

This book makes use of some material from books previously
published by Reed Consumer Books Limited

The publishers would like to thank the Energy Efficiency Office
for kind permission to use their diagrams as a basis for the
illustrations on pages 245 and 247

First published 1992
Hamlyn is an imprint of Reed Consumer Books Limited
Michelin House, 81 Fulham Road
London SW3 6RB
part of Reed International Books

A catalogue record for this book is available from the British
Library

ISBN 0 600 57520 9

Printed in Slovenia

Contents

Introduction

1001 HOUSEHOLD QUESTIONS ANSWERED contains a wealth of information on family and consumer matters. Written by a team of contributors who are acknowledged experts in their field, it provides solutions to a variety of domestic problems from stopping a dripping tap to protecting your home against intruders and offers sensible advice on a great range of subjects from writing difficult letters to giving parties.

The book is divided into 11 chapters, and begins with the all-important subject of health. KEEPING HEALTHY AND FIT shows how to achieve a balanced diet by sensible eating and describes the benefits of regular exercise. It tackles the problem of stress – both at home and at work – underlining the importance of a positive approach to life. The sections on pregnancy and childcare provide a useful guide to parenthood and the physical and mental development of the young child. After a comprehensive survey of common ailments the chapter on MEDICAL MATTERS discusses the treatment of a sick child, ending with a practical section on first aid and medical emergencies.

In FOOD AND COOKING the emphasis is on healthy eating, and the author describes the selection and preparation of all kinds of food from fish and shellfish, meat, poultry and game to the pastas which are becoming such a familiar part of our diet. CLEANING has a fund of useful tips on general cleaning and maintenance, including removing stains from fabrics and getting rid of household pests.

DIY AND HOME MAINTENANCE begins with a note on safety and security and then goes on to explain how to look after your property and how to decorate. The chapter concludes with some useful information on energy conservation, plumbing and central heating, and electricity, including tips on mending household appliances.

PARTIES AND FAMILY OCCASIONS shows how to organize the important events of life – weddings, funerals and christenings – and also provides some expert advice on dinner parties and children's parties. GARDENING describes how to create and maintain a fine garden, with particular emphasis on the flower garden, container and patio gardening, and the kitchen garden. COMMUNICATIONS offers a useful range of information on such topics as letter writing in general, job applications, fax machines and personal computers, and using the home as an office.

MONEY provides expert advice on ordering your personal finances, including general household budgeting, dealing with banks and building societies and using credit cards to the best advantage. It also contains detailed information on buying and selling a home, insurance and ways of saving. KNOWING YOUR RIGHTS advises the consumer about the law of contract as it applies to shopping in the supermarket, by mail order or by doorstep purchase. It also shows how to cope with repairs and services, how to complain to public utilities, and how to tackle holiday problems and noisy neighbours.

The chapter on LEGAL AFFAIRS deals with the law as it affects us, taking into account the most recent legislation, and covers a range of topics from accidents and personal injuries to marriage and divorce, motoring, and work and employment.

1 Keeping Healthy and Fit

INTRODUCTION

'How are you?' That question, in many different languages, is the almost universal way in which people greet each other. It is not just an enquiry after health, for after all we do not normally work on the assumption that people will be ill, but is one about general well-being.

How we feel and our well-being are scarcely separable. The problem is, however, how do we manage to attain the state of feeling good?

Clearly we can have no control over the blows that fate chooses to deal us, but we have a lot of control over how we treat our bodies and minds. If we are fit, we are likely to feel physically at ease, and less likely to succumb to ordinary illnesses. Then once we have experienced regular fitness, we are usually uncomfortable if we let it slip away, feeling out of sorts with the stale and sluggish feeling that follows. In this respect our bodies are a bit like cars: a well-serviced vehicle both runs well and sounds well, but one with dirty points, mucky oil and a badly tuned engine complains and labours all the time. Likewise, if we let ourselves get 'overweight', we are just that – carrying around more weight than we were made for. Every extra kilo of fat beyond our optimum weight is a 1000-gram burden distributed around the body – usually in those areas where it looks worst.

The key to both fitness and eating is balance. The dangers of overdieting are well recognized, but over-exercising can be harmful, too. It can cause injury, and leads to fatigue and greater susceptibility to illness. But both exercise and sensible eating have their place in the well-balanced lifestyle that is the root of happy living.

In our modern lives what most commonly takes us away from this well-being is stress. Stress is literally the application of pressure to one part of a structure. If the structure is strong and well made it can cope, and so too if we are fit and have plenty of energy we can cope with the stresses in our lives. But if we are tired or lethargic we are liable to give into stress. Stress itself is unavoidable; the problems arise when we give in to it. Then there is a vicious downward spiral: unhappiness leads to our letting ourselves go physically, to binge eating, and to illness, all of which make it harder to deal with stress. If, on the other hand, we lead a harmonious life, in which a sensible attitude to work, creative use of leisure, fitness and healthy eating all play their part, we are more likely to answer the question as to how we are with a genuinely enthusiastic 'Great!'

A Balanced Diet

In the Renaissance painters would portray their ideal females as beauties whose large amounts of flesh would keep them firmly out of any fashion magazine today. This taste prevailed into Victorian times, with the coining of the death-invoking term 'wraith-like' to describe the thin. But ideas of the desirable change, and what was once seen as a becoming roundness is now regarded as an undesirable fatness.

It can be argued that this is not simply a matter of fashion. Being overweight is a sure way of shortening your life expectancy. It can put a strain on the heart, lead to shortness of breath, give you high blood pressure and prevent you exercising your muscles in the way that they need in order to remain strong. It also stops you feeling good, in that the body is sluggish and lacking in energy.

The truth is that one needs to find the right balance. Apart from the psychological problem of anorexia, overweight is a greater problem in the West for the average employed person than undernourishment.

What actually is overweight is a personal thing, as there is no simple rule as to what is the right weight for a 5 ft 6 in woman or a 6 ft man – some people naturally have wider bodies than others. However, there is now a standard chart which gives guidance to desirable weights according to height and frame, and it provides a good starting point. Apart from that, the ability to look at yourself in the mirror without prejudice is the best guide: you can see if you are bulging in the wrong places. You can also certainly sense from your general feelings if you seem to be carrying round a few more kilos than you should.

THE BODY'S BUILDING BLOCKS AND FUEL

'Counting the calories' is now a familiar term for a way of assessing how much food we are eating. A calorie (abbreviated in figures to kCal as it is strictly a 'kilocalorie') is really a fuel measure, indicating the food value of a certain amount of a given substance. Pound for pound, some foods contain far more calories than others.

Certain numbers of calories are regarded as necessary to an adequate diet. Consume substantially fewer and you will become undernourished; consume more and they will cling on to you as fat. As you would expect, the amounts vary from individual to individual, depending upon their height and their notionally correct weight. For adults the normal requirement to maintain a good body weight is in the range of 1900 to 3500 calories, women requiring less than men, old people less than young. Lifestyle also determines needs: someone with a sedentary job requires fewer than someone who is physically active all day, for the simple reason that the active person is using more. If you do not know where you fit on the scale you can take medical advice first as to what figure is right for you.

Calorie counting, though, is not enough to ensure healthy eating. It is possible to consume the right number of calories for your size, but to be malnourished. This is because a calorie is only a measure of energy. We need not only different types of energy, which are mainly provided by carbohydrates and fat, but also protein to provide the building materials for the tissues of the body, including the brain, and vitamins to enable other foodstuffs to work properly. On top of that we have to consume a certain amount of 'roughage' or fibre.

We hear so much today about the evils of fat and carbohydrate that it is tempting to split foodstuffs into good and bad. However, we need all of them, in the right proportions. The trouble is that too much of any of them upsets the body's balance – it is even possible to get a form of poisoning from an excess of certain vitamins. The problem today is that many people eat too much of certain kinds of fat and carbohydrate, which especially congregate in those foods which are most tempting and which we are likely to overeat – the 'naughty but nice' syndrome.

The carbohydrates we eat come almost entirely in the form of starch, found in grains and legumes, and sugar, found naturally in fruit, dairy produce and vegetables, but produced on a huge scale as refined sugar. It is in this latter form that it is harmful because such large amounts of it are consumed, not only as table sugar, but in sweetened drinks, confectionery, and processed foods. This excess makes a major contribution to overweight, heart disease and sometimes to diabetes.

That sugary cream bun that you might have been thinking of eating carries a second potentially lethal weapon. Fats are essential to us, forming an excellent and efficient form of energy, and performing vital functions that cannot be carried out by other foodstuffs. The downside is that they are rich in calories.

To avoid another health hazard you have to differentiate between the three varieties of dietary fat: saturated, mono-unsaturated and polyunsaturated, according to their chemical constitution. Too much saturated fat, which is mainly found in meat, eggs and dairy products such as cream, promotes heart disease by loading the arteries with cholesterol. And heart disease is one of the main killers of people under 65 in the West, though with greater awareness of the role of diet, the incidence has started to fall.

Meat and dairy products are also a good source of protein, but they are not the only ones. Protein exists in all living tissue, plants as well as animals. The highest concentrations are found in meat and fish, but perfectly adequate amounts can be obtained from grains, pulses, nuts and many vegetables.

With vitamins the story becomes more complex, as there are fourteen major ones, all performing different functions, often in ways that scientists still do not fully understand. They are mainly found in fruit, vegetables and milk. Some are destroyed by heat, so a well-balanced diet has to include raw fruit and vegetables.

Finally, we need various minerals to keep the body in balance, most notably iron and salt. Unfortunately, although we could not survive completely without salt, nowadays we tend to get far too much of it, as it is commonly added to processed foods, whether tinned items such as baked beans, or dry snacks like crisps. Too much salt raises again the prospect of our old enemy, heart disease, as it constricts the arteries, leading to the increased possibility of heart attacks or strokes.

TRIMMING THE FAT

Taken by weight, fat contains over twice as many calories as protein or complex carbohydrate. Bodybuilders, boxers and other athletes looking to increase their size and physical strength therefore train on diets rich in fats, but the rest of us need to watch them. This does not just apply to foods that are obviously fatty: the oil in nuts is a form of fat, and a packet of cashew nuts is about the most waist-expanding nibble you can consume.

If you think that you might be consuming too much fat – and if you have an average Western diet you will be – there are several steps that you can take:

* use skimmed milk instead of full-fat milk
* cut out cream in favour of low-fat yoghurt, or better none at all. Do not replace it with Greek-style yoghurt, as it has cream added
* substitute vegetable margarine or low-fat spread for butter
* choose low-fat cheese, especially cottage cheese, in salads or sandwiches
* go for lean cuts of meat and discard all visible fat
* avoid nuts, unless you are vegetarian
* use vegetable oils in cooking and for salad dressings, rather than butter or lard
* keep away from cakes, biscuits, pastries, pies, chocolate, and most sweets.

There is some controversy now over the substitution of margarine for butter, as it has been claimed that margarine contains a substance that inhibits the natural chemical processes in the blood stream that break down cholesterol, but most doctors and scientists are not convinced.

Do not assume that all products that are derived from vegetable oil are free from saturated fats. If the food label says 'hydrogenated' vegetable oil, then it has been subject to a process that makes it chemically the same as animals fats. 'Polyunsaturated' oils, such as sunflower or safflower, actually lower cholesterol, while mono-unsaturated ones, such as olive oil, have no effect on it, either way.

CUTTING THE SWEET TOOTH

The average person in Britain consumes 100 g/4 oz of sugars a day, but the recommended maximum is only 60 g/2¼ oz, and you can manage perfectly well without it altogether. The rest goes on our waistlines.

Most of it is in the form of refined sugar, which is not only high in calories, but in 'empty' ones, meaning that the sugar has little or no other nutrients. Refined sugar is the great enemy of the overweight, doing little more than giving a quick energy fix and adding more bulk to their frames. It should therefore be resisted firmly. This is not always easy, for while the sugar you are putting in tea or coffee is perfectly obvious, it pops up all over the place, including many places where you might not expect it.

Watch out for the following:
* sweetened proprietary drinks, whether fizzy or still; they usually contain several spoonfuls of sugar per can or small carton
* confectionery
* canned fruit in syrup
* cereals with added sugar
* jams and conserves, especially ones not advertised as 'low-sugar'
* all canned food with sugar listed as a constituent.

It pays to get in the habit of reading food value labels, as sugar is so frequently added. Ingredients are always listed in order of relative proportion, so the nearer 'sugar' is to the top of the list, the greater proportion of the item it constitutes. Look out for 'fructose' and 'glucose' too, which are the chemical names of the two simple sugars that make up table sugar. There are alternatives to sugar, quite apart from the artificial sweeteners. Use honey on cereals, and dried fruit in baking.

HIGH AND LOW CALORIE FOODS

High calorie (per 100 g/4 oz)		Low calorie (per 100 g/4 oz)	
Cashew nuts 610	Deep-fried scampi 450	Celery sticks 10	Canned sweetcorn 80
Milk chocolate 600	Cheesecake 430	Tomatoes 16	Cottage cheese 100
Double cream 510	Pork pie 420	Fresh apricots 20	Plain boiled potato 100
Cheddar cheese 480	French fries 330	Low-fat yogurt 75	Peeled prawns 120
Roast breast of lamb 470	Avocado pear 260	Baked beans 80	Chicken breast 160

ALCOHOL

Liquid consumption is often overlooked by dieters. While sufficient fluid intake is extremely important for correct body functioning, especially of the kidneys, taking in too much liquid in the course of the day can create fluid retention, which may often contribute to weight gain. It may not be enough to replace sweetened drinks; watch the number of unsweetened cups of tea or coffee too.

Keeping an eye on liquid intake also includes alcohol, of course. Regular heavy consumption launches a two-pronged attack on your health. It produces high blood pressure, putting strain on the heart, and over a long period of time can cause severe and irreversible damage to the liver.

Alcoholic drinks are high in calories. Alcohol actually has more calories per gram than sugar – seven as against four. This applies to all alcoholic drinks, and while they may not produce the obvious stomach of the beer drinker, wine and spirits also add on weight. Like sugar's, these calories are 'empty', so that the heavy drinker who eats little may take in plenty of calories, but can suffer from malnutrition. And if that were not bad enough, alcohol limits the body's ability to absorb some important vitamins, so the full effects of what is eaten are lost.

The government has supplied simple guidelines of what is a safe amount for the average person to drink each week. This is measured in units of alcohol, a unit being half a pint of beer, a glass of wine or a measure of spirits. The recommended maximums are 21 units for a man and 14 for a woman. The reason for the difference is that on average women have more fat and less water in their bodies than men, with the result that alcohol stays in their bodies for longer, and in a more concentrated form. Don't be soft on yourself when adding up these units. The measures of wine and spirits are based on what you would get in a pub, not on the more generous quantities that most people pour at home.

Medical experts advise that it is better not to drink for a couple of days in the week than to consume a steady amount each night. This gives the body the chance to flush out the alcohol altogether.

A Sensible Diet

Snacking and bingeing are inconsistent with healthy eating. You may not need to lose weight yet, but if you are prone to nibble between meals, you may well be heading for that situation.

Eating regular meals is not a matter of establishing a boring routine, but is a way of giving the body the amounts of food it needs in the way it is best equipped to deal with them. Cutting out a meal can mean that by the time you get to eat, you are extremely hungry and eat a lot of food very quickly. Although the end result may not in itself make you any fatter, it certainly does not lead to the sense of feeling good that we are looking for, but produces a bloated sensation. Not eating regular meals is also more likely to make you snack instead, and one of the problems with snacks is that they are often just those sugary or fatty foods that help us put on weight without providing good nourishment.

This means starting the day with a good breakfast. This is the meal most commonly missed, but without it you will be low in energy by mid-morning. You then have the choice of either soldiering on, and making yourself tired, or consuming a cake, chocolate bar or biscuit that will provide an instant energy high, only to leave the energy levels even more depleted two hours later.

THE OVERWEIGHT TEST

Be really honest with yourself. Do you ever:

- nibble between meals?
- binge if you feel depressed, for 'comfort'?
- help yourself to seconds when you're not really hungry?
- skip proper meals and then indulge your hunger with easy-access junk foods?
- eat too many fatty, sugary foods?

If you answer 'yes' to two or more questions you are probably overweight.

Try not to eat too late at night. This is not only bad for the digestion, but there is also less chance to shift calories before you go to bed. Above all, eating regularly satisfies the hunger and makes you less likely to binge.

If, however, you cannot get through the day without some snacks, then prepare some celery or carrots in advance, or take an apple or orange with you.

BALANCED MENUS

Day 1

Breakfast   3 apricots or prunes with 150 ml/5 fl oz natural yogurt

Lunch   1 jacket potato topped with 50 g/2 oz cottage cheese with chives

Supper   100 g/4 oz lamb's liver, grilled or fried in a minimum of sunflower oil, with mushrooms, sliced green beans and 2 new potatoes

Day 2

Breakfast   1 slice wholemeal toast topped with 25 g/1 oz grated Edam cheese and grilled with 1 tomato

Lunch   1 hardboiled egg, sliced, with 1 teaspoon low-calorie mayonnaise, sprinkled with mustard and cress and served with plenty of mixed salad, accompanied by 2 crispbreads or slices of melba toast

Supper   100 g/4 oz monkfish, marinated in lemon juice and herbs and grilled as a kebab with spring onions and pieces of red pepper, and served with rice

Day 3

Breakfast   100 ml/4 fl oz freshly squeezed orange juice, 1–2 Weetabix with skimmed milk

Lunch   1 wholemeal bap filled with 50 g/2 oz corned beef, 1 teaspoon of your favourite pickle and lettuce and tomato

Supper   100 g/4 oz chicken breast, brushed with clear honey and spread with grain mustard, and baked, with broccoli spears and carrots

Day 4

Breakfast   Fresh fruit salad with a variety of fruits in season or compôte of stewed fruit, 1 slice wholemeal bread, toasted, with Marmite

Lunch   Salad of cooked brown rice, sweetcorn, beetroot and sardines

Supper   100 g/4 oz beef sausages, grilled, served with steamed cauliflower florets, grilled onion rings and tomato

Day 5

Breakfast   1 baked apple

Lunch   1 wholemeal pitta bread filled with tongue, sliced olives and shredded lettuce

Supper   100 g/4 oz salmon steak, foil-baked with herbs and cucumber, served with boiled potato and French beans

Day 6

Breakfast   Kipper kedgeree

Lunch   Celery sticks and 50 g/2 oz Brie

Supper   Baked aubergine stuffed with lean mince, tomato and chickpeas

Day 7

Breakfast   2 rings of fresh pineapple with 50 g/2 oz curd cheese

Lunch   Eggs and cress wholemeal sandwiches

Supper   Fillet of lamb, grilled, with diced root vegetables and stir-fried cabbage

---

How to balance your foods within these meals is a more tricky problem, but in July 1991 the Department of Health laid down daily nutrient intakes to meet the needs of most of the population.

As well as the figure of a maximum of 60 g/2¼ oz sugar already quoted, the report recommended 56 g/2 oz protein for men and 45 g/1½ oz for women, 70–80 g/2½–2¾ oz fat, 200–300 g/7–10 oz lactose (the form of sugar in milk products) and starches, and

18 g/½ oz dietary fibre. The amounts of vitamins varied from one to another, but in general terms we need a daily intake of vitamins A, B1, B2, B3, B6, B12, and C.

How food is cooked is important too. A potato baked in its jacket will provide necessary starch and some of the vitamins needed, but if you fry it instead you will remove most of the vitamins and whack in a dollop of fat. Stir-frying is an excellent way of cooking vegetables, meat, fish and seafood with only a minimum of fat while also preserving nutrients that may be destroyed in longer cooking methods. Other methods can be considered for other foods:

* steaming: good for vegetables, fish and shellfish
* grilling: small cuts of meat, chicken, fish and kebabs shed much of their fat
* dry frying: a special heavily ridged pan is good for steak, lean-mince burgers and chops, as the fat drains away
* baking: wrapping meat and fish in foil lets them cook without additional fat; likewise roasting bags for joints of meat
* pressure cooking: cooks vegetables quickly and, providing you follow the instructions, there is less chance of overcooking than when boiling.

DIETING

Dieting can become a fad, a form of obsession with food that is a close relative to the greed it supplants. There is evidence that many diets do not help in the long run, but lead only to short-term loss of weight that is then put on again soon after the diet ends. Much crash dieting produces a rapid loss of weight made up of water and glycogen rather than fat, which are quickly replaced from a normal diet. Over a long period of time crash dieting can have a harmful effect on the entire metabolism. It can also reduce the muscles, which if not exercised remain weak, and when weight is put on again it is in the form of fat.

Dieting should be seen as working in harness with exercise. While crash dieting will not go with heavy exercising as the one will be depriving the body of the sources of energy that the other needs, a well-toned and vigorous body will burn up the food that goes into it and establish a healthy metabolism.

Like exercise, dieting needs to be regular. You may find that you have to revise the eating habits of lifetime, which comes through developing an eating plan and becoming aware of what you eat. This awareness extends to how you feel, with the result that in time the gooey chocolate bar loses its appeal as you cease to enjoy the stodgy feeling it leaves in the stomach. Often the consequence is that you come to enjoy your treats more, because you eat them for the taste when you really want them, and not out of habit or in the search for comfort. It is important to continue to enjoy your food. A diet plan must be built around things you like eating, because otherwise you won't stick with it. It should also include variety.

Dieting to lose weight should not be very different from eating a sensible diet to stay healthy. The main difference is that you will be eating less and reducing the fattening foods in particular, rather than eating foods that you would not normally have. It is therefore more important to eat regularly, so as not to make yourself frequently hungry, and to observe the principles of a balanced diet.

Fasting is a drastic way of losing weight quickly, but you soon become light-headed and drained of energy. There is also no guarantee that the weight will not return afterwards. However, fasting for just one day on a regular but occasional basis, say once a month or once a quarter, can be beneficial. It helps lose a little weight as not only do you not eat for the day, but the stomach shrinks and you find you do not need to eat as much as usual for a day or so afterwards. It also purifies the system, giving the digestive tract the chance to eliminate all wastes. Do not, however, go without water, but sip regularly during the fast. Other drinks can do as well in terms of providing liquid, but bear in mind that fruit juices and tea or coffee with milk contain calories.

Here is a selection of suggestions for a week's balanced menus as part of a weight-loss plan. There is no need to stick rigidly to this, but you can regard it as a template on which you can substitute dishes of a similar nutritional make-up and calorie content. Add a dessert to either lunch or dinner in the form of fruit, either *au naturel* or as a fruit salad, with yoghurt or muesli, or stuffed with dried fruit.

Fitness

The initial question is: fit for what? The person aiming to run a marathon needs to reach a far more highly tuned physical condition than the one who just wants to be able to run for the bus without fighting for breath afterwards. But this is not to say that the marathon runner's condition is an ideal for everyone to aim at. The length and intensity of training that this requires places such a strain on the body that the ordinary person may feel physically tired for much of the time, and is likely to be susceptible to injury or illness – hardly the state that most people would regard as 'fit'. Most of us will happily settle for feeling healthy and full of energy, with an ease and flow to our movements.

'Exercise' is a relatively modern concept. Until this century most people did work which involved sustained physical effort, and even those who did not were likely to walk much more than their modern counterparts. For some today's sedentary lifestyle involves minimal physical effort, and this is now regarded as a major health hazard. It is as much of a problem as eating the wrong diet, suffering from stress, or even smoking. About 40 per cent of adults in the UK are overweight, and alarmingly increasing numbers of children are becoming so. No more than 10–15 per cent of the body's weight should consist of fat, but in the West the proportion is more likely to be 25–35 per cent.

The actual amount of progressive, vigorous exercise which experts advise as a basic requirement for keeping your body in adequate working order is quite small. It works out at 20–30 minutes at least three times a week – a total of about $1\frac{1}{2}$ hours, which is really not very much when you consider that most of us spend more than 50 hours a week asleep, and many of us 20 hours or more watching TV!

There's no mystique about getting your body into a trim, well-proportioned and healthy feeling condition. It's basically achieved in two ways:

* Eliminating excess body fat by eating the right kind of food, in the right balance to supply your body with all the nutrients it needs, in the right quantities to meet your energy requirements and no more.

* Toning and conditioning the muscles, to make them strong, flexible and resilient, by doing the right kind of exercise on such a regular basis that it becomes as much part of your everyday life as eating or sleeping.

Diet and exercise should not be regarded as alternatives, or as mutually exclusive: the quickest and most effective way to achieve – and, most important, keep – a state of physical fitness is by combining them.

THE BENEFITS OF EXERCISE

A heart working efficiently to provide the muscles with the nourishment they need plays a key role in any exercise programme. There is a mutual benefit as exercising the muscles improves the heart, which then serves the muscles better – and also makes you less prone to heart disease.

The extra demands made on the heart-pump by the exercising muscles for an increased volume of blood cause a dramatic rise in the heart rate. At rest, a normal heart beat will be about 72 contractions per minute. During strenuous exercise this may increase to 200 or so. Exercising regularly means that when the heart returns to its at-rest state after exercise, its rate will become lower, with fewer contractions per minute and lower demands made upon it. Body fitness also means that the heart rate returns to normal more quickly after exercise has been taken. Top athletes may have a resting heart rate as low as 38 beats per minute, but a heart-rate of 45–50 contractions per minute would indicate a state of fitness to be proud of.

Exercising regularly improves the efficiency of the lungs and heart as well as of the other muscles. There is evidence to show that exercise increases the size and strength of the heart and the elasticity and capacity of the lungs, and also enlarges the arteries, which dilate as they distribute blood to the working muscles. If you are also following a low-fat diet, you are cutting down on cholesterol, the fatty plaque-like substance which develops in the lining layer of the arteries, causing the narrowing and blocking which leads to cardiac arrest.

AEROBIC AND ANAEROBIC EXERCISE

'Aerobic', which means 'with oxygen', describes any exercise which relies for its performance on an increased supply of oxygen. By making special demands on the heart and lungs, aerobic exercise works to summon up the extra oxygen the muscles need to cope. 'Aerobics' are just one type of exercise; others are jogging and cycling.

Of all types of exercise, aerobic exercise does most to condition the way the heart, lungs and bloodstream supply the muscles with the oxygen and other nutrients needed to produce the energy they are required to expend. In this way, aerobic exercise is especially important for the development of muscular stamina, although it contributes significantly to flexibility and general muscle toning as well.

Unlike aerobic exercise, which is essentially more prolonged, anaerobic exercise does not rely on extra oxygen and is done in short periods or spurts – usually under 90 seconds in duration. This more static form of exercise characteristically involves individual muscle groups and, while effective for increasing muscle strength, does little for enhanced cardiovascular efficiency. Weight-lifting and callisthenic exercises like sit-ups and push-ups are a typical form of anaerobic exercise.

For overall fitness aerobic exercises are the ones to concentrate on, though anaerobic exercises are useful for toning specific muscles.

EXERCISE VALUES

When you embark on a fitness programme, some of the health-enhancing benefits you may enjoy include:

- Strengthened and enlarged heart muscle, whose fitness and pumping facility improve as it is made to work harder
- Increased volume and capacity of lungs, boosting oxygen intake and facilitating breathing
- Dilated arteries, enabling more oxygen-enriched blood to reach the muscles more quickly
- Reduced blood pressure levels
- Increased metabolic rate, burning up more calories, after and during exercise, and decreasing body fat

- Stretched and strengthened muscles, making for suppleness, stamina and good body support
- Enhanced skeletal tissue and bone mineral mass
- Increased energy and vitality

In addition, exercise may also help to:
- curb the appetite
- give up smoking
- control tension and stress
- create a sense of elation and well-being, by releasing the brain endorphins, the body's natural painkillers
- create quicker reflexes

Just as it needs to be done regularly, exercise should also be progressive. You cannot change the way your body works overnight – it's a gradual process.

A realistic but attractively varied exercise programme could look like this:
* 3 exercise sessions of 20–30 minutes a day, including warm-ups and cool-downs, either at home or in a fitness studio
* 1 weekly keep-fit, dance, yoga or aerobics class
* 1 weekly swim or jogging session plus plenty of brisk walking or cycling.

Easy does it Maintaining fitness is not just a matter of setting aside special times in the week, but is a way of life; remember that one of the main causes of ill health is our sedentary lifestyle. There are a surprising number of ways of incorporating gentle exercise into your daily round.

Climbing the stairs, for example, is excellent aerobic exercise, involving the same degree of exertion as relaxed running. In the same way, a brisk 20-minute walk every day is first-class exercise, so leave the car in the garage for those short trips to the shops. Alternatively, get on your bike! Cycling is obviously good exercise for the legs, but also benefits the upper body muscles. And many ordinary everyday tasks like cleaning the car, housework or gardening give muscles a good workout, especially if performed with a bit of vigour.

LOSING CALORIES THROUGH EXERCISE

A 10 stone/70 kg adult exercising for 15 minutes could expect calories used to work out as follows:

Walking slowly	55	Jogging	120
Cycling slowly	65	Cycling fast	168
Walking briskly	80	Running	200
Dancing energetically	85	Playing squash	230
Playing tennis	120	Swimming fast	255

EXERCISING REGULARLY

Becoming and staying fit means following a regular exercise routine, and not just doing it when you feel like it. This calls for commitment, and that means self-discipline.

Your motivation has to come essentially from you, from knowing that you are doing something really worthwhile for yourself. Encouragement from family and friends can be tremendously helpful in maintaining enthusiasm and not becoming disheartened. After a while it will be easy to stick to the routine as you come to prefer feeling fit to being unfit.

For exercises you decide to do by yourself at home, set aside a time that fits into your daily schedule easily. For example, if you are out at work all day, exercising when you return home, before sitting down to an evening meal, may be especially relaxing and invigorating. Some people find the idea of early morning exercise appealing, as a way of getting off to a good start, but it is not advisable to tax muscles that have not yet had a chance to warm up fully. You should not exercise for the first 20 minutes after rising, and over-strenuous exercise first thing may counteract the relaxing benefits of a good night's sleep. By the same token, exercising late at night may prove too stimulating and make it difficult for you to go to sleep easily.

Avoid exercising after soaking in a hot bath, when the muscles will be too relaxed to function at their best, or after a heavy meal, when making extra oxygen demands on the system will interfere with the digestive processes.

Joining a weekly exercise class at a set time on a set day is fun and a fine way of keeping yourself up to the mark on a regular basis.

CHOOSING YOUR EXERCISE

Walking Walking is strongly recommended as a basic component of any programme. Building up to 3–4 hours' brisk walking a week, and always ensuring at least 20 minutes per day, will show marked results in a matter of weeks. You should aim to be taking 90–120 steps per minute at the start of a walking exercise programme, and work up to a maximum of 140–150 steps per minute.

Walking has so many benefits and so much to offer:
* It can be enjoyed at any age
* Taking place in the open air, it is especially invigorating
* It is enjoyable both alone and in a group.

The disadvantages are that it leads to a limited level of fitness, and that it is not so enjoyable if you have to walk in the traffic fumes of city streets.

Jogging   When done correctly, jogging is excellent all-over exercise. Through the gently persistent, steady demands it makes on the body, it is especially beneficial to the cardiovascular system, increasing the capacity of the heart, speeding up the blood-flow to the muscles, flushing wastes from the arteries so that they expand and function better, and reducing cholesterol levels.

As with all exercise, you need to build up your jogging skills gradually and patiently. With jogging it is time, not speed or distance, that counts. 'Little and often' should be your golden rule. Don't make the mistake of trying to cover too much ground too soon: 5 minutes out and 5 minutes back is ample to begin with, increasing the time to $7\frac{1}{2}$ minutes out and back, until finally you build up to a 30-minute session, which you should practise at least 3 times a week.

As with other exercise, the secret is to make jogging part of your everyday routine. It is believed that jogging for 15–20 minutes a day over 18 months can *double* the elasticity and capacity of the arteries.

* Healthwise, jogging enhances the body system's ability to assimilate and make better use of oxygen
* It makes the joints more flexible through complete and constant movement of every part of the body
* Jogging can be done any time and in all weathers
* Apart from investing in a pair of good-quality jogging shoes and renewing them as necessary, it does not require expensive equipment.

The main disadvantage is that it stresses the lower limbs. Enthusiastic joggers are prone to knee and hamstring injuries.

Swimming   Swimming is often described as the perfect exercise. It is supremely relaxing, for the water counteracts the effect of gravity, making the body weightless. The water facilitates movement but at the same time provides natural resistance through its density. This serves to strengthen the muscles by making them work that much harder. *Fast* energetic swimming can burn up to three times as many calories as brisk walking.

Here are just some of its benefits:

* Swimming exercises all the major muscles of the body, improving overall flexibility, muscular strength and aerobic capacity
* Because the body is 'cushioned' by the water, risk of strain and injury is significantly less than in some other forms of exercise
* The force of gravity does not operate in the water, so there is no pressure on the joints, making swimming ideal exercise for people suffering from rheumatism or arthritis, or recovering from bone fractures
* Swimming is ideal for all age groups. Babies of 3–4 months who have had at least one polio immunization can be taken into the water by their mothers. It is never too late to learn to swim, either.

The main drawback is that you need water! Even if there is a pool near you, the times you can use it will be restricted, and there is also the expense. However, most pools offer reduced price season tickets.

Cycling Cycling is another superb form of cardiovascular exercise, considered by some experts to be as effective as running. It is splendid for all-over muscle toning and firming. As well as the strong, rhythmical, piston-like movement of the legs, the upper body is fully exercised as well, being used to balance and drive forward, while gripping the handlebars works on the arm and shoulder muscles.

The main problem with it is the cost of the bike – and a good quality one is essential for safety and long-term efficiency. However, if you use it instead of a car or public transport, in the long run it will save you money.

Rowing Rowing is excellent aerobic and firming exercise, though it is not advisable to take it up after the age 35, as it does impose extra strain on the back. Rowing is primarily powered by the back and leg muscles, especially the quadriceps at the front, and the hamstrings at the back of the thighs, with extensive use, too, of the arm, abdomen and buttock muscles. It therefore effects superb all-body muscle toning. For those who cannot join a club, rowing machines give an equally good aerobic workout on dry land, but without the bonus of the fresh air.

Exercising at home The shy, the busy, or those whose domestic commitments make it hard to get out need not forego exercise, as it is perfectly possible to do it at home, though it helps to be strong-minded as the distractions are considerable.

You need to choose a room that is warm in winter and cool in summer, with good ventilation and plenty of space. If it is not carpeted, then it is worth buying an exercise mat, so as to avoid slipping or hurting yourself if you do fall over.

Exercises suitable for doing on your own include sit-ups, stretches, leg-raises, bicycling in the air, press-ups, shoulder raises and turns. These are all good for toning muscles, and if you develop a 20- or 30-minute routine that leaves only short rest periods between each group of exercises, you will exercise aerobically too.

EXERCISE CLASSES

While exercising at home is particularly convenient because it can be done at any time to suit your general lifestyle and be fitted into the timetable of a particular day, joining an exercise class has many advantages too.

Regular classes help keep up morale and maintain motivation. A set time and place impose a discipline of their own, which makes a welcome change from self-starting exercise at home. However keen you are, there will always be times when you feel lazy, and at times like these there's nothing like a class to get you going!
* A class gets you out and about and brings you in contact with new people, which can be particularly welcome if you are housebound for any reason. If you are at home with small children, many classes provide crèche facilities.
* In a class you meet like-minded people with the same aims, and probably the same weaknesses and problem areas too!

* The common enthusiasm, energy and sheer body heat generated in a class are infectious and stimulating.

* Although in a class you are all working together, rather than in isolation, an element of friendly competition is often present too, and this can have very positive effects on the group as a whole.

* There are so many different kinds of exercise you can learn in class that there's no chance of getting bored.

* Some forms of exercise – yoga, for example – must be learned in class with a qualified teacher, to avoid the danger of strain and injury.

* Most important, you will be led by a teacher, whose role is not only to explain and demonstrate, but also to encourage, inspire, and transmit enthusiasm.

You're spoilt for choice when it comes to deciding what type of exercise class to join! Fitness studios, health clubs and sport and leisure centres will usually gladly allow you to sit in on a class to give you an idea of what's involved before you register.

WARMING UP AND COOLING DOWN

Both warming up and cooling down are very important before and after taking any exercise. Warming up stimulates the cardiovascular system: it gets the heart going, increases the circulation, and makes the increased blood-flow to the muscles gradual. This avoids the danger of pulls or strains which can occur when the muscles are overstressed. Warming the muscles gently increases their flexibility and loosens up the whole body ready for exercise.

Start all warm-ups by running on the spot for a minute or two, to speed up the heart rate – 100 beats per minute is ideal at this stage.

Now warm up the muscles all over your body progressively, starting with the lower legs and working methodically through the steps that follow.

1. Stand 1 m/3 ft away from a wall.
2. Keeping the feet flat on the floor, extend the arms and lean forward to touch the wall. Hold for 5 seconds.
3. Repeat 10 times.

Another excellent way of stretching the calf muscles is to:
1. Hold on to a table edge for support.
2. Bend your right leg at the knee and lunge backwards with your left leg, keeping it straight.
3. Holding the left leg in the straight position, *gradually and very gently* lower the heel of your left foot until it rests flat on the floor. Do not force your heel down. Hold to a count of 10.
4. Repeat with the other leg.
5. Do the exercise 5 times for each leg.

Here is an exercise for stretching the Achilles tendons which joggers will find specially useful:
1. Stand on a brick or thick book (a telephone directory is ideal) with your toes near the edge and your heels jutting out.
2. Supporting yourself by holding on to a table edge, gradually lower both heels until they are flat on the floor.
3. Slowly rise on to tiptoe, then repeat the exercise 10 times.

To loosen the lower back:
1. Lie flat on the floor, both legs out straight in front of you.
2. Clasp one knee with both hands and pull the knee as far into your chest as possible.
3. Repeat 10 times for each leg.

Local authorities run extensive exercise programmes catering for all those wishing to improve their general physical condition. You can find out all about these by inquiring at your local adult education college, library, or sports and leisure centre.

Keep fit The Keep Fit Association aims to encourage the understanding of the principles of movement, as well as exercise participation. Teachers specially trained in body mechanics and the use of music in exercise, as well as first aid, coach classes which still reflect the source of their founder's inspiration: the exercises are based on the movements of gymnastics – turns, stretches bends, lunges, etc. – rather than of dance. Devices such as hoops, balls, clubs and skipping ropes are used as part of exercise performance and add to the interest of classes.

Aerobics Although, as discussed earlier, any form of sustained exercise requiring extra oxygen is correctly described as 'aerobic', the word 'aerobics' is most often colloquially used to describe a fast-paced, demanding, competitive and achievement-oriented style of exercise.

Aerobics became fashionable in the 1970s, when Jane Fonda did much to give them their fashionable image. In fact the fast pace of this type of exercise can actually involve a quite high strain risk, and a form of 'low-impact' aerobics is now often preferred in classes, certainly for beginners.

Aerobics are tremendously popular because they are exciting, racy and full of variety. They draw on jazz dance, ballet, gymnastics and yoga for the exercise techniques they teach, to strongly pulsing, rhythmical music: musical tempo is a vital part of the enjoyment of aerobics. Excellent for cardio-vascular fitness, aerobics are also great for muscle-toning and body-shaping, working on all the muscle groups by means of bouncy, 'on the spot' exercises repeated many times.

You can practise aerobics at home, but as the basic movement is bouncing you need a rubber mat or springy surface. A class is far preferable, if only because the instructor is tremendously important in aerobics, calling out instructions, keeping up the tempo and checking on individuals' correct performance to avoid danger of strain or injury.

Yoga We have seen how dance steps and rhythms are incorporated into many forms of exercise, and the same is true of the movement awareness techniques of yoga. The Eastern philosophy of yoga, which originated in India some 5000 years ago, emphasizes the partnership of mental and physical discipline to achieve total fulfilment and control.

The type of yoga most commonly practised in the West is Hatha Yoga, which means the physical practice of yoga. In this students learn the importance of concentration and body awareness, getting to know their bodies by means of slow, quiet, sustained movements and special breathing techniques.

In yoga, body fitness is acquired by the regular practice of a series of precisely defined postures or *asanas*, intended to focus on specific limbs, joints and muscle groups, and to massage the internal organs of the body, improving the circulation and assisting the digestion.

There are hundreds of *asanas*, some of them very difficult, which can take years to learn. In most classes in this country only a relatively small proportion of these are taught, in a combination of standing, sitting and prone poses. They develop balance and poise, superb muscular toning and control, flexibility and suppleness. They also focus and absorb the practitioner's mental energies, resulting in the quiet, refreshed and revitalized mind, the state of total relaxation and inner peace which are the essence of yoga.

STAYING WITH IT

Whatever form of exercise you settle on, you should regard it as a part of your way of life. That does not mean sticking rigidly to one form of exercise until your last days, but if you do decide to give up what you are doing, make sure it is in order to take up something else. You will probably find that this becomes quite easy as exercise is itself enjoyable, especially once little-used muscles and joints have lost their rustiness and have started to function properly.

You are never too young to start exercising, but you are always too young to give it up. Unless you get carried away and overstrain the body so as to risk injury, remember that exercise does not wear the body out. On the contrary, it keeps it in a condition where it is going to function better for longer.

Stress and Happiness

Happiness is a natural state. Few of us are truly materialistic enough to think that we become happy by owning things, though we all may set our hearts from time to time on buying some particular object that will give us pleasure when we get it. Real happiness is something more lasting, that comes from within. Acquisition of objects or instances of good fortune give us only passing pleasure. If we think of someone we would characterize as being of a happy disposition we notice they are not so because they are fortunate in what happens to them, but that they have a quality which enables them to approach life positively, to enjoy thoroughly the good things and be able to cope with the bad ones.

Yet despite being reasonably healthy and reasonably well off, most of us do not seem to be happy. Just look at any crowd in a busy shopping street or on the way to work and you will see tension, worry and even misery in the faces. On the other hand, look at a group of young children. They will be running around, jumping, skipping, generally appearing to enjoy life. It would seem that they have a natural happiness that is covered up in adult life. It is not just that small children do not have mortgages to worry about or careers to protect, but that they live more immediately, in the moment. For adults our attitudes get in the way most of the time: our inner turmoil, worry, fretting, or the constant urge to move on to the next thing, never allowing ourselves real rest.

THE NEGATIVE EFFECTS OF STRESS

The word that most of us would use to describe the condition that takes us away from happiness is 'stress'. It is difficult to imagine being happy and stressed; the two run counter to each other. The word has come to take on a negative meaning in modern life, and so we look for ways of avoiding or mitigating it.

Stress not only wears us out and shortens our temper, it can often make us selfish because we become obsessed with our own situation. Stress also leads to illness, by lowering our physical condition and resistance to disease. In extreme form it can actually create illness. Certainly stress contributes in a major way to high blood pressure, heart disease, ulcers, headaches, and some forms of arthritis and asthma.

We are all bound to be subject to stresses from time to time, as life will change and put pressures on us. When we use the word we are usually thinking of stress as an adverse reaction, a negative mental condition. But 'stress' itself is neutral; it is the way we react to it that affects our happiness. For example, moving house will inevitably involve pressure – what makes it stressful is the amount of worry and apprehension with which we approach it. If we are sure it is going to be a bad experience, then it certainly will be. If we are nervous of the change, worrying that the removal men will break things, dreading having to settle in a new neighbour-hood, then the blood pressure will rise, the temper fuse will shorten and we will make a misery of the whole experience. But if we are calm and confident, then the experience can be handled with ease; it might even become exciting. The difference between the two reactions is determined by attitude.

THE POSITIVE SIDE OF STRESS

Stress is, in fact, all about energy, and as such it can be described as a dynamic and stimulating force. Life without stress would be dull and featureless – indeed in a totally stress-free existence nothing would ever be achieved. Any activity requiring effort creates stress, which can be seen, therefore, as a vital spur and incentive. It is stress in one form or another that gets us going – out of bed in the morning, and across the road in an alert fashion. Stress motivates us to earn our living and enables us to concentrate in order to do a job efficiently and give our best performance.

This understanding of stress can itself make a huge difference to our lives and increase our capacity for happiness. Nevertheless, whatever you may hear or may read in the papers, there is no magic way to happiness. We have lived with harmful stress for much of our lives, and just trying to think of it in a new light is not going to change much. However, it is possible to come to terms with it by developing a set of stress skills that are right for you as an individual, and also by learning how to harness it to your advantage. How one handles stressful situations will ultimately be a personal matter, but stress patterns and ways to deal with them occur in similar areas in all our lives, and there are useful guidelines to follow (see overleaf).

KEYS TO STRESS MANAGEMENT

The following 20 rules will act as a useful framework within which you can learn to control stress.

- Learn to appreciate the potential value of stress in creating incentive and sense of purpose.
- Get to know yourself and become fully aware of your personality type.
- Remember that stress is caused from within and can be best dealt with from within.
- Be aware of your own stress levels.
- Learn to identify the various sources of stress inherent in your own particular lifestyle.
- Be aware of your reactions to different sources of stress, so that these do not take you by surprise.
- Avoid perfectionism, when this means expecting too much of both yourself and others.
- Avoid unnecessarily provoking situations where possible.
- Avoid over-committing yourself; learn when to say 'no' without feeling guilty.
- Avoid fragmentation, which is often caused by trying to do several things at once.
- Know how to avoid causing stress to others.
- Beware of unnecessary worrying.
- Learn the value of positive thinking.
- Discover how effective a cheerful outlook can be.
- Be as sure as you can be of what your motives really are, and make sure that you are really happy with them.
- Acquire the habit of sorting out your priorities.
- Learn the art of effective delegation.
- Get into the habit of talking problems through rather than bottling them up.
- Don't forget that listening is as important as talking in effective communication.
- Learn to value physical fitness as a means to relaxation and antidote to stress, and do all you can to acquire it.

STRESS THERAPY

Stress has always been around, but it has become a particularly significant feature of modern life. As the pace of life has accelerated we have become under more pressure to react quickly, more decisions are required from us, and the opportunities to lean on a gate and reflect have diminished. People who have high-pressure jobs are, of course, perceived as being especially prone to stress, but it is in reality very widespread. If there is one single thing that acts as an antidote to stress, it is the art of relaxation. Methods may differ, but their purpose is the same – to gain control of stress signs and draw on inner strength to achieve equilibrium.

Physical exercise is very important, too, as a way of releasing energy and achieving relaxation, and the physical fitness that arises also helps you stand up to stress. Exercise helps you keep in touch with your body and makes you more alert.

STRESS AT WORK

Work is generally acknowledged to be one of the major sources of stress, and in our competitive society of high achievers it has perhaps assumed a disproportionate significance. Certainly most people spend more time at work during their working lives than they do at home.

As we have seen, stress is often associated with change and uncertainty, and this is especially relevant in the workplace, where poor communication, threats, and fluctuating priorities are all common and create a sense of insecurity. External pressures are a feature of most jobs – dealing with difficult clients, making presentations, contact with the public. Internal pressures are just as normal – getting on with the boss, handling subordinates, relating to colleagues. Environmental and physical conditions also contribute, whether it is suffering eye-strain from working with a VDU or sitting in an open-plan office where you never get any privacy. Do not underestimate the effect of these, and if you suffer from overcrowding, too much noise, or temperatures that are too high or too low, you don't have to suffer in silence and get worked up about them, but can complain creatively, pointing out how the conditions are affecting everybody's work.

KEYS TO COPING WITH UNEMPLOYMENT

- Help yourself deal with the sense of disorientation so often experienced by the jobless, by planning your day carefully, for example, getting up early and taking the day from there.
- Make every effort to look, and keep looking, for a job. Even if no opportunities arise immediately for the type of work for which you are qualified, it may be wise to consider alternative types of job, if available.
- Use the extra leisure time available to you constructively. Instead of regarding it as a bane, think of it as an opportunity for developing new interests and skills.
- Get out of the house as much as possible.
- Keep as fit as possible.

KEY TO COPING WITH WORK STRESS

A lot of damaging stress can be pre-empted if you know what is expected of you in your job. A clearly defined, sufficiently detailed job description is one of the best ways of avoiding stressful uncertainty. Make sure that you get regular feedback on your performance and anything else that you need to know, on a regular basis, from the person to whom who are answerable. Make sure it is clear in your mind and in his or hers how much your boss expects you to act on your own initiative, and how much you should consult on. Feelings always become stronger when bottled up, so share your difficulties: if you have problems talk them over with your family, friends and colleagues.

One of the best guidelines for minimizing stress at work is not to take things personally. It may not be easy to accept criticism if you are sensitive, but if you are aware of feeling slighted, adopt an objective attitude to it. Remember, too, that if your boss seems aggressive towards you, it may be that he is having an off day which is nothing to do with your performance.

Establishing boundaries However busy you are, it is always advisable to take a good lunchbreak in the middle of the day, so as to recharge the batteries. Avoid eating or drinking too much, or too quickly, and watch what you eat. A good diet is

> **PHYSICAL CONDITIONS**
>
> You will be more relaxed if your working conditions are comfortable.
> - If you spend long periods of the day seated, your chair should support you in a comfortable position and be in the right relation to your desk height for you to be able to work without back strain.
> - If you work on your feet, make sure you have somewhere comfortable and clean to relax during your breaks and that you have a proper lunch.
> - Do not work for long periods on VDUs, and take breaks to exercise your eyes.
> - Keep your work space free of clutter, especially when you finish at night.

an essential part of establishing the physical well-being necessary to combat stress.

Finally, shun the temptation to take work home. It will usually wait until the morning, and if not it is better to stay late or go in early than to put work into your briefcase. Work at home eats into your important unwinding time, and it nags away at the back of your mind before you actually get down to it, creating yet more stress.

STRESS AT HOME

A secure and stress-free home life is an infallible foundation for a happy life, and conversely, a happy home life is a safeguard against being overwhelmed by harmful stress outside.

Unfortunately, however, the demands of daily life are such that even harmonious families can be subject to stress, and too often the home becomes the arena of the most stressful conflicts of all, amongst the most common being marital differences, sexual difficulties, money worries, problems with children, and the act of juggling a job with home life.

Marital stress As with other forms of stress, one of the fundamental causes of conflict in marriage is change. People develop throughout their lives, and when there are two involved it might not be in the same direction. Expectations of life and of each other, aspirations, and the common ground on which the marriage was built in the first place, may gradually diverge over a long period until the differences emerge into the light of day.

To be aware of the possibility of such a pattern developing in your marriage, and to take preventative steps in time, can save you a lot of stress, and possibly even the marriage itself. Making time for each other can often be the soundest premise for a stress-free marriage. As one of the couple develops new interests these can be shared, or, if not, then appreciated with respect. A certain degree of independence – having some different friends and hobbies and spare-time pursuits – is a valuable component of a harmonious relationship.

Failed expectation is the other prime cause of distress in marriage. The romantic haze of the wedding will not last for ever, but those people who try to cling on to it will create an image that is impossible for their partner to live up to. No one other person can be expected always to create in us a warm and admiring glow, and the higher the pedestal we put our partner on, the more claylike his or her feet are going to appear.

Sex Sex is no surer a foundation for a happy marriage than is unalloyed romance. If it assumes excessive, or exclusive, importance, it stands in the way of the development of the other expressions of togetherness, such as companionship, friendship and shared interests. Sooner rather than later it will destroy the relationship altogether. Jealousy, the lack of trust in the other partner, is just as destructive.

More common than either of these are the various forms of sexual incompatibility, whether difficulties in making or enjoying love together, or differing expectations over type and variety of intercourse. Ultimately these can create considerable stress, especially if the couple do not face up to them. As with other problems, talking about them may do much to release the tension and open up a way to a solution. It may be enough just to talk to each other, but if not then marriage guidance organizations exist to help. GPs are often willing to give assistance, and some hospitals, health centres and family planning clinics provide special sex therapy for couples. Awareness and understanding are the best foundation from which to cope, rather than letting events take you by surprise.

Working couples Marriages in which both partners work are now the majority in Britain, but tiredness at the end of the working day and conflicting priorities create particular tensions. To avoid these:
* Try not to let your working and home lives overlap.
* Set aside some time, however short, in which to relax when you get home from work, to make the transition smoother.
* Share responsibilities like paying the bills, and household chores such as cleaning and shopping.
* Unless one of you really loathes it, share the cooking. There can be great pleasure in cooking a meal for someone else to enjoy, and it gives the non-cooking partner the chance to sit down and unwind.
* Even if your timetables prevent regular eating together, make sure some meals are shared every week.
* Establish a leisure activity that the whole family will enjoy, at least once a week.

CHILDREN

Bringing up children is one of the most rewarding of life's experiences, but also one of the most exhausting. Caring can also lead to a special kind of isolation for a parent at home all day, especially in the parts of the country where facilities for children are not readily available. To counteract this get out as much as you can. Join a mother and toddler group; find a friend to go shopping with. Once the first child is of school age it should be easy to make friends with other parents as the school gates serve as a great social club. Playgroups often provide the same network of parents. Also, watch out for the situation where children take over completely: keep part of your life

STRESS SCALE

In the late 1960s Dr Thomas Holmes and Dr Richard Rahe, of the University of Washington in Seattle, USA, published in chart form, in the *Journal of Psychosomatic Research*, the degrees of stress, based on a scale from 1 to 100, which their research showed as commonly associated with life events. Whether or not you feel your own stress levels coincide with the findings outlined in the chart, it provides a comprehensive checklist of stressors which affect us all.

	100		100
Death of spouse	100	Large mortgage or loan	31
Divorce	73	New responsibilities at work	29
Marital separation	65	Children leaving home	29
Jail term	63	Trouble with in-laws	29
Death in family	63	Outstanding personal	
Personal injury or illness	53	achievement	28
Marriage	50	Spouse begins or stops work	26
Losing a job	47	School or college ends or	
Marital reconciliation	45	begins	26
Retirement	45	Living conditions change	25
Illness of family member	44	Personal habits change	24
Pregnancy	40	Trouble with boss	23
Sex problems	39	Change in working conditions	20
New baby	39	Change in residence	20
Business readjustment	39	Change in school or college	20
Change in financial		Change in social activities	18
circumstances	38	Change in sleeping habits	16
Death of a close friend	37	Change in eating habits	15
Change in work	36	Holiday	13
Increased arguments with		Christmas	12
spouse	35	Minor violations of law	11

separate with your own time and interests, and share accounts of your respective days with your partner.

Small children produce a different stress in their parents, that of worrying constantly that they are going to hurt themselves. Practical steps here are needed, by making your home as childproof as possible, especially danger areas like the kitchen and stairs. A little time and care can save a year or two of tense and unrelaxed days.

HOLIDAYS

Holidays are meant to repair the wear and tear of normal life and put us back in a happy frame of mind. Yet they can be stressful experiences in their own right, and people have been known to return with the good friends who went away with them crossed forever off their social list, or with family members in a sullen silence that has lasted for days. Holidays are a bit like marriage: it is tempting to expect too much of them and not be prepared for the inevitable occasional mishap and upset.

Holidays represent a variety of changes: a change of scene, a different way of life, customs and traditions; different food; often a new language and currency to contend with. All of these can be stimulating, but they can also be disorientating and even threatening.

Key to stress-free holidays

* Don't be too ambitious when planning and turn it into a major challenge with a long list of things to do or places to visit.

* Do your homework to make sure the holiday is right for you – if you look after a family all year, for example, self-catering may not mean much of a break.

* Going to the same place every year might not sound exciting, but may be the best way of having a relaxing time, especially for young families.

* Book through a travel agent you trust.

* Take out proper insurance, and make sure you understand all the small print.

* Allow plenty of time to obtain traveller's cheques, visas, inoculation certificates, and any other documents you need.

* Make a list of any items you need to buy specially and leave yourself plenty of time to get them.

* Try to learn a few phrases in the language of the place you are going to. It won't make you able to conduct a conversation, but will give you confidence.

* Make the journey as easy as possible by rationalizing your luggage. Don't end up with an assortment of small carriers, nor one hugely heavy case.

Christmas   Although it is supposedly a time of joy, Christmas can create a great deal of stress. For the lonely it can be particularly painful, and the suicide rate always goes up over the holiday. But even for those with family gatherings to organize, it often seems to be a huge chore rather than a time of celebration.

One way to avoid this is to be well organized, and work out when you can do the bits of preparation so that they fit in with your schedule. Starting too early is just as fraught as starting too late, as you will have had enough of the whole thing before it even begins. Share out the jobs, especially with children, who are generally more than willing helpers at this time of year. Another way is to stop and remind yourself what Christmas is all about, and the essential simplicity behind its message.

TRAVEL

In the present age we all regularly travel distances that would have astounded earlier generations. However, the more people travel, the harder it is becoming for everybody. As a result getting into the car is rarely the prelude to carefree motoring it once was, and airports have come to resemble sheep pens.

Motoring   Traffic jams, other people's aggression and fatigue at the wheel seem as much a part of driving as buying petrol. You can do a certain amount of planning to avoid traffic jams by consulting traffic reports in the media, and can equip yourself with a good road atlas to show possible alternative routes. Otherwise, when they happen, accept the inevitable and put on a cassette that you enjoy.

Bad driving spreads like a virus, and once you are subject to somebody else's selfishness or stupidity, the temptation is to respond. But you will be far happier if you can manage not to retaliate by reminding yourself that confrontations on the road not only lead to stress but often to accidents.

Air travel Airports are often crowded and noisy and can be highly confusing to those unfamiliar with them. Flight delays and cancellations, which all too frequently happen at peak travel times, and long-drawn-out check-in, security and baggage retrieval procedures, can contribute to the feelings of apprehension that even seasoned fliers are prone to.

Deep breathing exercises can be highly beneficial during an air flight. The decompressed atmosphere in an aircraft creates unpleasant physical conditions, dehydration especially, which can be countered by taking plenty of fluid before and during the flight, but avoiding alcohol, coffee and carbonated drinks, which just exacerbate it.

On long flights wear loose comfortable clothes and get as much rest as you can. Take a good book with you, or some pastime you enjoy, so that if you are held up the time will not drag by.

RELIEVING STRESS

Growing recognition of the toll that stress can take has resulted in increased interest in recent years in tackling it on an everyday basis. Exercise, relaxation and a well-balanced diet are essential elements in this. However, even these need to be approached with a sense of balance and proportion; excessive exercise becomes an obsession, and can lead to injury and fatigue, while excessive relaxation can lead to boredom and torpor.

Exercise Physical exercise uses up excess energy, burns off the potentially toxic noradrenalin, and leaves you feeling calmer and more in control. A general sense of well-being often follows. Regular exercise keeps joints supple and muscles relaxed, dispelling stiffness caused by tension. It also leaves you mentally stronger, more resilient and able to cope. People who take to regular exercise find that they suffer less from mental fatigue and are able to sleep better, since when they go to bed they are physically tired and they do not find themselves with a body whose unused energies feed a roving mind. For more about exercise see Fitness pages 16–24.

Stress relief for the mind In a perfect world we would probably not need special means of relaxation, but for most of us relaxation has to be fitted in as something we do, much like other activities. While slumping in front of the television provides a relaxation of sorts, it does not help the body achieve the energy flow that exercise creates, and it leaves the mind free to continue turning over thoughts and worries. It is this mental activity that creates most tension and prevents us from being happy. For this reason many techniques have been developed or made available over recent decades as means of restoring mental poise.

Meditation The use of meditation in learning to control the mind and thus achieving a deep sense of calm, encompassed by an enhanced inner awareness, is an ancient and important part of Eastern philosophies. In its original context meditation has a profound spiritual significance, and many of those who have been practising it in the West would say that they find this to be true. However, many turn to it at least initially as a way of finding a sense of peace and inner well-being.

That meditation is of special value in reducing stress is confirmed by scientific observation of people practising it: their heart rates slow down, their muscles relax, and their brainwave patterns indicate a mental state that combines complete repose with total alertness.

Like physical exercise, relaxation through meditation needs to be progressive and to be guided by a qualified practitioner. The best known school internationally is the one founded by Maharishi Mahesh Yogi, which offers what it calls Transcendental Meditation, but there are many other organizations with their roots also in India or in the religions and philosophies of other Eastern countries.

Other Eastern teachings The East has produced many forms of physical exercise whose main aim is mental rest and alertness. Yoga is the best-known, particularly the type called Hatha Yoga. Various exercises are carried out to achieve bodily fitness, but this is not the end but merely a means to achieving mental control. Ultimately yoga leads to meditation, but even beginners will find that the classes involve a period designed to relax the mind and find inner rest.

It is similar with T'ai Chi, a Chinese discipline, which uses exercises of the body to stabilize and harmonize the ever-flowing energies of the body and mind. It is related to the martial arts such as judo, kung-fu and karate, all of which combine physical fitness and alertness with achieving increased consciousness and poise.

All of these should be taught by qualified instructors at regular classes, though they will also involve exercises being carried out at home.

Modern Western techniques Biofeedback has been developed over the last 20 years to promote awareness of stress by measuring physical responses to it. Special electronic metering and other devices detect subtle physiological changes that prefigure stress, so that the user can respond to and control it.

In contrast, the Alexander Technique uses no machines but manual guidance and verbal instruction. The Technique works on posture, seeing this as of vital importance to our mental and physical well-being. Students develop a sense of balance that enables them to observe tensions. According to Alexander, the natural balance mechanism can be made to work without undue effort by a system of postural reflexes.

Cultivating a Positive Approach to Life

If you can alleviate stress you will have taken a great step towards improving the quality of your life. The other thing to do is to develop a positive approach to life, so that you look for the good rather than the bad in every situation. Life is bound to be full of changes; indeed, if it was not it would be very dull. If we view changes with suspicion, always fearing the worst, then we will make ourselves unhappy.

This does not mean that you should try to sit on your natural feelings of apprehension. In fact, it is impossible to suppress any emotion, and to try to do so leads only to mental turmoil and distress. But you can control your attitude, and it is this that gives particular quality and colour to emotions. Take, for example, having to speak in public. Whatever appearance they give, most people experience some butterflies in advance, even very experienced speakers. You can respond to this feeling either by immersing yourself in it and letting it feed all sorts of ideas about personal inadequacy and the hostility of the audience, or you can see this feeling as the product of the adrenalin that you need to perform well. The first way will make you miserable for hours, but the second is the source of excitement and good humour.

Those who are happiest in life generally have a quality of balance. They seem neither to be the constant prey to external events, nor locked into rigid attempts to control their environment. A certain acceptance of fate is paradoxically an essential aspect of being in control, because you can never determine what will happen to you, and to resist all the time means that you will be fighting with life itself. This is not the same as fatalism. A certain willingness to accept means that, instead of burning up mental energy in anger and resentment, you are able to use the power of the mind to assess each situation and see what needs to be done.

Often what helps is having a clear set of priorities, and this involves self-knowledge. Establish what you really want in life or in any situation: whether, for example, your career is so important and fulfilling that you are happy to let it take up so much time as to curtail leisure activities; whether you have some hobby on which you truly want to spend most of your spare time; whether family life should come before everything else. Then we need to assess the amount of time we have, how much we can do in that time, and learn to read the signals of when we have had enough of any activity and not get hooked on it to the point of fatigue and irritability.

Finally, one of the great keys of happiness is being able to appreciate what you have. A fundamental characteristic of human beings is our desire to move on, advance, take on the next challenge. Without this urge to progress we would still be living in caves. But necessary as the urge is, it can obliterate the enjoyment of what we have achieved to date. It is a very unusual and unfortunate person indeed who has nothing in life that they can genuinely appreciate – family, friends, the ability to fulfil intellectual or physical pleasures – but unless you learn to appreciate whichever of these you have, happiness will always remain elusive.

Pregnancy

PREPARING FOR PARENTHOOD

Nowadays, with modern contraception, most couples can plan when to have their children. While problems with fertility can be distressing, many can be corrected, and in point of fact they only affect a small proportion of couples.

Men and women become fertile at puberty, when the reproductive organs mature. For girls, the onset of menstrual periods is the most obvious sign, which can occur between age nine or ten and 17 (this range is quite normal). The optimum time for a first pregnancy is between the ages of about 23 and 29, when a woman's body is at its peak of health. This is not to say that women both older and younger cannot have safe, healthy pregnancies.

The reproductive process Every month during a woman's fertile years, a signal from the pituitary gland in the brain stimulates the ovary to produce an ovum, in a process known as ovulation. At the same time the endometrium – the lining of the uterus, or womb – develops. If the ovum is not fertilized it disintegrates after about 14 days and the endometrium is shed during the four to five days of bleeding known as menstruation. Women are most likely to conceive a child during the middle three to five days of their menstrual cycle.

Spermatozoa (or sperm as they are more usually known) are constantly being formed in a man's testicles from puberty. They are about $\frac{1}{25}$ of a millimetre long and resemble tiny tadpoles. Millions of them are ejaculated through the penis at the moment of orgasm, mixed with seminal fluid.

In the developed world, women who are well nourished and fit menstruate earlier and remain fertile longer, so that pregnancies over 35 years of age are now quite common. Fertility ceases for women with the onset of the menopause at around the age of 50, whereas men can go on fathering children for many years longer.

DEVELOPMENT OF THE EMBRYO

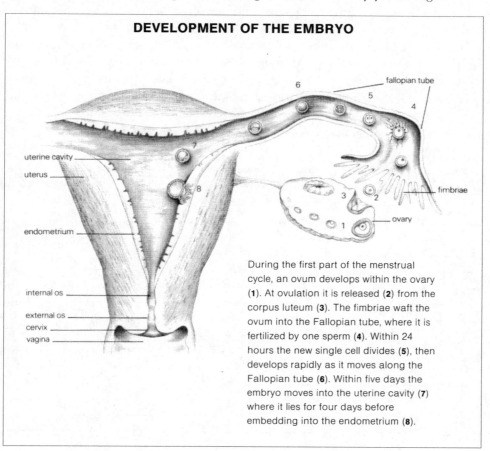

During the first part of the menstrual cycle, an ovum develops within the ovary (**1**). At ovulation it is released (**2**) from the corpus luteum (**3**). The fimbriae waft the ovum into the Fallopian tube, where it is fertilized by one sperm (**4**). Within 24 hours the new single cell divides (**5**), then develops rapidly as it moves along the Fallopian tube (**6**). Within five days the embryo moves into the uterine cavity (**7**) where it lies for four days before embedding into the endometrium (**8**).

How a pregnancy occurs During sexual intercourse, sperms contained in the man's semen are deposited in the upper part of the vagina. If they meet an ovum one of the sperms will fertilize it. The nuclei of the sperm and the ovum combine, thus incorporating inherited characteristics from both parents. The fertilized ovum then begins to divide, and divide again, into two, then four, then eight cells, and so on. Within five days the little 'ball' of dividing cells, the embryo, attaches itself to the uterine wall. There the outer cells burrow into the wall and connect with the mother's blood vessels. These outer cells eventually form the placenta, the organ which sustains the fetus, as the developing embryo is called, by transferring nutrients from the mother's bloodstream. The inner cells eventually develop into the baby.

PRE-PREGNANCY HEALTH

It is now recognized that the health of both mother and father before conception can affect the outcome of a pregnancy. Excessive smoking and drinking of alcohol can affect fertility as it depresses sperm production in a man, while smoking during an established pregnancy has been proved to affect a baby's health and normal development. It is a good idea to eat a sensible, balanced diet before embarking on pregnancy, and for the mother to maintain an appropriate body weight for her height. Being too fat during pregnancy can cause problems which affect both mother and baby.

It is also important to make sure that you are immunized against rubella (or German measles, see page 71). Although this is a mild disease in itself, if you catch it while you are pregnant it can cause severe congenital disabilities in your unborn child, particularly during the first three months of pregnancy.

PRE-PREGNANCY AVERAGE WEIGHT FOR WOMEN			
		Weight without clothes	
Height without shoes	Acceptable average	Acceptable weight range	
(ft in)	(st lb)	(st lb)	(st lb)
4 10	7 2	6 5	8 5
4 11	7 4	6 7	8 7
5 0	7 6	6 8	8 9
5 1	7 8	7 0	9 1
5 2	8 0	7 2	9 3
5 3	8 2	7 5	9 5
5 4	8 5	7 7	9 8
5 5	8 7	7 9	10 1
5 6	9 1	8 1	10 4
5 7	9 4	8 4	10 7
5 8	9 7	8 7	11 0
5 9	10 0	9 0	11 2
5 10	10 2	9 2	11 6
5 11	10 5	9 5	12 0
6 0	10 8	9 8	12 3

THE SIGNS OF PREGNANCY

- Missed menstrual period. This is the first sign for most women whose periods are regular.
- Enlarged breasts. Breasts can enlarge very quickly at the onset of pregnancy and become quite tender. They may feel rather lumpy as the milk sacs develop and fat deposits build up.
- Changes in the nipples. The nipples darken in colour, and small protruberances develop round the areola (the area round the nipple where it meets the breast.)
- Nausea. Many women experience 'morning sickness' right from the start, although it may not be in the morning, and is not often accompanied by actual vomiting. It usually goes away after the first 12–14 weeks of pregnancy as the hormonal balance stabilizes.
- Frequency of urination.
- Fatigue. Many women feel extraordinarily tired at the start of pregnancy, due to the profound physical changes taking place as their bodies adjust to accommodate the developing child.

Problems with fertility   The most common problems with fertility occur when a woman is failing to ovulate. Male infertility is often a result of low or non-existent sperm production. These and the many other reasons for infertility may require specialist investigation over several months or even years. However, the treatment of female infertility is one of the medical success stories of the past twenty years, although male infertility is still very hard to treat.

If you are having problems with fertility – and remember that doctors are unlikely to consider that there is a problem until you have been trying to conceive for about a year – consult your GP who will probably refer you and your partner to a specialist fertility clinic in the gynaecology department of the hospital.

Confirming the pregnancy   If you think you may be pregnant visit your doctor, who will arrange for a pregnancy test. This usually means supplying a sample of urine in which the hormones of pregnancy should be present and detectable. You can also buy commercial testing kits at chemists' shops. Most pregnancies can be confirmed by about the sixth or seventh week (see below).

If you are not sure of the date of your last period, or your cycle is irregular your doctor or midwife may try to establish the size (and therefore the age) of the fetus by means of a gentle internal examination or by an ultrasound scan at the hospital.

The length of pregnancy   The length of pregnancy is calculated in weeks from the date of the first full day of your last period, although in point of fact conception probably did not occur until about 14 days after that. Pregnancy is said to last 40 weeks, divided into three sections, or trimesters (weeks 1 to 12, 13 to 28, and 29 to 40). A normal pregnancy can be anything from 38 to 42 weeks. To calculate the estimated date of your baby's birth either count 40 weeks on from the date of the first day of your last menstrual period, or seven days plus nine months.

HOME OR HOSPITAL?

Once the pregnancy is confirmed, your doctor will ask you to think about where you want to have your baby, which may also determine the type of antenatal care that you are given. You can have your baby either at home or in hospital. The majority of babies in the UK are born in hospital as fewer doctors and midwives are available to supervise home births. However most maternity units are more relaxed than they used to be and your stay in the postnatal ward need not be longer than three or four days, even for your first baby.

As long as the mother is healthy antenatal care is often carried out by your own doctor or by a midwife at the local health centre. Some consultants run antenatal clinics in health centres to avoid pregnant women having to travel long distances to hospital, and some GP units pair up with hospitals to deliver their own patients' babies in hospital, but if the mother is healthy she can go home within 6 or 12 hours.

Discuss all the options with your doctor and the community midwife, if there is one attached to the practice. Even if your antenatal care is mainly to be carried out by your doctor, you will probably have your first checkup at the hospital. Your doctor will give you a letter of referral and, depending on the procedures, you will probably be given an appointment within the first 12 weeks of pregnancy.

HEALTH DURING PREGNANCY

The first antenatal checkup is one of the most important – thereafter you may have checkups as little as once every six weeks, but they are more likely to be every four weeks, until about 36 weeks when you will be checked fortnightly, then probably weekly. State-of-the-art ultrasound equipment is now commonly used to show the movement of the fetus inside the uterus, even at a few weeks of pregnancy.

Amniocentesis and chorionic villus sampling These relatively new techniques help to identify possible congenital problems in the baby during pregnancy. They are often offered to older mothers – the risk of congenital abnormality such as Down's syndrome increases rapidly after the age of 35.

Amniocentesis involves inserting a needle through the abdominal wall to withdraw some amniotic fluid from inside the uterus. The baby's cells which are floating in the fluid can be tested for abnormalities. This technique is done at about 18 weeks of pregnancy and the results take about three weeks, so if there is a serious problem and the mother is offered a termination, it can be distressing as she will have to be induced.

Chorionic villus sampling is an even more recent development, done at around ten weeks of pregnancy. It is available only at a few hospitals. As there is a fairly high risk of miscarriage associated with it, it is offered only to women whose babies are most at risk from various rare congenital disorders.

Diet While it is not suggested that mothers should go on a slimming diet during pregnancy, it is wise to avoid very fatty or sugary foods. A balanced diet including meat, fish, fresh vegetables and fruit, and plenty of dietary fibre is ideal. There is no need to consume a lot of fluids either – simply drink when you are thirsty.

Exercise Fatigue during the first trimester will probably slow you down anyway,

COMMON COMPLAINTS OF PREGNANCY

Anaemia This is quite common because the red blood cells are 'diluted' during pregnancy. Good nutrition can avoid it, or your doctor or midwife may supply iron pills.

Cramp Cramp in the lower limbs can occur in late pregnancy. There is no evidence that extra calcium or salt helps this.

Fainting This is not uncommon in pregnancy. Standing too long so that blood pools in the legs can lead to fainting so avoid it. Some women experience the sensation of fainting when lying on their backs due to pressure on the blood vessels. Avoid lying on your back in later pregnancy.

Headaches Many women experience headaches which can be treated with paracetamol. If they are persistent or very severe call the doctor at once.

Heartburn and nausea Nausea is common in the first trimester but if it persists and is accompanied by vomiting your doctor will treat it seriously, as there is a danger of dehydration. Heartburn is a type of indigestion which is caused by pressure on the stomach from the expanding uterus. The doctor or midwife will give you a safe medicine to take, and it is a good idea to eat little and often rather than large meals, and avoid fatty or highly spiced foods.

Insomnia Lack of sleep makes the general fatigue of pregnancy worse, and women often find it difficult to sleep in later pregnancy. Practising relaxation and taking an afternoon rest can help. Do not take sleeping pills during pregnancy as these affect the baby.

Nose bleeds Some women experience these because the blood vessels are dilated during pregnancy.

Maternal infections Genital tract and urinary infections are quite common and you should always report them to the doctor. They can easily be treated but the medication must be safe in case it crosses the placenta. Common colds and viral infections do not harm the baby but if they occur in early pregnancy and you have not yet told your doctor make sure she or he knows if you are likely to need antibiotics.

Oedema This means swelling, in pregnancy it affects the lower limbs and hands. It may be normal but can be associated with high blood pressure. Try to put your feet up at least some time during the day especially in the last trimester.

Sciatica Pain and tingling down the leg is due to pressure on the sciatic nerve. It is probably due to pressure from the baby's head, and it eases when the head descends.

Skin changes Some women develop patches of skin colouring on the face or abdomen. This is normal and fades after the birth.

Spots Spots and mild rashes occur, but these are nothing to worry about. Talk to your doctor if you think you have an allergy.

Stress incontinence Pressure on the bladder plus stretching of the pelvic floor muscles often results in leakage of urine when women cough, sneeze or laugh. Pelvic floor exercises help to avoid this. If it persists beyond pregnancy to the point of being embarrassing it can be corrected surgically.

Stretch marks As the abdomen distends the skin often develops scar-like marks. These fade after pregnancy but are not affected by creams or oils.

Vaginal discharge Natural secretions of mucus in the vagina increase during pregnancy. This may lead to irritation, so do not wear underwear made of artificial fibres. Ask your doctor for a cream to overcome this problem.

Varicose veins Action of the hormones in softening ligaments in preparation for childbirth also affects the valves of the veins, which can lead to varicosity. Women are also more prone to haemorrhoids (varicose veins in the anus) during pregnancy. Avoiding constipation by eating plenty of dietary fibre helps prevent this.

Weight gain Average weight gain is 12.5 kg/ 28 lb. Any more or less should be carefully monitored.

but again take the exercise you feel comfortable with. Walking is a very good idea as it improves the circulation in the legs, helping to avoid varicose veins. Swimming is also good especially late in pregnancy.

Sexual intercourse   There is no reason why you should not continue to enjoy sexual intercourse throughout pregnancy although at the later stages you may want to find different positions as the mother's abdomen enlarges. In the last weeks full penetration may also be uncomfortable.

Preparation classes   Most hospitals and health centres offer preparation classes for childbirth and baby-care, and there are other organizations like the National Childbirth Trust which provide classes for a fee in a home environment. It is worth joining such a course, partly because of the confidence it gives, particularly to new parents, and also to meet other parents having babies at about the same time as you who live locally. This helps to build up a mutual support network after the birth which is very important, especially if you are not used to being at home all day.

Classes typically involve information about labour and birth, the newborn baby's care and feeding. Most also include techniques for relaxation and ways to cope with uterine contractions during labour. Hospital classes also include a tour of the delivery rooms and postnatal ward.

WORKING MOTHERS AND BENEFITS

Many women are at work when they become pregnant. In the UK women have the right to time off from work without loss of pay for antenatal visits. A mother is also entitled to maternity leave and benefits – and to have her job back afterwards.

Provided that you have worked for your employer for six months or more before the pregnancy, you have the right to maternity leave from 11 weeks before your baby is due to up to 29 weeks afterwards. For 18 weeks of this time you are entitled to statutory maternity pay. Some employers have more generous arrangements, so check with your personnel officer or trade union representative.

If you don't qualify for maternity pay you can receive a maternity allowance from the Department of Social Security for the same period of time.

COMPLICATIONS OF PREGNANCY

There are some complications which may require special treatment, extra visits to the antenatal or ultrasound clinic, or possibly even a stay in the antenatal ward at the hospital.

Miscarriage   Miscarriage or spontaneous abortion is when the pregnancy is lost before 24 weeks. A baby born after that time is deemed to be premature. Most miscarriages occur early in pregnancy and, while distressing, are usually followed by successful pregnancies. If a mother suffers an early miscarriage she will usually be given a 'D & C' (dilatation and curettage) operation to make sure the uterus is completely cleared. Late miscarriage is more distressing, and is sometimes due to a condition known as 'incompetent cervix', in which the cervix does not remain completely closed, and as the fetus grows the bag of waters protrudes, often rupturing and bringing on premature labour at about 20 weeks. If this happens in subsequent pregnancies the mother will be given a cervical suture (stitch) under general anaesthetic at about 14 weeks of pregnancy, which keeps the cervix closed. It is removed at about 38 weeks, when the mother will probably go naturally into labour.

Premature labour   Premature labour is one that begins after 24 weeks of pregnancy; before that it is a miscarriage. If a mother feels she is going into labour early she should ring the hospital labour ward immediately. She may be given a drug to inhibit the uterine contractions and will probably be kept in hospital for bed rest.

FACTORS ASSOCIATED WITH PREMATURE LABOUR

- Multiple pregnancy
- Bleeding from the vagina
- A fetus that is growing slowly ('small for dates')
- Incompetent cervix
- Abnormality of the uterus
- Diabetes
- Too much amniotic fluid
- Infection, especially of the kidneys
- Previous history of premature labour

Bleeding during pregnancy   Vaginal bleeding in pregnancy should always be taken seriously and should be reported to your doctor or midwife immediately. In early pregnancy it could presage a miscarriage; in later pregnancy it may be due to a condition known as placenta praevia. This is when the placenta has developed so low on the uterine wall that as it grows it covers the cervix or neck of the womb. As the uterus expands and the cervix stretches the placenta may start to come away from the uterine wall causing painless bleeding. In addition a placenta praevia will obviously impede the baby's progress in labour. Placenta praevia can now easily be diagnosed with ultrasound. The mother is usually given bed rest in hospital. The baby is always delivered by Caesarean section.

Another possible problem in late pregnancy is bleeding behind the placenta, even though it is in a normal position. This is called placental abruption. It is accompanied by pain and, although vaginal bleeding may be slight, ultrasound scan may show up quite a lot of blood collecting between the placenta and the uterine wall. If the abruption is mild you will be kept in hospital and monitored carefully to preserve the pregnancy as long as possible. If it is severe the baby would have to be delivered quickly by emergency Caesarean section.

Multiple pregnancies   While multiple pregnancies are quite normal, they can be associated with complications and need to be monitored carefully. It is simply more work for the mother's body to nurture two or more babies. Twins occur in about one in 80 pregnancies – triplets and larger multiples have recently increased due to techniques of fertility treatment. Twins are either non-identical (when two separate ova are fertilized by two separate sperm) or identical (when one fertilized ovum divides into two separate embryos before being implanted).

The problems of twin pregnancies are mostly exaggerations of the minor problems of single pregnancies, particularly fatigue, joint pain associated with the extra weight, excess fluid, anaemia, insomnia and indigestion. Nausea is often much worse in the first trimester. There is also a higher risk of high blood pressure and of premature labour. However the main risk of a multiple birth is at the actual birth, when the second (or subsequent) baby may suffer distress especially if the labour is prolonged or the baby is breech (see page 44).

High blood pressure High blood pressure (hypertension) (see page 66) in pregnancy can be dangerous if it is not checked. When associated solely with the pregnancy it is called pre-eclampsia. It puts the mother at risk from kidney problems, and prevents the placenta from functioning properly so that the baby's growth may be inhibited. It can be associated with placental abruption (see page 41).

High blood pressure must always be taken seriously in pregnancy which is why it is checked at every antenatal appointment. As it is rarely accompanied by any other symptoms it may be difficult for the mother to accept the restrictions placed on her, but these are essential to the success of the pregnancy. If it is unchecked the life-threatening condition known as eclampsia may result.

Mothers are advised to rest and if the pressure rises to a dangerous level they may be admitted to hospital for bed rest. Severe cases will be treated with drugs, with the aim of maintaining the pregnancy to 36–38 weeks when the baby will be delivered. If the blood pressure rises uncontrollably the baby will probably be delivered by emergency Caesarean section any time after 24 weeks.

LABOUR AND BIRTH

Labour is the term used to describe the process by which the uterus contracts, the cervix opens and the baby and placenta are expelled through the vagina. It is divided into three stages. In the first stage the early contractions of the upper uterus thin (efface) the cervix. These may be practically painless and are often indistinguishable from the so-called Braxton Hicks contractions, which are 'practice' contractions felt throughout the third trimester. The cervix then begins to open (dilate) and contractions become more noticeable, more frequent, last longer and are closer together. The cervix has to dilate to about 10 cm/4 in to allow the head to pass through. The length of this stage is unpredictable, but is a matter of hours.

Once the cervix is fully dilated the second stage begins. During first stage the baby's head descends lower into the pelvis; at the second stage the contractions push the baby's head down the birth canal (vagina) which stretches to allow it through. Occasionally the perineum (the skin round the entrance to the vagina) tears slightly and the mother may need stitches after the birth.

The head rotates as it comes down so that it is facing the back as it emerges. When the baby's head starts to push against the perineum and can be seen by the midwife it is known as crowning. Once the head emerges the baby rotates again so that the shoulders can come out more easily.

The third stage is the delivery of the placenta and membranes, which emerge five to ten minutes afterwards. There are contractions but these are not as uncomfortable as first-stage contractions and feel rather like severe period pains.

What to do when labour starts   Once a mother is sure she is in labour, with contractions every five minutes or so, she should telephone the labour ward and be driven to hospital. If you do not have your own car you should call an ambulance or taxi – do not attempt to drive yourself in case the labour should be unexpectedly quick. Fathers are now actively encouraged to be present in many labour wards.

If the membranes rupture and you feel a warm rush of fluid, you should go to hospital as soon as possible, even if you are not experiencing pains. This is because there is a small danger of infection entering the uterus and because the cord may be trapped between the baby's head and the cervix causing possible fetal distress if the blood supply is inhibited.

Pain relief   Some women find they can manage contractions simply by using the breathing and relaxation techniques taught in their preparation classes. However most use some form of pain relief.

* Entonox. Sometimes known as 'gas and air' this is a mild analgesic combining oxygen with nitrous oxide, which can be inhaled through a mask at the height of a contraction.

* Pethidine. This is an analgesic administered by injection. It is not used as frequently as it used to be because it affects the baby during and after the birth.

* Epidural anaesthetic. This is a local anaesthetic administered by drip directly into the spinal column through a gap in one of the lower vertebrae of the spine. It completely deadens pain in the abdominal region but leaves the mother awake and alert. It can make the second stage more difficult as the mother cannot feel the contractions and does not know when to bear down, so doctors and midwives tend to administer it early in first stage so that it has more or less worn off by the time second stage is approaching.

Induction and acceleration of labour   Occasionally if labour is prolonged and the baby is showing signs of fetal distress such as slowed heartbeat, then labour will be speeded up with the use of an artificial hormone drug administered through a drip in the mother's arm. The same drug, oxytocin, is also used to induce labour from the beginning.

REASONS FOR INDUCING LABOUR

- If the pregnancy has gone on far beyond the date the baby is thought to have been due. After 40 weeks of pregnancy the placenta begins to deteriorate and the baby is in danger of being starved of oxygen
- High blood pressure
- A small-for-dates baby
- A baby that is already very large in proportion to the size of the mother's pelvis
- A diabetic mother

Caesarean section   A Caesarean section is the name given to the surgical delivery of the baby through the abdomen. It may be decided upon well before the baby is due because the mother's pelvis is too narrow to allow the baby's head to pass through, or because of placenta praevia (see page 41). In these cases the Caesarean section is booked in advance like any other operation. Emergency Caesareans are performed for various reasons which crop up during pregnancy or labour, one of the common reasons being a breech birth. This is when the baby is born bottom first instead of head first. Many mothers of breech babies go into labour normally and are able to deliver their babies vaginally, but sometimes the baby cannot pass easily through the pelvis and birth canal and gets stuck. Breech babies are always carefully monitored, and if the baby shows signs of distress then an emergency Caesarean will probably be performed. Sometimes the doctor in charge will decide well before labour that a Caesarean is going to be necessary and will arrange one.

Forceps and ventouse   Sometimes the mother may need help in delivering the baby at second stage. She may be too tired to bear down, the baby's head may be large and be lodged in the birth canal or an epidural anaesthetic may be preventing the mother from knowing when to help the contractions. When this occurs, the doctor will use either forceps or ventouse extraction.

Forceps cradle the baby's head inside the birth canal and the doctor gently draws it down and out. Ventouse extraction involves attaching a small cup to the baby's head by means of a vacuum, and again the doctor uses it to gently draw the head down the birth canal.

After the birth   When the baby is born the cord is cut and the baby's mouth is cleared of fluid. He is examined quickly by the midwife and given an 'Apgar score' – a quick check list to measure his health and responses. He will then be weighed and measured and wrapped to keep warm. In the postnatal ward the mother is encouraged to learn to feed and care for her baby under the supervision of the midwives. She is examined every day to make sure the uterus is starting to return to normal, a process which takes five to six weeks in all. The baby's progress will also be monitored, and before mother and baby are discharged from hospital, or when the baby is four to five days old, the paediatrician (or general practitioner if you are at home) will give the baby a thorough overall examination.

Childcare

Parenthood is a commitment for life, but it is the first years that make the most demands on the mother and father. Once children have started school they certainly still produce enough problems for their parents to have to deal with, but the day-to-day responsibility is taken off their hands, at least for some of the time. Before that parents can witness a rapid and enchanting succession of changes, amazing physical developments, and the formation of the personality.

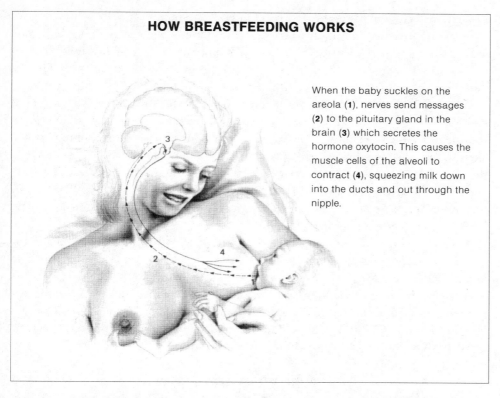

HOW BREASTFEEDING WORKS

When the baby suckles on the areola (**1**), nerves send messages (**2**) to the pituitary gland in the brain (**3**) which secretes the hormone oxytocin. This causes the muscle cells of the alveoli to contract (**4**), squeezing milk down into the ducts and out through the nipple.

BREAST OR BOTTLE FEEDING

This is the first decision new parents have to make. It is undoubtedly true that breastfeeding is more satisfactory, but it is not possible or practical for all. Breast milk is designed specifically for babies, it is always ready and always clean, and it is convenient and costs nothing. You can in theory breastfeed your baby anywhere. Recent research has also indicated that, statistically, breastfed babies may be more intelligent than bottle-fed ones. Almost any woman can breastfeed – the size of breasts or nipples is immaterial.

However, infant formulae are now very sophisticated and babies thrive perfectly well on them. But formula milk is not particularly cheap and the cost of equipment – a minimum of four bottles plus extra teats, sterilizing equipment, etc – and the inconvenience of having to remember to sterilize all the time are practical disadvantages. A baby should never be left with a propped up bottle unsupervised as he could easily choke.

Doctors and midwives encourage mothers to breastfeed at least at the start. This is because the pre-milk – known as colostrum – contains antibodies from the mother which protect the baby from illnesses which are dangerous in the first six to 12 months of life. Babies can be completely breast- or bottle-fed until they are about four to five months old – after this other foods can be introduced. Solid food should be introduced by six months, since the milk does not contain enough iron or calories to support the growing child after this age.

Length and timing of feeds It is recommended that babies are fed when they are hungry rather than adhering to a strict regime of four-hourly feeds. Your baby will indicate hunger by crying and mothers will experience the 'let-down reflex', when the sound of crying stimulates the pituitary to produce oxytocin and they feel the milk being squeezed into the milk ducts as a tingling or prickling in the breast.

Whether feeding by breast or bottle, there may be as little as one or two hours or as much as five between feeds to start off with, but gradually the baby will develop a routine of his own, which will probably average out at about four hours between feeds. If breastfeeding, it is a good idea to stop about halfway through and change to the other breast so that milk production is equally stimulated in both. It isn't always necessary to break during bottle feeding, but if the baby has a rest or seems uncomfortable, stop and lift him upright to see if there is any wind to come up. There is no need to spend a long time rubbing his back.

After a feed babies often bring up a little milk with a burp. This is normal and the only inconvenience is possible staining of the parent's clothes. However, repeated vomiting of whole feeds should be reported to the doctor.

Advice on feeding is available from the midwives in the hospital or the community midwife, and from the health visitor once the mother is back home. Organizations like the National Childbirth Trust and the La Leche League also provide specialist breastfeeding counsellors who advise and support mothers.

PROBLEMS WITH BREASTFEEDING

Blocked ducts A segment may become tender because a duct is blocked. This can be relieved by warm flannels and gentle downward massage. Put the baby to the breast as frequently as possible until the problem clears.

Cracked nipples If the baby does not latch on properly the nipples may become sore and cracked. It is painful, so can be a disincentive to breastfeeding. However it is important to continue, checking that the baby's gums are on the areola not the nipple itself. If it is very painful a nipple shield can help until the crack heals.

Engorgement This occurs about four to five days after birth when colostrum is replaced by true milk. The breasts feel swollen and full and need supporting with a bra. This can be relieved by warm flannels or baths, but frequent feeding is the best remedy.

Mastitis This is an infection of the breast possibly caused by a cracked nipple which has allowed bacteria to enter. It may be accompanied by a temperature and a sore, red area on the breasts. It is treated with antibiotics. There is no need to stop feeding.

THE MOTHER AFTER THE BIRTH

Once the mother is back home she is visited by the community midwife daily until the baby is ten days old, after which she is under the care of her general practitioner and health visitor. Bleeding from the vagina will gradually lessen after the first week, and will have disappeared altogether about three weeks after the birth. If there is any sudden bleeding the mother should report this to her doctor at once. There will be a baby clinic nearby to which mothers are invited to go and have their baby weighed, and to talk about any problems.

When the baby is six weeks old the mother will be given a full postnatal examination either at the hospital or by her general practitioner. The doctor will make sure the uterus has gone back to normal size, that there are no problems with residual bleeding, that breastfeeding is going all right and that the mother's health is generally good. The doctor will also talk about contraception if he or she has not already discussed it at the hospital.

Sex and contraception Sexual intercourse can usually be safely resumed within three or four weeks of the birth – if you are in any doubt consult your doctor or health visitor. It is quite possible for a mother to become pregnant again within two or three months of the birth if she does not take precautions, even if her periods have not apparently started again, so contraception is recommended. And while breastfeeding inhibits conception, it is not an infallible method of birth control.

CARING FOR THE BABY AT HOME

Sleeping and crying Babies vary in their sleep requirements, just like adults. Young babies sleep about two thirds of a 24-hour period. Their sleep patterns are quite random to start with and they have no concept of the difference between night and day. However, within a few weeks or months most start to sleep more at night and less in the day, although there will always be individual babies who continue to wake at night well into toddlerhood, and others who sleep through the night from three or four months old. Both are normal. Babies do not necessarily want to go straight to sleep after a feed and parents will recognize their babies' wakeful times quite early on. When being put to bed they should be laid on their side or on their backs until they are big enough to roll over by themselves. Laying a baby on his or her front has been implicated as one of the possible factors associated with 'cot death' (sudden infant death syndrome) and should be avoided.

Crying is the baby's distress call, the only way he can communicate his needs. He may be hungry, uncomfortable, perhaps need to bring up wind, have a dirty or wet nappy, be too cold or too hot, be tired or simply want a cuddle.

Colic Many babies have a wakeful irritable period, often in the evening, which can be accompanied by screaming, and which seems impossible to pacify. The baby may bend his legs as if in pain. This condition, sometimes called colic, has no known cause, but it often starts when the baby is about three to four weeks old and usually stops at three or four months. It most commonly happens in the early evening, which can be a strain for parents, especially if one is out at work all day.

Bathing and changing High standards of hygiene should always be observed with babies and young children to avoid bacterial infections. Always wash your own hands before feeding and before and after changing your baby's nappy. Nappies should always be changed when they are soiled and they should not be allowed to get too wet. Soreness can result from an infrequently changed nappy with resulting discomfort to the baby.

Frequency of dirty nappies varies from baby to baby. Bottle-fed babies especially occasionally suffer from constipation which is usually due to lack of fluid. Give the baby boiled water to drink in a bottle or on a spoon. Diarrhoea in the form of very wet, green or explosive stools should always be taken seriously in babies and young children (see page 62) and you should consult your doctor if this happens.

Babies do not have to be bathed every day. Many very young babies do not enjoy it, and the whole business can be an ordeal for them and the parents, but others like it straightaway and most come to enjoy it after a few weeks. It should be done in a warm place; bring the baby bath into another room if your bathroom isn't very warm. The water should be about 29 °C/84.2 °F, and should feel comfortably warm when you put your elbow in it. Always test the water first as a baby's skin is much more tender than an adult's and scalds more easily. Wrap your baby in a towel before and afterwards to avoid rapid cooling, and have all the equipment needed within easy reach before you start. Never leave the baby lying on a changing mat on a high surface – even the smallest baby can wriggle off and older babies learn to roll over very unexpectedly.

Very young babies often develop spots or a so-called milk rash, but they are harmless and disappear after a few weeks. They have nothing to do with milk. Dry skin can be smoothed with baby lotion or oil or you can put oil in the bath water, but be careful when lifting the baby out as the oil makes his skin more slippery. If the dry skin seems angry or irritates the baby check with your doctor as it may be infantile eczema (see page 63). Some babies develop dry crusts of skin on the scalp, known as cradle cap; this is harmless and disappears after the first few months. You can soften the crusts with olive oil overnight, then wash them off when you wash the baby's hair.

BABY AND CHILD DEVELOPMENT

Growth Growth is mainly measured through regular weight and length (height) checks. These are compared to your baby's weight and length at birth on a growth chart to make sure that his progress fits the expected rate of growth for his age and physical make-up.

Teeth Teeth start to come through at about six months, starting with the central incisors. Lateral incisors appear between about nine months and a year and the first molars are cut at about 14 to 17 months. The first teeth start being replaced by permanent teeth at the age of five or six. Tooth-cleaning habits should be begun as early as possible, and regular dental check-ups can start as early as two. The teeth can also be protected by paying attention to diet. Too much sugar, especially in the form of sticky sweets or drinks, can damage the teeth even before they appear through the gums. It can be cleaned away but it is better to avoid it altogether.

Sight At birth babies can see and focus on a face within about 20 cm/8 inches away. By six weeks they can focus on objects 45 cm/18 inches away and can follow a brightly coloured ball with their eyes. With more eye-to-eye contact comes smiling and the first signs of real communication between baby and parents. Small babies enjoy having a mobile hung over the cot.

By three to four months the baby will look at his hands, bringing them up to his face and playing with his fingers. He will start to recognize faces and smile spontaneously at people he knows by five or six months. At seven or eight months he may appear to become clinging and shy with strangers – he is able to see that they are different and that he does not know them.

Hearing Young babies respond better to high-pitched sounds rather than low ones. They will startle at sudden noises but soon learn to ignore familiar loud sounds. A baby by six weeks may turn his head to a sound, 'stilling' as he listens. Hearing is important in the development of speech, and parents are often the first to suspect hearing problems. Hearing is tested by the doctor and health visitor at the baby clinic between the age of seven and nine months; if there is any doubt about the baby's level of hearing he will be tested again by a specialist audiologist.

Muscle control At birth and for about six to eight weeks a baby's neck muscles are too weak to hold up his head, which is the heaviest part of the body at this age. Parents are often worried about their baby's lolling head – it does need supporting at this age. However, when lying on his front a baby can lift his chin up.

By six weeks a baby has sufficient head control to enjoy being propped in a bouncing cradle. This is much more interesting for the growing baby who may not want to sleep immediately after every feed and who will be stimulated by watching what is going on around him. A bored, frustrated baby lying alone in his cot is much less likely to settle than one who has had a time of activity first.

By three to four months head control is much better; he can lift his head right up when lying on his stomach and when you pull him up to a sitting position from lying flat he will bring his head up in line with his back. By five months your baby will be doing press-ups as a preparation for crawling, pushing himself right up with his hands and arms when lying on his front. He will also be learning to roll over, so this is the time to be especially vigilant about leaving him on a high surface which he could roll off.

By six months your baby will be sitting unaided for short periods, and by eight months will sit and be able to swivel his body without toppling over, reaching for toys and other objects which are within reach. There is only a short time at this stage before full mobility, as babies also grow in curiosity and the desire to explore the world increases their determination to move around.

Manual dexterity At birth your baby has a grasping reflex but this soon disappears. The movements of his hands appear random but gradually he will gain control of his arms, and by three months will be making efforts to reach toys nearby. At four to five months he can grab an object and hold it, soon learning to bring it up to his mouth for further exploration. This is the time to make sure that he does not get hold of things on which he could choke if he swallows them by accident.

From six months objects are transferred from one hand to the other. At this same age he grasps an object crudely in the palm of his hand like a scoop. At around nine months he begins to use fingers and thumb together to grasp things between them. From nine to 12 months he can hold objects in both hands and bang them together. He can also pick up a tiny object like a raisin between his thumb and index finger.

Crawling and walking The process towards mobility usually starts with crawling. Many babies find themselves going backwards, because as they try to push themselves forwards with their hands their legs are pushed backwards. Babies usually crawl at about nine months. They will be pulling themselves up to a standing position by nine or ten months and by 12 months may be 'walking' round the furniture, holding on. However, it can be a comparatively long time before they take their first steps unaided. Usually they will have stood unaided for a few seconds first. Most babies are walking by 15 to 18 months.

Occasionally a baby may not crawl at all but shuffle around on his bottom in a sitting position, and progress to walking that way. This is perfectly normal.

Communication and speech By three months smiling will be spontaneous and babies will squeal and babble. They begin to vocalize with distinguishable sounds like 'ba', 'ma' and 'da' at about nine months. By 12 months they have found at least one word which signifies 'mother' and 'father'. Nursery rhymes and simple books can be introduced as early as one year as babies learn by simple repetition, but the best way to encourage and develop your baby's speech is to talk to him. It doesn't matter what it is about – your baby will simply enjoy the two-way communication.

By 15 months your baby will be saying three or four words, but the use of sentences is a slower process – by 20 months to two years most children are making simple two-word sentences like 'baby cry', 'daddy gone'. By three speech is quite sophisticated, and your toddler will be able to understand quite complicated instructions.

FEEDING

Solid food in the form of milky cereal or puréed fruit can be introduced in very small amounts at about four to five months, depending on your baby's size. Solid food is usually only necessary once a day at first, and it is best to introduce new foods very gradually. By about six months the average baby will probably be having some solids three times a day and milk feeds will gradually be reduced, perhaps to one in the morning and one last thing at night, with dilute juice or water at other times.

At about six months you can introduce a cup – most parents prefer to use the type with a feeding spout to avoid spills, but in fact babies can learn to drink from an ordinary cup quite quickly. A cup with two handles is a good idea to start as the baby will want to hold it himself. By eight to ten months your baby will also want to hold a spoon and try to feed himself; this can be messy but it is worth encouraging.

Try to make your baby's diet as varied as possible and introduce new foods when you can. He will show likes and dislikes, but try to ensure that his diet contains a balance of protein, carbohydrate and fresh fruit and vegetables, so that he gets all the nutrients, vitamins and minerals needed for growth. At this time he will also be able to hold pieces of food like fingers of toast, rusk, banana or peeled apple and try to eat them himself, but do not leave a baby alone with food in case he chokes.

Once your baby is eating foods similar to the rest of the family don't leave him out at mealtimes. Bring his high chair up to the table so he feels part of the group. He is much more likely to learn to eat properly and develop acceptable eating habits if he has examples from an early age.

OUT OF NAPPIES

The secret with toilet training is patience and good temper. It takes a while for children to get the idea, and being angry when inevitable accidents happen is more likely to delay the whole process as children begin to associate it with their parents' disapproval.

Babies are physically incapable of controlling their bladders or bowels until they are about 24 months old. Occasionally a toddler becomes dry earlier than this but the parents can count themselves lucky. It is not worth trying to introduce toilet training as such until at least 18 months. At about this age a baby may become aware of being wet and may indicate to his parent or carer that he is uncomfortable. He may acquire a word for urine and become aware of when his bladder is full, though he may not able to hold it in yet. This is a good time to introduce the pot, gently showing your child that the two things normally go together. If you have a friend whose child is a little older and is already using the pot it is useful to have your toddler watch, as children respond to example.

Bowel control follows a similar pattern. Some parents find introducing the pot for bowel movements easier than for urine as it is a slower process and it is easier to spot the signs of a movement about to happen. However, some children resist using the pot for bowel movements for some time even when they may be dry. Once your child is using the pot for them, make sure you set up a pattern of hygiene so that he learns to wash his hands afterwards as a matter of course. While you will need to clean him yourself for some time, encourage him to try to do it himself as soon as practicable.

Even though your child may be using the pot during the day, it may be some months or even years before he has the control to last the night without wetting himself. Although the majority of children are dry at night by three and a half, around one in ten will still wet the bed most nights at age five. It is not necessarily abnormal, but if you are worried talk to your health visitor or doctor. Once your child seems to be waking with a dry nappy, leave the nappy off at night; he may well have been using the nappy out of habit. You will undoubtedly have some accidents but deal with these without fuss.

HEALTH CHECKS AND IMMUNIZATION

Your child's development will be checked at regular intervals during infancy and young childhood. Physical and intellectual development are always checked at six weeks, and again at 18 months, two and a half to three years and at school age (about five years), although these later ages vary slightly with different health authorities. Hearing and sight are also checked at seven or eight months. These checks are done by your GP, at the baby clinic, or in the case of the five-year-old check, by the school doctor. You can, of course, ask your doctor or health visitor to check your baby's development at other times if there is anything worrying you.

Immunization against childhood diseases which can be life-threatening if contracted young starts at about three months old. There has been some controversy over the immunization against whooping cough (see page 74) which may have affected one or two babies in the past but the risk is extremely small compared to the risk to a baby who contracts the disease. Go and talk to your doctor about this if you have any doubts.

IMMUNIZATION SCHEDULE

Age	Vaccine
Newborn	BCG for babies at risk from TB
3 months	Diphtheria, tetanus, pertussis (whooping cough) – known as DTP or Triple vaccine – and poliomyelitis
5 months	DTP; polio
9 months	DTP; polio
15–18 months	Mumps, measles and rubella (German measles) – known as MMR
School entry	Diphtheria, tetanus; polio
10–13 years	BCG (if no immunity to TB found)
11–14 years	Rubella (all girls, if no immunity already)
School leaving	Tetanus; polio

NON-PARENTAL CHILDCARE

In families where the mother goes back to work after the birth or in single-parent families, non-parental childcare may have to be considered. There are various options available, some more expensive than others: nannies, day nurseries and childminders.

Nannies should be trained with an NNEB nursery nursing qualification. They can either live with the family, or come in daily. Some families share a nanny, which can be helpful if one parent works part-time. Always interview your nanny as a couple and take up references; talk to the previous employer on the telephone as people are less open in reference letters. Nannies are probably the most expensive option for the working mother.

Day nurseries are private (fee-paying) or run by the local authority (which will probably mean that only the most deserving cases will be given places). They are usually open from about 8 am to 6 pm. Word-of-mouth recommendation is often the best way to choose a day nursery, but you should always visit it and spend some time there observing how the staff care for the babies and children.

Childminders are people (usually women) registered with the local authority to look after other people's children in their own homes. They often look after more than one child but are relatively inexpensive. Registered childminders have to adhere to certain standards of care; it is not a good idea to leave your baby with an unregistered one.

PRE-SCHOOL EDUCATION

Allowing your child to go to playgroup or nursery school for a few hours a day from about the age of three years is an invaluable preparation for school. Research has shown that children with some form of pre-school play experience settle into school better and grasp reading and writing skills more quickly than those without. Pre-school education involves skills in socializing and becoming independent, and provides a lot of the early learning skills which lead on to reading, writing and number work. It also gives children the opportunity for supervised play with things like sand, water and paint which might be difficult for you to supply regularly at home.

Playgroups are run by a committee of parents and usually involve the parents helping the full-time playleaders once a week. The fees should not be high. The groups are often held in hired halls.

Nursery schools are run by trained nursery teachers with the help of nursery nurses (NNEB-qualified) in purpose-built surroundings. Private nursery schools charge quite high fees; local education authority nursery schools are free. Some primary schools have a nursery class attached to them; this is an excellent introduction to school as the child is already familiar with the surroundings and will probably already have got to know the reception teacher before moving into the main school.

When your child starts a nursery or playgroup, you will probably be invited to spend the first few sessions there with your child to give him confidence. Gradually the playleader or nursery teacher will encourage your child to leave you and join the other children's activities, and may suggest that you leave for an hour or so. You may be surprised how quickly your child adjusts.

Sessions are usually only two or three hours at most, either in the morning or afternoon. If your child is still having a nap during the day try to enrol him in a session which doesn't interfere with this. In fact you may find that if he has given up

---

WHAT TO LOOK FOR WHEN CHOOSING A PLAYGROUP OR NURSERY

- Is there a welcoming atmosphere?
- Is there parental involvement?
- What variety of activities are available?
- What is the child/adult ratio?
- How do the staff interact with the children? Are they aloof or friendly?
- Do the adults talk to the children or to each other?
- What is the policy towards sexism and racism?
- Are children adequately supervised, and what are the safety precautions?
- How is a distressed or angry child handled, and what is the attitude to aggression?
- How do the staff help new children settle in?
- Do the staff seem to get on with each other?
- What is the level of communication between playleaders and parents?
- Do kitchen and toilet areas appear clean?

having a nap before he starts nursery he may well need one again for a while because many children find nursery very exciting and therefore exhausting. He may well show signs of regressing – such as starting to suck his thumb again or wetting the bed despite having become dry at night. Because of this it is quite important to think about what else is going on in your child's life. For instance, if there is another baby on the way, try to settle the child into the nursery well before the birth so that he does not feel rejected. If this can't be arranged, wait until your child has got used to the idea of having another baby in the family before starting him at nursery.

STARTING SCHOOL

In Britain the legal school age starts at five years, but in practice many children begin their formal education before their fifth birthday. If your chosen school has special links with the playgroup or nursery which your child is already attending, this makes the transition much easier. If not, spend some time looking at different schools well before the term your child is likely to start, and once you have chosen one and have been accepted (these things do not necessarily go together first time), see if you can spend a morning in school with your child.

The criteria for choosing a school are very similar to those for choosing a playgroup or nursery, although you will obviously want to look at the school's academic record as well. However, it is worth bearing in mind that a primary school in an inner city area may well be better than average in helping its children to succeed, given the social background of many pupils, while the idyllic little school in the countryside may well have happy but unambitious children. Thus academic test results may not always be the best guide to a school's overall success.

Starting school is a lot less difficult for children who have experienced pre-school education of some kind. But school days are much more structured and much longer, and some under-fives find it hard work even if they have grown out of their nursery schools. In any event it does help to prepare your child for school by making sure he can dress and undress himself for P.E. lessons, do up his own shoes and coat (if he can't manage laces choose buckle shoes or ones with velcro fastenings), can go to the toilet by himself, and can use a knife and fork if he is staying for school lunches.

Most reception classes now invite parents to come in with their children for a visit beforehand to familiarize the child with the school routine. The youngest children sometimes come in only for the morning or afternoon sessions for a while; at other schools it will be all day right from the start. However, all schools know that their youngest children need a period of adjustment, and arrange extra supervision in the first few weeks.

Medical Matters 2

A phenomenon that puzzles medical researchers has been dubbed the Churchill syndrome. It refers to the fact that Winston Churchill led a life that confounds all the prescriptions for healthy living, yet he lived into his nineties. He smoked heavily, drank large quantities of brandy, was overweight, kept irregular hours, and lived under considerable stress, yet he rarely had a serious illness.

Perhaps there is hope for those of us who are keen on the indulgent lifestyle. However, the fact that his circumstances are regarded as unusual actually shows that by and large it is by looking after ourselves that we increase our chances of living long and healthy lives. All the same, there are times when illness catches up with us. It is as well to understand what is happening to us then, what the symptoms of our illness are, and how soon and with what help we may expect to get better.

This is not, however, a licence for self-diagnosis. The first prerequisite of good health is to be registered with a good doctor, and the second is to know when it is necessary to visit him or her, and when it is not. Without this ability to judge but with a little imagination most of us can probably persuade ourselves that we are suffering from at least one or two of the illnesses described in the pages that follow. One of the reasons for this is not widespread disease but the human weakness for hypochondria; another is that many symptoms recur in different illnesses – headaches, feelings of nausea, faintness, loss of appetite. It is the particular combination of symptoms that marks any one disease, and on their own any of these common complaints can mean nothing more than being a bit run down. The descriptions that follow should not then be taken as replacing a visit to a doctor, nor as providing a means of doing his job for him, but as a way of telling us more about common illnesses.

The opposite applies to first aid. A working knowledge of the basics is really an essential for everybody, as the whole point of first aid is that you never know when it might be called upon.

2

Medical Matters

A-Z of Common Illnesses and Diseases

Acne A common problem in adolescence, acne is caused by an infection and inflammation of the oil-producing glands, or follicles, of the skin; the glands become blocked with infected skin oil. It is found mostly on the face, shoulders and back. Scratching or squeezing the spots should be avoided as they can introduce and spread infection. There are several commercial treatments available, some of which work, but the most successful treatment is to avoid greasy cosmetics and hair preparations, and to clean the hair and skin carefully and regularly. Where there is secondary infection a doctor may prescribe antibiotics to clear it up.

Appendicitis If the appendix becomes blocked with bacteria, inflammation sets in and there is a risk that it will swell and burst. The first sign is pain around the navel which moves towards the right lower quarter of the abdomen. It is generally accompanied by a mild temperature, nausea and vomiting, and the bladder may also become painful and make the patient pass water frequently. The same symptoms can also be produced by inflammation of the abdominal lymph nodes. As the appendix serves no useful function, in acute cases it is taken out. If there is only a slight inflammation, with the pain coming and going over a period of weeks, this is known as a grumbling appendix. Antibiotics may cure the condition, but if not then surgery is usually necessary.

Arthritis A painful inflammation of the joints which can affect almost any of the limbs. There are in fact two main types of arthritis which are of quite different origin: osteoarthritis and rheumatoid arthritis.

■ OSTEOARTHRITIS is the more common type. It is caused by wear on the joints, mainly on the large ones such as the hips, knees or spine. As such it is a disease that comes with age, though athletes sometimes suffer from it while still young because of the stress to which they subject their limbs. The first symptoms are minor discomforts in joints after use; these recur at intervals, becoming gradually more intense.

Dressing warmly in cold or damp weather helps alleviate the symptoms, as does heat treatment. Moderate exercise helps (though excessive exercise can aggravate it), as does physiotherapy. If you are fat you should lose weight, since obesity places greater strain on the joints affected. Painkillers like aspirin and paracetamol can provide relief; a doctor may prescribe stronger ones if these are inadequate. In severe cases surgery may be needed to replace the affected joint with an artificial one.

■ RHEUMATOID ARTHRITIS This is less widespread but more severe than osteoarthritis. It usually strikes between the ages of 25 and 55, and is three times more common in women than men. The cause is not known, though it is believed it may be a failure in the body's auto-immune system. It first hits the smaller joints, though it can spread to the larger ones. The disease often begins with a loss of appetite and a feeling of lethargy, followed by swelling and tenderness of the joints. As the disease progresses it can destroy cartilage and even bone tissue.

Sufferers should take plenty of rest and be given skilled physiotherapy. Anti-inflammatory drugs are often prescribed, and the patient may have to spend time in hospital with the joints in splints. These measures only help alleviate the symptoms and control the disease, as there is no known cure.

Asthma It is believed that asthma affects one in 10 children in the UK; about three-quarters of them grow out of it in adolescence, but for those adults in whom it persists it can be a serious condition, since it places a strain on the heart. Fortunately modern treatments are very effective.

True asthma is usually rooted in an allergy, and often runs in families. Attacks may be seasonal, when whatever it is that the sufferer is allergic to is concentrated in the atmosphere. What happens in an attack is that the walls of the bronchial breathing tubes produce mucus and go into spasm. The sufferer wheezes, and may struggle to get air in and, especially, out.

Asthma sufferers are given inhalers which contain drugs known as bronchodilators. These make the bronchial tubes relax, and hence limit the spasm and the obstruction. Sometimes steroids are prescribed. The doctor may also try to find out the cause of the allergy; the mite found in household dust is a common culprit, in which case regular cleaning and vacuuming can remove the source.

Parents of asthmatic children often wonder whether their child's activities should be restricted. This is not usually necessary, as the child will impose his own restriction. However, his school should be warned and be told what to do if he has an attack, and he should carry his inhaler at all times that he is likely to get excited.

Bronchitis An inflammation of the larger bronchial breathing tubes, bronchitis is generally caused by a virus. When it occurs in children they are rarely very ill. They have a cough and wheeze. Proprietary medicines can be taken for the cough, and antibiotics are often prescribed because of the risk of secondary bacterial infection. Children under five may suffer from 'wheezy bronchitis', caused by inflammation of the bronchial tubes. This may look like asthma, but only rarely develops into it. The child may be prescribed drugs to open up the bronchi. All children suffering from bronchitis should be kept in a smoke-free environment.

In protracted cases in adults the disease can eventually be a killer. In chronic bronchitis there is permanent infection which may be dormant for long periods but never goes away. Over the years the sufferer develops a constant cough which damages the lung tissue. Eventually emphysema develops. Antibiotics will help tackle infection during attacks and inhalers will help with the breathing. Smoking is a common cause, in which case the sufferer must give up smoking and avoid smoky atmospheres. Alcohol consumption must also be cut right down.

Bunions See **corns and bunions**.

Cancer A malignant growth of cells in the body that forms a tumour that grows rapidly and without restriction. One of its features is that it has a tendency to spread and to recur after it has been removed. The first cancer evident is known as the primary, and when it spreads into other organs they are known as secondaries.

Cancers can be found in almost any organ. The most common ones in the West are those of the lungs, breast, cervix, stomach and colon.

The exact cause is not yet known, although there is considerable research into the disease; likewise there is no simple cure. Surgery is often the first step, but removing the affected part of the body is no guarantee against the cancer's recurring, so surgery is normally accompanied with radiotherapy to destroy possibly cancerous cells and treatment with chemicals, known as chemotherapy. In some cases these treatments are given without prior surgery. Environmental factors, especially smoking and bad diet, undoubtedly increase the likelihood of cancer, possibly by as much as 70 per cent overall and by even more in specific forms of cancer, but cancer would still exist if we avoided all harmful substances and ate very prudently.

■ BREAST CANCER A major cause of death for women over 40, breast cancer is evident as a lump, or sometimes a depression, in one of the breasts, though it also often affects the lymph glands in the armpit. Although not all lumps are cancers, it is important for women to check their breasts regularly, and if they find a lump or depression to go to their doctor immediately.

Treatment usually consists of removal of the affected breast – a mastectomy – or of part of it, and the adjacent lymph glands. It is usually followed by radiotherapy, and women, especially those over 50, are given hormonal treatment with tamoxifen.

■ CERVICAL CANCER This type of cancer can be anticipated and treated at a very early stage, before malignant cells appear. A very simple procedure in which a smear is taken from a woman's cervix and tested in a laboratory detects the presence of abnormal cells at a pre-cancerous stage. They can then be removed without major surgery. Once women have started having sexual intercourse (the cancer has not been found in virgins) they should have smear tests at least once every five years, and preferably more frequently.

When cervical cancer has become established, the infected part of the cervix will be cut away and the whole womb may even be removed, followed by radiotherapy or chemotherapy.

■ COLONIC CANCER Cancer of the colon, or lower bowel, affects men and women more or less equally, though normally not before the age of about 50. Its first symptoms are bleeding from the rectum and often a blockage, followed by the patient becoming pallid and losing weight. The affected part of the bowel is cut away in surgery, and the healthy parts are joined together. If the cancer is very low in the bowel rejoining may not be possible and a colostomy is performed, after which the patient is equipped with a special bag into which the bodily wastes discharge.

■ LUNG CANCER This causes more deaths in Britain than any other form of cancer. As it is nearly always caused by smoking that grim pre-eminence may be lost with the decline in the number of smokers, although it is possible that at first there will be an increase amongst women, because of the higher numbers of late-middle-aged women who now have a lifetime of cigarette smoking behind them.

The first symptoms are a cough that brings up mucus which may be flecked with blood. This is followed by increasing breathlessness and chest pain. If you go to your doctor with these symptoms he will arrange for you to have a chest X-ray, but if you do not have all of them but think there is a likelihood of your having the disease it is still worth asking for an X-ray as it can detect lung cancer before the outward symptoms show. When caught early enough the tumour can be removed surgically, though sometimes radiotherapy is given without surgery.

The best way to prevent lung cancer is by not smoking. If you already smoke cigarettes, giving up will immediately reduce the likelihood of contracting the disease, a chance that decreases further with each day that passes without a cigarette.

■ SKIN CANCER This is believed to be caused purely by exposure to ultra-violet radiation, as it is most common amongst fair-skinned people who are exposed to a lot of strong sun. With the widespread practice of sunbathing and the depletion of the ozone layer, the incidence of skin cancer is forecast to rise dramatically over the next few years. The best form of prevention is therefore to avoid strong sunshine and to protect yourself with sun-barrier cream when you are out in it.

There are three types of skin cancer: rodent ulcers, squamous cell carcinoma and malignant melanoma, of which the first is the most common. The symptoms to look out for in any of the three are lumps in the skin, established moles that start to alter, or changes in the dark freckles that many old people have. The usual treatment is surgery to remove the tumours.

■ STOMACH CANCER Normally starts with a **peptic ulcer**, though many such ulcers do not develop into cancers. The first symptom is mild indigestion and loss of appetite, followed by pain and vomiting. As with lung cancer, early detection is essential if the sufferer is to have a good chance of surviving. If caught early enough the affected portion of the stomach is cut away, but if not drugs and radiotherapy are used to try to contain it. Stomach cancer is more common among men than women, and is most likely to strike over the age of 50.

■ TESTICULAR CANCER Generally confined to men under the age of 40. It is one of the most curable of cancers, through the simple measure of removing the affected testis. This does not impair the working of the other one, so men who have the operation need not fear that they will become infertile. The cancer is detectable as a lump on the testis, so men under 40 should inspect themselves regularly.

■ UTERINE CANCER This is the fifth most common form of cancer for women. For post-menopausal women the first symptom is usually slight bleeding through the cervix, and for pre-menopausal women it is spots of blood between periods, though it is rare in this age group. Soon there is a watery discharge flecked with blood from the cervix, followed eventually by pain in the pelvic region. The usual treatment is hysterectomy or radiotherapy, with or without hormonal treatment. Like cervical cancer, cancer of the uterus can be detected at a pre-malignant stage by a smear test.

Cataract The lens of the eye sometimes goes opaque with age, or more rarely because of injury or an infection. The vision becomes blurred and fades. Sight is restored in a simple operation to remove the lens; the eye can function perfectly well without it, provided that the patient is also given glasses to counter the consequent long-sightedness.

Chickenpox Although this is a disease of childhood, adults and adolescents who have missed it when younger can occasionally catch it. It is highly contagious.

Medical Matters

The first sign of the illness is usually a rash on the face and chest. It consists of crops of small spots, which burst, become pustular and dry over and scab. This process takes about seven days, during which the crops may be in different stages of development. The child becomes infectious a couple of days before the spots appear and ceases to be when they have all scabbed over. Chickenpox has an incubation period of one to three weeks. It is generally a mild illness. Its most disturbing feature is that the rash is itchy, but the child should be discouraged from scratching it. Often calamine lotion dabbed on to the affected areas provides relief.

Colds Usually caused by a virus. The symptoms are the familiar runny nose, generally accompanied by a cough, sometimes a slight fever, and an earache in children. Despite years of research there is no sure cure, though some people swear by various remedies such as massive amounts of vitamin C or camphor pills. Usually, though, you just have to let the illness run its course.

Conjunctivitis This can occur at any age; the cause is either bacterial or viral infection, in which case both eyes may be infected, or it may be due to chronic irritation by a dust particle or an inturned eyelash, in which case only one eye is affected. In its viral and bacterial forms it is highly contagious.

The outer membrane lining of the eye and the inside surfaces of the lids become inflamed, and there is commonly a whitish or yellow discharge. The eye feels painful and gritty, and the lids may be stuck together in the morning.

To treat conjunctivitis wash the eye regularly with plain boiled warm water, or a weak salt solution. This can be done with an eyebath, or in the case of a child who finds this difficult, by pouring water gently over the eye with his head over the sink. In younger children and infants moist cotton wool gently wiped over the eyes is adequate. In acute cases a doctor is likely to prescribe antibiotic eyedrops.

Constipation People who eat good diets with regular amounts of high-fibre foods should not suffer from constipation. They may think they have it merely because they have bowel movements less frequently than other people, but this is no guide as habits vary considerably from individual to individual. Children especially may go a couple of days without a bowel movement, and unless they complain of pain or otherwise seem ill, this is no cause for concern.

If you suffer from hard and painful bowel movements, then the most likely cause is eating too many refined foods, and the best remedy is to eat more whole foods – wholemeal bread, raw vegetables and fruit, and bran. Laxatives can clear up an attack of constipation, but overuse leads to dependency where the user will suffer permanently from the problem.

If constipation persists it could be a symptom of bowel disease, especially if the stools contain blood or the constipation alternates with bouts of diarrhoea.

Convulsions These are caused by abnormal electrical activity in the brain which is then translated into uncontrolled, rapid muscle activity, so that the limbs are moved jerkily and involuntarily. It is probably best known as a symptom of epilepsy, in which the sufferer may also foam at the mouth and go into a trance, but this condition is rare. Convulsions can also be caused by fever, a brain disorder such as **meningitis**, shortage of blood sugar, or certain drugs.

The most common form of convulsion in children is the febrile convulsion. It occurs between the ages of six months and five years and is associated with a rapid rise in body temperature. The fever itself can be caused by a simple infection such as one of the middle ear, or even **measles**. At the end of the convulsion the child may be semi-conscious or go into a deep sleep. He should be left to lie with his face sideways and down, while medical help is sought.

A doctor will treat the convulsion with drugs and will then treat whatever it was that caused the fever. After the first febrile convulsion many doctors recommend a lumbar puncture, which taps a little of the spinal fluid, as a test for meningitis.

Febrile convulsions can often be avoided. If a child's temperature shoots up cool him down by removing his clothes, opening the window and sponging him down with tepid water. Give paracetamol or aspirin to reduce the temperature further. When his fever has subsided he can be put back to bed and lightly covered.

Coronary heart disease   The first sign of a heart attack is a sharp pain in the heart, often spreading into the left arm or the throat. The pain may be so acute that you feel that you are dying, and you experience difficulty in breathing. What has happened is that an artery has become blocked, cutting off the flow of blood and oxygen to a part of the heart, which then perishes. In very bad cases this can be fatal, but usually the rest of the heart continues working and over a period of weeks other arteries grow and take over the function of the blocked one.

Arterial blockage is caused by fatty deposits (cholesterol) in the blood and weakened arterial linings, exacerbated by stress and smoking. It is therefore essential to rest fully for a few weeks after an attack, to cut out smoking and reduce the levels of fat in the diet, and to organize your life to minimize the amount of stress. After any heart attack the heart is permanently weakened, so unless you take these precautions there is a high chance of further attacks.

Corns and bunions   Both are caused by ill-fitting shoes. The best treatment is to buy more comfortable ones. Corns are hard patches of skin on or between the toes; bunions are swellings of the joint on the big toe. Plasters help alleviate the discomfort of corns. Bunions that refuse to heal can be removed by surgery.

Coughs   Colds are often accompanied by coughs, when they are merely one of the manifestations of the illness. However, a persistent cough can be a symptom of an infection such as **bronchitis** or **sinusitis**, or an allergy.

The type of cough often indicates the cause. For example, a child who wakes up in the morning with a cough often has a post-nasal drip. This is when secretions come from the nose and trickle down the back of the throat where they pool during the night. Treatment may involve the use of a nasal decongestant to unblock and dry the nose. It is not always wise to give a child a chemical cough suppressant, because if he is having an attack of asthma or has pneumonia, the cough helps clear the chest by

Medical Matters

removing infected or excess secretions. However, with an ordinary cough a cough mixture can help both the patient and other people in the house sleep, as they are more likely to be disturbed by the coughing than he is.

Croup A common form of **laryngitis** in a small child, caused by a virus. It manifests as a brassy cough, noisy breathing and often a fever. Croup is often distressing for the child, who may have difficulty in breathing. In bad cases the child might have real difficulty getting enough oxygen, and go blue. It is always worth having a child with croup seen by a doctor. If the symptoms are mild, the child can be treated at home; steam inhalations are sometimes recommended. In severe cases the child may need to go to hospital and be put in a humid croup tent.

Cystitis Inflammation of the urinary bladder, is more common in women than men. It is characterized by a dull pain in the abdomen, especially when passing water, and the urine may contain pus or blood. There is also a frequent need to urinate. It is treated by taking bed rest, keeping warm, and drinking plenty of fluids. Antibiotics are often prescribed. The condition can be caused by a microbe in the intestines which is wiped on to the urethra after a bowel movement. Women who are prone to it are therefore advised to wipe themselves away from the urethra.

Depression Everybody feels depressed at some time or other. Clinical depression arises when someone is not able to rise out of a fit of ordinary unhappiness, or else swings away from it into a highly energized but uncontrolled activity, only to return to the depression later (this is manic depression). It can be triggered by an external cause, or it may be inherent, arising for no particular reason.

The most notable feature of depression is how the sufferer feels, with no enthusiasm for anything, a pessimistic outlook, a feeling that life is just not worth living. Depressives also lack energy, lose their appetites, and are prone to wake early feeling wretched. The illness can strike at any time, but is most common in people in their twenties or over 50, and is more frequent in women than men.

Mild depression can sometimes be cured by taking exercise, and by consciously trying to put energy into one's activities. However, severe depression will not respond to such treatment, or to reason, but has to be treated with anti-depressive drugs and with psychotherapy.

Diabetes A disease in which the body has difficulty in metabolizing sugars, because of a deficiency of a hormone in the pancreas called insulin. It can strike at any age, arising spontaneously or possibly being caused by a diet with too much sugar. The sufferer complains of increasing thirst and passes urine frequently, and also loses weight. Older sufferers are also likely to experience infections of the skin, numbness and **high blood pressure**. Without treatment the diabetic may go into a coma. The treatment involves careful control of the carbohydrate content of the diet (sugar is a carbohydrate), and often daily injections of insulin.

Diarrhoea This is a matter of definition. To a doctor the term means frequent passing of watery stools, with little or no solid in them. Diarrhoea can be a symptom of a disease, such as **gastroenteritis** or bowel disorder, of **tonsillitis**, of food poisoning, or of an allergy. Unless accompanied by other symptoms, it is no more than a discomfort for adults, but children can become dehydrated and, regardless of the cause, should be given plenty of fluids. Proprietary electrolyte solutions, which replace both sugar and salt, are best, or flat soft drinks such as lemonade.

Diverticulitis   In people whose diet lacks roughage, small sac-like swellings often develop in the colon, or lower bowel, where impacted waste matter collects. If these become inflamed, the condition is known as diverticulitis.

The swellings themselves are relatively common in older people. Over a period the muscles in the colon have been strained through having to push for years without enough bulk to work on, and weak places begin to form in the colon wall. These then swell. Before the onset of diverticulitis a person will be aware of irregular bowel movements and slight cramps, and can avoid the inflammation by gradually increasing the amount of roughage in his or her diet. But if left, the symptoms develop into abdominal pain and tenderness, which may become severe. In this case the patient will be told to take bed rest, and also be put on to antibiotics. Severe diverticulitis can necessitate the removal of some of the bowel.

Dysentery   See **gastroenteritis**

Ear infections   Pain in and around the ear can affect children at any age, but may not in fact originate in the ear at all. It is often difficult to find whether it is coming from a part of the ear, or the teeth, the jaw or surrounding skin unless you can see an inflammation. However, the most frequent cause is the ear itself, especially in young children, whose ears often become infected by bacteria that originate in the nose or throat. Local treatment with a warm object such as a hot water bottle or an analgesic can relieve the pain, but if the ache persists antibiotics may be necessary.

■ GLUE EAR   An accumulation of fluid behind the eardrum. It generally follows an acute middle ear infection, and is associated with a blocking of the small Eustachian tube that leads from the back of the throat to the middle ear. There is often no earache, but the child's hearing seems to deteriorate. Treatment involves a decongestant drug and the insertion into the ear of small plastic tubes known as grommets. As inflamed adenoids can cause ear infection, and as repeated ear infection itself can lead to deafness, occasionally the adenoids will be removed too.

■ MIDDLE EAR INFECTION   Some 20 per cent of all children have had an infection of the middle ear by the time they have reached five years of age. The symptoms include earache, headache, fever, loss of appetite, slight deafness, and sometimes a discharge from the ear. Treatment generally involves an analgesic to relieve the pain and lower any fever, a decongestant, and antibiotics.

Eczema   A rash with rough, red and scaly skin lesions, especially on the face, cheeks, forehead, elbows and knees. It is usually due to an allergy, and is common in children of families with a history of **hay fever**. One cause in babies may be cow's milk, as it is rare in breast-fed babies. It can start as young as two months, but is also found in adults, and is often triggered by stress or an emotional crisis. Finding and removing the cause of the allergy is the ideal, but this is often not possible, and the problem can be treated only with steroid creams. Children who suffer should have their fingernails cut regularly so as to limit the damage done by scratching.

Emphysema   Over a period of years chronic **bronchitis** can gradually destroy the spongy tissue of the lung, leading to shortness of breath, malfunction of the lungs, and possibly a heart attack. This condition – emphysema – is generally caused by smoking. If you suffer from breathlessness and a bronchial cough, you should give up smoking immediately. Your lungs will not improve, but continuing smoking leads inevitably to further deterioration, and eventually the condition is fatal. You should also avoid smoky atmospheres and take moderate exercise. Your doctor will give you a bronchodilator, which is an inhaler that eases the airways.

Endometriosis   The problem of endometriosis begins before birth. Tiny clusters of cells of the female embryo's womb lining relocate into other parts of the abdomen. When the baby has grown into a young woman they are affected by the hormonal action of the menstrual periods and bleed during the monthly shedding of the lining of the womb (the endometrium). There is usually no indication of this for several years until in the late twenties they form blood blisters and cysts. The characteristic symptoms of endometriosis are heavy periods accompanied by back pain or pain in the abdomen. The treatment is a course of hormones, but if the condition does not improve a doctor may suggest a hysterectomy.

Fibroids   These non-malignant tumours that cause bleeding from the uterus are commonly found in the wombs of women over 35. They can cause discomfort in the lower back. If they grow large or are painful the womb is normally removed.

Food allergies   There has been a tendency in recent years to blame all sorts of illnesses on allergic reactions to certain foods, but they are probably not as widespread as this belief would have it. For example, it is true that some people are allergic to the gluten in flour, but this is a very rare condition. All the same, certain more common conditions such as **asthma** and **eczema** can be triggered by food allergies, more usually in children than adults, and an allergy to cow's milk is not uncommon in babies. Some children experience a condition known as urticaria, where areas of the skin erupt in itchy weals that look like nettle rash. If it does not clear up quickly this is likely to be a sign that it is caused by an allergy to a food.

Gallstones   The liver constantly produces a brownish fluid called bile which is stored in the gall bladder and which helps break down dietary fat. Lumps known as gallstones sometimes form here. They do not usually create much trouble, but they may block the duct, causing acute pain in the abdomen, a related pain in the right shoulder and shoulder blade, and a yellow colour in the skin and whites of the eyes. In such cases the gall bladder often has to be removed by surgery.

Gastroenteritis The leading cause of death amongst children in many underdeveloped countries, gastroenteritis is also widespread in the West, but prompt medical treatment means that it is rarely fatal. It is usually caused by a virus, but can be triggered by bacteria, often in food (food poisoning).

The patient suffers from regular vomiting and diarrhoea and does not feel like eating or drinking. There is a danger of dehydration, particularly in babies and young children, so it is important that they continue to take in fluids. The best are those that contain sugar and the chemicals that are depleted by the diarrhoea, such as flat lemonade or cola (the gas in the fizz can aggravate vomiting) or an electrolyte solution. If the patient becomes listless and refuses fluids, then he will be taken to hospital and put on a drip.

There is no treatment for the virus, but the disease normally clears up in a few days. Antibiotics may be given if laboratory tests on the stools show a bacterial cause. Both viruses and bacteria are infectious; careful hand washing is important as faecal/hand/oral spread is the most common means of transmission. If either the shigella or salmonella bacteria have been found the patient will be asked to go into some form of quarantine until they are no longer present.

Gingivitis A very common inflammation of the gums, often first evident as bleeding during toothbrushing. Regular and careful cleansing of the teeth, stroking the brush away from the gums to avoid aggravation, will usually cure it.

Glandular fever This is caused by a virus; it occurs worldwide and is particularly common where overcrowded housing and poor hygiene are found. It can strike any age group, but is most frequent in young adults. The illness has many symptoms: tiredness, aches and pains, a headache behind the eyes, high fever, a generalized reddish rash, and sore throat. Usually there are swollen lymph glands, particularly in the neck, but they are not tender, unlike the swelling that results from a throat infection. It is sometimes difficult for a doctor to make an accurate diagnosis without blood tests. The illness can linger for weeks, even months. There is no specific treatment for the illness, only the symptoms, e.g., bed rest is necessary for the tiredness, and adequate fluids and diet for loss of appetite. Do not share cups and other utensils used orally, since spread is by contact with infected body fluids such as saliva; in adolescence kissing is thought to be a common cause of cross-infection.

Glaucoma A common eye disorder in people over 60, glaucoma is caused by pressure of fluid in the eye, manifesting as blurred vision and haloes round lights. It is treated by inserting an artificial channel into the eye to drain the fluid. The operation is relatively simple, but must be performed early as glaucoma can irreversibly damage the nerve fibres at the back of the eye, leading to blindness.

Hay fever An allergic reaction to pollen, dust or animal fur. The sufferer has red and running eyes, a continual nasal discharge, bouts of sneezing, and may have a wheeze. It occurs more commonly in spring and summer. The treatment involves the use of antihistamine drugs and nasal decongestants, though bad sufferers can undergo skin and blood tests to try to locate and treat the specific allergy.

Hepatitis Infectious hepatitis is caused by a virus that attacks the liver, and is passed on by contact with infected body secretions. It is a relatively rare illness which can be either mild or serious. The first symptoms include a headache, general feeling of tiredness, nausea, loss of appetite, vomiting and abdominal pain. The stools frequently look pale. Jaundice sets in one or two weeks later, with the patient's urine becoming dark and the eyes yellow. Drugs are not recommended as the liver can have difficulty in treating them. Bed rest is the best treatment, with careful hygiene to avoid spreading the disease to other members of the family.

Hernia A bulge of soft tissue that has forced its way between weakened muscles, the most common site being the abdominal wall. Treatment often involves surgery, with the bulge being pushed back and the muscles sewn back together over it.

Babies sometimes have an umbilical hernia, where there is a protrusion of the intestine through a defect in the muscles around the umbilicus. This usually goes away by the age of five or six without treatment.

■ HIATUS HERNIA In this case a part of the stomach pushes through the gap in the diaphragm through which the oesophagus passes. It is often caused by obesity. The hernia itself causes little worse than indigestion, and it is unusual for surgery to be necessary. Dieting should be sufficient for it to go away.

Herpes The most common form of herpes is the ordinary cold sore, which forms small blisters by the side of the mouth. They normally clear up of their own accord.

Genital herpes is caused by the same virus, with the blisters appearing on the genitals. The condition may come and go and is difficult to treat. It can be transmitted from a cold sore during oral sex.

The herpes virus is a member of the **chickenpox** family, and the virus herpes zoster causes the chickenpox-related disease **shingles**.

High blood pressure The name, high blood pressure, accurately describes the condition, as it is one where the heart is pushing the blood through the arteries under excessively high pressure. Its other name, hypertension, is also descriptive as stress is a contributory cause. Three other major causes are obesity, heavy drinking and excessive salt. There are no visible symptoms until the condition is far advanced, and it has to be detected medically by taking a reading of the patient's blood pressure.

High blood pressure reduces life expectancy, and increases the chance of having a **stroke** or heart attack (**coronary heart disease**). The first treatment is to change your life style: lose weight, take less salt, stop smoking, cut down on alcohol, try to arrange things so as to be less stressed at work, and take up a relaxation technique. If these are not sufficient, beta-blocking drugs may be prescribed.

Hyperactivity A child who is always on the go, requires little sleep, is unable to finish simple tasks, gets easily bored, and is inattentive and easily distracted is thought medically to be hyperactive. The problem would seem to be that of a short attention span. The term 'minimal brain dysfunction' has been applied, but there is no obvious abnormality of the brain and no evidence of mental retardation. On the contrary, these children are often slightly brighter than average.

Many theories have been put forward, ranging from disorders of the brain chemistry to adverse reaction to artificial food additives. Changes in diet have a variable success rate, and there is no proven medical cure. Many children casually labelled 'hyperactive' actually have discipline and behaviour problems. Firm disciplinary limits need to be set for them, and an absolutely consistent approach applied by both mother and father.

Impetigo A surface bacterial infection of the skin frequently found in children. The most common site is the face, though the actual source of the bacteria is often another area of infection, such as a discharging ear. It usually starts as an area of redness, which then develops into pustules and blisters. Careful washing of the whole body with medicated soap is necessary to stop it spreading. The infected area can be washed with a solution of sodium bicarbonate, obtained from a chemist, and then an antibiotic cream applied.

Infestations We are hosts to millions of organisms, most of the time unknowingly because they are microscopic bacteria. Many are essential to our healthy functioning. Problems arise only when something bigger decides to make us its home, or larder. Most of these are pretty small, too, but the itching and sores they create are a source of discomfort, and they can spread disease or seriously weaken us.

■ CRAB LICE These are small insects that attach themselves to bodily hair, commonly in the pubic areas. They are so called because they are flat and have curved legs like a crab's. A common means of transmission is during sexual intercourse. A doctor will prescribe an insecticidal cream to kill them.

■ FLEAS There is a species that lives on humans, but the ones that normally bite us are dog and cat fleas. They do not live on the animal but in places that it frequents. They will generally prefer to bite your pet to you, but if they are hungry they will jump on to any mammal, and when they have bred profusely it is more than likely that there will be large numbers of hungry ones around.

Regular spraying of pets and the places they go to most is the best way of preventing infestations. The strongest insecticides have to be bought from vets. If they are not adequate and the fleas multiply, then call your local council who will send a specialist pest killer to come and spray your home.

■ HEAD LICE These are most common in pre-school and young school children, where they spread quickly by head contact. However, they are not limited to children; some older people carry them most of their lives without realizing. Amongst adults they prefer women's hair to men's. They are not a sign of lack of hygiene as they thrive in clean hair, and ordinary washing with shampoo and water does not destroy them.

The louse feeds off the scalp, laying tiny white eggs at the base of hairs. These are popularly known as nits. They look like small shining specks that will not go away with ordinary combing. Lice are more difficult to detect; they are tiny, flat, light brown or skin-coloured crab-like creatures. Although combing does not remove the nits, it is recommended for dealing with the lice as it can break their legs, which eventually kills them. The louse injects saliva which causes irritation, but the spots should not be scratched as this can produce **impetigo**. Because of the ease with which they spread the whole family and the whole class should be treated by soaking their hair with a special lotion that can be bought from chemists.

■ WORMS There are several types of parasitic worm that live in the human intestine, of which two are common in Europe.

Threadworms are extremely common in small children. They resemble tiny threads of cotton that can be seen in the anus and sometimes on the stools, in clothing and in bed clothes. The symptoms are itching, abdominal pain, nausea and **diarrhoea**. The worms lay their eggs in the lower bowel and round the anus. They cause an itch, the child scratches it, and the eggs then become embedded in the finger nails. They are later transferred to the mouth and the life cycle starts again. A doctor will prescribe a drug, usually in the form of pills.

Tapeworm is an infestation resulting from eating undercooked food, especially pork, beef and fish. Tapeworms live in the intestines, and diagnosis is usually made by seeing worm segments in the stools. Because they feed off the food before nutrients are fully digested, the host will eventually suffer from malnutrition even though he is eating a normal healthy diet. Drugs are prescribed to kill the worm.

Influenza The term 'flu' has taken on a dustbin-like quality; any illness with aches and pains, a temperature, and headaches sometimes accompanied by vomiting is commonly given that label. Doctors, however, shy away from the term now, unless you have influenza proper, and are likely to tell you that you have a virus, which is more accurate but scarcely any more specific. The illness will normally last a few days, and should be treated with bed rest and analgesics to mitigate the symptoms.

True influenza has the same symptoms but usually occurs in epidemics. You can be inoculated against influenza, and this is often advised for children, old people and anyone else whose resistance may be low. Unfortunately, the influenza virus has a habit of mutating, and there is no guarantee that a particular epidemic will not be of a new strain for which the immunization does not work.

Laryngitis Inflammation of the voice box (larynx) and vocal cords is known as laryngitis. As well as a sore throat, it is characterized by a dry cough, hoarseness and a loss of power in the voice. The treatment is to talk as little as possible and to inhale steam. The condition is dangerous in small children if it develops to the point that it threatens to block their air passages.

M.E. Myalgic encephalomyletes, to give M.E. its full name, has only recently been identified and named. There is still much to be discovered about the condition, including whether it is a single illness or whether there are several with similar symptoms. The patient experiences persistent tiredness, loss of concentration, and aches and pains. These may persist for several months, even years, with bouts of giddiness. The condition would appear to be caused by a virus or by different viruses.

Measles   One of the common infectious diseases of childhood, measles is caused by a virus which usually strikes between the ages of one and six. Ten to 12 days after it is contracted the child develops a runny nose and a cough, and may complain of sore eyes, vomit and have diarrhoea. He loses his appetite, his temperature rises, and small whitish spots appear in his mouth. Soon afterwards a red and blotchy rash appears behind the ears, then on the face, and finally on the trunk and limbs.

The child should be kept indoors and be treated for the fever (see **convulsions**). He should be given plenty to drink, and light palatable foods once he shows any inclination to eat. Measles can have serious complications, specifically **pneumonia** or **meningitis**. It is far less common than it used to be as most children are injected against it in a multiple inoculation against **mumps**, measles and **rubella**.

Meningitis   A serious infection, either bacterial or viral, that affects the lining of the brain and can strike at any age. Early diagnosis and treatment are necessary to avoid the possibility of brain damage.

The sufferer will complain of a severe headache, particularly behind the eyes, and will find light painful. There will be a high fever, vomiting, possibly a rash, and his neck will feel very stiff and he will not want to move it. A doctor is likely to carry out a lumbar puncture, at which fluid is taken from the spine in order to diagnose the type of meningitis. If it is bacterial the patient will be given antibiotics, and if viral painkillers. In either case treatment will be carried out in hospital.

Migraine   Quite different from severe headaches, migraines are a recurrent condition, with attacks often brought on by tension, fatigue, or the release from a long period of tension. A penetrating headache is accompanied by nausea, speech difficulty and sensitivity to light and sound. The sufferer has to lie down in a quiet darkened place, often for several hours until the attack passes.

Sufferers can often anticipate an attack through various signs, usually a shimmering in the vision or tingling or numbness in a hand. Once these are detected a full attack may be headed off, or at least mitigated, by taking prescribed anti-migraine drugs or just sleeping for a quarter of an hour. For some people attacks are triggered by cheese, chocolate, coffee or red wine, and avoiding them reduces the number of migraines they experience. Other people have found relief in treatments involving acupuncture and biofeedback. More than twice as many women as men suffer from the disease.

Multiple sclerosis   The cause of multiple sclerosis is unknown. It strikes young adults and the middle-aged, causing damage to the linings of the nerves in the brain and in the spinal cord. The first signs are attacks of poor sight, even double vision, giddiness and numbness or tingling. The attacks become more debilitating with loss of muscular co-ordination and difficulty with speech. They recur at unpredictable intervals, and can build up to a state of increasing paralysis. Whether the disease progresses to the point where the victim loses the use of his limbs is also unpredictable; in many cases it continues in occasional bouts without intensifying, and for some people it seems to clear up of its own accord.

Mumps   Before the spread of infant inoculation, mumps was a common viral infection in childhood. Two to four weeks after exposure to the virus the child complains of being unwell, loses his appetite, and has a fever and a headache. The salivary glands in the cheeks and lower jaw become tense, painful and swollen, and the mouth dry. Treatment can deal with the symptoms, not the cause: paracetamol or aspirin and regular mouth rinses can be used to make the child feel more comfortable. He will probably only want drinks and a little light food, and should be kept isolated until seven days after the face swelling has begun to subside.

Once the disease has been experienced the child is generally immune to it for the rest of his life. Adults who have not already had the disease as children can contract it; in men it is often painful and can make them sterile.

Peptic ulcers   Erosions in the lining of the stomach and digestive tract are known as peptic ulcers. They are caused by an excess of acid in the stomach, which can result from long periods of nervous tension, heavy smoking and drinking, and lack of sleep, or a combination of all these factors. There are two common types: gastric ulcers, which are those in the stomach, and duodenal, which are in the duodenum, or passage leading out of the stomach. Gastric ulcers are far more common than duodenal, and are found in roughly equal numbers in both sexes, while duodenal ulcers occur four times as often in men as in women.

The symptoms of both are the same – recurring bouts of pain in the region of the stomach, which is worse later in the day, heartburn, a burning sensation in the gullet, abdominal pain. The main treatment is bed rest and stopping smoking. Antacids are often prescribed to counteract the excess of acid in the stomach. In some cases surgery is necessary to remove part of the stomach or to by-pass the duodenum.

Pharyngitis   The area at the back of the mouth, the pharynx, can be infected by a virus, creating a sore throat and a temperature. If the tonsils are swollen the illness is more likely to be **tonsillitis**. Treatment only alleviates the symptoms, involving taking regular fluids and a drug to relieve the temperature, and it normally clears up in a few days.

Pleurisy   This is inflammation of the membrane around the lung. It is not itself a disease but a product of a lung infection, such as **pneumonia** or tuberculosis. The symptoms are pain in the chest, especially during coughing or deep breathing. The infection is countered with antibiotics but the underlying cause has also to be identified and treated.

Pneumonia   An infection of the lungs, pneumonia can be caused by either a virus or a bacterium. Segments of infected lung may collapse and become solid. With the infection the patient will have a high fever and a cough, which may or may not bring up mucus, and his breathing will be faster than usual and shallow.

Treatment involves physiotherapy to clear the lung of infected secretions, antibiotics and reduction of the fever by cooling and by analgesics. It is important for the patient to keep up fluid reserves, and occasionally oxygen has to be given.

Roseola infantum This disease, which is thought to be caused by a virus, strikes children between the ages of six months and two years. It starts with a high fever lasting three to four days, which then abruptly settles, and a scattered, reddish, non-itchy rash appears over the body. This rash fades quickly over the next two to three days and the child feels very much better. No specific treatment is necessary, but the temperature may be high enough to cause a **convulsion**.

Rubella (German measles) Rubella is a common childhood illness that can also affect adults. It starts with a general feeling of tiredness and a temperature. There is then a rash over the face, body and limbs. The rash looks like a milder version of **measles**, but there is no runny nose at the onset. The patient's lymph glands swell, particularly those at the back of the neck, the eyes appear red and the throat may be sore. Adults who suffer from it also experience pains in their joints. It has an incubation of two to three weeks, and is infectious from seven days before the rash appears to about five days afterwards.

The illness is mild in children, but is dangerous when contracted by pregnant women, especially in the first three months of pregnancy, as it can seriously damage the eyes, ears and heart of the developing fetus. It is therefore very important that anyone with the disease is kept away from pregnant women. Girls who have not had the disease by their teens are strongly advised to be inoculated against it, though now many infants are injected when about 15 months old with a single vaccination that immunizes them against rubella, **measles** and **mumps**.

Schizophrenia A very distressing mental illness in which the sufferer is prone to experience delusions and hallucinations, the most common ones being hearing voices. He has difficulty in coping with reality, and may become completely withdrawn, illogical or obsessed with the idea that there is some conspiracy against him. The condition can come on without apparent trigger at any age, though most often in the late teens in men and in the mid-twenties in women. The cause is unknown but it seems to involve some distortion of the brain's chemistry; patients are treated with strong tranquillizers and other drugs to bring the mind back on to an even keel, though therapeutic activity is also required.

Sexually Transmitted Diseases (STD) Otherwise known as Venereal Diseases, or VD. Until recently only two diseases were considered to be spread by sexual intercourse – gonorrhoea and syphilis. To these are now added genital **herpes**, NSU (non-specific urethritis) and the most serious and most recent of them all, AIDS (Acquired Immunity Deficiency Syndrome).

■ AIDS Unlike syphilis and gonorrhoea, AIDS is often passed on by means other than sexual intercourse. The virus that causes the disease lives in the blood of the host, so it can be caught by a transfer of blood from an infected person. Hence there are many cases of drug addicts catching AIDS from each other because they have shared needles, and patients in hospital have caught the disease by innocently being given transfusions of infected blood. The latter instance, however, is now unlikely as hospitals routinely screen all blood to be used for transfusions.

The virus that causes AIDS is properly known as the Human Immunodeficiency Virus (HIV). People carrying it are known as HIV positives; although they might not have any symptoms of AIDS, they can still pass on the virus. However, once a person has contracted HIV full-blown AIDS can start at any time (or never), manifesting initially in loss of weight, diarrhoea and swollen glands. Gradually it destroys the immune system of the body, making the sufferer prone to viral and bacterial infections. He is slowly weakened until finally there is an infection which the body no longer has the resources to counter. There is as yet no cure.

Despite its publicity the disease is still relatively rare, although the incidence is growing. In the West it was originally found mainly in homosexual men and in drug users, but it is becoming increasingly widespread in the heterosexual population.

■ GONORRHOEA AND NSU These diseases are far more common than syphilis, and are found more in men than women. The symptoms of the two are much the same; the difference is that the bacteria that cause gonorrhoea have been identified, while the exact cause of NSU is not yet known. Both diseases first show in men as an inflammation of the urethra, with discomfort in passing water and a yellow discharge. In women the inflammation is of the vagina. Both conditions are treated with antibiotics and, providing that they are dealt with early there are no permanent effects, but if left gonorrhea can lead to sterility and serious complications.

■ SYPHILIS This was once regarded with as much fear and concern as AIDS is today as it would lead eventually to permanent brain damage and death. However, it is now rare, thanks to penicillin. It starts with a hard but painless sore on the penis or in the vagina, or on the rectum if transmitted through anal intercourse. A rash appears after a few weeks over the whole body apart from the face. The rash then disappears but if untreated the disease attacks the heart and nervous system.

Shingles A disease caused by a variety of the herpes virus, known as herpes zoster. These viruses are part of the **chickenpox** family, and shingles is often contracted by adults who have had chickenpox in their childhood.

The virus lodges along the distribution of a nerve, often starting on the side of the chest or abdomen, causing pain which spreads across the chest or back. A rash then appears in the same places, and usually lasts about a week. There is no cure but there are drugs which can speed a recovery, and rest is important. The pain of the rash can be alleviated by dabbing it with calamine lotion.

Sinusitis The sinuses are four cavities in the head: above the nose, behind the nose and two in the top of the skull. These are lined with mucous membranes which can become inflamed, especially those around the nose. Sinusitis rarely occurs in early childhood as the sinuses do not develop until five or six years of age.

Sinusitis often starts with a cold, or with cold-like symptoms. However, the catarrh does not clear up but becomes thick and often green, and the sufferer has a dull pain in the head and sometimes in the teeth. Treatment is usually with antibiotics, which tackle the infection, while steam inhalations help move the catarrh. Recurring sinusitis is usually a sign that one of the nasal passages is blocked and this has to be cleared surgically. Sinusitis can also be caused by an allergy.

Stroke Similar to a heart attack (see **coronary heart disease**), but in a stroke it is the blood supply to part of the brain, not to the heart, which is cut off. It too is usually caused by a blockage in an artery, but it can also be brought about by haemorrhaging from a ruptured blood vessel in the head. The immediate symptoms vary according to the part of the brain affected; there may be speech difficulties, partial loss of sight, loss of sensation in one side of the body, or difficulty in swallowing. Afterwards there is a lasting paralysis in the parts of the body governed by the damaged area of brain, but physiotherapists are now able to help patients overcome this. A common cause of a stroke is **high blood pressure**, so those who have suffered strokes are counselled to lose weight, cut out smoking and take up a relaxation technique.

Thrush A fungal disease found in babies, young girls and in women. In babies it commonly occurs in the mouth, where small whitish flecks can be seen on the tongue and cheek. The inflammation can make the baby irritable and interfere with his feeding. It is passed on from the mother at birth, or from badly sterilized bottles. Thrush can also occur around the buttocks as a red and raw nappy rash.

In women thrush most commonly occurs in the vagina, creating discomfort and a whitish discharge. It is also sometimes found in the vaginal area of girls of school age. The fungus thrives in a warm damp area, such as can be created by artificial underwear materials that do not let the vagina 'breathe'. Vaginal deodorants can encourage it by killing the acid-producing bacteria in the vagina that normally destroy the fungus. Thrush is treated with an antibiotic cream or pessaries.

Thyroid problems The thyroid gland, which is situated in the neck, secretes a hormone called thyroxine that controls the metabolic rate of the body. In hyperthyroidism the gland is overactive, and the sufferer becomes shaky, fidgety and hot, and cannot relax. The eyes often bulge, and he – or more likely she, as women are more prone to the condition than men – is likely to have a bulge in the neck, known as a goitre, because of the swollen condition of the gland. The treatment is usually to give an anti-thyroid drug, although surgery may also be necessary.

The opposite condition, in which the thyroid is underactive, is known as hypothyroidism. Again the condition is more common in women than men, being especially prevalent at the time of the menopause. The sufferer slows down, becomes easily tired, puts on weight and looks puffy. She becomes constipated and her hair thins. The treatment is very simple: the patient is given hormone tablets to make up for the underproduction of thyroxine.

Hypothyroidism is also found in babies, usually due to a deficiency of iodine in the diet, and if it is not treated the baby does not develop properly and becomes a cretin.

Tonsillitis A bacterial or viral infection that causes inflammation of the tonsils, which are lymph nodes on either side of the back of the throat. They become swollen and tender, and the sufferer complains of a sore throat and fever. The glands can often be felt by a gentle prodding of the fingers. Treatment involves taking plenty of liquids, gargling with soluble aspirin and, if necessary, a further analgesic for the temperature. If the doctor thinks the cause is bacterial he will prescribe antibiotics.

Those who suffer recurrent tonsillitis may be advised to have their tonsils removed, although this operation is not as common as it used to be.

Travel sickness A fairly common complaint in young children who, however, usually grow out of it. It is caused by a disturbance in the balance mechanism of the inner ear during movement, which results in the child becoming pale, dizzy and nauseous. Simple measures like avoiding big meals before setting out on a journey, opening car or train windows for fresh air, and strictly limiting the number of sweets consumed, can prevent it; travel sickness tablets may also help. It is advisable for the parents not to make too much fuss about it, as anxiety makes it worse.

Urinary tract infection Infection of the urinary tract can occur at any level in the system – in the kidneys (pyelonephritis), the ureters (the tubes connecting the kidneys to the bladder), the bladder (**cystitis**), or the urethra. Infection is more common in females than in males, except in the case of newborn babies where it is found equally in both sexes. The symptoms include pain either locally over the kidneys or in the bladder, or on passing urine, together with more frequent passing of urine day and night. There may be other non-specific symptoms such as irritability, vomiting, **diarrhoea**, and a mild fever, and in children bed-wetting.

These infections are treated with antibiotics. With children the infection may be a sign of an abnormality in the urinary tract structure which will require surgery. Urinary infections can also contribute to the formation of kidney stones.

Varicose veins When their valves do not work properly veins swell up and turn blue. Once this has happened they remain permanently distended and discoloured, and are prone to ache when the person is tired. When found on the testicles varicose veins are known as haemorrhoids, and as varicoceles when in the scrotum, but are most normally found in the legs. Varicose veins often arise in pregnancy, and are very common over the age of 40, especially in women.

Some relief can be given by resting with the feet higher than the chest, or by wearing support stockings. As standing a lot can contribute to their formation, sitting as much as possible also helps. In severe cases the affected veins can be removed by surgery, in which case the surrounding blood vessels take over their job.

Whooping cough This can be a serious disease in children. Its main symptom is a repeated spasmodic cough which comes with a characteristic whoop. It can last for weeks and does not respond to cough medicines. The disease is more severe in children under one year of age, and the spasms of coughing can be so marked that the child is unable to breathe properly, with the possibility of damage to the brain due to a lack of oxygen. Occasionally there is pneumonia because of a secondary infection. The treatment is with antibiotics, and in cases where extra oxygen is thought necessary the child is admitted to hospital.

There has been some controversy over the inoculation of children against whooping cough because of a slight risk of complications, but the chance of suffering brain damage from the disease is greater than that of getting it from the vaccination. However, vaccination acts against only one type of the bacteria that causes whooping cough – albeit the most common one – so it does not provide a complete guarantee against contracting the illness.

The Sick Child

INTRODUCTION

It is not always easy for a parent to know when a child is truly ill. In addition, many parents worry about bothering their doctor unnecessarily. Although this is understandable, doctors are normally convinced that, despite their own doubts, parents are still the best judges of their child's health. So be confident in your own observations and go to the doctor when you feel it necessary.

With a very small child there is an added complication in that he does not have the words to say he feels unwell or to tell you just where it hurts. In this case you have to rely on your own intuition. Often the only guide is that the child behaves differently from usual: the tearaway toddler suddenly starts moping, the infant who previously slept regularly becomes constantly irritable and difficult to feed and to console.

In general the child who is unwell will lose his appetite, may sleep more than usual, and may develop a temperature. The temperature itself is not necessarily a cause for concern, unless the child has a tendency to develop convulsions (see page 60). Over and above these there are a few symptoms that are grounds for worry and for seeking immediate medical advice:

* a gradual loss of consciousness
* laboured breathing
* a convulsion
* suggestions of prolonged or severe pain
* continued vomiting and diarrhoea
* abnormal bruising and bleeding
* a rash other than known eczema.

In general, if you are in doubt it is better to seek advice than to wait to see what happens. If your child has got a serious complaint, it will be harder to treat the longer it is left.

CALLING THE DOCTOR

Unless you think the source of the trouble may be an infectious disease, it is normally best to take the child to the surgery. The doctor will have all the equipment there that he is likely to need to make a diagnosis, and can perform simple investigations, such as urine and blood tests. If the cause of concern is more urgent, for example if the child shows any of the symptoms listed above, or if he has had a major accident or you suspect poisoning, telephone the doctor immediately. He may suggest a home visit or arrange for the child to go to the local hospital.

In all cases it is important that you have the advice of a doctor that you trust. Problems sometimes arise where the regular doctor cannot come and you are not sure how much to trust the judgment of the unknown person deputizing for him. However, most doctors will err on the side of undertreatment rather than overtreatment, which is how it should be. You can always seek a second opinion if you are not happy with the child's progress.

TREATING A CHILD AT HOME

As with adults, the best cure for children who are poorly is rest. In fact, children are usually more sensible than grown-ups about this; they don't have so many ideas about other things that they ought to be doing, and will stay in bed when ill and want to get up only when they feel better.

When you have been prescribed a medicine for your child, make sure you know what effect it is meant to have and how you can tell whether it is working. Make sure too that the instructions are clear. After each time you give it to the child, check that the top is securely replaced. All medicine should be kept in a locked cabinet out of reach of small hands.

Not all medicines are designed to cure specific diseases; some merely control the symptoms and make the patient more comfortable while nature takes it course. Antibiotics are not a cure-all, but are only of use in tackling specific bacterial infections. They have no power against viruses, but may be prescribed as a preventative measure by a doctor if he is not clear about what the cause of a particular infection is.

Tablets and liquids   Few children under the age of five can swallow a tablet whole, nor can many older ones, so break them up in halves or quarters. If your child still cannot take it, crush it up and mix it into a spoonful of food or honey. There is no loss in the efficacy of the pill if you do this.

With smaller children medicine is frequently prescribed in liquid form. This is often as a suspension in a syrup, so extra care should be taken afterwards with the cleaning of the child's teeth. Without this precaution tooth decay can be a problem for children obliged to take medicine on a regular basis.

Eye, nose and ear drops   If you have to give your child eye drops, take care not to frighten him by approaching too quickly. Start by comforting him, and if he is old enough tell him what is going to happen. Wash his eyes first, with cottonwool soaked in lukewarm water in which you have dissolved a little powdered salt, slightly more than a pinch to a cupful. Then rest his head backwards and gently put the drops in.

For nose drops, if the child is old enough encourage him to blow his nose first. Then, with his head tilted backwards, put the drops into each nostril individually and ask him to take a deep breath through his nose.

Eardrops are put in directly. Do not clear the ears out first, as there is a danger that you might force any wax in further, possibly infecting the ear or even damaging the ear drum.

Taking a child's temperature A high temperature is only a symptom of an illness, and unless it is getting high enough to cause a convulsion the main purpose in lowering temperature is to make a child more comfortable, rather than providing a cure. However, monitoring the child's temperature is useful as a way of measuring the progress of the illness.

There are two main types of thermometer, the rectal and the oral. Taking a reading in the rectum will give a truer indication of the deep body temperature, which is normally about 1°C higher than an oral reading. However, it is more practical and more comfortable for the child if you use an oral thermometer and take a reading from his mouth or from under the arm.

Before taking the temperature the thermometer should be washed in a mild disinfectant or soapy water and then rinsed in cold water, or should be sterilized if it is for a baby. Shake it vigorously in order to get the reading down. Then leave it in the child's mouth or armpit for between 30 seconds and one minute. Do not give it to a child orally if he has just had a hot drink since it will have raised the temperature of his mouth.

Children's temperatures, especially babies', swing much faster than adults', and often rise higher. If it goes above 38 °C/100.4 °F it is probably worth cooling the child by uncovering him and giving him small doses of an analgesic. If the temperature rises to 39 °C/102 °F or higher, then cool the room (but do not make it draughty) and sponge him down with tepid water.

Food and drink In most circumstances no special diet is necessary when a child is ill. Parents should recognise that sick children lose their appetites just as adults do, and that force-feeding is not a good idea. However, a sick child should be encouraged to drink plenty as dehydration can be a major complication, especially for one suffering from diarrhoea or vomiting.

TAKING A CHILD INTO HOSPITAL

Not all illness or accident emergencies require a child to be taken to hospital, but it is important to call your doctor straight away if such a situation arises, or to dial 999 and ask for an ambulance if it seems particularly serious. There are some conditions, where the child is in great pain or where life itself seems threatened, when this is essential.

Hospitalization is not just for emergencies. Your child may have a condition which needs examination over a couple of days, or may be required to come in for a routine operation, such as inserting grommets into the ears, removal of tonsils, or repairing a hernia.

Examinations are often performed without the need for an overnight stay. In that case your child will be given an outpatient appointment. Turn up with him at the appointed time, and explain to him what is going to be done. Most hospitals will have some play equipment to keep children entertained while they are waiting, but it is best not to rely on this and to bring your own toys and books so as to be prepared, if necessary, for a long delay.

The Sick Child

2

EMERGENCIES

Take your child to hospital yourself or call an ambulance in any of these situations:

- signs of severe illness, weakness or floppiness, or if the child goes very pale or bluish, or becomes semiconscious
- convulsions – with shaking limbs or stiffening of the body; he may not need admission to the hospital but should be examined by a duty doctor there if it is the first time it has happened
- severe pain, even if you do not know the cause of it
- persistent diarrhoea and vomiting with signs of dehydration, such as a dry mouth, fast heartbeat, lethargy
- persistent bleeding from an injury
- accidents, such as burns, scalds, head injuries, electric shock, or swallowing of poisons, medicines or solid objects
- unconsciousness, but treat this as outlined on page 83 while waiting for the ambulance
- breathing difficulties

PREPARING FOR A HOSPITAL STAY

It is very important to explain carefully to the child why he is going into hospital and what to expect. If it is an emergency reassure him that he is going to the best place for him, where people will know how to make him better. Children should also be reassured that they are going to get better and come home again. Young children in particular may need to be dissuaded from thinking that hospital is a form of punishment, as some feel that if they are being removed from the security of their home it must be because they have done something wrong.

Although a children's ward will have plenty of toys, take along some favourites to help the child feel secure, as well as some much loved books and games. It is now common for hospitals to provide a bed for a parent to spend each night with his or her child. You may not get much sleep yourself because of the unfamiliar noises of the ward, but it is well worth it for the security it gives the child to have you there. This is particularly the case with under-fives. This does not mean that you should spend 24 hours of every day with the child, but explain why and when you are going away, and when you expect to return. In any stay of more than a couple of nights parents should alternate the night duty so that they can each get some rest.

During the early part of the hospital stay, it is valuable to explain to the child what is going on around him so that he is not bewildered, and to maintain a sense of normality by wearing your everyday clothes and bringing some mementos of home, such as family photographs.

Some hospitals permit parents to go down to the operating theatre with their children, and if you are not allowed at least as far as the anaesthetist it is probably for practical reasons, not because it is not a good idea. Explain to the child about how he is going to be given something to make him go to sleep and reassure him that no more than is necessary to his health will be removed in surgery.

Going home   Children are often difficult when they return from a hospital stay, and may well be clinging, irritable and babyish. Many start wetting their beds again. How long this condition lasts varies, but it is easier to cope with if you are prepared for it and can meet it with understanding.

First Aid

INTRODUCTION

It is a rare person who will go through life without at some time encountering an accident or medical emergency that requires immediate action. That is where first aid comes in. It is designed to contain and reduce the effects of the injury before the injured person can be seen by qualified medical staff. Basic first aid skills should therefore be a part of everybody's mental luggage, as you never know when they might be called on to save someone from death or lasting disability.

SAFETY MEASURES

The best first aid measure of all is prevention. With a few rare exceptions accidents are caused by people – not by the inanimate objects which actually inflict the damage – and common sense can prevent most of them. On average every day in Britain 18 people die as a result of accidents in the home, and each year $1\frac{1}{2}$ million people require hospital treatment.

Special attention is needed with old people or children. Children are usually less aware of the dangers inherent in fires or electricity, and old people can be badly hurt in simple falls that would only cause minor bruising to younger people. We are all more likely to cut ourselves or bang our heads if we are ill or harassed.

The kitchen No part of the home is potentially more dangerous than the kitchen. It is a busy room, and it contains sharp knives, naked flames or hotplates, boiling water and hot irons. Keeping it tidy and well-lit is one of the basic precautions; others are to turn off all appliances when not in use, to turn the handles on pans inwards so they do not protrude into the room, and to keep sharp knives on a magnetic wall-mounted rack. Wipe up spills from the floor straight away. These measures are doubly important if you have small children. It is a wise precaution to keep a fire extinguisher and fire blanket in the kitchen, and to install smoke alarms.

Another kitchen hazard is poisoning. Most kitchens contain bleaches, polishes, oven cleaners and other substances that should never be ingested. Everything of this nature should be kept well away from food and out of the reach of children.

Power utilities Properly fitted electrical appliances used correctly should be 100 per cent safe, but they can become lethal when tampered with. Never carry out an electrical repair unless you know exactly what you are doing. Many accidents are caused by the humble electrical plug not being properly fitted. Wiring up the terminals correctly is only the beginning; the right fuse for the appliance must be fitted, and the cable-clamp fully tightened.

Last thing at night turn off all electrical appliances not in use, as a precaution against fire.

Modern domestic gas is non-poisonous, but it can still explode or kill by asphyxiation. If you smell gas you should extinguish all naked flames and open all windows and doors. Then check to see if a gas appliance has been left on unlit, and if not, turn off the gas at the meter and call the gas company from a neighbour's telephone. Do not operate electric switches. Do not go back into the house until you are given the all-clear, and never attempt to mend a gas appliance yourself.

Use fixed fireguards around every type of fire if there are crawling babies or toddlers about, as curiosity will draw a young child to a flame or glow. Fireguards should also be used with open fires if there are older children. Never go near an open fire wearing an inflammable synthetic garment.

SAFETY IN THE GARDEN

Domestic hazards do not stop when you go out of the house:

- rotary mowers can throw up stones at great speed, injuring feet and ankles if they are not protected by boots
- electric mowers trail cables which can be run over and cut
- power hedge-trimmers can snag in a hedge or swivel out of your hand in some other way
- garden chemicals are often poisonous
- deep or dirty garden cuts carry the risk of tetanus

Dealing with an Emergency

In any emergency it is essential that you remain calm. After an accident, you must rapidly assess the degree of injury, and decide on the measures to be taken.

Examination check list Quickly and methodically examine the casualty to assess the extent of his injuries. This should be done as far as possible with the casualty in the position in which he was found. In any case, do not turn an unconscious casualty on to his back.

1. Check – is the casualty breathing? If *not*, turn to page 84 immediately.
2. Check – is he bleeding? Feel carefully over and under for dampness.
3. Then, starting at the head, look for any wounds. Speak to the casualty and assess level of consciousness. Try to reassure him – even if he is unconscious, he may be able to hear you.
4. Check the pupils. Are they 'pinpoint' or unequal?
5. Check for bleeding from ears, nose or mouth.
6. Check for fluid, froth, burns and stains to the mouth. Remove any potential obstruction from airways, e.g. dentures.
7. Check for any odour on the breath.

8. Examine the rest of body: neck, spine, trunk, arms and legs, feeling with the flat of your hand.
9. An unconscious casualty should be searched for medical cards, e.g. Diabetic, Steroid or Anti-coagulant card.
10. Take the pulse, noting rate, rhythm, strength.

If the injury is minor, you may decide to treat it yourself. If not, first aid must be given as an interim measure only, until proper medical treatment is provided.

Having assessed the immediate needs in dealing with the accident, enlist the aid of anyone who is nearby, provided they appear able to cope calmly with whatever needs to be done.

If the injury is not serious, get someone to organize car transport to hospital. Travel with the casualty in case emergency treatment proves necessary.

If the accident is more serious, telephone the emergency services by dialing 999, and ask for 'ambulance'. Always give the number of the telephone from which you are calling, and the address or exact location of the place where the casualty is being given first aid. If this is not possible, mention any prominent landmark. Give brief details of the type of accident and the condition of the casualty.

If the casualty has been badly injured and you have to undertake immediate first aid, send a helper to make the 999 call. Never give a badly injured person food or drink. He may become unconscious or, if he has to be operated on, need a general anaesthetic. In either event, on a full stomach he could vomit or choke. The only exceptions are that anyone who has been badly burnt may have small sips of water, and anyone who has swallowed corrosive poison should be given tepid water (milk if available) in small sips, and even with these do not attempt to give liquids if the casualty is unconscious.

Fire Your immediate priorities in the event of fire are to get all the occupants out of the building, close all doors and windows as you leave to prevent the fire from spreading, and call the Fire Brigade by dialling 999. Then stay well clear.

Small fires can be put out with water (except where live electrical equipment is the cause), by smothering them with a rug, or by using a fire extinguisher. Be very careful if there is a lot of smoke, as you may be overcome by fumes.

Do not continue to fight a fire if the fire spreads despite your efforts, or if there is a risk that your escape route may be cut off by fire or smoke.

If a casualty's clothes are burning, lay him down and smother the flames with coats, rugs or blankets. Do not roll him round and round as this would expose even more of his body to the flames.

Treat **burns** as described on page 90; **shock** as on page 89.

Carbon monoxide poisoning Car exhaust fumes and defective household heating appliances are the main causes of poisoning by carbon monoxide. The gas itself is odourless and colourless, and the symptoms of carbon monoxide poisoning are easily mistaken for other ailments. Unexplained headaches, nausea and lassitude are the first signs. In more serious cases a victim will appear confused and sleepy, and

Dealing with an Emergency

2

81

perhaps become unconscious.

To give effective help, speed is vital:

1. Before attempting to reach the casualty, take several deep breaths of fresh air yourself – and hold your breath while in the gas-filled room or car. Otherwise you put your own life at risk. If there is more than one casualty, repeat this action before each return to the gas-filled area.

2. Get the casualty into the fresh air.

3. Turn off any appliances that are burning in the room. If a car exhaust has caused the accident, switch off the engine.

4. Open all windows and doors wide to allow toxic fumes to disperse quickly.

5. Give whatever emergency treatment is required. See **Unconsciousness** and **Artificial respiration**.

6. Dial 999 for an ambulance.

Electric shock It is essential for the rescuer to exercise great care and ensure that he does not touch a casualty still in contact with electrical wires or terminals.

■ ACCIDENTS CAUSED BY HIGH TENSION CABLES OR RAILWAY CONDUCTOR RAILS If the casualty is thrown clear by the shock, treatment for severe **Burns** and **Artificial respiration** can be given without delay.

If he remains in contact with the high tension current under no circumstances even approach him. Keep at least 20 m away to be safe. *Do not* attempt to move the casualty clear with a piece of wood or any other object, as the current can bridge a considerable gap and your own life will be at risk.

Dial 999 and ask for an ambulance. Explain the full situation and all the necessary services will be despatched automatically. Return to the site of the accident and stay there to point out the spot, but do nothing further.

■ ACCIDENTS CAUSED BY DOMESTIC ELECTRICAL SUPPLY Your first objective is to separate the casualty from the current.

1. Break the electrical contact by switching off or unplugging the current, either at the socket or, if this cannot be safely reached, by turning off at the mains. Do not touch the casualty or his clothes until this has been done.

2. If you cannot disconnect the supply, make sure that you are standing on a dry floor, to prevent any possibility of current being earthed though your body. If the floor is damp, stand on a piece of dry wood or cardboard.

3. Even then, do not touch the casualty with bare hands; use an insulated object to move him away, such as a walking stick, rolled newspapers, a bundle of clothing, or a looped clothesline.

The casualty will probably need **Artificial respiration**. The current has a serious effect on the heart, and **Heart massage** may also be needed. There will almost certainly be electrical **Burns**. These may look insignificant but they are often very deep and may have serious after-effects. Sometimes, there are **Broken bones** caused by sudden muscle contraction due to the electric shock.

Dial 999 for an ambulance without delay.

Car accidents Keep bystanders well back from a motor accident, unless there are people among them who can help, and prevent helpers and bystanders from smoking to minimize fire hazard.

Turn off the ignition.

If there are several casualties, check rapidly to see who requires first aid most urgently. Do not try to get casualties out of a crashed car until you have determined the extent of their injuries, unless there is an obvious fire hazard. You could do more harm than good. If they are unconscious or have spinal injuries, leave them in the car until medical help arrives, but make sure they can breathe by supporting the head.

If there is no telephone box nearby, stop a passing motorist – better still, stop two going in opposite directions – and ask both to telephone for the emergency services. Make sure that they each have all the relevant information:

1. The location of the accident.
2. Number injured and extent of injuries.
3. Whether anyone is trapped.

Never attempt to move a car in order to lift a casualty clear, however necessary this may be, without having adequate help to move it safely.

If a motorcyclist is the casualty, do not remove the crash-helmet unless his airways are blocked.

Keep the casualty warm and do not move him more than necessary. Usually a casualty will instinctively adopt the position most natural to his comfort.

Treat injuries as described in the appropriate section of this book, bearing in mind that the casualty may be in shock.

Drowning   In drowning, first aid is intended to supply air to the lungs, restore breathing and make sure that the heart is beating. Do not try to drain water from the lungs; this will be expelled when the casualty starts to cough, as breathing is restored. Begin mouth-to-mouth resuscitation in the water if possible, and continue while the casualty is being pulled ashore. Otherwise, carry out artificial respiration on the beach, or in a boat. Do not wait until the casualty can be carried indoors or made more comfortable.

Continue with mouth-to-mouth resuscitation until medical help arrives. Do not give up, even after an hour. When the casualty starts to breathe, be prepared to continue resuscitation until normal strong breathing is restored. Then turn the casualty into the **Recovery position**. Be ready to recommence artificial respiration if breathing weakens. The casualty must be removed to hospital urgently; even after apparent recovery there may be serious lung inflammation.

While waiting for an ambulance to arrive make sure that the casualty is kept warm, as hypothermia is possible after even a short immersion in cold water.

Unconsciousness   Many accidents can lead to unconsciousness, and your first priority must be to preserve life by ensuring that the casualty is breathing properly.

Use your fingers to remove any obstructions from the mouth: dentures, food, vomit, blood, or broken teeth. Use a handkerchief to remove remaining blood or vomit. Loosen clothing at neck, chest and waist. Remove glasses, if worn.

Turn the casualty into the recovery position, shown on page 84, unless he is so badly

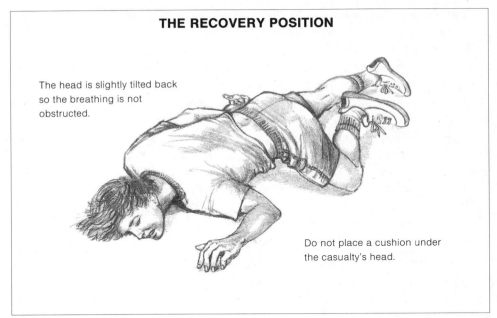

THE RECOVERY POSITION

The head is slightly tilted back so the breathing is not obstructed.

Do not place a cushion under the casualty's head.

injured that it would be dangerous to move him; in which case try to turn his head to one side. First, kneel beside him and place both his arms close to his body. Then cross his far arm and leg over his body and pull the far hip over so that he is lying on his side – protecting his head with your free hand as you do so. If help is available, and the casualty heavy, ask the helper to cradle the casualty's head as you turn him.

Now place the casualty's top arm and leg at right angles and tilt his head slightly back with his chin jutting out to keep his tongue clear of the back of his throat. Loosen any restrictive clothing but keep the casualty warm.

Breathing problems If a casualty appears not to be breathing, check quickly before commencing first aid. Study his lips and nose, and try to feel a current of air. Watch to see if the chest rises and falls, or feel the stomach just below the ribs to see if it rises and falls. If the casualty is not breathing, you have less than five minutes in which to start the breathing again. Otherwise, permanent brain damage or death follow quickly.

Air passages can become blocked naturally if a person is deeply unconscious, as the tongue drops back into the throat. This usually happens if the casualty is lying on his back. The blockage may be caused by vomit, blood, loose dentures, or large pieces of food. Quickly remove any obvious obstructions from the casualty's mouth. Reach well into the back of the throat with your fingers in order to make sure that nothing is still wedged there. At this point, many casualties begin to breathe again without further help.

If breathing has not started, roll the casualty on to his back and tilt his head well back by lifting his chin – holding him firmly below the chin and by the top of the head. This will lift the tongue away from the back of his throat leaving a clear airway. Loosen clothing at the neck, chest and waist. Check quickly to see if breathing has started. If not, begin artificial respiration immediately.

Artificial respiration In adults, use the mouth-to-mouth technique ('kiss of life'); for children use mouth-to-mouth and nose.

In mouth-to-mouth hold the casualty's head fully extended, as shown below, pinch the casualty's nostrils shut between your finger and thumb, take a deep breath, then seal your lips firmly around his mouth. Blow out steadily into the casualty's mouth, until the chest rises as air enters the lungs.

Remove your mouth, and watch the chest fall again.

Continue the cycle of blowing into his mouth and watching his chest rise and fall, at a comfortable natural rate of breathing.

If the chest does not rise and fall, or there is resistance to breathing into the casualty's mouth, there is probably still an obstruction in the throat. Check again.

Turn the casualty on his side, still with his head held well back, and thump him sharply on the back, between his shoulder blades. Remove dislodged material from the mouth and resume artificial respiration.

With babies and young children, place your lips over their mouth and nose together. Blow gently into the lungs and watch for the chest to rise. Otherwise, proceed exactly as for adults.

Continue artificial respiration until the casualty is breathing normally, then place him in the recovery position, and send for an ambulance.

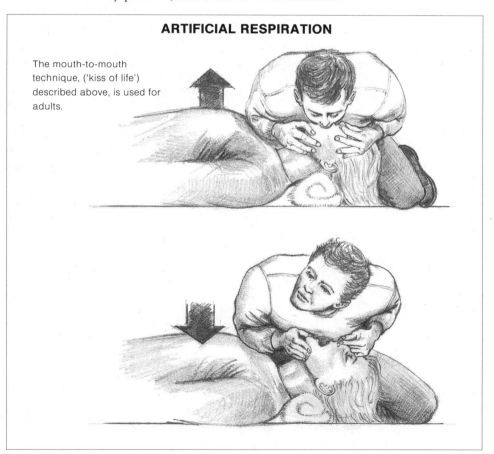

ARTIFICIAL RESPIRATION

The mouth-to-mouth technique, ('kiss of life') described above, is used for adults.

Heart Failure If the heart stops beating, or beats with a weak, quivery action, there is immediate risk to life.

Because he is not breathing, the casualty will already be a bluish-grey colour. After only a few breaths of artificial respiration, this colour should improve. But if the casualty remains bluish-grey, the heart may no longer be functioning properly. A further sign is that the pupils of the eyes become dilated and do not contract when the eyelids are held open.

Lay the casualty flat on his back, and thump the chest hard with the side of the hand, towards the lower end of the breastbone, and slightly to the left of his chest. The heart may start to beat again without further treatment. If not, repeat once or twice.

In babies, use two fingers to give a sharp tap on the chest; this should restart the heart. In either case, adult or baby, if this simple first aid measure does not work, external heart massage will be needed. This is more difficult, and if it were carried out while the heart was still beating, serious damage could be caused. Check carefully the three important signs that the heart is not working:

1. Blue-grey skin colour.
2. Dilated pupils (i.e. over-sized pupils).
3. Lack of pulse beat.

■ HEART MASSAGE Heart massage (heart compression) is carried out as follows. Kneel to one side of the casualty and locate the lower end of the breastbone. Place the heel of one hand on the chest near the centre of the breastbone, with the fingers and palm lifted clear of the chest. Place your other hand over this hand, again resting on the heel of the hand.

Hold your arms stiff, then rock your body forward to press down on the casualty's breastbone, which should press in (in an adult) by about 3.5 to 5 cm/$1\frac{1}{2}$ to 2 inches.

Rock your body back to let the breastbone rise, then repeat the whole manoeuvre, in a smooth rhythm. In adults, press at a rate of about 60 times each minute. In children, press more gently, with one hand only – but faster, about 80 to 90 times each minute. In babies, use only two fingers for compression, and press higher, towards the middle of the breastbone. Press very lightly and quickly, at 100 times each minute. In all cases you should avoid violent movement which could cause internal injury.

Restarting of the heart is shown by a rapid recovery of more normal colour, normal responses of the pupils, and the return of the pulse in the side of the neck.

Broken bones A broken or fractured bone may break clean across, crack, or be completely shattered. In a very bad break, broken ends of the bone can penetrate through the skin, with a risk of later infection. Sometimes, however, it is not so easy to tell if there is an actual break. Possible signs and symptoms of a break are:

1. The casualty may have felt, or heard, the bone snap, or may be able to describe the accident in such a way that there is no doubt about its result.
2. Pain at or near the site of the break will be very severe. Movement of the affected part will be difficult or impossible.
3. The whole area will be extremely tender to the touch.

4. There may be a deformity, such as twisting or bending of a broken limb.

5. The area of the break will swell rapidly, due to bleeding into the tissues.

6. Movement may appear unnatural, if possible at all. The casualty may feel a grating sensation in the damaged part.

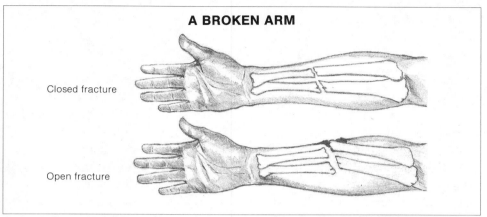

A BROKEN ARM

Closed fracture

Open fracture

Treat other serious injuries such as bleeding, breathing difficulties or severe wounds before dealing with the fracture. Fractures where broken bones have penetrated the skin should be covered immediately. Do not attempt to clean such wounds yourself, or touch them with your fingers. Cover them with a sterile dressing, or if this is not available, with any clean material.

Immobilize or support the damaged part so that no further injury occurs. Do not attempt to straighten or move the injured parts, and avoid all unnecessary movement of the casualty.

A broken leg is best immobilized by tying or bandaging it to the other, uninjured leg. If both legs are broken, splints have to be used. Arms are easily immobilized by tying them to the side or chest. With broken ankles, feet, or toes, do not remove footwear, as this helps support the damaged part.

First aid treatment for a broken spine consists of immobilization, and immediate expert help. Do not move the casualty. If a broken neck is suspected, the head must be immobilized without moving it. This can be done by making a collar from a rolled-up newspaper, and gently, carefully tying it around the neck with a bandage, steadying the head as you do so to prevent it rolling to one side.

If a rib is broken, there will be very sharp pains in the chest. The casualty takes shallow breaths because of the pain. If the broken rib has punctured a lung, blood will be coughed up. In a very bad break there may be an open wound to the chest, which allows air to be sucked in. This must be sealed immediately, preferably with an adhesive plaster dressing, or otherwise by covering with any suitable clean material, held securely in place by hand or by firm bandaging.

If the casualty is conscious, prop him up in a comfortable sitting position, or leaning over towards the injured side. If he is unconscious, lay him on his injured side, with his head slightly down.

Call an ambulance for all but minor breaks, such as a broken wrist. In the case of these it is usually possible to take the casualty to hospital by car.

Bleeding (Haemorrhage) External bleeding is obvious, but bleeding from an internal organ may not be so apparent. The signs to look out for are:

1. Pale skin.
2. Coldness, especially of hands and feet.
3. Rapid but weak pulse – 100 beats per minute or more (this can be felt at the wrist with the finger tips).
4. Sickness and thirst.
5. Shallow breathing, gasping for air.

Your aim is to stop blood loss as soon as possible and to obtain urgent medical attention. Call 999 for an ambulance.

■ SERIOUS EXTERNAL BLEEDING Make the casualty lie down and, if possible, raise the injured part and keep it at rest. This allows blood to drain back into the body, and gives a blood clot the chance to form without disturbance.

Apply pressure to the wound, preferably with a sterile dressing. If no dressing is available, and the wound is bleeding badly, use any clean material or even your hand or fingers to exert pressure until a proper dressing can be applied. If the wound is very large, press its edges together with the fingers and hold them in place until help arrives, or a clot has begun to form – this takes about 10 minutes.

Once the bleeding stops, carefully remove any dirt or surrounding foreign bodies, but only if this can be done without the need for probing the wound.

If you have to leave a foreign body embedded in, or protruding from the wound, put a sterile padding of gauze (do not use cotton wool) round the wound before applying a clean dressing, to prevent direct pressure. Hold the dressing in place with a firm bandage.

If blood soaks through the dressing, apply more dressings on top. Do not disturb the original dressing, as to do so might dislodge the developing blood clot.

If treating a scalp wound, there may be an underlying fracture, so do not apply direct pressure. Apply a sterile dressing much larger than the wound, puckering the dressing at the centre to raise it clear of the wound, then circle this with a large ring pad to prevent pressure and bandage firmly in position.

Keep the casualty still and give reassurance. When the bleeding stops, get him to hospital, provided you can do this without disturbing the wound. If the bleeding shows no sign of stopping after first aid, or if blood loss is considerable, call the doctor or an ambulance immediately.

■ INTERNAL BLEEDING Internal blood loss can follow a fall, blow or certain medical conditions. It can be very dangerous, so get the patient to hospital quickly.

While this is being arranged, help control the bleeding by getting the casualty to lie down and rest. Raise the legs on a chair or any other convenient object, to improve the blood supply to the brain and heart.

Keep the casualty warm and comfortable, give reassurance and treat any obvious external wounds. Do not give him anything to drink or eat, and remove him to hospital as fast as possible.

■ BANDAGING Bandaging holds a loose dressing firmly in place. It must be tight enough to ensure that the dressing cannot shift, but must never be so tight as to reduce the circulation. Signs of a too-tight bandage are numbness or whiteness of fingers or toes.

When using a roller bandage, it is important to match its width to the job it is to do. For hands and fingers, narrow bandages of 2.5–5 cm/1–2 inch width are necessary. For arms and legs, 5–8.5 cm/2–3½ inch-wide bandages are suitable, and for bandaging the trunk, even wider.

Bandages must be applied under tension. They are kept rolled, with the loose end being applied to the wounded part. First a loose loop is made around the injured part, and a light pull is given to the rolled bandage to secure it. The *outer* surface of the rolled bandage is applied to the skin.

Then the rolled bandage is passed round and round the injured part in a spiral, overlapping each previous turn by about two-thirds. Keep steady tension on the bandage as it is applied.

Sometimes several layers of bandage will be necessary for security, spiralling along and then reversing direction. Complete the bandaging by making a final straight turn above the injury, doubling the end over, and securing it with a safety pin or strip of adhesive plaster.

To ensure that bandages on limbs stay in place, start nearest the foot or hand, and work inwards towards the body. If the bandage covers the knee or elbow, pass the bandage around the limb, first above, then below the joint, to make certain that it is not dislodged as the limb flexes.

In an emergency, bandages can be improvised from any clean fabric, such as a shirt, sheet or tablecloth.

Bandages can be applied in first aid for several purposes, not just to control bleeding:
* *To keep a dressing in place over a wound*
* *To reduce the risk of wound infection*
* *To prevent further injury*
* *To prevent movement*

Shock   In any accident, the casualty may suffer shock. The symptoms are: cold, clammy skin, extreme pallor, sickness and giddiness, fast but shallow pulse and breathing, and confusion or restlessness.

Shock casualties may gradually lose consciousness and enter into a coma. Call for medical help urgently and, while waiting for this to arrive, do what you can to make the casualty comfortable. If he is conscious, reduce the strain on his blood circulation by laying him down. Raise the lower limbs slightly and, if there is a possibility of injury to the head, chest or abdomen, prop up his head and shoulders, with his head turned to one side.

If he vomits, or loses consciousness, turn him into the recovery position. Loosen any restrictive clothing, but keep him warm with extra cover, such as a blanket or coat. Do not use any artificial source of heat, e.g. hot-water bottles. Be prepared to give **Artificial respiration** if breathing fails. Do not give drinks, even if the casualty complains of thirst. Simply moisten his lips with water.

COMMON INJURIES

Back injuries If there is the slightest suspicion of damage to the spine, do not move the casualty at all. Keep him flat and immobile, and if help is a long while arriving, cover him with a coat or blanket to prevent chilling.

A very common back injury, generally incorrectly referred to as a 'slipped disc', often occurs while bending, or straining to lift a heavy object. This can be very frightening, as it is often too painful for the casualty to move at all. But if possible get the casualty indoors and lying flat. Give painkillers like aspirin or paracetamol, and call the doctor to make sure there is no serious damage.

Torn or 'pulled' muscles in the back, caused by falls, or by sudden twists, usually while carrying heavy loads, are very common and painful, but not at all dangerous. These, too, are treated by immobilization in bed, plenty of rest, and painkillers.

Burns and scalds Burns are among the most serious of common accidents, but only the smallest can be safely treated by yourself. Cool the injury under a cold running tap, or immerse it in water, and keep it there for at least 10 minutes, except in the most minor burns. This greatly lessens the extent of the injury, and reduces the amount of medical treatment which will be needed.

In chemical burns, use the same technique of washing the injured area with cold water for at least 10 minutes. Give a conscious casualty small amounts of a cold drink at frequent intervals, but do not give alcohol. Never attempt to give drinks to an unconscious casualty. This could cause vomiting and possibly choking.

Under no circumstances should you apply grease, ointment, or antiseptic to any burned parts. Do not touch the injury with cotton wool or any fluffy material which could stick to the wound.

Choking Choking is caused by any obstruction of the air passages to the lungs. In true choking, the lungs become completely blocked off by whatever was inhaled. The casualty rapidly becomes blue, and loses consciousness. You may be able to hook out the obstruction from the mouth, using your finger, but it may have been inhaled more deeply and be out of reach.

In this case, swiftly give a series of hard blows between the shoulders. Depending on age, position the casualty as follows:
* Hold babies upside down by the ankles, and slap them between the shoulders
* Lay children face down over the knee, and slap the back hard
* Get an adult casualty to lean over the back of a chair so that his head is lower than his chest and strike hard between his shoulders, using the flat of the hand.

If the casualty remains limp or blue, or if he does not seem to be breathing properly, follow with **Artificial respiration** or **Heart massage**. Even if the blockage remains you may be able to blow life-saving air past it.

Concussion If the casualty has been knocked out, even for a moment, a doctor's advice should be sought. Unconsciousness is accompanied by paleness, clammy skin and shallow breathing. As the casualty recovers, he may vomit. There is usually loss of memory of events just before and just after the accident.

Concussion always needs urgent medical attention. First aid measures are as for **Unconsciousness**, plus treatment for any visible injuries. If the pupils of the casualty's eyes are abnormal, his face flushed and his breathing noisy, he is likely to have brain compression, caused by a skull fracture or bleeding within the skull. He may also be conscious for a while before slipping into a coma. This is an extremely serious condition, and medical aid must be obtained urgently. While waiting for it to arrive, take all precautions to maintain the casualty's breathing (see **Unconsciousness**).

Crushing Injuries may range from fingers pinched by a closing door to extensive injuries to large parts of the body caused by motor accidents. For most minor crush injuries, apply a cold compress of towelling or other material soaked in cold water, and replace it frequently with fresh compresses. For more serious injuries, raise the injured part to reduce the leakage of fluids, and bind firmly with a crêpe or elastic bandage. In extensive crushing, internal injury may be serious. Lay the casualty flat with the legs raised. Call for medical help urgently. While waiting for help to arrive keep the casualty warm.

Dislocations The symptoms of a dislocation are very similar to those of a broken bone, except that a dislocation always occurs at a joint, causing it to be unnaturally fixed, whereas a broken bone is unnaturally mobile at the site of the fracture. However, the pain is such that the casualty will seldom even attempt to move, often feeling very sick. As with a break, first aid treatment is to support the injured part. Never attempt to replace the bones in their normal position. Support injured parts on a pillow or pad, or immobilize them firmly as described for **Broken bones**. Keep a close watch for signs that the circulation may be affected, such as whiteness of fingers or toes, or loss of sensation. If this occurs, straighten the limb very gently, but do not use traction.

Eye injuries If the eye is splashed with any chemical, wash it out immediately, with lots of water. Turn the head so that the chemical will not be washed into the good eye. Pull the eyelid back with your fingers, and allow a gentle flow of water to run directly sideways over the eyeball, for at least 10 minutes.

For any eye injury, other than a small foreign body which is easily removed, hospital treatment is urgently needed. Close the injured eye, cover it with a soft dressing and bandage gently around the head to keep the dressing secure. Take the casualty to hospital as soon as possible – do not wait for the doctor or ambulance to arrive.

Small objects inside the lower lid can be removed with the corner of a clean handkerchief or a swab of damp cotton wool. If the irritant is under the upper eyelid ask the casualty to look down and gently put the eyelid out and down over the lower lid. If this doesn't work, get the casualty to blink the eye repeatedly under water.

Fainting If the casualty has passed out completely, lay him down, loosen clothing at the neck and waist, and raise his legs to a higher level than his head. Upon recovery, give him sips of water. Treat any associated injury. Use your discretion as to whether medical treatment is necessary.

Penetrating wounds A puncture or stab through the skin leaves a deceptively small hole. The wound beneath may be very deep, and the object which caused the wound may have been dirty. Contamination could be carried deep within the wound, and infection is probable. For this reason, make no attempt to check the bleeding, which carries dirt out of the wound. When the bleeding stops naturally, apply a dressing and get the casualty to a doctor, unless the wound is small and shallow and can be treated with a plaster or small dressing.

Poisoning Two major groups of chemicals cause poisoning when taken by mouth. These are:

1. Poisons acting directly on the mouth, throat, stomach, and the rest of the digestive system. Symptoms caused by absorption into the system may occur later. Typical of these poisons are contaminated or rotten food, and some poisonous plants. Some of these poisons are corrosive, causing immediate burning and pain. Examples are: bleach, petrol, disinfectants, strong acids, and alkalis like caustic soda (sometimes included in oven cleaners).

2. Other poisons act on the nervous system after absorption into the body. Their effects are therefore delayed and, because immediate first aid may not be undertaken, they are doubly dangerous. Once symptoms appear, it is usually too late to remove the poison from the system by inducing vomiting. Among these poisons are aspirin and other pain-killing drugs, sleeping tablets, and poisonous toadstools. If you suspect that someone has taken poison by mouth, act very rapidly. While the casualty is conscious, ask what poison they may have taken. If the casualty knows he has taken a corrosive poison, or if the mouth and lips are sore or blistered, give him large quantities of water or milk to dilute the poison. Wipe away poison from around the mouth. Do not try to make the casualty vomit. Arrange transport to hospital by car as fast as possible and have someone telephone the hospital to tell them the casualty is on the way.

If you are sure that the poison was non-corrosive, and the casualty is conscious, make him vomit by pushing two fingers right down the back of his throat. Protect your fingers from bites by jamming a rolled-up handkerchief in the corner of the casualty's mouth. Let the casualty drink plenty of water between each bout of induced vomiting, to flush out the poison. Watch carefully to make sure that no vomit is inhaled. Remove the casualty to hospital quickly. Do not induce vomiting if the casualty is unconscious.

Unconscious casualties should be turned into the recovery position. Call for emergency medical assistance, and be prepared to give **Artificial respiration** if breathing stops.

Do not attempt to give liquids to an unconscious casualty.

Agricultural chemicals and garden pesticides are powerful nerve poisons, and can cause a wide range of symptoms, including twitching muscles and convulsions.

Sometimes symptoms occur several hours after handling or using pesticides. These require immediate medical attention, as they could be the forerunners of serious poisoning. Casualties must rest completely while awaiting medical aid. Strip off clothing splashed with chemicals, and wash the body thoroughly. If a pesticide has been taken by mouth give large quantities of water to drink.

Sleeping tablets and tranquillizers affect breathing, and **Artificial respiration** and **Heart massage** may be necessary while waiting for medical assistance. A person who has attempted suicide by overdosing with medicines should be made to vomit, as these substances are unlikely to be corrosive. **Artificial respiration** may be necessary.

If the attempted suicide was by drinking disinfectant or bleach (usually detectable by smelling the breath) treat by giving copious drinks of water or milk. Do not induce vomiting.

Get urgent medical assistance.

Strains and sprains A strain is damage to a muscle, usually caused by overstretching it in a sudden jerk or fall. Sometimes muscle fibres are torn. There is sharp muscular pain, and perhaps swelling.

Minor strains are treated by resting the damaged muscle. A cold compress reduces later swelling, and firm binding with a crêpe bandage provides support. Severe strains need medical treatment, and must be immobilized while transporting the casualty to hospital.

A sprain is quite different, affecting only the joint, being limited to tearing of the tendons which hold the joint together.

Sprains are very painful, and the casualty must immediately take all the weight off the damaged limb and support it in a comfortable position. Apply cold compresses to the joint to reduce later swelling, then bandage firmly but lightly with a crêpe bandage, to provide support.

THE HOME MEDICINE CHEST

A kit for first aid and home treatment should include the following:

Perforated film (non-stick) dressings; small, medium and large

Triangular bandages for slings

Rolled gauze bandages; assorted sizes

Adhesive plasters; assorted sizes

Adhesive plaster strip, 1 roll, for attaching dressing and securing bandages

Sterile cotton wool

Safety pins; assorted sizes

Scissors; preferably blunt-tipped

Crêpe bandages, for sprains and strains

Aspirin 'soluble' tablets BP, or paracetamol tablets BP

Calamine cream or lotion

Antihistamine cream

Disinfectant; medicinal quality

Tweezers; with fine points

Travel sickness tablets

Medical thermometer

Cotton wool buds

Kaolin and morphine mixture, to relieve diarrhoea

Sodium bicarbonate powder

3 Food and Cooking

Food is an essential part of our lives. The human body needs a regular supply of a variety of nutrients – protein, fat, carbohydrate, vitamins, minerals and fibre – and must get a balanced share of them all from the food we eat.

Just eating anything will not do. Our health and length of life depend very much on our choice of food – our diets. In recent years there has been considerable worldwide research into the connection between diet and health. While much of this has caused controversy, with theory and counter-theory being argued loudly in the world's media, it has, on the whole, become accepted that we in the West eat too much animal fat, sodium (salt) and sugar and not enough fibre. We could greatly improve our general health and reduce the incidence of fatal heart disease and other illnesses by eating less fat, especially the saturated fats found in red meat and dairy products, salt and sugar, and replacing them with fresh vegetables and fruit, pulses and grains.

It is not suggested that we should eliminate the 'fat/salt/sugar' foods from our diets. Remembering that 'there are no unhealthy foods, only unhealthy diets', we need to plan our food buying, preparation and cooking accordingly, and achieve a well-balanced diet that is a pleasure to eat.

This chapter aims to help the process, offering a guide to the great range of foods available to us in such abundance, giving hints on what to look for on those often bewilderingly laden supermarket counters, and suggesting preparation and cooking techniques for the foods we take home.

It also deals with the kitchen itself and how best to store foods, explaining which items should be kept in the refrigerator, the storecupboard and the freezer. It covers, too, electrical equipment for the kitchen, in particular the microwave oven and its advantages for busy people.

Fish and Shellfish

Fish is a valuable source of first-class protein, minerals and vitamins, with oily fish like mackerel and herring being particularly rich in vitamins A and D, as well as highly unsaturated fats. Fish also has a low carbohydrate content.

Many varieties of fish are available in Britain, with a varied choice of fresh fish and shellfish on sale all year round. March–May is generally the leanest time of the year for buying top-quality fresh fish.

FISH

While fish may be categorized as freshwater, salt (or sea), flat or round, it is more usually divided into white and oily groups.

White fish have a firm white flesh and a low fat content; the oil in them is found mainly in the liver and is usually discarded (to be used, in the case of the cod, in vitamin A- and D-rich cod liver oil), so that the fish is rather more easily digested than oily fish.

White fish available in Britain include bass, bream, brill, cod, coley, dab, dogfish, flounder, gurnard, haddock, hake, halibut, John Dory, monkfish (angler fish), plaice, skate (ray), Dover sole, lemon sole, turbot and whiting.

Oily fish In these the oil, which is distributed throughout the body, contains nutritious polyunsaturate fats. Even so, they seldom have more than a 20 per cent fat content – far less than the equivalent weight of meat. The flesh of oily fish is richer, darker and rather coarser than that of white fish.

Oily fish generally available in Britain include carp, eel and conger eel, herring, mackerel, grey and red mullet, pike, pilchard, salmon, sardine, smelt (sparling), sprat, rainbow trout, river (brown) trout, sea (salmon) trout, tuna (tunny) and whitebait (the fry of sprats or herring).

Smoked fish Both white and oil fish may be smoked, a centuries-old method of preservation involving salting the fish and then hot- or cold-smoking it. Smoked fish retains the protein content of fresh fish, but loses calories. Smoked fish available in Britain include Arbroath smokies (haddock), bloaters (inshore herrings), buckling (herring), kipper (herring), mackerel, eel, haddock (Finnan haddie), halibut, salmon and trout.

Other preserved fish are **pickled** and **salted** fish such as gravlax (raw pickled salmon), rollmops (raw pickled herrings), soused herrings, salt herrings and anchovies; and **dried** fish, particularly cod and – in Indian cooking – Bombay duck, which is cured bommaloe fish and smells quite dreadful until it is cooked.

Cephalopods available in Britain are squid (calamari) and octopus, available frozen all year round and fresh for much of the year. Watch out, too, for cuttlefish.

PREPARING A SQUID

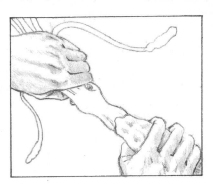

1 Hold the squid in one hand and pull the head and tentacles sharply. Most of the innards will come away. Cut off the tentacles and discard the head.

2 Pull the transparent backbone from the body and rinse the cavity. Peel the skin from the body and discard. Remove the skin from the tentacles. Rinse.

The great ocean fish – tuna, swordfish and shark, in particular – are to be found much more regularly in fish shops than was once the case. Usually sold as steaks, they tend to have a dry flesh which benefits from cooking in wine, lemon juice and other liquids in which they have been marinated.

SHELLFISH

These come in two main groups: crustaceans, which have protective external skeletons and legs, and molluscs, which have shells and no legs.

Shellfish generally available in Britain (though, in many cases, not all year round) include crawfish (spiny/rock lobster, *langouste*), crayfish (*écrivisse*), clam, cockle, crab, lobster, mussel, oyster, prawn, Dublin Bay prawn (scampi, *langoustine*), Pacific prawn, scallop, brown, common and pink shrimp, whelk and winkle.

BUYING FISH

When buying fresh fish, either oily or white, points to look out for include: plump, firm flesh; clear, full and shiny eyes; a moist and shiny skin; clean and bright red gills; and a fresh, not overly fishy smell. With ready-cut steaks and fillets, the flesh should be firm and the flakes closely packed. A watery appearance is a strong hint that the fish is stale. Fresh fish is best cooked and eaten on the day it is bought. Smoked fish should be eaten within three or four days of purchase, though it will keep in the freezer for up to three weeks.

As with fish, many varieties of shellfish are available frozen (or thawed from frozen – a fact which fishmongers should clearly indicate). To ensure real flavour and freshness, shellfish are best bought both fresh and live, to be killed and cooked at home. Live lobsters and crabs should be lively and the lobster's tail should curl under its body. The shells of live mussels, clams and oysters should close when tapped; any which do not house dead shellfish and should be discarded.

Since, where crustaceans at least are concerned, the killing is not a task for the squeamish, most fishmongers and supermarkets sell fresh lobster, crayfish, crab and other crustaceans ready-cooked. Cooked crustaceans should have dry, bright shells and feel heavy for their size; a floppy specimen is likely to be stale. Cooked shrimps and prawns should be a bright pink; they lose both colour and weight as they get older.

Like fresh fish, shellfish should be cooked and eaten the day they are bought. Shellfish that are not absolutely fresh can be toxic.

PREPARING A CRAB

1 Twist off the legs and claws at the joint with the body.

2 Holding the crab with both hands, pull the body away from the shell.

3 Remove the greyish-white stomach sac and the long white dead men's fingers and discard. Scoop out the meat from both shells, keeping brown and white separate. Crack the claws and remove the meat.

COOKING FISH

All kinds of fish and shellfish cook surprisingly quickly. The structure of fish flesh tends to be based on muscle fibres which are shorter and finer than those of meat, packed together in flakes with only small amounts of connective tissue. If overcooked, fish tends to become dry and tough, with the flakes falling apart. The cooking process, whichever one is chosen, should be short and gentle.

Frying both deep and shallow, is a quick and simple way of cooking fish. Usually, fillets or whole small fish such as whitebait are fried. The fish should first be coated with egg and breadcrumbs, batter, flour or oatmeal to protect the delicate flesh. A vegetable oil should be used for deep frying, and a tasty combination of butter and oil for shallow frying.

Food and Cooking

PREPARING A LOBSTER

  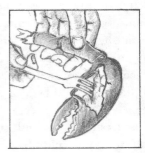

1 Twist off the claws and remove the legs. Cut away the thin undershell of the tail section and carefully pull out the flesh.

2 Place the lobster on a board and cut in half along its length with a sharp knife. Remove the grey vein of intestine running along its length. Scrape out the red coral (if present) and reserve. If liked, add the grey-green liver (near the head) to the flesh.

3 Carefully lift out the bony part of the head and break it into pieces. Using a lobster pick or skewer take out the flesh and any remaining liver and roe. Pull away the spongy gills and stomach sac from the head and discard. Crack the claws and pull out the meat. Wash and dry the shell.

Grilling is suitable for whole fish, steaks, fillets and cutlets. If the fish is on the bone, it is scored with a knife to ensure quick and even cooking. It should also be dotted with butter or lightly coated with oil to prevent it drying out. It is a good idea to line the grill pan and rack with foil to prevent fish smells lingering.

Baking is good for whole fish. The fish may be brushed with oil or butter and stuffed and cooked in an open pan or lightly covered. They may also be cooked in a liquid such as stock, wine or a sauce.

Poaching ensures that fish retains its moisture, since it is cooked in a liquid such as fish stock, wine or water, flavoured with herbs, vegetables or lemon juice. The fish may be cooked on top of the stove or in the oven, covered or uncovered. The cooking liquor is often turned into a sauce to accompany the fish at table.

Steaming prevents the fish's natural juices escaping into the water. The fish can be placed between two buttered plates or on a heatproof plate and covered in foil.

En papillote cooking involves the fish being wrapped in foil, greaseproof paper or cellophane with various flavourings, such as herbs and vegetables, and then poached, steamed, baked or deep-fried. This is one of the best ways to cook fish since all its flavours and juices are retained.

Meat and Offal

Lean red meat – beef, lamb and pork – and offal are very good sources of iron and other minerals, and protein, all essential in a healthy diet. Modern production methods have considerably reduced the amount of fat in meat, making it more acceptable to the health-conscious. Offal, especially liver, is generally very lean.

Since red meat is muscle, the tenderest kinds will come from parts of the animal that have little work, or from small, young animals rather than large, older ones. Thus, with beef the fillet, lying under the rib bone, is the tenderest meat, while the hard-working neck muscle is a tough meat, needing long slow cooking.

BUYING MEAT

Generally, all fresh meat should look fresh and moist, though not watery, and should smell fresh and sweet. It should not be sticky or sweaty looking – a sign of age.

Beef may look quite a deep brownish-red colour within a relatively short time of being cut. A dark red colour indicates beef which has been well hung and which should be tender and with a good flavour. Very bright red meat may not have been hung long enough.

Veal The meat from a very young calf should look a very light pink and be soft and moist, but not really wet; its very small amount of fat should be firm and white or very faintly pink. Stale veal looks dry, brownish and mottled and is to be avoided.

Lamb should be pink with a touch of red-brown, and its fat should look crisp and white.

Pork The lean part should show a pale pink colour and be slightly marbled with fat. It should have a good outer layer of firm white fat.

All these meats, if bought fresh, should be cooked within three days of buying, and stored, loosely covered, in the refrigerator well away from cooked meats.

Offal – liver, kidney, brains, tripe, sweetbreads, oxtail and tongue – should look bright and shiny and be clean-smelling when bought. It does not keep as long as red meat and, ideally, is cooked the day it is bought.

MEAT CUTS AND COOKING METHODS

Beef provides an abundance of cuts, suitable for a wide range of cooking methods.

Cuts for roasting include sirloin (which is also cut into steaks) and the various rib joints – wing rib, top rib, back rib and fore rib. An expensive roast is a baron of beef, which is the sirloin on the bone, from both sides of the back.

ROASTING TIMES FOR BEEF		
Type of Joint	Slow Method Moderately hot oven (190°C, 375°F, Gas Mark 5)	Fast Method Hot oven (220°C, 425°F, Gas Mark 7)
Meat on the bone		
Rare	20 mins per 450 g/1 lb plus 20 mins	15 mins per 450 g/1 lb plus 15 mins
Medium	25 mins per 450 g/1 lb plus 25 mins	20 mins per 450 g/1 lb plus 20 mins
Well done	30 mins per 450 g/1 lb plus 30 mins	25–30 mins per 450 g/1 lb plus 25 mins
Meat, boned and rolled		
Rare	25 mins per 450 g/1 lb plus 25 mins	20 mins per 450 g/1 lb plus 20 mins
Medium	30 mins per 450 g/1 lb plus 30 mins	25 mins per 450 g/1 lb plus 25 mins
Well done	35–40 mins per 450 g/1 lb plus 35 mins	30–35 mins per 450 g/1 lb plus 30 mins

Topside, or top round, may also be roasted, provided it is well barded, but it is probably better pot-roasted or braised, a cooking method which keeps the meat moist. Pot-roasting or braising is also good for the aitchbone (top rump or thick flank) and for brisket.

Brisket is also available salted and pickled, though salted silverside (round) is the traditional joint for boiled beef and carrots.

Among beef cuts best suited to slow stewing or casseroling are chuck and blade (the best stewing beefs: look for cuts with not too much thick fat on the outside); neck, clod, leg and shin all need very long and slow cooking.

Steaks, suitable for grilling or frying, include fillet, the only fat-free steak and the most expensive, cut from the tail end of the whole fillet. Chateaubriand is a thick steak cut from the large end of the fillet. Rump steak, from the joint next to the sirloin, is less tender than fillet but has a good flavour, especially the cut called the 'point'. The sirloin provides two steaks, porterhouse and T-bone, and thin steaks called 'minute' steaks which are cut from the upper part of the joint. An entrecôte steak is really the meat between the ribs of beef, though a slice from the sirloin or rump which is thin rather than thick can also be called an entrecôte steak.

Veal because it has so little fat, must be cooked with great care to prevent it drying out. Veal for roasting is usually barded with pork fat or fatty bacon. Cuts suitable for roasting are the leg, a prime cut which can be divided into others, including the knuckle; loin, another prime cut, taken from the back; and shoulder, which is often boned and rolled for roasting or pot-roasting.

While veal fillet can be roasted whole, it is usually sliced into escalopes, the most popular – and expensive – veal cut. Escalopes should be cut from the fillet end of the leg in slices 5 mm–1 cm/$\frac{1}{4}$–$\frac{1}{2}$ in thick, cut across the grain.

Veal knuckle, though bony, provides meat suitable for stews, pies and casseroles and for mincing. It is the cut for the classic osso buco, when it is sawn across into rings, with a marrow-filled piece of bone in the centre.

Breast is a fairly cheap cut, usually sold boned and rolled.

Veal chops come from the loin: chump chops from the bottom and cutlets from the top end. Both are suitable for frying, grilling (though they must be well basted) and pan-frying.

Pork, bacon, ham and gammon Pork comes in a wide range of cuts, suitable for all kinds of cooking. It should always be well cooked, and never served 'rare' like beef or lamb; a meat thermometer, pushed right into the centre of a joint, should show 85 °C/185 °F to indicate well done pork.

While most joints of pork may be roasted, some are better suited to this type of cooking than others. The leg may be roasted whole, but is more often cut into smaller joints, including the half leg and a boneless leg joint. The knuckle, or shank end, is a good roasting joint with plenty of crackling. Other pork roasting joints are spare rib, hand and spring, and loin. When boned, belly of pork, with the fat removed and the flesh stuffed and rolled, also roasts well.

Cuts of pork suitable for braising, stewing and casseroling, either on top of the stove or in the oven, include hand (the lean foreleg), spare rib chops, and blade bone (shoulder of pork).

Ideal for grilling, frying and barbecuing are loin chops, chump chops, belly, leg steaks and fillet (tenderloin). Spare ribs, which are well-trimmed slices from the belly, also grill or barbecue well.

Bacon (preserved or cured pork) comes in several joints and in three types of the familiar rasher – back bacon, middle or throughcut, and streaky. Joints include: collar, taken from the shoulder and suitable for boiling, braising and casseroling; forehock, a fairly lean joint with a good flavour and usually sold boned and rolled for boiling, braising or pot-roasting; and gammon or ham, the most prized part of a side of bacon, and often sold ready-cooked either on or off the bone. Raw joints are whole or half gammon, or smaller cuts called middle, corner and gammon hock; all are suitable for boiling, baking or braising.

A cured whole leg of pig is called 'gammon' when eaten hot and 'ham' when served cold. Special hams, removed from the carcase and cured and cooked according to the manufacturers' special recipes, include York, Bradenham, Old Smokey and Virginia-style hams.

ROASTING TIMES FOR PORK		
Pork on the bone	Hot oven (220°C, 425°F, Gas Mark 7)	25–30 mins per 450 g/1 lb plus 25 mins (depending on the thickness of the joint)
Pork, boned and rolled	Moderately hot oven (190°C, 375°F, Gas Mark 5)	30-35 mins per 450 g/1 lb plus 30 mins (depending on the thickness of the joint)

Lamb sold in Britain includes a great deal of home-produced meat and meat imported from other countries, especially New Zealand. A fairly high-fat meat, lamb is also very tender, and much of its fat can be trimmed off either before or after cooking. Unless it is very lean, a joint needs little basting during roasting.

While the leg and shoulder are the two most popular roasting joints, offering 8–10 servings, depending on size, best end of neck (rack of lamb) is also much used as a roasting joint, either singly or with two joined together to form either a guard of honour or a crown roast. The saddle (double loin) is a large roasting joint, comprising the whole loin from both sides of the animal, with the breast trimmed off, and providing an impressive joint for a special occasion.

Cuts of lamb suitable for the slower cooking methods, braising, stewing or pot-roasting, are middle neck, chump end chops and diced lamb, usually taken from the shoulder.

Tender, quick-cooking lamb is ideal meat for grilling, frying and barbecuing, whether as chops, steaks or fillet cut into cubes for kebabs. Lamb chops are: chump chops, the largest and with a small round bone in the centre; loin, the 'traditional' chop with a good eye of meat and a tail of meat and fat curled round it (called a 'noisette' when boned and rolled); and best end cutlets, consisting of the meat on one rib bone.

Generally, only mutton, which is seldom to be found in butchers' shops, is boiled, or, rather, simmered gently in liquid. Onion or caper sauces are the traditional accompaniments for boiled mutton.

ROASTING TIMES FOR LAMB		
Type of Joint	Slow Method Moderate oven (180°C, 350°F, Gas Mark 4)	Fast Method Hot oven (220°C, 425°F, Gas Mark 7)
Meat on the bone	30–35 mins per 450 g/1 lb (depending on the thickness of the joint)	20 mins per 450 g/1 lb plus 20 mins
Meat, boned and rolled	40–45 mins per 450 g/1 lb (depending on the thickness of the joint)	25 mins per 450 g/1 lb plus 25 mins

Offal Offal, or 'variety meats', is amongst the most nutritious of meats, being a very good source of iron and vitamins. It is also tasty and – apart from that great delicacy, calf's liver – very economical. Liver is considered to be the most nutritious of the various types of offal, with kidneys the next best.

All fresh offal should have a bright appearance, be moist and smell fresh. Liver should have little if any smell, and kidneys should smell fresh and show a good colour. Sweetbreads should be pale and look bright, as should brains, the colour of which should be a pinky-grey. Fresh offal should be cooked on the day it is bought. It can be frozen, however, and will keep in the freezer for 2–3 months. Wrap kidneys separately and separate slices of liver between freezer film. Cooked offal dishes which have been casseroled or braised may be frozen for up to a month, but grilled or fried offal should not be frozen because it dries out too much.

■ LIVER is virtually fat-free and is excellent nutritional value. Calf's liver is the finest, with a delicate flavour and tender texture. It needs only very light cooking, either grilling or frying. Lamb's liver, being less expensive than calf's, is the most popular. It may be grilled or fried in slices, or cubed and added to casseroles. Pig's liver is rather coarser and pungent. It can be grilled, fried or casseroled and is probably the best liver for pâtés. Ox liver is the cheapest, but is also fairly tough and very strongly flavoured. It is best casseroled or added to pâtés.

■ KIDNEYS include ox, calf's, pig's and lamb's. The first two are many-lobed, coarse and strongly flavoured, and are often used with stewing steak for steak and kidney pies and puddings. Pig's and lamb's kidneys are smaller, with lamb's kidneys having the more delicate flavour. Both may be fried or grilled, the quick cooking keeping them tender.

■ TONGUE, either ox or lamb, can be served hot as well as cold. Both can be bought either fresh or salted. Salted tongues require considerably less cooking time than fresh ones, though they need several hours' prior soaking. Ox tongue, which has the better flavour, may be boiled or braised, and lamb's tongues need the longer cooking time for casseroling or braising.

■ OXTAIL makes a delicious casserole. Sold ready skinned and jointed, it is best cooked the day before it is needed so that it can be chilled and any fat removed before it is reheated for serving.

■ HEART is the one type of offal that is often roasted, with lamb's and pig's hearts being the usual choice for stuffing and roasting. Ox heart and calf's heart are both best suited to slow cooking methods, such as casseroling and braising.

■ SWEETBREADS, either calf's or lamb's, require quite a lot of fiddly preparation before cooking, including soaking, then simmering in water and lemon juice before the outer membrane and any tubes can be removed. Once dry, they can be coated in egg and breadcrumbs and braised or fried.

■ BRAINS come from lambs and calves. A set of lamb's brains will make one portion, while calf's will make two. They must be bought, prepared, cooked and served while very fresh.

■ TRIPE is the stomach lining of the ox, and three types are sold: smooth or 'blanket' tripe; 'honeycomb' tripe; and 'thick seam' tripe. All should be thick, firm and white. Tripe is usually sold dressed, which means it has been partly boiled.

Also available from butchers are pig's and sheep's heads, the best brawn being made from pig's heads. Pig's cheek is the basis of 'Bath Chaps', and pig's trotters, more popular in continental cuisines than British, provide meat for brawn and can also be par-boiled and roasted. Calf's trotters are used for aspic.

Poultry and Game

Poultry and game, which are, on the whole, low-fat meats and good sources of protein, are no longer seasonal foods; intensive farming and deep-freezing have meant that we can choose our chicken or turkeys fresh, chilled or frozen at any time of the year and a wide range of game birds and other game either fresh when they are

Food and Cooking

in season or frozen at other times of the year. While free-range poultry and well-hung game in season tend to have a better flavour and texture than frozen birds, chicken, turkey and other mild-tasting meats lend themselves so well to being cooked with flavour-adding herbs, vegetables and sauces that the economical cook loses little by choosing frozen poultry.

Fresh-chilled poultry, which has been killed, gutted and immediately stored at just above freezing point, has a good texture, although it is rather less flavourful and tender than poultry – whether battery-reared or free-range – which has been hung, complete with head, feet and innards, for 2–3 days before being drawn and trussed ready for sale.

All fresh poultry should be eaten within three days of purchase. Frozen poultry should be thawed thoroughly and completely before cooking so that there is no chance of bacteria inside a still-icy body cavity not being destroyed during cooking.

CHOOSING AND COOKING POULTRY

Chicken Several types are available, their names mainly indicating the size and age of the bird.

■ POUSSINS are very small chickens, weighing 350–900 g/12 oz–2 lb and aged only 4–8 weeks. Larger ones, sometimes called double poussins, will serve one, but really little ones may need to be served in pairs. Tender and delicate, they should not be cooked with overpowering ingredients. They may be roasted, pot-roasted, casseroled or grilled.

■ BROILERS are also quite small and usually about 12 weeks old. Weighing from 1.25–1.5 kg/2½–3½ lb, one broiler will give 3–4 portions. They can be cooked by any method.

■ SPRING CHICKENS are small broilers, weighing about 900 g/2 lb and aged about 6–8 weeks. They can be cooked in many ways and will serve 2–3 people.

■ LARGE ROASTERS are usually hens or young cockerels which have been specially fed so that they grow large quickly. Aged about 10–15 weeks, they should weigh about 1.75–2.25 kg/4–5 lb. One bird should feed 5–6 portions. Quite flavourful, they can be roasted, pot roasted and casseroled.

■ CAPONS sold today are not the true capons of yesteryear, which were neutered and specially fattened young cockerels. Today's 'capon-style' chicken is a specially fattened bird with a good flavour and tender flesh. Weighing up to 4.5 kg/10 lb, one bird should give up to 10 portions.

■ BOILING FOWL are older birds and fairly tough, as they are often over 18 months old and may have been former egg-layers. They have an excellent flavour and respond well to long, gentle simmering or stewing for about three hours, with vegetables being added towards the end of the cooking time.

All fresh chicken ready for sale should have a firm texture and look shiny. The breastbone of a young, fresh bird should feel soft and pliable. Generally, the larger the bird, within its category, the better its value as it will have a higher proportion of meat to bone. Check a chicken for bruising on the legs and breast, avoiding any which show this.

When buying frozen chicken, avoid any which show freezer burn, as they will probably be dry and tasteless, and any which have sizeable chunks of ice between the carcase and the wrapping – a sign of partial thawing and re-freezing.

Once brought home, a fresh chicken should be unwrapped, its giblets (if any) removed and stored separately, and both put in the refrigerator, loosely covered. A frozen bird will need some hours to thaw completely – about 12 hours for a 900 g/2 lb bird at room temperature or a cool place and double that time in a refrigerator.

CUTTING UP A RAW CHICKEN

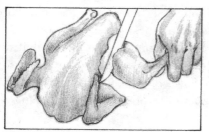

1 Cut through the leg joint where the thigh joins the body. Cut between the ball and socket joint to free the leg.

2 Press down the shoulder then cut through the skin at the base of the wing.

3 Place a knife inside the carcass and slit along the ribs to detach the breast from the lower carcass.

4 Cut down on one side of the breastbone to give two breasts.

ROASTING TIMES FOR POULTRY

Type of Bird	Oven Temperature	Cooking Time
Chicken	200°C, 400°F, Gas Mark 6	20 mins per 450 g/1 lb, plus 20 mins over
Guinea Fowl	200°C, 400°F, Gas Mark 6	20 mins per 450 g/1 lb, plus 20 mins over
Duck	190–200°C, 375–400°F, Gas Mark 5–6	25–30 mins per 450 g/1 lb
Goose	*Either* 200°C, 400°F, Gas Mark 6	15 mins per 450 g/1 lb, plus 15 mins over
	Or 180°C, 350°F, Gas Mark 4	25–30 mins per 450 g/1 lb

Guinea fowl, which are about the size of a spring chicken, have a rather more gamey flavour than chicken, and are best bought when they have been hung for two days. They roast very well.

Duck Intensive farming of the domestic duck has done much to change its old image of a bird with a lot of fat and not much meat. Most duck sold today has an acceptable amount of meat. Even so, it is wise to avoid duck weighing less than 1.5 kg/3 lb as it is likely to be mostly bone with very little flesh.

An average duck will weigh 1.75–2.25 kg/4–5 lb, and will not yield more than four reasonably-sized portions.

When choosing duck, look for one with a soft underbill, pliable feet and a breast which feels meaty. Because of their high fat content, ducks freeze well without losing their succulence or much flavour, though that fat content also means that ducks should not be frozen for more than about three months, as the fat can turn rancid.

Duck, whether whole or in the breast portions available in supermarkets, is best roasted. It is traditionally roasted unstuffed, as any stuffing will absorb a lot of fat.

Goose, which has a fine, slightly gamey flavour and texture, is much more readily available, both fresh and frozen, than was the case not so long ago. Because it is a bony bird with a low flesh-to-body size ratio, it will not feed so many people as the equivalent size turkey. An oven-ready goose weighing about 4.5 kg/10 lb will feed 6–8 people.

Goose should be young – ideally no more than 7–8 months old (a bird under six months is a gosling); look for soft yellow feet, a pliable yellow bill and yellowish fat. The skin should look creamy with an apricot tinge and with no sign of brown or blue.

A goose is best roasted. It should be trussed, pricked all over with a skewer to allow fat to escape, and stood on a rack in a roasting pan so that it does not stew in its own fat. It may be stuffed, but the stuffing is more often cooked and served separately.

ROASTING TIMES FOR TURKEY

It is recommended that all sizes of turkey should be cooked at 180°C, 350°F, Gas Mark 4.

Weight	Without foil	Wrapped in foil
2.25–3.5 kg/5–8 lb	2–2½ hours	2½–3½ hours
3.5–5 kg/8–11 lb	2½–3¼ hours	3½–4 hours
5–6.75 kg/11–15 lb	3¼–3¾ hours	4–5 hours
6.75–9 kg/15–20 lb	3¾–4¼ hours	5–5½ hours
9–11.25 kg/20–25 lb	4¼–4¾ hours	Not recommended

Turkey is probably the most versatile and economical of all the various kinds of poultry. It can be cooked in many different ways and is available in cuts and pieces to suit all pockets and all kinds of meal. As well as the whole bird, which can vary in size from the relatively small – around 2.25 kg/5 lb or so – to the huge (13.5 kg/30 lb), turkey is available in boned and rolled 'roasts', and as wings, thighs, drumsticks, escalopes, fillets and steaks.

HOW TO CARVE A TURKEY

1 Remove a drumstick, leaving the thigh on the bird and slice the meat from the drumstick.

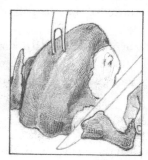

2 Carve slices from the thigh then remove the wings and strip the meat off neatly.

3 Carve thin slices lengthways from the breast taking in the stuffing as you reach it.

A good fresh turkey will be broad and compact-looking, with a fresh but not overly moist-looking skin and a creamy white flesh. Since turkey meat is at its best when it has been hung for a minimum of three days, a fresh turkey will make more flavoursome and succulent eating than a frozen turkey, which will probably not have been hung at all between killing and freezing.

A frozen turkey will need at least two days' thawing time in the refrigerator (three days for an extra-large bird), plus a few hours at room temperature to ensure it is completely defrosted before cooking.

CHOOSING AND COOKING GAME BIRDS

Some game bird seasons in Britain are:

Pheasant:	October– February
Partridge:	September– February
Red Grouse, Ptarmigan:	August– December
Black Grouse (Blackcock):	August– December
Wild duck:	mainly September– January
Pigeon:	no close season
Quail:	no close season

The main game birds are:

Pheasant probably the best-known and most popular of all, and available both fresh and frozen. It is often sold by the brace – a cock and a hen bird together. The hen is plumper and more succulent. Young pheasant are best roasted, but more mature birds, which are tougher though they have a good flavour, are best slowly casseroled, braised or pot-roasted. One roast pheasant will serve 2–3 people.

Partridge small game birds with a delicate flavour. Thought to be at their best in October, one bird will serve one person. Best roasted, they may also be spatchcocked (backbone removed and then flattened out) to grill or barbecue.

Wild duck are often not hung at all as their flesh deteriorates quickly. Because they are virtually fat-free wild duck are very dry and need to be covered liberally with fat before roasting. Timing is important with roast wild duck, since they are best served slightly – but only slightly – underdone. A mallard or large wild duck should serve two people.

Grouse, of which there are several species in Britain, including red grouse (the finest), black grouse, ptarmigan and capercaillie. Grouse are usually only available fresh and should be well hung. Young birds should have bright eyes, soft pliable feet and smooth legs. The breast bone should feel soft and pliable, too. Young birds are best roasted, but older birds can be marinated and casseroled, made into pâtés or pies or potted. One grouse will usually make only one portion.

Quail the smallest European game bird. Since they are now farm-bred, quail are available more often than when only the wild, migratory bird was summering in Europe. One bird is usually a reasonable portion, though big eaters might need two. They are generally roasted, then eaten with the fingers. They should be barded, or wrapped in fatty bacon before being cooked.

Pigeon (wood pigeon) are in season all year, but are thought to be best from March to September, when they are young. Pigeons do not need to be hung. They should be plucked and drawn immediately. One plump, young bird will make a portion; two squabs (fledglings) will make a portion; and a larger, older bird will serve two if casseroled with other ingredients. A roast bird needs to be barded well.

ROASTING TIMES FOR GAME BIRDS		
Type of Bird	**Oven Temperature**	**Cooking Time**
Pheasant	220°C, 425°F, Gas Mark 7	45–60 mins, depending on size
Partridge	220°C, 425°F, Gas Mark 7	30–45 mins, depending on size
Grouse	220°C, 425°F, Gas Mark 7	30–45 mins, depending on size
Wild Duck	220°C, 425°F, Gas Mark 7	30–50 mins for mallard 30–40 mins for widgeon 20–30 mins for teal and other small birds
Pigeon	200°C, 400°F, Gas Mark 6	about 30 mins, depending on size
Quail	180°C, 350°F, Gas Mark 4	20 mins

Vegetables, Fruit and Nuts

To make a very broad distinction, vegetables are savoury foods, usually eaten cooked with salt, and fruit are sweet foods, often eaten raw or, if cooked, with added sugar. The former is most often eaten during a meal, either as part of a meat course or, if the meal is vegetarian, as its main course. Fruit is most often served as an end-of-meal dish.

The distinction breaks down at many points. A great many vegetables are eaten raw in salads, often mixed with fruit, and the acidic quality of fruit makes them excellent accompaniments for meat – apple with pork, plums with beef, melon with ham, and apples or oranges with duck. An enzyme in papaya and kiwifruit gives them a role as meat tenderizers. Some fruits, botanically classed as such, have a savoury rather than sweet taste and are used as vegetables. The tomato and the avocado both fall into this category.

VEGETABLES

While most vegetables contain a high percentage of water, they also contain, in varying quantities, protein, vitamins, carbohydrate and fat. They are good sources of dietary fibre, particularly if eaten unpeeled.

Choosing and storing vegetables Freshness is the key to buying vegetables, since they tend to lose vitamins and nutrients after they have been picked or harvested for some time. Avoid any that look dull or discoloured, that were damaged during harvesting or transport, or that are limp and wilted. A less-than-fresh smell is also a bad sign. Leaf vegetables should be looked at carefully for signs of garden pests, while any that are wet on the outside, perhaps because of rain, could be rotten inside. Heavy frost could also have left vegetables like Brussels sprouts rotten inside, while looking all right on the outside.

Most vegetables are best stored in cool conditions and at the correct humidity. At home, storage in aerated plastic bags in a cool place can often achieve a good balance of temperature and humidity. Some recommended storage conditions are as follows:

In the refrigerator, in a plastic bag or wrapped in cellophane – asparagus, brassicas (cabbage, cauliflower, broccoli and calabrese, Brussels sprouts, kohlrabi, kale and spring greens), carrots, celeriac, celery, endive, globe artichokes, leeks, the various kinds of lettuce and salad green, parsnips, fresh peas and mangetout, radishes, salsify, sweetcorn, turnips and watercress.

In a cool larder or the salad compartment of the refrigerator, uncovered – aubergines, courgettes, cucumbers, okra, peppers and tomatoes.

In a cool place – aubergines, avocados, sweet potatoes and tomatoes.

At room temperature or in a cool place – garlic, onions and potatoes. Ideally, potatoes should be kept in the dark, too; a heavyweight, double-thickness paper bag is a good idea.

Cooking vegetables Vegetables contain starch and cellulose, and the purpose of cooking them is to break down their starch and cellulose, thus making them more easily digestible. Heat will do the breaking down, but not much of it is needed, and most vegetables should be cooked as briefly as possible, so as not to destroy vitamins and nutrients. Vegetables should be prepared for cooking quite simply, with a minimum of trimming and peeling, since many vitamins lie in or just below the skins. They should not be exposed to the air or soaked in water for any length of time before cooking since this, too, causes them to lose vitamins and nutrients.

Vegetables should be cooked until they are only just tender when prodded with the sharp point of a knife or skewer. Many vegetables do not even have to be put in the water, but may be steamed over it. Water in which vegetables have been cooked should not be drained down the sink: it will contain some of the flavour and nutrients of the vegetables and can be used as stock or the basis of a soup.

Other alternatives to cooking vegetables in water are stir-frying, which involves rapid cooking at high temperature, and pressure-cooking and microwave cooking, neither of which destroy vegetable nutrients as much as does boiling in water.

■ FRUIT

Fruit is a good source of vitamins and minerals and is, on the whole, low in calories. Like vegetables, but on an even greater scale, fruit is imported in vast quantities from many parts of the world, so that our supermarkets are never without a varied and colourful array of fruit of all kinds. Even so, the 'seasonal' aspect of fruit buying has not gone, and it still pays to be aware of peak times, especially for home-grown fruits, when many varieties become considerably cheaper.

Choosing and storing fruit When buying stoned fruit – apricots, cherries, mangoes, peaches and nectarines, plums and greengages – choose fruit that is firm to the touch, is not bruised and is free of soft spots, discoloured skin or splits in the skin.

■ SOFT FRUIT, which should be bought the day it is required as it does not keep, should never look wet or mouldy (carefully check the undersides of plastic boxes or punnets of soft fruit). Strawberries, raspberries and currants should all be firm.

■ APPLES AND PEARS should also be firm to the touch and be free of soft spots, bruising or breaks in the skin. Rough brown patches on some varieties of apple is 'russeting': russet apples are good cookers and go particularly well with cheese. Although town shops and supermarkets are selling a wider choice of apple varieties than was once the case, it remains true that farm shops and country stores are the places to find many of the older varieties of English apples.

■ CITRUS FRUITS range from the tiny kumquat to the large grapefruit and ugli fruit, with a splendid array of oranges, lemons, limes, mandarins and tangerines, clementines and satsumas in between. Citrus fruit is not grown in Britain, so it is fortunate that it travels well. Most citrus fruits remain in good condition for many weeks after picking, provided they are correctly transported and stored. Choose fruit that feels heavy for its size – an indication of plenty of juice. Good quality citrus fruit will have no sign of bruising, damp or soft patches.

■ IMPORTED EXOTIC FRUITS range from the familiar banana, pineapple, melon and grape, through the less familiar but increasingly plentiful kiwifruit (Chinese gooseberry), mango and passion fruit to the wonderfully coloured and shaped Sharon fruit, rambutan and carambola. Exotic fruits generally reach the shops in prime condition, but the same rules apply to buying them as to other fruits. Soft and damp fruit, wrinkled skins, black patches and a generally wilted look all indicate fruit to be avoided.

If fruit is to be kept for just a day or two before eating, it should be checked over regularly. Ripe fruit gives off a gas which speeds up the ripening of any fruit near it, so fruit should be removed from the fruit bowl as it ripens. Coversely, unripe fruit can be ripened more quickly if it is put in a paper bag with a piece of already ripe fruit.

Recommended conditions for several days' storage are: in the refrigerator in aerated polythene bags – apples, apricots, berries, cherries, figs, grapes, peaches and nectarines, pears, persimmons, plums (including greengages and damsons), pomegranates and rhubarb. In a cold cupboard or the salad compartment of the refrigerator, uncovered – cranberries, grapefruit, lemons, limes, lychees, melons, oranges and small citrus fruit. In a cool place – bananas, grapefruit, guavas, mangoes, melons, papayas, pineapples.

For long-term storage of hard fruit such as apples and pears a cool, dry and airy place is essential, where the fruit can be laid out, not touching, on shelves where air can circulate. The fruit must retain its stalk and be completely blemish-free. Apples can be allowed to ripen on the tree but pears should be picked before they are ripe. The fruit must be checked regularly and any ripe pieces removed.

Cooking fruit Fruit, unless it is to be soaked in wine or liqueurs, especially fruit-based ones, should be prepared just before it is to be cooked or served. Fruit which goes brown after being peeled or cut, including apples, pears, peaches and bananas, should be dropped into acidulated water (water with added lemon juice).

Most fruit has a high acid content, which means that it should be cut with a stainless steel knife, as the fruit can both stain an ordinary steel knife and be tained by it. Fruit should not be cooked in an aluminium saucepan, since the acid in it can dissolve some of the aluminium off the pan and into the fruit.

Soft fruit to be served fresh should be left sugar-free as any sugar, in drawing out the juices, would turn the fruit flabby.

Fruit being stewed should be not quite covered by the water or syrup it is to be cooked in, and it should be cooked at a gentle simmer only, for as short a time as possible, as it softens and breaks up very quickly.

NUTS

Nuts are high in fibre, and rich in vitamins, protein, calcium, iron and oil. They are also extraordinarily versatile, providing flavour and texture for all manner of foods, including soups and sauces, meat and poultry dishes, desserts, cakes and biscuits, savouries and sweetmeats. Their oils, including walnut, groundnut (arachide, peanut), hazelnut and pistachio, and essences give wonderful flavouring to salads, puddings, cakes and many other foods, while 'milk' made from almonds and coconuts make delicious and cooling drinks. Their high protein content makes nuts invaluable foods in vegetarian and vegan diets.

Because their high oil content can turn rancid in response to temperature change, nuts are best bought in small quantities and stored in airtight jars (not tins) in cool conditions.

MUSHROOMS

Mushrooms are edible fungi, of which some countries in Europe have more than 80 different species. In practice, about a dozen or so species are regularly available during the year.

Wild mushrooms are generally available fresh in the autumn. Since the two best woodland mushrooms, the cep (cèpe, boletus) and the chanterelle, have a world-wide distribution, modern transport can greatly extend the boundaries of 'autumn'. Other wild mushrooms regularly available include the morel, which appears in the spring, blewit, horn of plenty and oyster mushroom.

Cultivated mushrooms are available all year round and include three sizes of the cultivated mushroom, *Agaricus bisporus* – the familiar button mushrooms, cup mushroom and open or flat mushroom sold in great quantities in greengrocers and supermarkets. Shiitake mushrooms are used widely in oriental cookery; like the wood ear, the shiitake is cultivated in China and Japan. Both are available fresh or dried.

The cep, chanterelle and morel are also sold dried. Dried ceps and chanterelles should be soaked for up to 30 minutes before use and both they and their soaking liquid can be used in cooking. Dried morels need only 10–15 minutes' soaking before use.

Truffles are the rarest and most expensive of fungi; they are tubers that grow near the roots of oak or beech trees. The most sought-after are the black Perigord truffle from France and the white Piedmontese truffle from Italy. Fresh truffles are gathered in the autumn, with the help of pigs or specially trained truffle hounds, and most are marketed locally, leaving more distant truffle lovers to make do with specimens in cans or jars.

Using mushrooms Fresh cultivated mushrooms are best bought in small quantities and used quickly, though they will last for 4–5 days in the refrigerator, kept in an open plastic bag. They should not need skinning. Wiping with kitchen paper or a damp cloth is all that should be necessary in the way of cleaning. If really dirty mushrooms need washing, the job should be done as quickly as possible, and the mushrooms should not be allowed to soak in the water.

Fresh wild mushrooms do need to be carefully picked over for dirt and insects and morels may need a quick washing to get rid of grit. If you have picked them yourself, they should also be checked against a mushroom textbook to make absolutely sure you have not gathered poisonous fungi by mistake. Fresh wild mushrooms are at their most delicious when eaten as soon as possible after picking.

PULSES

'Pulses' is the general term for the ripe, dried and edible seeds of legumes (peas, beans and lentils), foods with a high nutritive value. They are major sources of vegetable protein as well as good sources of iron, phosphorus and several B vitamins, and are comparatively low in fat. They have a much higher fibre content than other protein foods (meat, fish, eggs and milk). If pulses are eaten with a cereal 30 per cent more of their protein is released; hence the many dishes to be found in all cuisines combining pulses with rice or bread.

Pulses commonly available include a wide range of beans, from the small green mung bean (best-known in its sprouted form, beansprouts) and reddish-brown aduki bean to the much larger broad bean, butter bean and red kidney bean; chick peas, used in salads, stews and Mediterranean dishes such as hummous; Continental (green or brown), red and Puy lentils; and dried peas, both whole and split.

The small, round, yellowish-cream soya bean is the richest in food value of all pulses, being very high in protein. It is the basis of bean curd, or *tofu*, much used in oriental cooking, and of soy milk and soy sauce. Soya beans are also ground down into a high-protein flour and are used in TVP (textured vegetable protein) foods. The hardest of the pulses, soya beans require 3–4 hours cooking after long soaking, though 'soya splits', requiring only 30 minutes' cooking, are available.

Buying and storing pulses   Contrary to popular belief, pulses do not have a particularly long storecupboard life; long storage can cause them to harden so much that they will not soften during cooking. Pulses are best bought in small quantities, from a shop that has a quick turnover, and used soon after purchase. If stored in a cool, dry place, they should be used within 6–9 months at most.

Many pulses, including red kidney beans, cannellini beans, flageolets and chick peas, are sold canned, ready to use. These will keep for several months.

Cooking pulses   Most pulses benefit from being soaked before cooking, since soaking speeds up cooking time and makes them more digestible. Lentils are an exception, though Continental lentils will need $1\frac{1}{2}$ hours' cooking time if unsoaked and only 30–45 minutes if soaked first.

Pulses may be cold-soaked or soaked after an initial short cooking. Pulses to be soaked cold should be completely covered with cold water and left to soak for 6–8 hours, or overnight. The shorter soaking method involves putting the pulses in a saucepan of water, which is then slowly brought to the boil. They are boiled vigorously for 3 minutes, then taken off the heat, covered and left to soak in the water for one hour. After soaking by either method, the pulses should be drained thoroughly, then rinsed in a sieve under running water until the water runs clear. This gets rid of residual starch.

Pulses should be cooked in a large, heavy-based saucepan or casserole, completely covered in salt-free water or stock; salt toughens the skins of pulses and prevents them cooking properly, so should be added near the end of cooking, as should such acids as lemon juice, vinegar and tomatoes, for the same reason.

Once brought to the boil, dried beans, especially red kidney beans, should be boiled vigorously for the first 10 minutes of cooking to destroy any potentially harmful toxins.

Pulses may be cooked on top of the stove or in the oven. Cooking pulses in a pressure cooker reduces the cooking time by up to two-thirds. A bouquet garni (see page 121) added to the cooking water gives real flavour to the cooked pulses.

Cereal Products

Cereals provide starchy carbohydrates, essential in human nutrition. They are edible grains from cultivated grasses, including wheat, oats, corn and rice and, in a wider context, the foods deriving from them, especially flour-based foods such as bread and pasta.

RICE

There are estimated to be more than 7000 varieties of rice cultivated in the world. In practice, our choice is limited to white and brown rice from various countries, with a selection of grain sizes for each, plus wild rice, which is not a rice at all, but the seeds of a grass grown in the United States and the Far East.

This still gives us a sufficient choice of rice types for a wide range of dishes, both savoury and sweet. The type of rice needs to be matched carefully to the desired result: pudding rice will not provide the separate grains essential for a pilau, for instance, and long-grain Basmati rice will not give the moist clinging texture characteristic of the best risottos, for which Italian Arborio rice is needed.

Brown rice   is the rice grain with nothing but the outer inedible husk removed. Because it retains the bran, brown rice is superior in food value to white rice, and has a nutty flavour and texture. White, polished or pearl rice, is the rice produced when the bran has been removed by milling. Both brown and white rice come in three grain sizes: short, medium and long.

Long-grain rice   Basmati and Patna from India and Carolina from the United States are the long-grain varieties most commonly available. The grains are fluffy and separate when cooked, making the rice ideal for salads and with curries, stews, and meat and chicken dishes. Delicately flavoured Basmati is the traditional rice in Indian cooking.

Medium- and short-grain rice   These are shorter, fatter and stubbier grains than long-grain rice and include the Italian rices, such as Arborio, the glutinous rices widely used in Chinese cooking, and pudding rice. Sticky medium-grain rices are generally used for savoury dishes where the rice needs to cling or be moulded together, as, for example, in risottos and rice rings; short-grain rice is best for sweet dishes and desserts.

Rice flakes, produced by steaming and rolling, from both brown or white rice, are used for cereals, muesli and in baking.

Ground rice or rice flour This is made from rice ground to a fine powder and is used as a thickening and in cakes, biscuits and puddings.

Wild rice, used in savoury dishes, especially poultry and game stuffings, is appreciated for its brownish-black colour. It is expensive and not widely sold.

Preparing and cooking rice Brown rice may contain bits of husk, and should be put in water before cooking so that any unwanted pieces can float to the surface to be skimmed. Most kinds of white rice should be washed before cooking to get rid of loose starch, and to help prevent the grains sticking together during cooking: put it in a large sieve and hold it under running water. Wild rice and brown rice both take twice as long to cook as white rice. When measuring rice for cooking, allow about 50 g/2 oz per person.

■ ABSORPTION METHOD This is an easy way to cook rice, ensuring the grains stay separate and fluffy. For each cup of rice to be cooked, allow 2 cups of water or stock plus $\frac{1}{2}$ teaspoon of salt. Bring the water to the boil, add the salt and the washed rice, stirring to separate the grains. As soon as the water boils again, reduce the heat, cover the pan with a very tight-fitting lid and cook for 15 minutes for white rice, 45 minutes for brown rice. Do not lift the lid, as steam will escape and alter the cooking time. When the 15/45 minutes have elapsed the rice will be tender and fluffy, ready for serving immediately.

To cook rice by the absorption method in the oven, use the same proportion of rice to water, but put the rice into an oven-proof dish with a tight-fitting lid and pour the boiling salted water or stock over it. Stir well and cover with foil and the lid. Cook in a preheated moderate oven (180 °C, 350 °F, Gas Mark 4) for 30–40 minutes for white rice, 1 hour for brown, until all the liquid has been absorbed and the rice is tender.

■ STEAMED RICE, CHINESE-STYLE Soak the rice for at least 1 hour, then drain. Fill the bottom half of a steamer, or large pan, with water. Line the steamer with muslin and spoon in the rice, folding the ends of the muslin over the rice. Cover and steam 25–30 minutes, or until the rice is tender.

Boiling rice Allow 600 ml/1 pint water and $\frac{1}{2}$ teaspoon salt per 50 g/2 oz rice. Bring the water to the boil, add the salt, sprinkle in the rice, return to the boil and simmer for 12–13 minutes for white rice, 25 minutes for brown, until the rice is *al dente* (soft on the outside but with a 'bone' in the middle). Drain the rice in a sieve to serve.

PASTA

'Pasta' is the generic name for all forms of spaghetti, macaroni, ravioli, noodles etc, of which Italy is the world's main producer. There are two main types: the factory-produced dried pasta (*pasta secca*) made from hard wheat (durum wheat) semolina flour; and fresh pasta made with flour and eggs (*pasta all'uovo*). Although homemade *pasta all'uova* should ideally be made with semolina flour, all-purpose flour is an acceptable substitute. Pasta can also be made from buckwheat or wholewheat flour.

While most pasta is a creamy-yellow colour, both pasta ribbons and shapes come coloured green (with added spinach) or red (with added tomato purée).

Pasta's various shapes and sizes are not simply decorative, but are designed to affect the body, character and taste of the pasta and determine how it will be served, as there is a particular form of sauce suited to each shape, or a filling specifically designed for it.

Cooking pasta Pasta should be cooked in plenty of boiling water – at least 4 litres/ 7 pints for 450 g/1 lb of pasta. One or two tablespoons of olive oil in the water will help prevent the pasta sticking as it cooks. The water should be boiling rapidly when the pasta is added and brought back to the boil as quickly as possible.

Test the pasta at intervals when it is cooking; as soon as it is *al dente*, drain it into a large colander; it will continue cooking in its own heat. Toss the cooked pasta in butter or oil to give it a delicious flavour and texture. Pasta that is to be served with a sauce should be cooked when it is required, not before.

Suggested cooking times for dried pasta:

Spaghetti, 9 minutes; long macaroni, 10 minutes; lasagne, 10 minutes (add it to the boiling water a sheet at a time); cannelloni, 10–12 minutes; ravioli, 15 minutes; tagliatelli, 10 minutes; vermicelli, 5 minutes.

Homemade fresh pasta needs much less time, from seconds for fine pasta, 3 or 4 minutes for ribbons, and about 7 minutes for dumplings or stuffed pastas.

Storing pasta Freshly made pasta is best eaten on the day it is made or purchased, but it will keep in the refrigerator for up to 24 hours. The dough, or shaped dough, stores well in the freezer for up to 3 months.

Dried pasta keeps well in sealed jars or containers for up to 9 months, but the container must be dry and airtight. Pasta is best stored in a dark cupboard.

OTHER CEREAL PRODUCTS

Bread wheat from which comes numerous varieties and grades of flour, is the world's most important cereal crop; its high gluten content is what gives bread its lightness and elasticity. Other flours used in bread-making – rye, barley and maize – do not have this high gluten content and therefore are usually combined with bread wheat flour for bread-making. Cakes and pastries are made from a soft flour, with a lower gluten content, which may be called all-purpose, soft, plain or cake flour.

Other cereals regularly sold in health food shops and, increasingly, in supermarkets, are:

Barley a cereal with high levels of protein, calcium, iron, B vitamins and fibre. Used in stews and puddings, it does not need soaking before cooking. Pot or Scotch barley and pearl barley are both refined types, with much of the B vitamin content lost. Flaked barley is quicker to cook than the other types.

Buckwheat Really the seed of a herbaceous plant, buckwheat can be used like most grains, though it is most usually cooked in its flour or noodle form.

Bulgar (burghul, cracked wheat) is a processed form of wheat, much used as a substitute for rice in the Middle East. Bulgar is the basic item in the well-known salad, tabbouleh. Bulgar needs to be soaked in cold water for about 20 minutes, or brought to the boil in water and simmered for 2 or 3 minutes, before being drained, squeezed dry and then used.

Cornmeal (polenta, maize meal) Corn or maize is a staple cereal in many parts of the world, but in the UK it has been used mainly for cornflakes and cornflour. Italian polenta, coarsely ground maize cooked to a golden purée, is now taking a larger place on supermarket shelves here. It has a high protein content.

Couscous is made from the inner part of the wheat grain – the semolina. Semolina grains are dampened and rolled into a flour. The type of couscous sold in Britain has already been par-cooked and needs to be steamed only for about 20 minutes before being used as the basis for a salad or stuffing or as the basis for a pilau and similar dishes.

Dairy Foods and Eggs

Dairy products have essential roles to play in cooking and in the maintenance of a well-balanced diet, if used in moderation and with an understanding of their food values, especially their saturated fat and cholesterol content.

MILK PRODUCTS

Milk contains protein, vitamins and minerals, especially calcium, sugar and fat, as well as water. Most milk sold today is pasteurized, i.e., it has been heated to a temperature where potentially harmful bacilli are killed. Unpasteurized (raw) milk can be sold only from herds certified as being bacteria-free.

Milk is available in various grades, depending on their fat content. The fat and energy content of skimmed and semi-skimmed milk is less than that of full-cream milk, but their nutritional content is much the same. Most long-life milk, which will keep for several months if unopened, is UHT milk, that is, pasteurized milk that has been ultra-heat treated by being taken to a temperature of 132–140 °C/270–284 °F for one or two seconds. Homogenized milk retains the cream content of full-cream milk, but with the cream evenly suspended in the milk, rather than being allowed to float on the top. It makes good ice cream, but sauces made with homogenized milk take longer to cook.

Other milks available are buttermilk, soured milk, and evaporated and condensed milk. A very useful non-cow's milk is goat's milk which is highly digestible and is often given to babies and children who cannot digest or who are allergic to cow's milk.

Cream Of the various creams taken from milk, clotted cream has the highest percentage of fat (55 per cent) and single cream (18 per cent) and half-cream (12 per cent) the lowest. In between come double cream (48 per cent), whipping cream (35 per cent) and sterilized cream (23 per cent). To be whipped successfully, cream needs to have a fat content of 30–42 per cent. It should also be whipped straight from the refrigerator, as warm cream goes grainy when whipped.

Crème fraîche, or crème double, is a French cream treated with a special culture to make it keep longer. It has a delicious, slightly sour taste.

Yogurt is made from milk which has been allowed to curdle. It can be made from any kind of milk except condensed milk. When made at home a small quantity of live yogurt or culture must be added to the milk. Commercially produced yogurt has a lactic starter added. While cow's milk yogurt forms the bulk of yogurt sales, yogurts made from goat's and sheep's milk are also sold.

Yogurt used in cooking, especially if it is homemade, needs to be stabilized to prevent it curdling: heat the yogurt, stir in a little cornflour and water paste (about a teaspoon of cornflour to 300 ml/$\frac{1}{2}$ pint of yogurt) and let the mixture simmer for about 10 minutes until it thickens.

Butter is made from cream and can be unsalted or salted. Unsalted butter has the sweeter flavour, but salted butter keeps longer. All butters should be kept, wrapped and well away from strong-smelling foods, in the refrigerator and, ideally, used within 7 or 8 days of purchase, though they will keep safely for longer.

CHEESES

Most of the hundreds of cheeses sold in Britain are made from cow's milk, though cheeses from goat's milk and, to a lesser extent, sheep's milk, are also available. A variety of the Italian unripened curd cheese, Mozzarella, is made from buffalo milk, though most are now made from cow's milk.

Cheeses may be categorized according to flavour and texture:

Fresh and soft cheeses are easily spread cheeses, made from unripened curds, as in curd cheese and cottage cheese, or briefly ripened cheeses, such as cream cheese. They have a high percentage of moisture and fat. Brie, Camembert and Boursin are French-produced soft cheeses made from cow's milk. Italian Ricotta and Greek Feta may be made from both goat's and sheep's milks.

Semi-hard cheeses are matured cheeses with less moisture than fresh cheeses and which cut easily. Into this category fall such home-produced favourites as Cheddar,

Cheshire, Double Gloucester, Lancashire and Caerphilly, the Swiss Gruyère and Emmental and the Dutch Gouda and Edam.

Hard cheeses are those which have been matured for a long time. They have a low moisture and high fat content. Hard cheeses include the grainy Italian cheeses Parmesan (or Parmigiano Reggiano) and Pecorino and the pale-green Swiss Sapsago (green because of the clover added to the curd).

Blue cheeses contain mould cultures which give them a blue veining. Into this category fall such noble cheeses as British Stilton, French Roquefort and Italian Gorgonzola.

Vegetarian cheeses are ones which are prepared without animal rennet, making them suitable for vegetarians. Once the preserve of health food stores, vegetarian varieties of cheeses like Cheddar are now sold in supermarkets.

CHOOSING AND STORING CHEESE

Cheese is best bought from a supplier with a quick turnover, whose cheeses are likely to be in prime condition. Avoid any that look dry, sweaty or have a blue mould on the surface. Test soft cheeses for ripeness by pressing the top lightly with the fingers: the cheese should yield slightly. There should be no chalkiness in the centre.

Ideally, cheese should be stored in a cool, draught-free larder or cellar. The refrigerator is the next best place. Cheese should be wrapped in foil or paper, then put into a plastic bag before being placed in a temperate part of the refrigerator, such as the salad cooler or a door compartment. It should be brought out and unwrapped at least an hour before it is to be eaten.

Most cheeses freeze well, though soft and cream cheeses for not more than six months, and cottage cheese not at all. Hard cheeses tend to become crumbly with freezing, but retain their flavour. Cheese should never be re-frozen and thawed cheese should be used up quickly, as it does not keep.

When using cheese in cooking, take care that the heat applied is not too fierce, as the protein breaks down and the cheese become rubbery and stringy. Cheese should be melted, rather than cooked; grating helps hard cheese melt into a sauce.

EGGS

Eggs are probably the most indispensable item in cooking. Highly versatile, they may be used in all manner of dishes including soups and sauces, main dishes, puddings and cakes. They may be boiled, coddled, poached, scrambled, baked and pickled. They are also the basic ingredient of such dishes as omelettes and soufflés, and can be used to thicken or emulsify other foods, or to bind, coat or glaze them.

Eggs are rich in protein, which is found in both the white (albumen) and yolk. There is no nutritional difference between a brown-shelled egg and a white-shelled one, nor between eggs laid by free-range or battery hens.

Eggs contain an air space in the blunt, rounded end which increases in size as the eggs age: the fresher the egg, the smaller the air space. Eggs may be tested for freshness by putting them in a bowl of water: a fresh egg will lie flat in the bowl and a slightly stale egg will tilt slightly. A really stale egg will float to the surface; its contents should be checked before the egg is cooked. If it has a bad smell throw it out. A fresh egg, when cracked open, should show a thick white, clinging to the yolk.

Eggs are sold in seven sizes, graded by weight in all EC countries, from size 1 (70 g/ $2\frac{1}{2}$ oz) down to size 7 (below 45 g/$1\frac{3}{4}$ oz). Most baking recipes call for eggs in the size 2 or 3 range. They are best eaten within 2 weeks of purchase and should be stored in a cool place, blunt end up, so that the yolk rests on the white rather than on the air space. If they must be stored in the refrigerator, they should be used quite quickly since conditions in the refrigerator can make eggshells moist, allowing bacteria to penetrate into the egg. Free-range eggs are also best used quite quickly since the conditions in which they are laid often means they have to be washed before sale, a process which removes the protective coating on the shell.

Hen (or chicken) eggs are the only ones to be produced on a large scale in Britain. Other eggs are available, including smaller chicken eggs from bantams and pullets. Also sold are eggs from game birds – quail, pheasant and partridge; duck eggs, which are rather oily tasting and need to be eaten when very fresh; and goose eggs, also oily tasting and which should be used very fresh. The Chinese delicacy, 100-year-old eggs, are raw duck eggs preserved in lime, pine ash and salt for 50–60 days, after which they are usually shelled, sliced and steamed before being served cold.

Herbs and Spices

Herbs and spices are used in cooking to give extra, distinctive flavour to foods during cooking and other processes, such as pickling and preserving.

HERBS

Most herbs are best used fresh, when flavour and texture are at their best, but many herbs can be dried successfully, allowing them to be used when fresh herbs are not available. Some may also be frozen. Fresh herbs should be wrapped separately in absorbent kitchen paper, then kept in plastic bags in the storage compartments at the bottom of the refrigerator. They will keep well for up to a week.

Fresh herbs wanted for more long-term storage, such as drying or freezing, should be picked just before they flower, to get them at the time of maximum flavour. Ideally, they should be gathered on a dry but cloudy day. Herbs can be tied in loose bunches for drying, either hung up in muslin bags (to catch any loose bits) or laid on absorbent kitchen paper on a tray or rack in a warm place. Large-leaved herbs like bay, mint or sage can be dried this way or they can be dipped in boiling water for a minute, shaken dry and then put in a slow oven to dry completely.

Once dried, herbs can be crushed and stored in airtight glass jars, preferably out of direct light. Dried herbs are much more concentrated than fresh ones; one teaspoon of dried herbs equals a tablespoon of fresh ones.

Some herbs, notably basil and coriander, lose so much of their flavour when dried that drying them is really not worth the effort. Like most tender herbs, they will freeze well, retaining their flavour but darkening in colour when thawed. They should be put in airtight boxes for freezing, to prevent their scents permeating other foods in the freezer.

Herb mixtures Two classic herb mixtures much used in cooking are:
- BOUQUET GARNI – literally, a bouquet of fresh herbs, tied together before being put into stews, casseroles and certain sauces as they cook, but also available as dried herbs tied in muslin or cheesecloth. The herbs traditionally used in a bouquet garni are bay leaf, thyme and parsley; others added to it may include rosemary, marjoram, fennel or savory. Sometimes the whole bouquet is tied into a stick of celery. A bouquet garni is always removed from the dish at the end of cooking.
- FINES HERBES – a delicate mixture of finely chopped tender herbs, usually parsley, chervil and chives, sometimes with tarragon added. It is used with such delicately flavoured foods as eggs and white fish; in tartare and bearnaise sauces; and in mayonnaise accompanying shellfish and eggs. With a squeeze of lemon juice, fines herbes are often added to melted butter to make a delicious sauce for veal escalopes and chicken.

SPICES

Most spices used in the kitchen come from the tropical regions of the world, so it is not surprising that the many cuisines of these regions should owe much of their individual and distinct flavours and styles to the use of spices.

Spices should be bought in small quantities and used fairly quickly since, if they are stored for too long, they lose pungency and flavour. They are best bought whole, too, and cut into small pieces, or ground and crushed into a powder, as and when required. Many spices can, in fact, be used whole or in single pieces; whole cloves, vanilla, cardamom and star anise pods, cinnamon sticks, whole black or white peppercorns, are all used in cooking, though most are removed from the cooked dish before it is served.

Dry-frying whole spices before grinding them for use in cooking, a procedure much practised in oriental cookery, helps release the essential oils in spices, thus heightening their distinctive flavours. The dry-frying should be over a moderate heat, with the spices being stir-fried for about five minutes until they turn a little darker and begin to give off a delicious aroma. Let them cool before grinding them, either in a pestle and mortar or in an electric coffee grinder reserved for the purpose.

Spice mixtures
- FIVE-SPICE POWDER is used by Chinese cooks in a variety of savoury dishes, but especially with pork. Its basic spices are star anise, cloves, fennel seed, Szechuan pepper and cassia (or cinnamon).
- GARAM MASALA is a basic mix of dry spices used in Indian cooking, which may

involve up to 20 different spices, depending on the dish to be cooked.

■ QUATRE EPICES usually contains white pepper or allspice, nutmeg, cloves and cinnamon. It is used in European cooking in pâtés, pies and sausages.

■ SEVEN-SPICE SEASONING (*SHICHIMI TOGARASHI*) is a hot mixture from Japan, used as a condiment. It contains chilli, hemp seeds (mustard or rape), poppyseeds, nori seaweed, seasame seeds and dried mandarin peel.

■ ZATHAR is a Middle East blend of 2 parts dried thyme to 1 part sumac, sprinkled over breads before cooking or hot from the oven or served with crudités.

Storage and Equipment

IN THE REFRIGERATOR

Perishable foods which are to be cooked or eaten within a short time of purchase are ideally kept at a temperature just above freezing point: the recommended standard refrigerator temperature in the UK is 5 °C/41 °F.

Especially sensitive perishable foods like raw meat, poultry and fish should be kept near the bottom of the refrigerator, the coldest part. They should be covered or wrapped (preferably in foil rather than the supermarket's tight plastic wrapping) and kept so that they cannot drip blood or juices on to cooked meats.

Most foods in a refrigerator should be wrapped or covered, or stored in plastic bags or boxes. Covering food prevents moisture evaporating from it into the refrigerator, which can make it frost up and operate less efficiently.

Hot or warm foods should never be put into the refrigerator. They will cause the inside temperature to rise above its safe levels. Cooked food should be cooled down quickly, perhaps by putting it in a bowl and standing it, uncovered, in a basin of cold water. Unless eggs are to be used very quickly, they should not be kept in a rack in a warm kitchen; although a cool larder is the best place for them, a temperate part of the refrigerator, such as a door compartment, is safer than a warm kitchen.

Pre-packed chilled foods, which should never be eaten after the manufacturer's eat-by date, should be kept in as cool a part of the refrigerator as possible, and certainly not above 5 °C/41 °F.

Points for a safe refrigerator

1. *Make sure it is big enough for your needs; an overloaded refrigerator will not work efficiently.*

2. *If the refrigerator does not have an automatic defroster, defrost it regularly; an iced-up refrigerator does not keep low temperatures.*

3. *Check the rubber door seal regularly, replacing a broken or perished one.*

4. *Use a refrigerator thermometer to check the temperature, adjusting the temperature dial if necessary.*

5. *Do not open the door more often than is necessary, or leave it open.*

RECOMMENDED FOOD STORAGE TIMES IN THE REFRIGERATOR

At temperatures as close as possible to 0°C/32°F:

Fresh meat (including offal, sausagemeat, minced meat)	1–3 days (4 days for large joints)
Fresh poultry (remove giblets from inside)	1–3 days
Fresh fish, shellfish, smoked fish	1–2 days

At temperature range of 0–5°C/32–41°F:

Milk, cream, yogurt	3–5 days
Fresh-made mayonnaise and products containing it (e.g. coleslaw)	1–2 days
Soft cheeses	4–5 days
Raw pastry, unbaked dough, pizza bases	1–2 days

At temperatures up to 8°C/46°F:

Bacon, smoked (slightly less for green bacon)	7–10 days
Butter and fats	2–3 weeks
Hard cheese	8–9 days
Salads and green vegetables	1–5 days
Soft fruits	1–5 days
Eggs	2 weeks

IN THE STORECUPBOARD

Cupboards and shelves used for storing food should be clean and free of food dust and crumbs, so as not to attract mice and other pests, and cool, damp-free and as well ventilated as possible. Ideally, all their contents should also be visible at a glance, with no dark and inaccessible corners for food to get lost in.

Before putting food away in a cupboard, its 'best before' date label and any storage instructions should be noted. Reduced-sugar jams, for instance, are better kept in the refrigerator, even before opening.

Check cans for dents, rust or leaks; do not use such cans.

Remember to transfer bottled products, including mayonnaise, pickles, tomato sauce and purée to the refrigerator once they have been opened.

RECOMMENDED FOOD STORAGE TIMES IN THE STORECUPBOARD

Up to one year:
Cocoa, drinking chocolate, instant coffee and malted milk; cornflour, custard powder, instant desserts, jellies; syrup, treacle, icing sugar; gelatine, pasta, rice, wholegrains, marmalade.

Up to six months:
Unshelled nuts, oils (will keep longer, depending on conditions), breakfast cereals, herbs, spices, dried fruit, dried beans (will keep up to nine months, but will need longer cooking), flour (though is better used before six months), cake and pastry mixes, dried yeast.

2–3 months:
Baking powder, bicarbonate of soda, instant low-fat or skimmed milk powder, savoury biscuits.

Up to 1 month:
Shelled nuts, tea, non-vacuum packed coffee.

ELECTRICAL EQUIPMENT

Electrical equipment for the kitchen is on the whole pretty expensive, so it is worth making quite certain that the use which is made of it will repay the expense of buying it. Probably the most generally practical small electrical items for everyday cooking are a **hand-held beater**, invaluable for practical cake-making and beating egg whites, and an **electric blender**, which makes easy work of soups and purées. Many blenders come with a smaller, dry-goods grinder as an extra – useful for grinding coffee or chopping nuts.

Food processors are the ideal electric accessory for the busy cook or one who cooks for a number of people. They work very fast, chopping, slicing, grinding, mincing, puréeing and mixing; most of them have extra attachments for making juice, pasta or for mixing bread dough.

Apart from the refrigerator (see page 122–3), which has become as basic and essential a part of kitchen equipment as the storecupboard, two larger electrical items, the microwave oven and the freezer, have revolutionized the way we use our kitchens.

Microwave ovens allow busy people to prepare good food quickly. They contain a magnetron generating microwaves which cause the moisture in food to vibrate at such a high speed that enough heat is generated to cook it. The heat inside the oven (which has a vent to allow excess steam to escape) is moist, which prevents food drying out but also stops it browning.

The microwave oven's power output varies from 450 to 700 watts. Some microwave cookers, suitable for defrosting, reheating and simple cooking, have only full power (100%) or low power (30%). Others have completely variable power, permitting much more versatile cooking.

Provided that the microwave oven is correctly used – and all microwave ovens come supplied with detailed instruction books which should be thoroughly mastered at the very beginning – it is ideal for cooking portions of food quickly. Even if the food is frozen and has to be defrosted first, the microwave carries out the thawing and cooking processes much more rapidly than a conventional oven possibly could. Moreover, food may also be efficiently reheated in a microwave without loss of taste, texture or food value.

There is no greater nutritional loss in food cooked in a microwave than there is in a conventional cooker, nor are more vitamins destroyed. Moreover, some foods cook better in a microwave than in a conventional oven: fish, for example, likes the moist heat of a microwave, and vegetables and fruit keep their colour and shape better.

Most foods – boiled eggs and deep-fried foods are exceptions – can be cooked in a microwave, but some, including roast meats, pastry, cakes and breads, work better in a conventional oven – hence the development of the combination microwave cooker, which includes either a conventional or a convection oven and, often, a grill for browning.

Points for a well-used microwave oven:

1. *Do not switch on the microwave when empty; the magnetron will be damaged.*

2. *Use only dishes suitable for use in the microwave: heat-resistant glass, china, firm plastics and polythene, roasting and boiling bags and – for warming up foods – paper, wood and wicker. Do not use metal dishes or dishes with metal, silver or gold trims, crystal or cut glass, unglazed earthenware and pottery, soft polythene or foil.*

3. *Most foods need to be covered for microwave cooking. A solid lid or microwave-suitable clingfilm can be used for most foods; absorbent paper is used over bacon, sausages and chops to prevent fat spattering and to wrap breads and cakes to absorb excess moisture. If vegetables and fruits such as potatoes, tomatoes and apples are cooked uncovered, they should be pricked first to prevent them bursting.*

4. *Use only special microwave thermometers not ordinary kitchen thermometers.*

The freezer correctly used, can be the busy and budget-conscious cook's most helpful kitchen appliance. Unlike other preserving methods, such as salting and canning, keeping food in a freezer preserves its original quality, in terms of nutritional value and flavour, almost intact.

Points for a safe freezer:

1. *The temperature should be maintained at a steady − 18 °C/0 °F; hot or warm foods should never be put into the freezer.*

2. *The freezer should be de-frosted and cleaned regularly. This means, on average, 2 or 3 times a year for an upright freezer and once or twice a year for a chest freezer. As a general rule, when the ice has built up to a thickness of more than 5 mm/$\frac{1}{4}$ inch inside the cabinet, it is time to defrost. The job is best done when stocks are low.*

3. *To help food remain in optimum condition, it should be frozen as quickly as possible to prevent too many ice crystals forming, and packaging should be as airtight as possible. Open-freezing fruits and vegetables on trays before putting them in freezer bags allows them to freeze quickly (and prevents them forming a solid block).*

4. *To ensure that moisture does not get into food and damage it, the right kinds of packaging should be used, including freezer bags and plastic containers.*

5. *All foods in a freezer should be labelled with either the date on which it was frozen or its use-by date.*

6. *Thawed frozen food should never be re-frozen, unless the thawing has been only partial, with ice-crystals still round the food. Fully thawed food should be used as soon as possible, and not left lying about at room temperature.*

Storage times recommended in freezing instructions and recipes and by manufacturers of commercial foods usually err on the safe side. Food will not normally be harmful if eaten shortly after the recommended date, but the quality in terms of colour, flavour and texture will not be as good.

Foods that will not freeze successfully are: eggs, cream of less than 40% butterfat, fruit high in water content, bananas, avocado pears, celery, boiled potatoes (but mashed ones to which milk has not been added are all right), salad vegetables, tomatoes, custards, jelly, yogurt, soured cream, soft meringue, icings, mayonnaise, carbonated drinks and dishes containing garlic.

4 Cleaning

INTRODUCTION

Anyone who has ever added up, for insurance purposes, the value of the contents of their homes and their wardrobes, will know that they represent a large financial investment. It makes good sense, then, to give our homes and our possessions, including our clothes, the benefit of the regular care and cleaning that will extend their life and usefulness.

This chapter is concerned, in the main, with making the best of the everyday items in our homes, including furniture and fabrics, china, glass and cutlery, and the contents of kitchen and bathroom. It is concerned with the fabric of the home, too, giving hints on cleaning walls, windows, floors and doors, and on eliminating pests and smells. A long section is devoted to clothes care. Not included here are notes on the care and cleaning of antiques, valuable works of art or antiquarian books and maps; these are matters for experts.

Many of the cleaning materials suggested in this chapter are basic, multi-purpose items. Where the use of commercially manufactured products is suggested, always give preference to those which are environmentally friendly. Read the labels: a good range of CFC-free, ozone-friendly aerosols and sprays, from furniture polishes to pest killers, is available and should be sought out.

Maintaining a Clean House

The basic rule for keeping a house pleasant and safe to live in is to clean regularly but not obsessively. Some areas, particularly in the kitchen and bathroom, need daily attention, but other parts of the house will need attention only in relation to how often they are used. On the whole, though, it is better to clean lightly and often rather than to undertake a major clean a couple of times a year.

While there are proprietary products to cope with almost any cleaning job, many of them are expensive, one-job items. Much of the general cleaning of a house and its contents can be done with just a few versatile products: bleach, washing soda, washing-up liquid and a general-purpose cream cleanser; and some basic chemicals, such as acetone, ammonia, paraffin, turpentine and white spirit. Nor should ordinary water be forgotten: it is as good as, if not better than, most disinfectants at removing harmful bacteria from household surfaces.

The most important cleaning machine in the average household, apart from the washing machine, is the vacuum cleaner. This will operate most efficiently if its cleaning bag is changed before it becomes too full and its filter before it is clogged up with dust. Though it sounds economical, it is not really a good idea to reuse the vacuum cleaner's paper lining bag. Reused bags tend to become less porous and impede the flow of air through the cleaner.

CLEANING AND MAINTENANCE TIPS FOR THE HOUSE

Doors A good thick doormat at outside doors will keep a surprising amount of dirt and dust out of the house. Outside doors are particularly vulnerable at the base, both from rising damp and from driving rain forcing water underneath. If a door has become rotten it should be replaced and the cause of the damp corrected. A properly fitted weatherboard across the bottom of the door will keep out rain. Door hinges that are stiff or noisy are usually cured with just a drop or two of lubricating oil.

Drains A solution of 15 ml/1 tablespoon salt to 600 ml/1 pint hot water is useful for clearing a drain and getting rid of any nasty smells.

Floors Always vacuum clean or sweep a floor before either washing or polishing it, as a damp mop will not gather up particles of dirt while an electric polisher will simply grind them into the floor with the polish. Most floor surfaces should be washed with a damp mop and not soaked since over-wetting can cause cork tiles to lift and woodblock tiles to warp, while water allowed to run under units can cause damp patches and wood rot. **Ceramic** floors should not be polished after washing: they will become dangerously slippery. Unsealed **cork tiles** can be polished, provided a non-slip wax polish is used.

Alkaline floor cleaners, such as borax, washing soda solution or soap-based liquid solutions, should not be used on **vinyl** floor coverings, since they can cause shrinkage and cracking. Both **vinyl** floorings and **linoleum** benefit from a rinse with a bucket of clean water to which 1 cup of white vinegar has been added. This will remove any film left by the cleaning product used and give the floors a sparkling finish.

To remove white patches from **quarry tiles**, mop with a weak vinegar solution: 60 ml/4 tablespoons vinegar to 4.5 litres/1 gallon of water. Let the solution dry on the tiles. Repeat if necessary.

Paintwork Painted woodwork can be cleaned with sugar soap and water, working up from the bottom to avoid dirty streaks.

Walls and ceilings A simple solution for washing walls is $\frac{1}{4}$ cup washing soda, $\frac{1}{2}$ cup ammonia and $\frac{1}{4}$ cup white vinegar mixed into a bucket of warm water. Work up from the bottom, then rinse downwards to prevent streaks of dirty water running down already-cleaned sections. Difficult stains may be removed with neat washing-up liquid or household cleaner, which must be rinsed off thoroughly.

Soot may be scrubbed off **stone** or **brick walls** with clean water and a fibre (not metal/wire) scrubbing brush. **Polystyrene ceiling tiles** should not be painted over, since this could be a fire hazard. A wedge of white bread makes an effective tool for rubbing dirt and grime off **wallpaper**. For grease spots on wallpaper, try laying a piece of blotting paper over the spot and pressing it with a warm iron.

Windows Effective home recipes for window cleaners are either a few drops of household ammonia or 30 ml/2 tablespoons vinegar in a bucket of clean water, or a capful of cold water detergent to 1 litre/2 pints of clean water. The windows may be polished up after cleaning with crumpled newspapers, which prevents smearing. Windows should always be cleaned when the sun is not shining on them, so that they do not dry too quickly and leave smears.

CLEANING AND MAINTENANCE TIPS FOR HOUSE CONTENTS

Baths and sinks Preventing tidemarks, which will form particularly easily in hard water areas, makes bath-cleaning easier; add a little washing-up liquid to the bathwater (bubble bath, which is the same thing with a scent added, is also effective, of course, but more expensive).

When cleaning baths and sinks, use a cream cleanser with a nylon pad – not metal, which can scratch the surface. A neglected bath can be restored by filling it with very hot water and adding three or four cupfuls of washing soda. Let this mixture soak in the bath for at least two hours, then empty the bath, rinse it with a hand-held shower and rub down the surface.

Washing soda is also effective in preventing fat building up in the drain pipes of kitchen sinks: sprinkle a good cupful of washing soda into the sink, then pour at least a kettleful of near-boiling water over it. This should be done regularly and not just when fat has been accidentally poured down the sink. (Fats and drippings from cooked meats should never be drained down the sink: pour unwanted fat into old cans, harden them in the refrigerator, then throw out with the kitchen refuse.)

Old toothbrushes are useful bath and sink cleaners. Use one dipped in disinfectant to clean out overflows, and one with a little bath cleaner to clean behind taps. Stainless steel sinks can be polished with wads of damp (not wet) newspaper.

Carpets A good vacuuming should always be given to carpets before and after shampooing; the underside of rugs and movable carpets should not be forgotten. It is a good idea to lay strips of foil under pieces of furniture that cannot be moved during shampooing to prevent marking. Anchor the foil under furniture feet or castors. Carpets must not be over-wetted or scrubbed during shampooing – the pile will be distorted. Always test an out-of-the-way section of carpet with the shampoo first.

Small patches of squashed carpet pile can be raised by steaming: put a damp white cloth (not a coloured one which might lose dye on to the carpet) over the area and press gently with a hot iron. When the cloth is dry, take it up and brush up the pile with a stiff brush.

Dents made by heavy furniture in wool carpets can be removed by putting two or three small ice cubes in the dent and leaving them to melt. When the area is dry, go over it with the suction nozzle of the vacuum cleaner.

China Everyday china should always be washed up soon after it is used, then dried and put away. If dishes need soaking, this should be done in cold, soapy water – hot water will bake foods like egg on to the china. Tea or coffee stains can be removed from mugs and cups with an overnight soak in washing powder solution. Light staining on modern china and ceramics will usually respond to soaking in a solution of household bleach and water; rinse well afterwards.

Regular dusting will help prevent a build-up of dust and grime on china and porcelain ornaments. For more serious cleaning, lay the piece to be cleaned on a soft foam mat or a cloth in a plastic basin of warm, soapy water. Rinse it, and dry thoroughly. Pieces should be washed separately, to prevent edges, handles and the like knocking against each other in the water.

More serious stains may be taken off china and porcelain with a damp cloth dipped in bicarbonate of soda or borax. Vinegar and water, rubbed over firmly, will take off most hard water marks.

Lime scale (calcium carbonate), built up on ceramic pot plant holders through regular watering of the plant, can be removed using spirits of salt (hydrochloric acid), obtainable from chemists, and **handled with care**: always wear old clothing, rubber gloves and safety glasses. Add the acid to water, **never** the other way round. Put the pot to be cleaned in a bowl, add water to cover the stain, then slowly add the acid until the lime scale begins to bubble. Stop adding the acid and leave the pot to soak until the lime scale has been dissolved. When the work is finished, pour the acid solution down an outside drain and rinse the article thoroughly.

Cookers and ovens Ammonia is an inexpensive oven cleaner, but it must be handled with care: wear rubber gloves and do not let it splash into your eyes. If a non-self cleaning oven has not been cleaned for some time, an overnight 'soak' is very effective. Turn the oven on to a moderate heat for 20 minutes to warm up, switch off and put an ovenproof bowl of strong ammonia on the top shelf and a dish of boiling water on the bottom. Close the oven and leave the ammonia and water to work overnight. Next morning, remove and discard them and clean the oven with a solution of washing-up liquid and water. Oven walls can be cleaned with a solution of bicarbonate of soda and water, a job which is most effective if the oven has been warmed first, though turned off before work starts. Where food is burned on to the bottom of the oven, let it cool, then sprinkle on dishwasher powder. Cover with a damp towel and leave overnight; next day, wash off with warm water.

Only manufacturers' recommended products should be used to clean halogen hobs, and certainly not cream cleanser, which will leave a film.

It is not a good idea to try to keep grill pans free of burnt-on stains by lining them with aluminium foil; fat can collect in pools on the foil and may catch fire.

Furniture No matter how meticulously **wooden** furniture is dusted and polished, over the years a layer of dust and old polish will build up on the surface of the wood, leaving it dull and its grain hidden. It may also become stained, from carelessly abandoned wine glasses, spilt liquids and the like. The grimy layer can be removed with a reviver: either a mixture of four parts white spirit to one part linseed oil, or equal parts of raw linseed oil, turpentine and methylated spirits. Mix the reviver in a screw-top jar and shake well. Rub the reviver over the furniture with a clean cloth. The cloth should be refolded during the work so that a clean surface is always presented to the wood. This process will not affect stained or polished surfaces but it will lift the wax off stripped and waxed pine and other waxed woods.

If the furniture is really dirty, the reviver can be applied on a ball of 000 grade wire wool. Whether using a cloth or wire wool, do not apply too much pressure and work in the direction of the grain. To finish off, wipe the wood with a clean cloth dampened with white spirit. Finally, apply a fresh coat of wax or French polish.

Some stains left on polished wood furniture – ring marks from wet glasses, splashes of alcohol or nail polish remover – often penetrate no further than the top layer of polish, and may be dealt with at home, removing them with a liquid metal polish applied on a soft, damp cloth. When the stain has disappeared completely, the area can be repolished. Candle wax dripped on to polished furniture should be left to go solid then picked off, either with a fingernail or a piece of stiff plastic. A reviver will wash off any remaining wax.

Dirty **cane** or **rush** furniture can be wiped over with a well wrung-out cloth which has been dipped in warm, soapy water. Rinse thoroughly, as soap residues could encourage mould, something which rush is particularly prone to: dry it in the sun, if possible. Canework can become very dry and brittle in a centrally-heated house; prevent this by using a humidifier.

To lift greasy deposits off **painted** and **lacquered** furniture, use warm, soapy water on a soft rag, wrung out so there is not enough water to flood joints in the furniture or get under veneers – the joints could swell and the veneers lift. Large items should be washed a section at a time, working upwards to prevent streaking. The furniture should be rinsed gently with clean water, again using a wrung-out cloth, and then rubbed over with a dry cloth.

Great care is needed when treating the special finishes of **leather** furniture: clean according to the manufacturers' instructions. The main problem with leather desk-tops is usually ink and speed is essential in dealing with the spill or streak. Blot up quickly and wash the area with water for fountain pen ink and milk for ballpoint.

Glass This cleans quite easily, but the work needs to be done carefully since most glass is quite fragile. Drinking glasses are best washed individually: antique glasses should never be put in a dishwasher. Wash glasses in a plastic bowl with a soft pad in the bottom and filled with warm water and washing-up liquid. A few drops of ammonia in the water is a good idea if the glassware is greasy or very dirty. Rinse glasses in clean water then stand them upside down on a cloth (to prevent chipping) to drain. Glassware must be dried thoroughly since damp can cause staining.

As wine and sherry decanters are used largely for show, it is important that they look sparkling clean. To remove any tidemarks or dregs stains, half-fill the decanter with water and add a handful of uncooked rice. Stop the top and hold firmly; swish the water and rice around until they have done their job. Rinse out with hot water. The insides of decanters can be dried with a hairdryer.

To clean a glass vase stained by hard water, rub with a gentle scouring paste or pumice powder; pad a wooden spoon handle with a cloth and use this if you cannot get right into the vase. Wash in warm soapy water and rinse well.

Clean glass tables and shelves with a cloth soaked in methylated spirits. Use an old, soft toothbrush to clean the crevices of cut crystal.

Never immerse glass with metal mounts, such as claret jugs, in water. Clean such glass with damp cotton wool, keeping the metal parts dry.

Ivory Whiten ivory piano keys that have turned yellow with a cloth moistened with lemon juice. Ivory goes yellow more quickly in the dark, so leave the keyboard cover up on a piano.

Laminates Most kitchen worktops are now made of plastic laminate which does not get dirty or stain easily. Never use a kitchen worktop as a chopping or slicing board, since knives will scratch and cut the surface, allowing grime to sink in. Where there is a stain on a laminate surface – turmeric, for instance, causes stains which are very difficult to remove – use a cream kitchen cleanser or a little dry bicarbonate of soda on a damp cloth. Tea stains on white laminate can be treated with a mild bleach solution: 1 teaspoonful bleach to $\frac{1}{2}$ litre/1 pint water. Rinse this off well. Do not use it on coloured or patterned surfaces, as it may remove more than just the tea stain.

Lavatories These should be cleaned regularly. The best time is last thing at night, so that the lavatory bowl has several hours to be soaked by the cleaner. Bleach cleaners should never be used at the same time as powder, cream or liquid cleaners, since poisonous chlorine gas could result.

Marble Table tops and fireplace surrounds made of marble can be given a shine by rubbing them with a slice of lemon wrapped in a clean cloth and dipped in borax. Since lemon juice is an acid, it should be rinsed off after only a couple of minutes to prevent it damaging the marble. For fume stains from the fire or from cigarettes, rub the marble with a cloth soaked in vinegar, then rinse well.

Metals All metalware benefits from regular cleaning, preventing rusting or corrosion. If rust or corrosion do occur, use one of the numerous proprietary cleaners available to deal with them.

■ BRASS if new or newly cleaned will stay cleaner longer if a layer of clear polyurethane varnish or clear lacquer is painted or sprayed on. A little lemon juice with the brass polish will also help keep brass clean and bright longer. Neglected brass can be treated with a strong ammonia solution before it is cleaned. Washing alone will not clean brass, and proprietary metal cleaners are needed to remove tarnishing. A commercial rust remover will be needed for badly corroded brass showing signs of verdigris.

■ BRONZE This should never be cleaned with abrasives or metal polishes; simple washing in warm soapy water, followed by thorough drying, is the best treatment. A thin coat of wax polish could be put on bronze to be left outdoors.

■ CHROME A soft brush and soapy water are also a good cleaner for chrome, which can be polished up after cleaning with a mixture of two parts paraffin to one part methylated spirits. A solution of one part ammonia to one part water will remove corrosion from chrome. To remove hardwater deposits round chrome taps, rub in a paste of salt and vinegar or ground white chalk and vinegar. Rinse off and rub with a dry chamois leather.

■ COPPER A good cleaner is a mixture of two egg whites, a pinch of salt, a small glass of vinegar and four soup spoons of plain flour. Use this mixture on copper pans and kettles, rinsing off with warm water. The salt and vinegar paste recommended for chrome (*above*), or half a lemon dipped in salt, can also shift stains on copper.

■ PEWTER This does not rust as some other metals do, so it can be washed in warm soapy water. If a dull, dark film builds up, clean this off with metal polish. Use methylated spirits on a cloth for bad spots and stains, or try fine wire wool dipped in olive oil, working *with* the lines of the article, rather than in all directions.

■ SILVER This tarnishes quickly on exposure to air, so the best type of cleaner is a long-term silver polish which provides a chemical barrier. Silver dishes and cutlery should be washed in hot soapy water every time they are used and before they are polished to prevent grains of dirt scratching the metal during polishing.

Provided the silver coating is not wearing thin, silver cutlery can be cleaned in washing soda solution: lay the cutlery on a strip of metal foil in a plastic washing-up bowl, sprinkle a handful of washing soda over it, then cover with hot water. When the soda stops bubbling, take out the silver (wear rubber gloves!) and rinse it. When it is dry, buff with a soft cloth.

Upholstery A mixture of one part detergent to four parts boiling water will cool to a jelly. Whip this up with an egg beater and use the resulting foam to clean fixed upholstery covers. A commercial upholstery shampoo, of which the foam only is usually used, should always be tested first on an inconspicuous part of the upholstery.

Remember that dirt and dust can permanently damage upholstery fabrics, whether fixed, as on sofas and chairs, or loose as in curtains, or cushion covers. While regular cleaning is important, weekly attention with a vacuum cleaner or simply shaking out dirt and dust, will greatly extend upholstery life. Dirt-repellent sprays, used on new fabrics and reapplied after cleaning, will help preserve most fabrics.

COMBATING UNWANTED SMELLS

A fresh-smelling house is a pleasure to live in. Regular cleaning, plus bowls of pot pourri or dried lavender, will keep houses welcoming most of the time, and a little forethought can prevent many potential nasty smells actually doing any harm. Even unavoidable smells can be dealt with – if you know how. Here are some tips.

In the kitchen

* If you are cooking something like curry or fish with a smell that you would not want to penetrate to all corners of the house, work with a saucer of vinegar nearby; it will absorb most of the smell.

* A few drops of lemon juice in the water prevents the smell of cooking cabbage spreading beyond the kitchen, without affecting the taste.

* Adding chopped celery to cooking oil when frying fish helps disguise the smell.

* Washing does not always remove the smell of foods absorbed by a chopping board. Try rubbing a paste of bicarbonate of soda into the board, rinsing it off, then washing as usual. To get rid of the smell of onion, rub the board with coarse salt before rinsing with cold water.

* If silver cutlery has a fishy smell, add a drop of mustard to the washing-up water. A little vinegar added to the water will remove fish smells from china.

* Refresh a clean saucepan that still smells by boiling a little white vinegar in it.

* Wash hands smelling of onion or garlic as soon as possible in cold water; if the smell persists, rub with lemon juice or vinegar, then wash with soap and water.

* Clear the refrigerator of lingering odours by smearing a paste of baking soda around the inside. Rinse with clean water. Charcoal, baking soda or simply crumpled-up newspapers may also absorb smells. Alternatively, switch off and wipe it with a solution of the sterilizing fluid used for babies' bottles, avoiding the metal parts. Rinse the inside and leave it to dry before turning it on again.

About the house

* The smell of fresh paint can pall very quickly. Remove it by leaving a small dish of kitchen salt in a newly painted room overnight.

* Remove strong chemical smells by using a peeled onion in a bucket of water.

* A mothball in the bottom of a dustbin improves its smell and keeps away flies.

* If a little-used cupboard has become rather musty, put a saucer of bath salts on the floor.

* For drawers that have not been aired, pop in lemon peel or small pads of cotton wool with a little vanilla essence. Perfumed drawer lining papers help keep drawers smelling sweet.

When entertaining

* Place a small bowl of vinegar in a room where people are smoking to absorb the smell. It is also possible to buy special candles which do this job as they burn.

* When guests have left, get rid of lingering smoke by whisking a damp towel round the room.

Coping with pets

* If a cat or dog is sick on the carpet, a quick squirt from a soda siphon will help to eliminate the smell once the mess has been cleared up.

* If a cat has sprayed or soiled anywhere in the house, the area must be cleaned so thoroughly that the cat is not tempted by smell to use the place again. Wash with clean water, then with a solution of sodium hypochlorite (this is a bleach, so should be used carefully). Once the area is clean, sprinkle round baking soda to absorb any remaining water: this can be easily vacuumed once it is dry. Various proprietary deterrents are available to keep cats away from areas where they have sprayed or soiled. Solutions, pellets and powders are longer-lasting than sprays.

HOUSEHOLD PESTS

Few houses or flats, however well maintained, can hope to escape completely from invasion by some kind of household pest. Many creatures, such as ants, wasps and mice, come in from outside, attracted by the presence of warmth and food. Others may indicate a point of weakness in the house: if woodlice are a constant problem, for instance, there could be dampness in the plaster or woodwork that the woodlice are happily feeding and breeding on. Other pests may indicate a problem with hygiene, either within the home or outside it. With all pests, prevention is better than cure. So that your house does not attract pests:

* Never leave scraps of food around. Sweep up crumbs after every meal and try to stop children eating crisps, biscuits and apples in every room of the house, leaving tasty morsels, or even their school lunch, under beds, and so on.
* Put away or cover all food when it is not set out for a meal. This includes pet food: it is not a good idea to give a cat a large bowlful of food in the morning and let it sit around all day.
* Keep the lid firmly on the dustbin. Make sure there are no holes through which rats could drag food. Flies will lay eggs on any foodstuffs in or out of the dustbin.
* Be aware of the address and telephone number of the local authority's Pest Control Office, and get in touch with it at the first sign of any major infestation.

Ants Black garden ants are the usual invaders, coming in after protein, fatty foods and anything sweet. See where their nest is, then pour boiling water over it. There are also various proprietary products, including powders. Poisonous ant-bait should not be necessary and should not be used where there are children or pets.

Bees and wasps These are generally harmless, unless provoked. Wasps are, in fact, predators of insects more harmful to people. Nesting wasps can be a worry, however, and if the nest can be reached, it should be treated with a special wasp-killer, puffing it into the entrance at dusk when the wasps are inside. Wear gloves as a precaution and move away as soon as you have finished. You can also make an old-fashioned wasp trap by hanging a jam-jar half-filled with jammy or sugary water near the nest. Similar wasp-traps on window sills can keep wasps out of the house. A swarm of wasps or bees needs expert attention and the local Pest Control Officer or Environmental Health Officer should be called at once.

Carpet beetles The preferred food of these small brown and cream, ladybird-shaped insects and, more particularly, of their larvae, is carpet, feathers or wool. They are fast becoming a more serious carpet pest than moths. To get rid of them, spray with a persistent insecticide (the larvae will often survive onslaughts from short-lived preparations) and dust between the floorboards and under the carpet underlay, with an insecticidal powder. If stored blankets or woollen clothes are affected, wash or dry clean them, then store with a cotton bag of paradichlorbenzene crystals (from chemists) or use a proprietary mothproofer. Fur coats infested with carpet beetles must be treated professionally; never spray them.

As a preventive, clean carpets regularly and spray the folded-over edges of fitted carpets and areas of carpets which are left undisturbed for long periods (such as under heavy furniture) with a residual insecticide.

Cockroaches   These dark-brown 2.5 cm/1 inch-long insects carry diseases that affect humans, spreading them in their excrement. They also smell nasty. They favour warm, moist spots around pipes, sinks and stoves, and are found more in older properties with plenty of inaccessible hiding places. Cockroaches are difficult to get rid of. The insecticide must penetrate right into the places where they hide, which is not always easy. Clean everything thoroughly and cover all food. If the cockroaches seem out of control, call the Pest Control Officer.

Earwigs   These are usually seen at night and do no real harm. They do not live naturally indoors, but come in from the garden, often being brought in on cut flowers. Simply sweep them up and throw them outside. If they have settled in wall or floor crevices, use an insecticide powder.

Fleas   These usually come from cats and dogs and breed happily in our centrally-heated, well-carpeted homes. Pets should be checked regularly for fleas and treated, if necessary, with specially formulated flea sprays. Their bedding should also be treated, and the places where they usually sleep or rest, including carpets and furnishings. Vacuum all treated areas within a day to pick up stray fleas and eggs.

Flies   Flies and bluebottles are prolific carriers of bacteria and should be kept out of kitchens and wherever there is food. Discourage flies from frequenting the dustbin by washing it out regularly and disinfecting it. Sprinkle the dry dustbin with soap powder or drop in a mothball. Keep any garden compost well away from the house. Flies can be got rid of with sprays (note, though, that aerosol insecticides can affect people and pets, so a slow-release fly-killer is safer), old-fashioned fly-papers and plastic strips impregnated with fly-killer. Flies dislike and will avoid some herbs, so use these in the fight against them, including oil of lavender rubbed on the woodwork round windows, and bunches of bay leaves hung in the larder.

Mice and rats   Both these rodents are attracted by food, both carry diseases and both will gnaw at just about anything, including electric wiring and gas pipes, to sharpen their incisors. If you suspect there are mice in the house, act quickly – they breed rapidly. Find the mouseholes and put down dishes of turpentine or wads of cloth soaked with oil of peppermint to repel them. Mouse poison, used in dosages small enough to be harmless to people or pets, can be effective but generally only in the short term. The best long-term answer to a mouse problem is, in fact, a cat – even the smell of a cat can be enough to send mice away. If rats are the problem it is advisable to inform your local Pest Control Officer.

Mosquitoes Though not as serious here as in many other countries, mosquitoes are still a pest and the bite of the female can cause considerable pain and unpleasant swellings. If there is a stagnant puddle, pond or even water butt where they could breed, a drop of paraffin on the surface will prevent the larvae from developing. Indoors, keep a pot of fresh basil in the room – mosquitoes dislike it.

Moths The larvae of moths are responsible for tiny holes in woollen clothes, bald patches on fur and even holes in wine bottle corks. The larvae are most often found in stored clothes and blankets and are covered by a fluffy substance. Brush them off the fabric, checking underneath collars and pocket flaps. If you find signs of moth larvae in a carpet, kill them by steam ironing with a warm iron and a damp cloth. Do not press down hard with the iron, but let the steam do the job.

Prevent moths returning by lining drawers with newspaper so the larvae cannot creep back in through the bottom, and use mothballs or moth-repellent strips. Never put clothes away dirty, as moths are attracted by the smell of greasy stains. Freshly cleaned clothes and blankets can be sprayed with moth repellent – test spray an unobtrusive section first.

Silverfish These are small wingless silvery insects about 1 cm/$\frac{1}{2}$ inch long. They thrive in damp conditions and are typically found in the bath, under kitchen sinks or at the back of cupboards. They live on carbohydrate – starch – products, including wallpaper paste and book-binding glue. If there are no young children in the house, a sprinkling of a mixture of one part sugar and one part borax in places where silverfish have been found will get rid of them. Or use an insecticidal powder.

Ticks These small (about 5-mm/$\frac{1}{4}$-inch long) insects are usually associated with the country and farm animals, but since they occasionally turn up in town, it is useful to know how to deal with them. If they land on a family pet or a child, they will bite and swell up with the blood they take.

Do not try to pull a tick off. It will probably break, leaving its jaws embedded in the skin, which can lead to infection. Soak cotton wool in methylated spirits and take hold of the tick with this. The spirits will make the tick ease its hold and you can get it off in one go.

Woodlice Harmless in themselves, these tiny grey crustaceans are a sign of damp – unless their colony site is near an outside door and they have just wandered in. Get rid of them with insecticide and draw a barrier with an insecticide pen to discourage them from coming into the house. Just in case they have been attracted by damp in the house, look for and treat the source of any damp.

Woodworm Woodworm can spread so always inspect any second-hand furniture before bringing it into the house. The obvious signs are little piles of fresh sawdust and holes in the woodwork or furniture. The holes are made by the grubs of the wood-boring furniture beetle which lays its eggs on the surface of the wood. When the grubs hatch they bore into the wood, leaving no sign of their entry, and may remain there for up to ten years. While small items can be treated with a proprietary liquid squirted into the holes, anything more serious requires professional help.

GETTING RID OF PESTS SAFELY

It is necessary to use chemicals to get rid of most household pests, often made up in the form of baits, puffers and aerosol sprays. There are also insecticidal smokes and fumigants. Whatever is used, it is essential to follow a few safety rules:

* Always read the manufacturer's instructions carefully and follow them precisely.
* Store all chemicals, during and after use, where children cannot reach them.
* Never decant pest control chemicals into old lemonade or soft drink bottles that children could mistake for the real thing.
* Always label bottles, jars or tins. Using the wrong chemical can be very dangerous.
* Take great care when handling chemicals. Wear rubber gloves, wash splashes off the skin at once and always wash your hands when the job is finished.
* Most sprays are both highly toxic and inflammable. Avoid inhaling the vapour from aerosols and always use them in a well-ventilated room, making sure that pets and children are well out of the way. Keep clear of food and afterwards clean any nearby work surfaces. Never smoke when spraying or have any naked flames nearby.
* Before using an aerosol, make sure the spray hole is pointing towards the area you want to spray. Never puncture an empty can or put it on a fire: it will explode.
* Flush any left-over liquid chemicals down an outside drain if they are not to be kept; then pour buckets of cold water after them.

Stain Removal from Fabrics

The newer a stain, the easier it is to remove, especially if tackled in the right way. Keeping a basic stain-removing kit ready to hand is obviously a sensible move.

A basic selection of stain removers, which as well as proprietary products could include amyl acetate, ammonia, glycerine, hydrogen peroxide, lighter fuel, methylated spirits, nail varnish remover and white spirit, should be kept together in one place. Since all these substances are poisonous, they must be kept in well-stoppered, clearly labelled bottles and stored in a secure place.

Also in the stain removal kit should be pieces of clean sponge, old sheeting to make a pad to work over, cotton buds for precise application on very small stains, a nail brush or old toothbrush, and an old medicine dropper for dripping very small amounts of cleaner on to a small area or for squirting it through a stained fabric so that the stain is removed on to a backing pad.

REMOVING STAINS FROM FABRICS

ADHESIVES
Sticky Tape
Use methylated spirits.

Contact and Clear Adhesive
Dab gently with acetone (or nail varnish remover), except on acetate fabrics.

Epoxy Resin
Start removing the resin before it sets. For natural fabrics, apply methylated spirits; for synthetics, use lighter fuel.

Latex
Use cold water to remove as much as possible before it dries. Then peel off and dab any mark left with grease solvent.

Modelling Cement
Remove with acetone or a non-oily nail varnish remover (except on acetate fabric).

PVA Glue
Apply methylated spirit.

Superglue
Hold under running cold water or use a wet pad.

ALCOHOL
Beer
Washables: Rinse in lukewarm water, soak in biological washing powder, then wash.

Non-washables: Blot off as much as possible, dab with white vinegar, blot again.

Spirits
Washables: Rinse in cold water.

Non-washables: Blot, sponge with methylated spirits. Blot, sponge with cold water.

Red Wine
Washables: Mop up surplus red wine, then sponge immediately with white wine, then treat as if white wine (see below).

Non-washables: Sponge with warm water and blot. Sprinkle with talcum powder and leave for an hour. Sponge and blot again.

White Wine
Washables: Rinse in warm water, sponge with borax solution if necessary. If stain has dried, loosen with glycerine before laundering.

Non-washables: As red wine.

Bird Droppings
Washables: Scrape off and soak in biological powder before washing as usual. For droppings coloured by berries, see Fruit Juices.

Non-washables: Scrape off, sponge with solution of 1 part ammonia to 6 parts water (test coloureds first). Soak up excess moisture; dab with white vinegar.

Blood
Washables: Soak in a strong salt and cold water solution for five minutes; rinse, soak again in clean, cold solution. Repeat until the stain has gone. Soak stubborn stains in a solution of hydrogen peroxide plus ammonia (1 tablespoon 20 vol. strength hydrogen peroxide to 7–8 tablespoons water plus $\frac{1}{2}$ tablespoon ammonia). Do not use on pure nylon.

Non-washables: Soak up blood, then sponge with a few drops of ammonia in cold water. If traces still remain, apply a paste of starch and water. Let dry.

Dried Blood
Washables (not wool or silk): Soak overnight in biological powder.

Non-washables: Dampen with lemon juice, sprinkle with salt, iron between two sheets of slightly damp white blotting paper.

Candle Wax
If possible, freeze affected item until wax is hard enough to scrape off. Cover stained area with clean white blotting paper and use a warm iron to remove the rest. Repeat ironing if necessary. Use a solvent for any last traces or methylated spirit for coloured wax.

Carbon Paper
Washables: Sponge with undiluted liquid detergent and rinse well. If stain persists, dab with methylated spirits, then treat with liquid detergent and a few drops of household ammonia.

Non-washables: Sponge repeatedly with white spirit or methylated spirits.

Chewing gum
Washables: Soften with egg white or grease solvent and scrape off, then wash. *Or* freeze till hard and peel off. Remove any residue by ironing over with brown paper or treat with methylated spirits, or white spirit or proprietary chewing gum stain remover.

Non-washables: Freeze and peel off, remove last traces with grease solvent.

Chocolate
Washables: Scrape off any solids, then wash in cool soapy water. If necessary, sponge with a warm borax solution: 25 g (1 oz) borax to 600 ml (1 pint) water. *Or* sponge with warm water, sprinkle with dry borax, rubbing it in gently and leave for half an hour. Rinse and launder as usual. Use a proprietary grease solvent if any stain lingers.

Non-washables: Scrape off, then use a grease solvent.

REMOVING STAINS FROM FABRICS

Coffee and Tea

Washables: Rinse out in suds as soon as possible. If necessary, soak overnight in biological powder. For immediate results, sponge with warm borax solution.

Non-washables: Sponge with borax solution, then blot. If necessary use a grease solvent.

Correction Fluid (Tippex)

Washables: Allow to dry and pick off as much as possible. Dab stain with acetone or nail varnish remover, except on man-made fibres. For these, wash or take to dry-cleaner.

Non-washables: Allow to dry, pick off as much as possible, then dry-clean.

Crayon

Washables: Treat with methylated spirits, then wash. *Or* rub with undiluted detergent and rinse thoroughly. Remove any remaining colour with methylated spirits.

Non-washables: Dab with grease solvent or take to dry-cleaner.

Dyes

Washables: Add a few drops of ammonia to methylated spirits and sponge gently, but be sure to test first on coloureds or man-made fibres. *Or* rinse well in cold water and soak in biological detergent. Treat any remaining dye on white fabric with a proprietary dye stripper.

Non-washables: Take to the dry-cleaner immediately.

Egg

Washables: Scrape off solids, rinse in cold water, wash in biological powder.

Non-washables: Scrape off solids, then treat with a grease solvent.

Food Colouring

Washables: Sponge immediately with cold water, work in undiluted liquid detergent, then rinse. If stain remains, dab with methylated spirits.

Non-washables: Sponge with cold water, then treat with methylated spirits.

Fruit Juices

Washables: Rinse in cold water. If colour remains, stretch garment over the basin and pour hot water through it. For beetroot, sprinkle powdered borax over stain before treating with hot water.

Non-washables: Sponge with cold water, then with glycerine. Leave for an hour, then sponge with white vinegar. Finally, sponge with cold water.

Grass and Leaf Stains

Washables: Wash in warm soapy water. If stain remains, sponge with methylated spirits and wash.

Non-washables: Make up equal quantities of cream of tartar and salt into a paste with water and rub this into the stain. Leave for 15 minutes, then brush off.

Gravy

Washables: Wash at once in cold soapy water. Rinse. Use a solvent to remove any greasy traces.

Non-washables: Sponge with soapy water. Blot dry, then use a solvent.

Grease

Most fabrics can be treated with a proprietary grease solvent. Sponge on the *wrong* side.

INK

Ballpoint

Washables: Rub with warm soapy water, then wash. Use nail varnish remover for any stain that remains (except on acetates).

Non-washables: Dab with nail varnish remover (except on acetates). Alternatively, use a proprietary ballpoint stain remover.

Felt-Tip

Washables: Remove as much as possible with pads of cotton wool or paper towels. Small spots can be dabbed with methylated spirits (except on acetates). Wash with soap powder or flakes and rinse well. Alternatively, use a proprietary felt-tip stain remover.

Non-washables: Small spots can be tackled with methylated spirits, otherwise take to the dry-cleaner.

Fountain Pen

Washables: Treat with liquid detergent as soon as possible. Rinse. Stretch fabric over a bowl, cover stain with salt and pour the juice of a lemon over it. Leave for at least 2 hours, then wash as usual.

Non-washables: Sponge with cold water and blot well. Alternatively, use proprietary stain remover spray, or take to the dry-cleaner.

Indelible

Treat at once with a proprietary indelible ink stain remover.

Typewriter

Sponge with methylated spirits and/or a dry-cleaning solvent.

REMOVING STAINS FROM FABRICS

MAKE-UP

Lipstick

Washables: Most stains will wash out. If stubborn, apply a suitable proprietary make-up stain remover.

Non-washables: Apply a proprietary make-up stain remover.

Mascara

Washables: Sponge with washing-up liquid, then with ammonia, and rinse.

Non-washables: Treat with a dry-cleaning fluid.

Metal Polish

Treat with white spirit. When stain is dry, brush gently to remove any dried bits of polish.

Mildew

Washables: If the usual wash does not remove it, soak in 1 part 20 vol. hydrogen peroxide to 6 parts water, but watch for possible bleeding of colour.

Non-washables: Take to dry-cleaners.

Nail Varnish

Simply dab with nail varnish remover (except on acetates). If you are not sure what the fabric is, test on inside seam first or use amyl acetate.

PAINT

Oil-Based/Gloss/Enamel

Washables: Dab with white spirit or turpentine. Sponge with soapy water, then wash.

Non-washables: As above but do not wash.

Emulsion/Water-Colour

Sponge with cold water. Dry cleaning may be necessary for delicate fabrics.

Perspiration

Washables: If washing in a biological washing powder does not work, sponge with weak solution of ammonia, then rinse and wash.

Non-washables: Sponge with a solution of 1 teaspoon white vinegar to 250 ml (8 fl oz) warm water.

Putty/Plasticine

Washables: Freeze until hard, scrape off as much as possible, then sponge with grease solvent. Wash.

Non-washables: Freeze and scrape. Sponge with grease solvent. If stain remains, take to dry-cleaner.

Rust

Sponge with a solution of 1 teaspoon oxalic acid to $\frac{1}{2}$ litre (1 pint) water. (N.B. oxalic acid is poisonous, so be careful.)

Scorch Marks

Washables: Slight marking may be removed by soaking in cold milk. After this, if still necessary, dab with soapy water containing 1 teaspoon borax, then rinse out.

Non-washables: Keep sponging with a solution of 2 teaspoons borax in $\frac{1}{2}$ litre (1 pint) warm water. Then sponge with cold water.

Shoe Polish

Treat with white spirit or a dry-cleaning fluid.

Suntan Oil

See Grease. If any colour remains after treating, soak washables in warm water with 1 teaspoon borax added. Then wash in detergent and rinse well.

Tar and Oil

Washables: Scrape off, then sponge from wrong side of fabric with eucalyptus oil. Remove any remaining traces with lighter fuel, then wash as usual.

Non-washables: Scrape carefully. Loosen with glycerine, then rub gently with lighter fuel and dab with a cloth wrung out in warm water.

Urine

Washables: Soaking in biological powder is usually enough.

Non-washables: Sponge with cold water and blot up, then sponge with a solution of 2 teaspoons white vinegar to 1 litre/$1\frac{3}{4}$ pints water. (This will also help to banish any smell.)

Vomit

Washables: Scrape, soak and wash in biological powder.

Non-washables: Scrape and sponge repeatedly with warm water to which a few drops of ammonia have been added.

Precautions to take when using any stain-removing solvent:
* *Wear rubber gloves*
* *Do not smoke or work in a room with an open fire, a radiant heater or a pilot light*
* *Keep windows and doors open*
* *Before using a stain remover, scrape or blot off as much as possible of the cause of the stain; test the remover on an out-of-the-way part of the stained article*
* *Work from the outside of the stain in to the middle, to prevent it spreading, gently using a dampened cloth or sponge.*

Do not attempt to remove stains from silk chiffon, brocade, watered silk, silk jersey, velvet or lurex (unless it is clearly labelled as washable). These delicate fabrics need specialist attention.

Final warning: stain removal is always a tricky business, with some risk of damaging fabric. The methods suggested in the chart have been tried and tested, but they cannot be absolutely guaranteed.

Upholstery and Carpets

Once something has been spilt on a carpet, cushion or other upholstery, blot it up as quickly as possible, not rubbing but pressing down with a wad of tissue or absorbent kitchen paper; replace it with a fresh wad as soon as it is soaked or stained.

For individual stains, follow the advice in the stain removal chart above, adapting the instructions as necessary. Where a carpet cannot be 'rinsed', spray instead with soda water or mop it with a clean damp cloth. Where the instructions say 'wash', use a special carpet shampoo. In general, avoid overwetting the carpet by blotting up the cleaning liquid as you work. Some upholstery can be treated with proprietary upholstery shampoo. While many fabrics can be shampooed, cotton velvet, chenilles, tapestry, silk and wool are best left to professional cleaners. Acrylic velvet and many other sofa coverings can be cleaned using the foam only from upholstery shampoo.

Clothing Care

Regular and correct cleaning and laundry, along with prompt mending of holes and tears, sewing on of buttons etc, help clothes and textiles last longer while retaining a good appearance. Good washing practice requires forethought and planning in the way you sort, complete and carry out the wash.

BEFORE THE WASH

Brush mud and dirt from clothes as soon as they are dry. Check all garments for objects left in pockets (just one paper handkerchief can leave little bits of paper fluff over everything else in a load). Turn clothes inside out to minimize fading and close zips, Velcro openings and buttoned openers. If left open they can snag other fabrics. Tie up loose tapes or strings to prevent them being pulled off.

To check an item for colour fastness, try it out first in warm soapy water; if the colour runs, wash it separately. Another way of checking colour fastness is to dip part of the garment in water then place it between two sheets of blotting paper on the ironing board and press it with a warm iron. If the colour either comes through on to the paper or alters in any way as the iron heats it, the garment must be washed separately. If the instruction label on an article says to wash it separately 'the first few times', do just that, then test it for colour fastness before adding to a load.

Sort the washing according to care labels. Articles with different care labels can be washed together, so long as a programme is chosen which suits the most delicate fabrics in the load. The same rule applies if the label lists only fibre content with no specific washing instruction: wash according to the most vulnerable fibre listed.

Carry out any pre-treating necessary. If a shirt has a dirty collar and cuffs, give it a head start by soaping and scrubbing with ordinary soap or by spraying with a proprietary pre-wash spray. Pre-wash soaking is also helpful. Soak whites overnight and coloured articles for 2–3 hours. Use hand-hot, not boiling, water and **never soak** wool or silk or anything not colourfast. Some fabrics with special finishes, e.g. showerproof or flame-resistant, are damaged by soaking as are garments with metal trimmings. Do not soak white nylon fabric with coloured fabrics as the nylon will pick up loose dye.

IN THE WASHING MACHINE

Follow the manufacturer's instructions as to the load the machine will take and still do its job efficiently. If the load cannot rotate freely it will not be washed or rinsed properly. Always wash full loads, if possible, since this is a more economic use of water and detergent. Do not use a machine's half-load facility for washing a small load of synthetics; they need a full load of water to prevent them creasing.

Use the recommended detergent for the machine: a low-lather powder gives a better performance in an automatic machine. With ordinary powder, the froth can fill up the drum and prevent good washing and rinsing; it can also damage the machine. Low-lather detergent should also be used in front-loading machines.

Avoid using biological detergents for baby clothes or if anyone in the family suffers from eczema or has a very sensitive skin. Such detergents may cause irritation.

Proprietary whiteners can be added to the wash if there are items in it which need whitening or brightening up. Follow the instructions on the container.

Fabric conditioners may also be used in a washing machine. They keep washing soft to the touch and reduce the build-up of static electricity in synthetics. The correct amount of conditioner should always be used. Too much makes clothes greasy and eventually causes fabrics to fail to absorb detergent and thus stay dirty.

CARE LABELLING AND WASHING SYMBOLS

A standard range of symbols indicating textile care during washing is used on all care labels. An older range of symbols, using numbers for temperature range, still appears on much clothing, although a simple temperature number is now used on its own:

TEXTILE CARE LABELLING CODE: WASHING

 wash at 60°

The tub symbols used on fabric care labels indicate the three variables in the machine washing process – water temperature, agitation and spinning. Maximum water temperatures are shown in degrees Celsius inside the tub. 100°C is boiling; 95°C is very hot; 60°C is hot – hotter than the hand can bear; 50°C is hand hot; and 40°C is warm – pleasantly warm to the hand.

AGITATION AND SPINNING are both shown by the use of a bar or broken bar under the tub:

 Single bar denotes reduced machine action (agitation and water extraction)

 Broken bar denotes the much reduced machine action necessary for machine washable wool (with normal spinning)

Other labels indicate

 handwashing

 not washable

BLEACHING

 Triangles are used to indicate whether articles may be treated with **chlorine (household) bleach**:

 A triangle containing the letters Cl indicates that the article may be treated with chlorine bleach.

 A triangle crossed out means that chlorine bleach must not be used.

TUMBLE DRYING

Most textile articles can be safely tumble dried, and there are label symbols indicating which drying method is safest:

⊙ Tumble dry on a low heat setting

◯ Tumble dry on a high heat setting

⊗ Do not tumble dry. Where this symbol is used, other instructions, e.g., 'dry flat', should be given in words.

Care of the washing machine It will give longer, more efficient service if it is cared for. It should be wiped free of condensation after use and the casing polished occasionally with a wax-free spray polish. If it is being used in a hard water area, a water softener should be used in it. The washing powder or detergent will work more efficiently and the machine parts will not become encrusted with limescale. It is a good idea to run through the standard wash cycle with clear water 3 or 4 times a year to clean out the machine. The filter should also be cleaned regularly. Check the rubber door seal regularly and replace it if necessary.

IRONING

Not all clothes or fabrics need ironing. Modern synthetic fabrics are often best just put straight on to hangers after tumble drying. Most clothes benefit from being allowed to hang for a while after ironing; clothes put on immediately after ironing tend to crease quickly. If steam irons are not allowed to reach the required temperature before use, they tend to drip water on the articles they are pressing.

DRY-CLEANING

A circle symbol on a label indicates that the article can be dry-cleaned. It should never appear on its own, but with additional information indicating the types of cleaning solvent which may be used:

IRONING

The **ironing** symbols on care labels have four variations. The temperatures shown in brackets are the maximum sole plate temperatures indicated by the dots in the symbol:

Hot (200°C). Cotton, linen, viscose or modal (modified viscose)

Warm (150°C). Polyester mixtures, wool

Cool (110°C). Acrylic, nylon, acetate, triacetate, polyester

DO NOT IRON. Ironing would be bad for the fabric.
(Does *not* indicate that the fabric is necessarily crease-resistant.)
In addition to the symbol, the words 'Cool', 'Warm' or 'Hot' may also appear on the label.

DRY-CLEANING

Goods normal for dry-cleaning in all solvents.

Goods normal for dry-cleaning in perchloroethylene, white spirit, Solvent 113 and Solvent 11.

Goods normal for dry-cleaning in white spirit or Solvent 113.

Do not dry-clean.

When the circle containing P or F is underlined, do not 'coin op' clean, as this indicates that these materials are sensitive to dry-cleaning and require special treatment.

Coin-op dry-cleaning machines are not suitable for all garments or fabrics. They should not be used for duvets, blankets and other bedding, as the fumes from the dry-cleaning solvents can linger in them, with possibly fatal consequences.

Clothes, curtains and upholstery that have been dry-cleaned should always be hung out to air after cleaning, to ensure that toxic fumes do not linger. For the same reason, do not take the dry-cleaning home in a car with the windows shut.

CLEANING LEATHER, SUEDE AND SHEEPSKIN

For all their strength and versatility, leather, suede and sheepskin are very vulnerable to most cleaning products. Generally, except for very minor marks, regular cleaning needs to be done by professionals.

■ LEATHER COATS AND JACKETS Remove any surface dirt with a soft cloth, wiping off grease or oil as quickly as possible so that it does not sink into the leather. Serious stains will need to be handled by a dry-cleaner specializing in leather. If the garment is part of a set, such as a suit, then the other piece should be cleaned at the same time, as cleaning tends to alter the colour of leather a little.

■ LEATHER GLOVES Remove dirty marks from kid gloves by rubbing gently with a soft clean eraser. It is also possible to use bread: crumble white bread between the palms while wearing the gloves and roll it round on the marked areas.

■ LEATHER HANDBAGS AND BRIEFCASES Colourless beeswax furniture polish keeps these looking good and helps prevent staining. They can also be cleaned with saddle soap: apply with a small sponge, working it in with a circular movement, then rinse with a cloth dipped in water. When the bag is dry, it may be polished.

■ SUEDE Although professional cleaning is recommended, the odd mark may be dealt with at home. Rub Fuller's earth into the mark and leave for 15 minutes before brushing out with a soft (**not** wire) brush. Do not use any sort of chemical fluid as it may ruin the colour of the suede or, at least, leave an unsightly ring.

■ SHEEPSKIN Coats may be freshened up with a dry (hair) shampoo, lightly rubbed into the woolly side and left for an hour. Shake and brush the shampoo out, in the open, if possible. As with suede, for the odd mark sheepskin may be treated with Fuller's earth, but regular cleaning must be done by professional cleaners. Sheepskin rugs may be cleaned using the lather only from a bowl of soapflakes in warm water. Work the lather in with a brush, not too energetically and being careful not to overwet the rug. Dry it away from direct heat, then vacuum clean it.

CARING FOR SHOES

■ LEATHER BOOTS AND SHOES should be polished regularly to preserve the surface and kept in shape with shoe trees or pads of newspaper. Before polishing with a good wax polish or cream, any dirt should be removed with a damp cloth.

A common stain on leather in winter results from the salt spread on roads and paths to melt snow. The tidemarks can be removed by rubbing in a solution of half vinegar, half water. Leave to dry then polish as usual. Brown shoes stained by rain and looking patchy will benefit from a rub with turpentine. Work it in and leave overnight, then polish.

■ FABRIC shoes may be cleaned with proprietary shampoos, though these tend to lighten the colour, and the shampoo should be tested on an unobtrusive part, such as the tongue of the shoe, first. A number of fabric shoes, especially light trainers, are designed to be washed in the washing machine: read the labels carefully first.

■ PLASTIC, PATENT AND WET-LOOK shoes can be sponged clean, then wiped dry. A little Vaseline, or milk, rubbed into patent leather shoes, will give them a good shine. Patent leather shoes should always be put away with shoe trees in them to prevent creases in the leather turning into cracks. Vaseline helps keep them supple.

■ SUEDE shoes should be sprayed with a proprietary protective spray before they are worn at all. The spray makes the leather look soft without shiny patches and also protects it. Everyday dirt should be brushed off suede shoes with a stiff bristle (**not** metal) brush.

STORING CLOTHES

Clothes to be stored for any length of time – winter clothes during the summer, for instance – must be cleaned first. Perspiration can cause permanent stains in fabrics, even in clothes that have been worn just once.

Clothes for long storage also need to be protected from moths. Soft plastic wardrobe boxes which can be stored under beds or in a dry attic are useful, though white garments, such as wedding dresses are best stored in boxes lined with acid-free tissue paper: plastic bag storage for any length of time can cause white to yellow.

Generally, though, plastic is useful for storing clothes. Folding clothes over rolled-up plastic bags before packing them helps prevent creases. Man-made fabrics are best rolled up, rather than folded, for storage or packing, as they crease less.

5 DIY and Home Maintenance

Whether to do the work themselves or call in the professionals is the question all home owners ask when faced with the sometimes daunting responsibility of maintaining and improving their properties. It requires a realistic assessment of one's abilities and spare time. This is easier said than done but an objective starting point would be to talk to friends with DIY experience and see how they feel about various jobs. You will soon see a pattern emerging of jobs which are worth doing yourself. Don't forget to include the enjoyment factor in your assessment. If, for example, you hate heights there is no point scaring yourself to death to replace a roof tile, even though it may be a simple job in essence.

For more involved projects call in a professional to find out how much the job will cost, what's involved and how long it will take.

With this information you will at least know what you stand to save. Often you would be lucky to complete the work in anything less than three times as long as it takes a professional, and if your schedule involves lots of stops and starts, allow for these.

A compromise might be to take on some of the work yourself but leave the difficult bits to someone else. Many small builders are now prepared to collaborate on DIY/professional projects and will often oversee the whole job, but it does depend upon good co-operation. Similarly, you could barter your skills and talents with a friend or neighbour provided you trust them and they you.

The kinds of job where the DIYer has a clear advantage are the fairly simple, small ones where the call-out fee for the tradesperson is more than the cost of doing the work. An example is replacing an electrical fuse. In these cases you may even have difficulty in getting a professional to carry out the job, particularly if it is of an urgent nature. Here DIY becomes not so much a matter of choice as survival.

This chapter can therefore be regarded primarily as a survival guide, to help you through the jungle of pipes and wires in your home. It will also help you prepare for larger projects by pointing you towards specific sources of information. On a general note you should also supplement this by consulting specialist books or a DIY encyclopedia; talking to tradespeople is also helpful. The more you learn beforehand the less you will have to learn as you go along, and this will be reflected in the time taken to complete a job and in the results.

If you do decide to call in a professional the list of trade associations given on page 171 should help protect you from the worst of the predators. It is also worth asking friends and neigbours to recommend people they have used – they may also tell you who to avoid. Use the following check list to help find a reputable person:

* Does the tradesperson come through the recommendation of trade organization and/or a personal contact?
* Will they provide a detailed written quotation and specification of the work to be done and a written guarantee if applicable?
* Can they/will they provide references?
* Do they carry adequate public liability insurance?
* What method of payment is required and when? Be wary of deposits and never make them in cash.
* Are there any extra charges, such as transport, VAT, or hire of special equipment?

The Office of Fair Trading gives good advice on employing professionals in a booklet called *Home Improvements* which is available by phoning 071-242 2858.

Safety and Security

It is one of life's ironies that we are accustomed to wishing each other a safe journey, but have no equivalent sentiment for staying at home. Yet statistically we are more at risk in our homes than anywhere else.

Falls Falling from heights can have severe consequences; even falls from stepladders can result in broken bones that might put you out of action for several months, so never be complacent.

By securing a ladder the risk of falls is greatly reduced (most people fall because the ladder moves). A stepladder can be steadied by another person, but a longer ladder should be tied because it takes a lot of strength to hold a long ladder with a person on it if it starts to shift.

A scaffold tower is safer and more comfortable to work from than a ladder and will give you a place to put materials, but don't forget that a tower can also topple, so it is just as important to secure it. Be sure to fit a kickboard to prevent tools from falling off the edge of the platform.

Tools Tools in good working order are inherently safer than those which have been neglected. They are also a pleasure to use. Store them safely, especially if there are children about, and make sure they are used only for the purpose intended. Power

5

DIY and Home Maintenance

tools are particularly hazardous in inexperienced hands, so avoid distractions when using them and ensure that you fully understand the operation of each tool before use.

* Keep fingers away from blades.
* Tie back long hair.
* Remove loose bits of clothing, particularly ties.
* Always protect your eyes with safety glasses.
* Keep electric flex over your shoulder, away from the danger area.
* Never interfere with or remove the safety guards on power equipment.
* Do not use power tools outside in wet or damp conditions.
* Unwind an extension reel fully before use and check it for damage afterwards.
* Use an RCD circuit breaker on power tools and any type of outdoor supply.

Many power tools are supplied with a two-part flex connector so that they can be easily isolated from the mains supply for adjustment. It is most important that these connectors are installed with the plug portion (pins protruding) on the flex attached to the tool and the socket portion (no pins) on the flex running to the mains supply.

Hidden hazards When drilling or sawing beware of hidden services – wires and pipes buried beneath floors and plaster. They can sometimes be located by using a wire and metal detector. Some detectors show which wires are live, but do not trust them totally – turn off the electricity if you intend to disconnect or cut a wire.

Curious children It isn't only cats that are curious. Children are also attracted by the unusual – it's how they learn. For parents of small children, unplugging power tools and picking up anything sharp becomes a matter of course but when work is going on this is a virtual impossibility. Don't try and mix DIY and small children.

Chemicals A great deal of effort goes into labelling and packaging chemicals so the user is aware of the precautions required. Sadly, much of this information is never read because people believe that nothing so dangerous would be allowed for DIYers. Don't be fooled. If the instructions say wear goggles and gloves then that is a minimum requirement, not an optional extra.

* Store chemicals safely.
* Use them only for the recommended purpose in the recommended way.
* Learn what to do in case of an accident.
* Ventilate the area.
* Wear protective clothing.

Glass safety Following a large number of accidents in which people were injured by glass, legislation was brought in to help reduce the risk. A glass merchant is now required to supply the correct thickness for a given area. This is to ensure that large thin panes are no longer fitted in vulnerable positions but it does not entirely eliminate the danger and does nothing about glass fitted before these regulations.

For all low-level windows or picture window panes, toughened or laminated glass is the best answer, but where it is impractical to change existing panes a transparent plastic safety film will help stop the glass flying in the event of a breakage.

If you intend to fit toughened glass or any form of double glazing first read the paragraph on Escape below.

FIRE PRECAUTIONS AND SMOKE ALARMS

The ever-present risk of fire can be greatly reduced by taking some simple precautions. In high-risk areas such as the kitchen it is worth keeping an extinguisher and fire blanket by the door.

Escape Most fatalities are caused by the effects of smoke rather than the flames themselves. The risk is greater when people are asleep. Waking up in time means there is a good chance of survival. A few well-positioned smoke alarms are essential for providing those vital seconds of warning which so often save lives. A quick escape from the building is vital, so plan escape routes from every room – it will save essential seconds in an emergency. Doors must be easily opened, with keys to hand. At least one openable window in each room should be large enough to climb through. Once out don't go back – dial 999 for the fire brigade.

Smoke alarms The importance of smoke alarms cannot be stressed too highly. They are easy to install, usually requiring just two screws to hold them in place, and battery operated. Some also include an emergency light. The usual place to fit them is in the hall, but in multi-storey houses one should be fitted on each floor. The fitting instructions give specific advice about where (and where not) to fit them. Some

FIRE PREVENTION

Fire blankets
Use for smothering chip pan fires and for preventing further harm if clothing catches fire. Keep near but not over cooker. To use, hold the fire blanket with your palms upward so your hands are shielded.

Before going to bed. Ensure all occupants know positions of keys to main exit doors; close all doors; unplug TV; check ashtrays.

Emergency exits. Each room must have one openable window. Double-glaze opening sashes and casements separately.

Dangers in the kitchen. Cooker near door or curtains; unattended chip pan; towels drying over cooker; frayed flex; overloaded socket.

Dangers in other rooms. Unguarded open fire; unswept chimney; portable fire too close to furniture or clothing; moving or filling lit oil fire; folded or creased electric blanket; smoking in bed.

alarms can be interconnected so that if one is triggered they all sound together. Press the test button once a week to check when battery replacement is due.

GAS SAFETY

Gas has a good safety record. Stringent safety precautions are taken in the design and manufacture of gas appliances but if the installation and maintenance are not carried out to the same high standards the users and even their neighbours are put at risk. Any work on gas must be carried out by a CORGI registered engineer.

If you smell gas:

* Turn off the gas supply. (Check now to see that it will turn off easily; if it doesn't, ask the gas company to service their stopvalve.)
* Open windows and doors.
* Do not operate electrical switches.
* Use a neighbour's phone to call the gas company's emergency number listed under Gas in your directory.
* Do not go back into the building until you are given the all clear.

Good ventilation Many gas appliances take their air for combustion from within the room. This must be replaced to ensure safe operation of the appliance.

* Make sure an air brick is fitted to rooms with conventionally flued gas fires or boilers.
* Do not block up any air bricks.
* If you fit an extractor fan in a room with a gas appliance have the appliance checked to ensure the fan is not pulling poisonous fumes down the chimney.

BURGLARY AND THEFT

Protecting your home against intruders provides peace of mind and in many cases the bonus of a reduction in insurance premiums. Before carrying out any security work consult your insurers to see what their requirements are to qualify you for a discount. It is not easy or always desirable to make your home impregnable (living behind bars is not much fun and can be dangerous in a fire) but a reasonable level of security will deter the opportunist thief who is not particularly skilled or determined.

Make it difficult for a thief.

Door viewers and safety chains Fish-eye lens door viewers are cheap and require only a drill and screwdriver to fit. They are essential for flats and houses where you cannot see who is at the door before opening it. The second line of defence should be a door chain which will allow the door to be opened just enough to conduct a conversation and check the identity of a caller. Remember that thieves and con men are very plausible people. If in any doubt, do not open up – call the police.

Door locks The old adage 'you get what you pay for' applies particularly to locks. The British Standards kitemark is the best guarantee of quality.

CRIME PREVENTION

GENERAL PRECAUTIONS

Insurance   Check that you are well insured for buildings and contents.

At night   Lock and bolt all external and garage doors, locking all accessible windows including upstairs if near drainpipe or flat roof.

Every time you go out   Lock all external doors and windows, including vents, and don't leave keys hidden under mats etc.; don't leave doors of empty garage open. Leave on lights in some rooms in evening (*see security lights*).

Before you go on holiday   Cancel all deliveries – newspapers, milk, etc.
Cut lawns, and trim hedges so that house isn't hidden from road.
Ask neighbour to clear letterbox of circulars, move mail from doormat, put lid on dustbin, open and close curtains.

DOOR LOCKS

Final exit door   5-lever mortise deadlock or automatic deadlocking rimlatch; mortise rack bolt or surface bolt at top and bottom; door viewer (if solid door); door chain or limiter.

Side/back door   5-lever two-bolt mortise deadlock; bolts as for final exit door.

French doors   Hook-bolt mortise deadlock; rack or flush bolt at top and bottom of first-closing door; hinge bolts if outward-opening.

Patio door   Cylinder-operated hook-bolt lock; sliding-door lock at top and bottom of fixed frame.

SAFES AND VALUABLES

General   Keep a list of all serial numbers, mark valuables with house number and postcode using security marker (ink invisible in normal light) and take colour photographs of them.

Wall safe   Mounted in brickwork of wall; may be removed by professional thief.

Floor safe   Mounted in reinforced concrete under floor; larger and easily concealed.

WINDOW LOCKS

General   Drill out screwdriver recesses on all exposed screw heads, or use clutch-head screws, to prevent locks from being unscrewed.

Pivoting/hinged window   Four basic types: separate lock to secure casement to frame; cockspur handle restraint; locking cockspur handle; restraint for stay. State if for timber or metal window when buying lock.

Sash/sliding window   Standard sash fastener should be of Fitch or Brighton type.
Secure timber types with sliding-bolt lock; dual screw or screw-stop both sides. Secure metal types with small sliding-door lock.
Alternative locking positions allow opening for ventilation.

Louvre window   Secure glass with epoxy adhesive or fit expanding metal grille.

ALARMS AND LIGHTING

Burglar alarms   If you have an alarm professionally installed, make sure that the installer is a member of the National Supervisory Council for Intruder Alarms (Telephone 0628 37512).
Domestic components may include, in addition to alarm and control box, infra-red detector, magnetic-reed door and window sensors, pressure mats (which should not be used alone as system will not operate if wires are cut), door-chain switch and panic buttons. Great care is needed during installation to avoid false alarms.

Security lights   Plug-in time-switch can operate table-light at selected times; security wall-switch gives varied switching of main light and can 'learn' switching times; outside lights prevent dark corners.

OUTDOOR SECURITY

Shed/outbuilding   Secure door with hardened steel locking bar, fixed with coach-bolts, and close-shackle 5-lever or 6-pin hardened padlock; lock away tools, and chain and padlock ladder to secure wall-bracket.

Side gates   Bolt or padlock on inside, barbed wire or carpet-gripper on top.

Drain pipes   Coat with anti-climb paint from 2 m/6 ft above ground upwards.

It is essential to have one deadlock (rim or mortise) on each exit door from the building, as much to stop the burglar from walking out with your valuables as getting in. Burglars generally like to have at least one quick and easy escape route.

Window locks These vary according to the type of window.

■ CASEMENT WINDOWS can be locked by a single device screwed to the frame or alternatively by a device to restrict the opening handle of the window. If this seems too cumbersome, go for a replacement locking handle.

■ SASH WINDOWS are locked by restricting the sliding operation. This can be done by an extra device or by replacing the catch with a key-operated one.

■ SLIDING WINDOWS and doors need an additional lock set into the channel, at top and bottom for maximum effect. Do not rely on the single lock provided.

Alarms The 'cry wolf' syndrome has served to discredit household and car security alarms, but modern systems can be set to minimize the nuisance of false alarms and thereby give the devices more credibility when they do go off. The features to look for are two-stage sirens which sound inside the building, then again after a period outside as well, and self-cancellation and resetting. DIY systems with code or key operation are very easy to fit and, provided you follow the instructions, offer all the reliability of professional systems at a fraction of the cost. An alarm should be fitted only as a back-up to secure locks – never instead.

Looking after the Building

Time and weather take their toll on buildings but if you learn to recognize the tell-tale signs of trouble you can deal with it before it becomes a major expense.

Woodrot Use a sharp bradawl to test various parts of exterior wooden window frames and other structural timbers for rot. If it pushes in easily the frame is rotten.

■ DRY ROT is a serious problem which requires specialist treatment. It usually occurs in unventilated areas and often results in cuboidal cracking of the timber. Bright red dust and a musty smell are further indications. Dry rot spreads through brickwork and even dry timber, carrying moisture with it through long stringy 'tentacles'. Do not leave infected timber lying around as the spores spread.

■ WET ROT occurs only in timber and flourishes in alternate wet and dry conditions. Softening of wood, opening of grain and dark brown or black discoloration are common signs. Wet rot can be halted but not reversed by using preservative pellets, which you implant using a small drill.

Cracks When cracks appear in walls it does not always mean the house is falling down. Some are due to the natural expansion and contraction of building materials, others are due to a fairly new building settling, and there are also old cracks from previous movement or even bomb damage.

More serious are cracks caused by movement of the foundations but even some of these require no action. Of all the cracks that people notice in their homes only a small percentage mean having to underpin the foundations. To the untrained eye the difference is difficult to detect – even surveyors often have to monitor cracks over a period to find out what is happening. If you need further advice contact your insurance company, the local authority building inspector or a surveyor.

Small superficial cracks should be filled with flexible sealant which will allow for some future movement. Some exterior cracks will let in rain and should be sealed, even if only temporarily, pending more extensive work.

Pointing Rain penetrating through decaying mortar brick joints means the pointing is defective. Repointing should not be put off indefinitely because other damage such as rusting wall ties or rotting floor joists can be taking place unseen. Large-scale pointing is best left to professionals but small areas can be repointed following instructions in a DIY book.

Damp Painting brickwork is not an effective long-term remedy against penetrating damp. Penetrating damp will show up as discoloration on interior walls but it may also be caused by condensation. To tell the difference tape a square of polythene to the wall. If damp shows underneath it during wet weather, then the cause is penetration from outside or rising damp. Rising damp will not climb above 1 m/36 in and may be accompanied by white salts known as efflorescence. If these signs are not present look for other causes such as condensation.

Condensation Water running down walls and windows during the winter, mould in cupboards and peeling paint and wallpaper are all classic signs of condensation.

Fit extractor fans in the kitchen and bathroom to draw out moisture-laden air at source. Improve the distribution of heat to warm up cold surfaces. Any musty smells are usually caused by damp rotting the fabric of the building. Follow your nose and trace the smells to their source. Ventilation is essential to combat damp in enclosed spaces such as floor voids and cupboards.

Air bricks should be checked for blockages. In the loft you may need to fit special eaves ventilation grills to assist the through-put of air.

Damp leads to decay in structural timber (see woodrot). Reduce the moisture by increasing ventilation and treat the timbers with a wood preservative.

Woodworm This can be treated by painting or spraying timbers with a light application of woodworm fluid. Choose the type that also protects against rot.

For widespread infestations use professionals who will give a guarantee against future attacks.

Decorating

Interior decorating is an all-year-round job but is best done in the winter when there are fewer demands on your time. To minimize disruption, work room by room.

SURFACE PREPARATION

WALLS, CEILINGS

Previous treatment	New treatment	Preparation	Comments
DISTEMPER	Paint – oil-based or emulsion (latex)	Wash off all old distemper; or wash down and use lining paper	To test for distemper, wipe over the surface with a damp rag – if a powdery substance comes off on the rag the paint is distemper. You cannot paint over distemper except with more distemper, as it will break through the new painted surface, causing it to flake off. If lining prior to painting make sure any paste is removed from the front before painting
	Wallcovering (paper, vinyl)	Wash down and key with abrasive paper; size or use stabilizing primer if necessary	
	Tiles	Wash down, make sure surface is sound	
	Wood cladding (siding); fabric	Clean thoroughly. No other preparation necessary if fabric or cladding to be fixed on wooden strips; cross-line the walls if fabric is to be stuck	
OIL-BASED PAINT (gloss or eggshell/lustre)	Paint – oil-based or emulsion (latex)	Wash down, key lightly. Use undercoat for oil-based paint	
	Wallcovering (paper, vinyl)	Wash down, key lightly	
	Tiles	Wash down and key	
	Wood cladding (siding); fabric	Wash down; key if fabric to be pasted on	
EMULSION (LATEX) PAINT (water-based)	Paint – oil-based or emulsion (latex)	Wash down; key a silk vinyl. Matt emulsion (latex) can be an undercoat for oil-based paint	
	Wallcovering (paper, vinyl)	Wash down	
	Tiles	Wash down; key a silk vinyl	
NEWLY PLASTERED WALLS (must be completely dried out)	Paint – emulsion (latex)	Sand lightly, use thinned-down coat as an undercoat	Newly plastered walls may show signs of shrinkage, cracks or efflorescence during drying, and painting is usually recommended. Do not use vinyl wallcovering as it will not let the wall breathe
	Wallcovering – use paper, *not* vinyl	Must be left for six months; apply coat of size	
	Tiles	Key to provide grip for adhesive	
	Woodcladding (siding); fabric	Attach wooden strips to completely dry walls. Do not paste fabric on	

WALLCOVERING Paper Vinyl Special wallcoverings	Paint – all types	Check to see if colour-fast; if so, paper or vinyl can be painted over. Make sure covering is adhering firmly to the wall; slash and restick bubbles or peeling seams; wipe any adhesive off front; prime any metallic inks	If wallpaper is hand-printed and not colour-fast it will smudge; it will have to be stripped, or the wall lined. Sand down other papers to hide any obvious joins and to remove old adhesive from the front before painting. Always make sure any old wallpaper adhesive is completely removed with water and a scraper before painting or re-papering; walls can again be sanded smooth if necessary
	New wallcoverings	Strip off old wallcovering, fill and smooth walls; if necessary size. If using special wallcovering, cross-line first	
	Tiles	Strip, fill and key	
	Wood cladding (siding); fabric	Clean thoroughly. No other preparation necessary if fabric or cladding to be fixed on wooden strips; cross-line walls for fabric	

WOODWORK *Doors, shutters, mouldings and window frames*

PAINT (oil-based)	Paint – oil-based, gloss or eggshell/lustre	Wash down, scrape or burn off flaking or blistered paintwork. Sand down, fill cracks and holes and sand smooth. Treat knots with knotting and prime bare wood; undercoat	Always use the manufacturer's recommended undercoat to match the top coat
	Polyurethane varnish or oil	Strip off previous treatment, wash down, fill, sand and prime; treat any knots and apply varnish or oil. The first coat forms an undercoat	If sealing or oiling wood to show off the natural beauty, all old paint or stain will have to be completely removed.

POLYURETHANE VARNISH	Paint – all oil based types	Remove varnish with chemical stripper, sand, prime and undercoat. If varnish is in good condition, sand and paint over	
	Stain	Remove varnish with chemical stripper, and sand	
	Polyurethane varnish or oil	As described for previously painted wood	A darker varnish can be applied over a keyed, varnished surface

NEW WOOD	Paint – all oil-based types	Sand, fill cracks and prime	
	Stain	Sand; where necessary sand	

The great variety of decorating materials means that you can select appropriate paints and wall coverings for each room. Anti-condensation paints are made for kitchens and bathrooms.

Vinyl wallpapers are also suitable for such areas but make sure they aren't applied to walls with rising or penetrating damp. Locking the moisture in does more harm than good. Don't apply new wallpaper on top of old – the results are always uncertain. Use a steam stripper to remove difficult wallpaper; score impervious surfaces first. Sealing paints for masking nicotine or soot stains are useful in cutting down preparation time. Gloss paints are very durable and popular for woodwork but good alternatives for interiors are the eggshell or satin finishes which help to mask blemishes and give a more professional touch.

Making good Before decorating a certain amount of preparation and making good needs to be done. This is the laborious part of the job which many people are inclined to rush, but the finished results always reflect the preparation or lack of it.

Small areas of damaged paint can be sanded smooth at the edges and 'brought up' with primer and undercoat. If the paint comes off very easily it is best to remove it altogether using chemical stripper or a warm air gun. Take care not to char the wood – paint will not stick to burnt surfaces.

Filling cracks Cracks in plaster work should be prepared by raking out with a steel blade or scraper and undercutting the edges slightly. This gives a better key and helps allow for shrinkage by giving a tapered edge to the filler.

If you use a flexible filler it should not be sanded, so make sure you damp it and smooth it with a filling knife just before it sets hard.

Patch plastering Small areas of plaster are easily repaired using a universal one-coat renovation plaster which will stick to most surfaces.

Five easy steps to patch plastering:

1. Dampen the surface.
2. Apply the plaster with a trowel.
3. Level with a wooden or steel straight-edge using a sawing motion.
4. Allow plaster to become fairly dry, so that your finger barely makes an impression.
5. Splash with clean water and polish with a smooth trowel.

Energy Conservation

Reducing the amount of energy we use at home helps fight pollution and saves money. Insulation and draught-proofing are good DIY projects which will reduce heat loss. The recommended minimum thickness for loft insulation is 150 mm/6 in, and existing insulation can be topped up to this level. Any electrical cables in the loft space should be repositioned over the top of the new insulation.

The next most significant saving is to replace old or inefficient heating appliances.

FOUR YEARLY EXTERIOR MAINTENANCE SCHEDULE

YEAR ONE: HOUSE TIMBER

Windows and doors. Check for rot. Repair timber, replace cracked glass, prime bare wood, then maked good putty. Undercoat and gloss. (A modern alternative to paint is microporous preservative stain. Choose a high-build type for window frames and doors.)

YEAR TWO: ROOF AND METALWORK

Roof. Inspect with binoculars and if possible also from inside the loft for any sign of leaks. Seek professional help if you aren't good at heights.
Gutters. Check when raining. Repair or replace.

YEAR THREE: MASONRY

Walls. Check for cracks. Repair pointing or damaged sand and cement render.
Inspect the earth around the house. It must be more than 150 mm/6 in below the damp course. (A physical damp-proof course is recognizable by a thin black horizontal line near the bottom of the brickwork. A chemical damp-proof course will be seen as a row of filled holes in the same position.)

YEAR FOUR: GARDEN PATHS, DRIVES AND FENCES

Inspect paths and drives for cracks and damaged edges. Fences. Check for rot. Replace rotten boards, rails and gravel boards.

Most modern boilers and fires are much more efficient than their predecessors but condensing gas and oil boilers give the optimum efficiency by removing latent heat and sending the burnt gases out practically cold.

Modern electronic controls take energy saving one step further by precise monitoring and regulation of heat outputs according to changing conditions. Thermostatic radiator valves help regulate the heat in each room – you can even set them to give no more than frost protection in spare rooms.

Double glazing This comes in two forms:
- SECONDARY DOUBLE GLAZING fits on the inside of an existing window to form a separate barrier. Its success at screening out noise and reducing heat loss is determined by the size of the gap between the panes. Around 20 mm/$\frac{3}{4}$ in works best for heat, but noise is best reduced by bigger gaps of perhaps 100 mm/4 in.
- REPLACEMENT DOUBLE GLAZING – both windows and doors – consists of sealed units, two pieces of glass sandwiched together. The close-fitting frames and draught stripping does as much to reduce heat loss as the glass itself.

Plumbing and Heating

Plumbing and heating systems vary enormously. The one shown here might not resemble the one in your home but by understanding the basic principles you should be able to draw a diagram of your own system and mark the various control points. Knowing where and how to turn off the various parts of your system will enable you

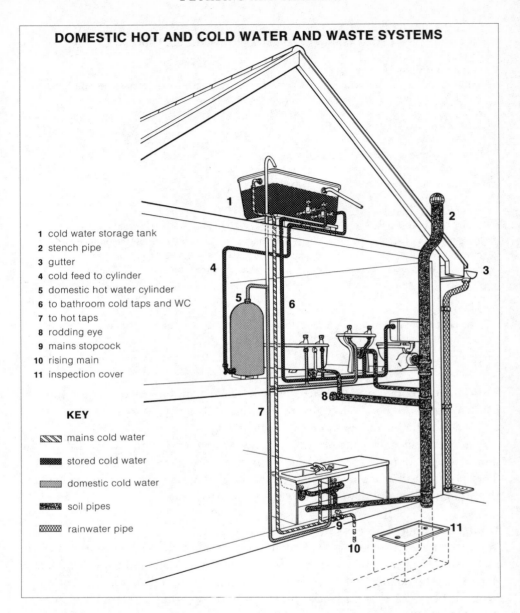

DOMESTIC HOT AND COLD WATER AND WASTE SYSTEMS

1 cold water storage tank
2 stench pipe
3 gutter
4 cold feed to cylinder
5 domestic hot water cylinder
6 to bathroom cold taps and WC
7 to hot taps
8 rodding eye
9 mains stopcock
10 rising main
11 inspection cover

KEY

mains cold water

stored cold water

domestic cold water

soil pipes

rainwater pipe

to carry out repairs and alterations without the risk of a flood. It will also help you cope with an emergency, providing a breathing space to consider your next move. That way you stand a better chance of steering clear of 'cowboys'.

GETTING TO KNOW YOUR PLUMBING

Start at the point where the mains water enters your home. There should be a stopcock buried in the ground either just inside or just outside your boundary. If you cannot locate it ask the local water company for assistance; it belongs to them anyway so they should be able to trace it or provide a plan. Check that the stopcock works – it is your first line of defence. If it does not turn off the water, the water company will repair it.

Next locate the consumer stopcock at the point where the mains water enters your home. This could be under the sink or in a cupboard. You can often trace the mains by listening and following the pipes with the kitchen cold tap running. Check that your stopcock works. If it doesn't it might simply need rewashering. To do this turn off the outside stopcock and follow the instructions given here for rewashering a tap.

Trace your mains water pipe up to the loft or highest point of your plumbing, commonly the cold water tank. Here you will find the high pressure ball valve feeding the tank.

Follow the pipes from your tank to the hot water cylinder and the cold water supply to the bathroom. Somewhere on these pipes you should find two gate valves. The one leading to the hot water cylinder turns off your hot water by preventing cold water entering at the bottom and pushing out the hot water.

DEALING WITH PLUMBING EMERGENCIES

SYMPTOM	POSSIBLE CAUSE	CURE
Running tap	split washer	new washer
Overflow pipe dripping	faulty ballvalve	new washer or seating
No water at hot taps	air lock	blow out
	dry tank, grit in ballvalve	dismantle valve
No water at cold tap in kitchen	mains fault	check with neighbours; contact water authority
No water at cold taps in bathroom	air lock,	blow out
	blocked ballvalve	dismantle valve
No hot water (cold)	boiler out	relight
	motorized valve stuck	use manual lever
	pump jammed	use manual restart
	immersion heater burnt out	replace
Noise in pipes (mains)	pressure too high	turn down, check ballvalve
Leaking radiator valve	worn gland packing	repack gland
Leaking radiator	corrosion hole	turn off valves; replace radiator
Cold radiator	air in top	bleed with key through the top vent screw
WC does not empty	blockage	rod through or plunge
WC won't flush	faulty mechanism or diaphragm	remove plunger and replace diaphragm
Waste-pipe gurgling	blockage developing	plunge or chemically clean
Boiler making noises, kettling or banging	scale	descale
Boiler sending hot water through vent pipe	thermostat	replace thermostat

Plumbing and Heating

5

DRIPPING TAPS

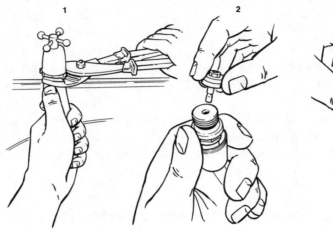

FITTING A NEW WASHER

Turn off the water supply. **1** Loosen and remove the head (there is no need to remove the shroud). **2** Remove the washer from the end of the jumper plate. **3** Push on the new one.

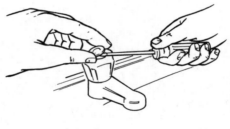

LEAKING SPINDLES

Quarter-turn ceramic disc taps do not need rewashering but occasionally they drip and the cartridge must be replaced.

1 Turn off the water supply, then remove the disc to reveal the fixing.

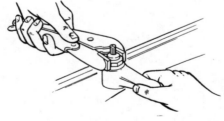

2 Unscrew the headgear.

3 Slip a new O-ring on to the spindle, then reassemble.

The cold water supply feeds all the low-pressure (non-drinking) taps and possibly the WC, though this might be fed from the mains.

Label all your shut-off points and check them at least once a year. They will benefit from being exercised, particularly if your water produces limescale.

Common variations If you do not have a cold water tank, then your system is mains-fed. A good way of checking this is to turn off the mains water at the consumer stopcock. If the hot taps stop working almost immediately this is an indication that the hot water system is mains fed. Any maintenance work or repairs to the hot and cold water system can be carried out using this single control.

Replacing ball valves The least reliable components in most plumbing systems are the ball valves in the main cold water tank and the WC cisterns. A sign that something is wrong is water coming from the overflow warning pipe. Don't ignore it – the problem will simply get worse. Remedying the fault is in most cases just a matter of rewashering. However, if your ball valve continues to give trouble after rewashering it is better to replace it. Ball valves are either high or low pressure. High-pressure valves are fed from the mains water supply; low-pressure valves are fed via a tank. Be sure to ask for the right one. If in doubt, turn off the supply to the valve, remove it and take it with you to the plumbers' merchant.

CENTRAL HEATING

The central heating system is usually fed by a small header tank which tops up the water from time to time. This tank should contain no more than 100 mm/4 in of water, in order to leave room for expansion as the water heats up when the boiler is first switched on. Check that the ball valve is not jammed by gently pushing the float down. It is not advisable to have a stop valve on the pipe leading from this tank to your boiler as it might accidentally be turned off, thereby closing the cold feed.

Leaking radiator valves Radiator valves often weep around the spindle when they are turned on or off. Remove the cap and tighten the tiny gland nut down half a turn. If this doesn't stop the leak, the gland needs repacking. Some radiator valves, such as those marked *Belmont*, can be repacked without draining the system. Take the plastic head along to a plumbers' merchant to identify the correct replacement 'O' rings before you dismantle the valve.

Draining and filling the system To empty the heating system, turn off the mains water supply into the feed and expansion tank. This can be done by tying up the ball valve arm. Turn off the electrial supply to the boiler and pump; this may be a plug and socket or a switch. Turn off the pilot light inside the boiler. Drain the boiler and radiators by attaching a hosepipe to the drain cock at a low point on the system. Run the hosepipe to the outside of the building.

To refill the system close the drain cock and turn on the mains. You will have to bleed the air from the radiators by inserting and turning a small radiator key in the air cock at the top of the radiator. Do not turn more than twice as the small screw will drop out. There may be other air cocks located on the high points of the system, which will also need bleeding. Once water appears the air cock is bled.

To work on the central heating system (if you have one) you will need to drain the radiators in this way. If you are in any doubt about the way your system works consult a plumber or a specialist handbook.

DRAINS

It is understandable that most people do not give much thought to their drains until they go wrong, which usually means they have become blocked. Calling in professionals to carry out even the most simple jobs on drains can be surprisingly expensive, especially at weekends. Often the work and the tools needed are not complex. Clearly it is the unsavoury nature of the job that gives it such a high price tag. Yet there is hardly ever any need to do more than poke a few rods down a manhole, provided that you understand how the drains are laid out and which way they flow. A basic set of rods and attachments can be bought as an inexpensive kit or you can buy the pieces separately. Alternatively, visit a tool-hire shop.

The most useful attachment is the plunger head. When fed into the drains on the end of a few rods this can be worked vigorously back and forth to create alternate suction and compression which will clear all but the most stubborn blockages. It is far better than trying to push a blockage through.

Electricity

Despite the importance of electricity in our lives, it still remains a mystery to many people. This might not be so bad were it not that, while readily professing a complete ignorance of the subject, they happily wire up plugs, replace fuses and cobble together everything from Christmas tree lights to garden power points. It is little wonder that so many domestic fires are caused by electrical faults and so many home fatalities by electrocution. Those who want to carry out extensive repairs and alterations are urged to make a more thorough study of the subject than is possible here, by consulting specialist books and, if still in any doubt, a qualified electrician. The following information is intended only as a guide to the domestic wiring in the average home and is not to be taken as specific instruction.

TURN OFF THE POWER BEFORE STARTING ANY ELECTRICAL WORK

The main supply Like other services, such as gas and water, electricity enters our homes via a service main. The supply becomes the responsibility of the householder only after it has passed through a main fuse and a meter to two tails (thick circular-section cables).

In modern houses the fuse is usually 100 amps. This is the maximum power available to the property. It may well be that when you add up all the fuse ratings the

SAFETY TIPS WHEN WORKING WITH ELECTRICITY

* Never attempt any electrical work unless you know what you are doing, you understand how to do it and you are confident that you can carry out every stage of the job.

* Always turn off the main switch before beginning any electrical work. As an additional safeguard, hang a sign on the switch saying that the supply has been turned off so that no one will turn it on again.

* If you are working on one circuit only, remove the appropriate circuit fuse, or switch off the circuit MCB, before turning on the supply to the other circuits. Keep the fuse in your pocket until you have finished, so that no one can replace it in the fusebox without your knowledge.

* Double check all the connections, whether within accessories, plugs or appliances, to make sure that the cores go to the correct terminals, that the terminal screws are tight and that no bare conductor is exposed.

* Never touch any electrical appliance or fitting with wet hands, or use electrical equipment in wet conditions (in particular, out of doors). Never take a portable appliance into a bathroom on an extension lead.

* Always unplug an appliance before attempting to inspect or repair it.

* Turn off the switch before replacing an electric light bulb.

* Do not use long trailing flexes or overload sockets with adaptors; fit extra sockets. If you have to extend a flex, use a proper flex extender; don't just twist the cores together and wrap them in insulating tape. If using an extension cable on a drum, always unwind it fully first or it may overheat; check the flex rating if the cable is supplying heaters.

* Check plug connections and flex condition on all portable appliances at least once a year, remaking connections and replacing flex as necessary. Replace damaged plugs or wiring accessories immediately.

* Never omit the earth connection. At accessories, take the earth core of the cable to the terminal on the mounting box or accessory as appropriate; on appliances with an earth terminal, use three-core flex and connect its earth core to the terminal. Bad earth connections can cause serious electric shocks.

* Teach children about the dangers of electricity. The biggest danger areas are socket outlets (fit ones with shuttered sockets to stop them poking in metal objects) and trailing flexes (unplug appliances not in use).

* Never overload sockets or run appliances from lampholders.

total exceeds this figure, but the diversity factor (not having every appliance running at the same time) means that in normal use the load on the fuse board should never exceed the capacity of the main fuse.

Circuit breakers Some power supplies, particularly the overhead type, have a circuit breaker where they enter the home. This safety feature should automatically cut out if there is a dangerous fault in the system.

Modern consumer units or fuse boards also include two systems of protection. One is the individual miniature circuit breakers (MCB) which protect the circuits from overload. The other is the main automatic circuit breaker which shuts off the supply when an earth fault occurs, primarily to protect the occupants of the home against electric shock. Main circuit breakers are now of the residual current device (RCD) type which are much safer than any other kind, but their increased sensitivity means that the slightest fault will 'trip' the switch. It can even happen that a fault outside the building causes nuisance tripping, where the power is shut off for no apparent reason. It may well be that once the switch is reset the system operates perfectly well. If the switch continues to trip frequently or will not reset, then the fault must be located. To prevent nuisance tripping from affecting appliances such as freezers and computers, some consumer units have one or more fuseways controlled by a conventional main switch while the remaining circuits are RCD-protected.

Tracing a fault The first place to look for a fault is in the various appliances you have connected through plugs and sockets. If you were actually using an appliance at the time this could give a clue but it might be a coincidence. To be sure, unplug all

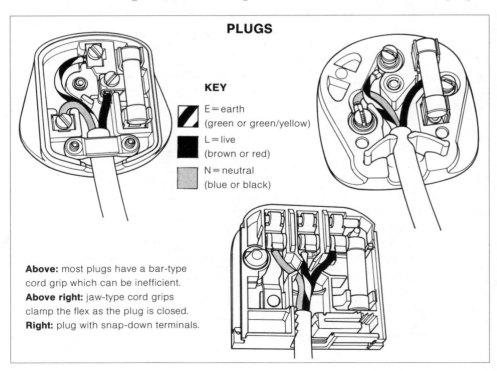

PLUGS

KEY

E = earth
(green or green/yellow)

L = live
(brown or red)

N = neutral
(blue or black)

Above: most plugs have a bar-type cord grip which can be inefficient.
Above right: jaw-type cord grips clamp the flex as the plug is closed.
Right: plug with snap-down terminals.

ELECTRICAL CIRCUITS

LIGHTING CIRCUIT WITH JUNCTION BOX AND LOOP-IN METHOD

Modern lighting circuits are connected up using loop-in ceiling roses: the circuit cable loops from rose to rose, and switch cables run from the rose to the switch position; junction boxes connect branch circuits. Pull cords should always be installed in bathrooms.

1 ceiling rose
2 junction box
3 plateswitch
4 loop-in ceiling rose
5 lampholder

6 two-way switches for landing light
7 meter
8 consumer unit

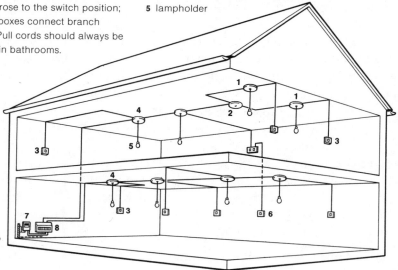

POWER RING-MAIN CIRCUIT WITH TWO RADIALS

A typical ring-circuit installation. Note the separate radial circuits to cookers and fixed appliances.

1 socket
2 immersion heater
3 spur from ring main socket
4 spur from junction box

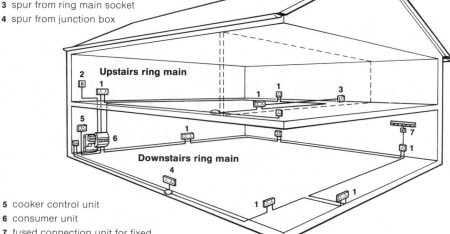

5 cooker control unit
6 consumer unit
7 fused connection unit for fixed appliance

appliances and plug them back in one by one until the fuse or circuit breaker goes.

If none of these causes a problem turn off all the lights and repeat the process of turning them back on one by one. You should also check the central heating and water heaters by turning them on and running through the programmes.

If the fault can't be traced to anything obvious you will need a qualified electrician. The more you can tell him about the nature and origin of the fault the better. Make a note of the time of day when the fault occurred, what appliances were in use, which lights were on and anything else you feel might be useful.

Cable and flex Cable is used for all fixed wiring. It is usually flat in section, and the insulated solid cores are coloured red and black. The bare earth core is insulated with green/yellow sleeving wherever the cable terminates. Flex is used to connect appliances (with the exception of high-powered appliances such as cookers and showers) to the fixed wiring. It is often circular in section. The fine stranded cores are all insulated and coloured brown, blue and green/yellow.

The circuits From the main switch or circuit breaker the current is distributed to the various circuits. The red live conductors are fed through individual fuses or circuit breakers. The sizes of some fuses have been altered to European Standards but they should correspond to one of the following figures and may be colour-coded according to their rating in amps.

White 5/6 amps	Lighting circuits
Blue 15/16 amps Yellow 20 amps	Radial circuits feeding fixed appliances such as water heaters, fires and showers.
Red 30/32 amps Green 45 amps	Ring and radial power circuits, and radial circuits to larger appliances such as powerful showers and cookers.

It is helpful to identify which fuse or circuit breaker severs which circuit. A space is provided inside the fuse cover for labelling.

Types of circuit

■ RADIAL CIRCUITS have a single cable looped in and out of the points which they feed, terminating at the last one. In the case of a **power circuit**, any number of sockets and fused outlets may be connected within a floor area of 20 or 50 square metres, depending on the cable size and the type and rating of the circuit protection device.

■ RING CIRCUITS form a closed loop, feeding any number of sockets and fused outlets within a floor area of 100 sq m/1076 sq ft. Spurs are sometimes taken off ring or radial power circuits to serve individual outlets.

■ LIGHTING CIRCUITS usually loop in and out of the ceiling roses and terminate on the last one. Junction boxes may be used instead of loop-in ceiling roses for looping in the main supply cable and making the switch connections. Because of the diversity factor a maximum of 18 lampholders may be connected to any one 5-amp circuit.

Earthing The requirements for earthing cause a lot of confusion. This is hardly surprising since it seems illogical and alarming that a possible fault occurring, say, in an electric immersion heater could be transferred to every water tap in the house through this system of electrical cross-bonding.

On modern electrical installations you should have a green and yellow wire running, independently, from the plumbing back to the consumer unit (the fuse box). This forms the equipotential earth bonding for all the metal pipes and fitments in the house. If you haven't got this earthing system, then the wiring needs to be updated.

Ideally the fault should run to earth and blow a fuse or circuit breaker, but this cannot always be relied upon. If the pipes and fittings were not cross-bonded anybody touching the hot and cold taps at the same time could complete a circuit to earth and receive a possibly fatal shock. With cross-bonding the circuit is already completed, so the taps and every other piece of metal plumbing are equal in electrical potential, i.e., no current will flow from one to the other.

Areas outside the equipotential zone, such as the garden or garage, present a special risk since any stray current can find an easy route to earth through a person, especially in damp conditions. In such situations each circuit must be additionally protected with its own RCD. These are available as plug-in adaptors, but as they rely upon the diligence of the user, a better method is to use a permanently wired-in device. Socket outlets with built-in RCDs provide this facility in a single device, and it is a requirement that one RCD-protected socket is fitted in all new homes for such uses.

With so much riding on the provision of good earthing, the earth wire must be of the correct cable size and the connection to the main earthing point must be incapable of working loose. It is recommended that this should be secured and tested by a professional. Connections to the pipework should be made with special earthing clamps.

REPLACING A FUSE

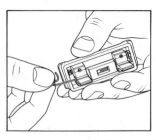 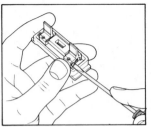 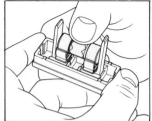

1 If a rewirable fuse blows, turn off the power and pull out the fuseholder. Unscrew terminals. Remove burnt wire.

2 Thread in new wire of the correct rating and fix to the terminals. NEVER use any other metallic object as a fuse.

3 With some cartridge fuse-holders, the fuse is a simple push-fit. Fuses of different ratings are different sizes.

DIY and Home Maintenance

Calculating fuse requirements The cartridge fuses fitted in plugs and in fused connection units for fixed appliances are rated at either 3 or 13 amps. Additionally there is a 5-amp fuse for certain appliances.

The wattage and voltage of an appliance are given on a metal plate attached to it. For an appliance of up to 3 amps fit a 3-amp fuse; for one which is greater than 3 amps, fit a 13-amp fuse, unless otherwise specified. The amperage is calculated as follows:

$$\text{amps (A)} = \text{watts (W)} \div \text{volts (V)}$$
$$\text{e.g.} \qquad 850\,\text{W} \div 240\text{V} = 3.5\text{A}$$

A 3-amp fuse would not be enough, so a 13-amp fuse should be fitted.

Exceptions to this rule are appliances such as vacuum cleaners where there is a momentary high surge of current on starting up. These are usually designed to operate on a 13-amp fuse. 5-amp fuses are sometimes specified for appliances such as colour televisions. In all cases you should always follow the manufacturer's recommendation.

Flex sizes The size of flex is measured in mm^2. The current carrying capacities of different sizes of flex are shown below.

0.5mm^2	3 amps
0.75mm^2	6 amps
1.0mm^2	10 amps
1.5mm^2	13 amps
2.5mm^2	16 amps

The capacity of the flex must be equal to or greater than the rating of the plug fuse. Where flex is connected directly to the fixed wiring without a fuse (e.g. as in the case of the flex from a ceiling rose to a lampholder) the size of flex must relate to the rating of the circuit fuse in the consumer unit.

Wiring a three-pin plug Flex may have two or three cores. If there are only two cores – brown and blue – the appliance should be marked with this symbol ▣ to show that it is double-insulated and therefore does not require an earth connection. Alternatively, it may be a non-metallic table lamp, for example. Three-core flex, with a green/yellow earth core, should be used for other appliances.

* Always use flex not cable.
* Strip the end of the outer sheath using a purpose-made, wire-stripping tool set to the exact size of the flex.
* Check that the insulation on the inner cores has not been damaged by the removal of the outer sheath.
* Remove the plug top and cut the brown live and blue neutral wires (and the green/yellow earth wire, if present) to suit the positions of the L, N and E/ ⏚ terminals. The earth wire must remain longer in most plugs.
* Set the wire-strippers to the inner core size and cut through the insulation at approximately 3mm from the end. Strip off the end insulation.
* Slacken the cord grip screws and feed the flex beneath the clamping bar. Some

plugs have two angled inserts which grip the sheathing.

* Lightly twist together the strands in each wire so that they form tidy ends.
* Secure each conductor to its terminal by tightening the screw. If there is no green/yellow wire in the flex, no connection is made to the terminal marked E or ⏚.
* Gently tug each wire to check it is secure.
* Tighten the cord grip to hold the outer sheath securely.
* Replace the plug top.

Mending Household Machines

Many of the sophisticated machines and pieces of equipment we use in our homes today are not made with repairs in mind. You may have encountered the 'cheaper to buy a new one' response that seems prevalent among the larger retailers of everything from portable radios to home computers. This is an economic fact of life which we have to acknowledge but the attitude has percolated through to manufacturers of relatively simple appliances, such as electric kettles, vacuum cleaners and domestic irons.

Inevitably this results in otherwise perfectly good appliances being thrown away because of a simple fault, such as a loose wire or a burnt-out element. Provided that you have a basic knowledge of wiring circuits and are prepared to spend a little of your time many faults are easily rectified, but if you are uncertain about what you are attempting, follow the retailer's advice or seek out one of the few remaining small repair shops.

Maintaining machines Preventive maintenance can save time and money in the long run.
* Check and clean filters on vacuum cleaners to prevent the motor from overheating.
* Clean dust from moving parts of all machinery:
    Extractor fans can vibrate noisily if dust is allowed to build up on the impellers (rotating blades).
  Tape recorders and video recorders are easily damaged by dust and moisture.
  Dust building up in the back of television sets can cause a fire.
  Clean lint filters in tumble driers after each use.
* Regularly clean the filters in washing machines and dishwashers to prevent debris from blocking the waste mechanism.
* On some electric shower heads scale can cause overheating. Remove scale by soaking in a solution of vinegar.
* Lubricate locks with spray lubricant or graphite powder to make them easy to open and close.
* Clean lawnmowers thoroughly with the power switched off to prevent dry grass unbalancing the blades.
* Avoid using too powerful a bulb in a light fitting or table lamp. Most shades and fittings are labelled with the maximum wattage.

Checking continuity

FIRST UNPLUG THE APPLIANCE.

Most faults can be traced by checking continuity. To do this you can use a purpose-made, battery-powered circuit tester or make up your own battery and bulb test device.

The principle is to test each section of the circuit and by a process of elimination isolate the part with the fault.

Check the plug

Connect the wires to the live and neutral terminals of the plug.

If it doesn't work

Test or replace the fuse.

Is the fuse OK?

Test each conductor of the flex to the appliance.

Test across the switch terminals. Does it switch on and off?

Test the element. With motor windings the test may not be conclusive, but if every other part of the appliance works, by default it must be this.

Replace the faulty part with the correct spare part if it is economical to do so.

FAULT-FINDING USING A BATTERY CONTINUITY TESTER

DOES IT WORK?

NEVER		**SOMETIMES**
↓		
UNPLUG		UNPLUG
↓		↓
*CHECK FUSE	[LOW VOLTAGE TESTING]	*CHECK PLUG
		↓
		TRY OTHER SOCKETS
*FUSE→OK →		↓
	*CONTINUITY TEST FOR	← *CHECK INTERNAL
↓	BAD CONNECTION OR	WIRING WITH
	BROKEN WIRE	CONTINUITY TESTER
*REPLACE WITH		
CORRECT SIZE	OK	
FUSE BLOWS		
↓		
*CONTINUITY TEST		
FOR SHORT CIRCUIT		
↓		
*ISOLATE SECTION	SPARE PART	
WHERE SHORT	MAY BE NEEDED	
OCCURS →	↓	
	IS IT ECONOMICAL	
	TO REPAIR?	

*Test to be carried out with appliance unplugged

USEFUL TRADE ORGANIZATIONS

Looking after the building and Exterior maintenance

Building Employers' Confederation
82 New Cavendish Street
London W1M 8AD

Tel: 071 580 5588

Federation of Master Builders
4 Great James Street
London W1N 3DP

Tel: 071 242 7583/7

Scottish Building Employers' Federation
13 Woodside Crescent
Glasgow GG3 7UP

Tel: 041 332 7144

The British Wood Preserving and
    Dampcourse Association
Building No 6
The Office Village
4 Romford Road
London E15 4EA

Tel: 081 519 2588

National Federation of Roofing Contractors
24 Weymouth Street
London W1N 3FA

Tel: 071 436 0387

Decorating

National Federation of Painting & Decorating
    Contractors
82 New Cavendish Street
London W1M 8AD

Tel: 071 580 5588

National Federation of Plastering Contractors
82 New Cavendish Street
London W1M 8AD

Tel: 071 580 5588

Energy conservation

National & Cavity Insulation Association
P.O. Box 12
Haslemere
Surrey GU27 3AH

Tel: 0428 654011

British Plastic Windows Group
British Plastics Federation
5 Belgrave Square
London SW1X 8PD

Tel 071 235 9483

Glass & Glazing Federation
44–48 Borough High Street
London SE1 1XB

Tel: 071 403 7177

Plumbing and heating

The Council for the Registration
    of Gas Installers (CORGI)
4 Elmwood
Chineham Business Park
Crockford Lane
Basingstoke
Hants RG2 0WG

Tel: 0256 707060

Institute of Plumbing
64 Station Lane
Hornchurch
Essex RM12 6NB

Tel: 04024 72791

National Association of Plumbing, Heating
    and Mechanical Services Contractors
Ensign House
Ensign Business Centre
Westwood Way
Coventry CV4 8JA
Tel: 0203 470626

Scottish & Northern Ireland Plumbing Employers'
    Federation
2 Walker Street
Edinburgh EH3 7LB

Tel: 031 225 2255

Heating & Ventilating Contractors' Association
34 Palace Court
London W2 4JG

Tel: 071 229 2488

Electricity

Electrical Contractors' Association
34 Palace Court
London W2 4HY

Tel: 071 229 1266

Electrical Contractors' Association of Scotland
Bush House
Bush Estate
Midlothian EM26 0SB

Tel: 031 445 5577

National Inspection Council for Electrical
    Installation Contracting
Vintage House
36–37 Albert Embankment
London SE1 7UJ

Tel: 071 582 7746

6 Parties and Family Occasions

It is no accident that we say of parties that we *give* them. A party is something that we provide for other people, so that they can enjoy good company, food and drink. The degree of pleasure that the hosts draw from the occasion is related precisely to that gained by the guests. Though, of course, no excuse need ever be necessary for holding a party. The special landmarks in life call out for them: weddings, births, coming of age. At such times we share our happiness by asking other people to join in celebration. It is a two-way process, as it is only by having other people there that we are able fully to celebrate properly. It may at first seem odd that this applies even to funerals, but one of the reasons for holding a reception after a funeral is that people can celebrate together the life of someone they loved.

Parties are also about socializing, seeing old friends and getting to make new ones. Hence the host and hostess need to make sure that their guests feel at ease and have the chance to mix. Ritual plays a part in this, even down to the most casual of parties where the customary handing over of a small thank-you gift or bottle at the beginning lessens that slightly awkward sense of obligation. Formal parties exhibit the reassuring power of ritual in a more pronounced way: the rules about dressing up, the correct way of serving dinner and seating the guests, the opening of different bottles of wine with each course – all are actually designed to put people at ease.

The secret of success in parties lies in planning. Start well in advance by writing lists of things to be done, beginning with when to send out invitations and ending with what time to light the candles. The better organized the host and hostess, the less in a flap they are likely to be on the night.

The other point of good organization is that it frees the host and hostess to go round making sure that everyone is enjoying themselves and has somebody to talk to. Sacrificing yourself to some wonderful culinary concoction may produce food that everyone will remember, but their overall impression of the evening will not be a happy one if they spent half their time staring at your wallpaper.

That also means not trying to do everything yourself, especially at the larger functions. We all know people who are genuinely happiest when they are helping, so it is far from a hardship for them to spend some time in the kitchen beforehand, or to take round plates of food or drinks as the party is getting underway. All the same, it is worth bearing in mind that the word 'host' is a verb as well as a noun: it implies positive activity on the part of those giving the party. For all the help and preparation, at the end of it all you are more than likely to be feeling quite exhausted, but it will be tiredness resulting from having had a truly good time yourself.

Weddings

In every century, in widely differing cultures, marriage has been held to be one of life's most important events; hence the ceremony and tradition attached to the wedding day. The various elements of wedding pageantry – the ring, the cake, the bouquets – all contribute to creating a special atmosphere, a memory to last a lifetime.

No couple today is likely to follow custom slavishly, but while some prefer to throw it all aside and do their own thing, many more find that weddings bring out the tradition-loving side of their nature, and that the ceremonious dignity of wedding etiquette enhances the occasion.

The rules of 'who does what' have relaxed a good deal over the last two decades, and the days when the wedding preparations were entirely the province of the bride and her mother, with the bride's father waiting with an open cheque book, are long gone. Couples are now more likely to share expenses, but most find that their family's hopes and wishes still play an important part in shaping their decisions.

THE ENGAGEMENT

Engagements no longer have any legal basis but most couples still regard them as a public announcement of their intention of sharing their lives permanently. Parties to celebrate engagements are not part of the wedding tradition, but equally you would not offend against some unwritten protocol by throwing one. Also, it can be as small and intimate or as large and as glossy as you like. Engagement presents are not usual, though some members of the family might like to give something to mark the occasion. On the other hand, they are an integral part of a popular American custom that has established a toehold in Britain. This is the 'shower party'. It is a strictly female occasion which is normally organized by one of the bride's friends and held in her home. Each guest brings a small present for the bride's new home, according to a preordained theme of the party: at a kitchen shower, presents could be an egg whisk, a cake tin, an ice cream scoop or something similar; at a linen shower they would be tea-towels, pillowcases, a tablecloth, and so on.

You might want to announce your engagement in a newspaper, especially if you have a large and well-spread circle of friends. *The Times* and the *Daily Telegraph* are the usual choices, as are local papers.

ADVANCE PLANNING

With the wedding itself, the first thing to decide on is the day and the sort of wedding you want to have. Most couples marry on a Saturday, especially if they want a full-scale reception, since this is the day on which their friends and family are most likely to be free to join them. As the Jewish sabbath is Saturday, Sunday is the popular day for Jewish weddings. More and more registry office weddings, however, are taking place on Fridays. Registry offices close on Saturday afternoons, so couples who want an evening reception find Friday afternoons a convenient time for the ceremony. Spring is still a popular time of the year, although there are no longer the tax advantages to be gained by marrying before 5 April.

The simple choice of venue is between a church, chapel or synagogue and a registry office. If you do not want a religious service you can still marry in all the traditional dress, complete with bridesmaids, in a registry office, though the actual ceremony lacks much of the ritual of a church wedding.

You may wish to combine the two, and have a civil ceremony followed by a service of blessing. As many bishops and individual vicars do not agree with divorced people marrying in church, this is an option for those couples of whom one or both has been married before. The blessing, unlike the actual marriage service, does not have to be performed in church, so you can ask a vicar to bless the union in a romantic spot of your choosing. There is, however, no guarantee that he will agree!

When to book It is possible to arrange wedding ceremony, reception and honeymoon at a couple of weeks' notice, but it takes both stamina and luck. It is far more realistic to think in terms of months.

Churches get booked up some time ahead, particularly at popular times of the year, and even registry offices cannot be guaranteed to have spaces at short notice. Hotels can hold only one, or possibly two, receptions a day, and photographers and car hire companies both have long lists of bookings for peak wedding times, so it is a good idea to stake your claim with them as soon as your main arrangements have been made. Printed invitations should be ordered at least nine weeks ahead, so that you can send them out in good time, and as soon as that is done you should be thinking of hiring morning suits. If you want elaborate flowers from a popular florist you should give a few weeks' notice to them, too.

Counting the cost Weddings can be very costly and your choice of clothes, the length of your guest list and the place chosen for the reception will probably depend on what you want to spend. Listing the possible costs early on, before you make any firm decisions, is sound policy. Divide them into sections like 'clothes', 'reception' and so on; then you can look at the estimated total for each section and, if you need to prune, decide where you will make the cuts.

The guest list The planning of a wedding will go much more smoothly if the two sets of parents get on together. No one expects them to accept each other immediately as bosom friends, but it is a good idea for the two sides to meet at least once before the wedding. If the bride's parents are going to foot the bill, they will need to explain to the couple and to the groom's parents what they have in mind and the number of guests, and agree the numbers to be invited by each side.

However large your wedding, you will probably have to leave out *someone* with a distant claim to be there, so it is better to decide on the boundaries of the guest list right from the beginning. There are plenty of possibilities:

* As many relatives, friends and colleagues as you can pack in
* Family only, with all relatives on both sides invited
* Close family only
* All relatives and a few close friends
* Close family and close friends only
* Relatives only at the reception and a party for friends afterwards
* Relatives, friends and colleagues invited to the church but a reception only for those you would normally invite to a party.

WHO PAYS FOR WHAT

For those who want to follow tradition the division of costs is clear cut, and for those sharing the cost more equally it provides a starting point:

The bride's family pay for
Engagement and wedding announcements in the press
Wedding stationery: printed invitations, order of service leaflets, menus, place cards, printed thank-you notes if required
Engagement and pre-wedding party, if any
The bride's dress, accessories and going-away clothes
The bridesmaids' and attendants' clothes – these days they would normally make a contribution, at most
Photographs, videos, tape recordings, etc.
Flowers for the church or reception
Cars for the bride's family to the church and the bride's parents to the reception
All costs for the reception

The bride pays for
The bridegroom's ring, if required

The bridegroom pays for
Engagement and wedding ring
Marriage licence
Registry office fees or church expenses
Bride's and bridesmaids' bouquets
Buttonholes for himself, the best man and ushers
Corsages for the two mothers
Presents for the bridesmaids and best man
Cars for himself and the best man to the church

The best man pays for
His own wedding clothes

The music   The atmosphere of a church wedding will depend to a large extent on the music you choose, so it is worth taking the time to plan a balanced, effective programme. Of course, your choice will be governed by the quality of the organ and the organist; remember that the organist – and the choir if there is one – will probably best perform pieces that they know and like.

The music is most effective if it builds up all the way through, so that the climax comes as bride and groom walk down the aisle together. In the Church of England ceremony there are five musical phases to think about: before the bride's entrance;

Parties and Family Occasions

the procession to the altar; the hymns; while the register is being signed; and the recessional. For the last Mendelssohn's Wedding March is by far the most popular choice, but if you find it hackneyed Purcell's 'Trumpet Tune', Verdi's 'Grand March' from *Aïda*, or some other stirring but not too martial piece, will send you down the aisle in an equally imposing and upbeat manner.

Personal flowers   You should not choose the bridal bouquet until you have settled on a dress, and a conscientious florist will want as much information as you can give about it. What is in season will be the next consideration in deciding upon the selection. The aim in making your choice is to arrive at something imposing enough to stand out, but not so large as to be an encumbrance.

When choosing bouquets and headdresses for bridesmaids, bear in mind the colouring of the girls themselves, as well as the colour of their dresses. Flowers for young bridesmaids should be light and easy to carry. Flowerballs, rather than posies, may be a good idea; children often find them more interesting and they are less likely to be dropped or crushed. An alternative for a child bridesmaid is a basket of flowers.

Buttonholes are worn by the bridegroom, both fathers, the best man and the ushers. Traditionally these are white carnations.

PLANNING THE RECEPTION

In most cases the style of the reception will fit in with the style of the whole day, with a large morning dress wedding followed by a formal 'wedding breakfast' or an elegant buffet in a hotel banqueting room, and a small, no-fuss ceremony by an informal party at home, the pub or perhaps a local hall.

Where?   Hotels have a great deal to recommend them as reception venues. The rooms are usually large and well-decorated, the staff experienced in organizing functions, and the facilities designed to cater for large numbers.

When you look at menus and consider estimates, remember to check on the following:
* Does the estimate cover catering only or is the cost of the reception room included?
* Are VAT and service included?
* Are tips normally expected in addition to a service charge?
* Are flowers included?
* Can the hotel provide a toastmaster, and what will this cost?
* Do you have to pay extra for cloakroom staff?
* Is there a time limit on your use of the rooms?
* Does the package include a changing room for the bride and groom, and is there any discount for staying overnight?

A reception at home can be intimate and welcoming, as well as far less costly than a hotel. However, it can entail an enormous amount of extra work and last-minute upheaval. It also limits the number of guests: the average house will hold about 30 people in reasonable comfort; a large house will manage 50. Though guests can spill over into the garden on a fine day, it would be foolish to count on good weather, even

SEATING PLAN FOR A SIT-DOWN WEDDING MEAL

1 2 3 4 5 6 7 8

1 Chief bridesmaid	5 Bride
2 Groom's father	6 Bride's father
3 Bride's mother	7 Groom's mother
4 Groom	8 Best man

in summer. However, if both your garden and pocket are big enough, you can get round this and heighten the romance by hiring a marquee.

The catering Hiring a hall allows for a large reception, with the option of a sit-down meal, but, if you are doing your own catering, there will be many journeys to and fro and to add to the work, and if you hire outside caterers the saving on hotel prices may not be as substantial as you had hoped. Also, halls often have very limited cooking facilities and can be very drab and depressing.

Outside caterers to provide and serve the food are also a possibility for the reception held at home. Standards and prices vary wildly from one to another, so it is wise to ask around for personal recommendations. If you do need to hire a firm without a recommendation, find out how long they have been in business and ask them for details of other weddings where they have handled the catering.

Compare menus and prices from several rival firms and check the following:

* Does the price include providing glasses, crockery, linen, etc?
* Are tea and coffee included?
* How many people will be serving?
* Is hot food included and if so, what are the arrangements for keeping it hot?
* Are they able to provide a toastmaster and cloakroom staff, if required?
* Will they clear up afterwards at no extra cost?
* Are VAT, service and insurance included?
* Are tips normally expected in addition?
* What time will they arrive to begin work?

Only those with a flair for organizing and plenty of willing and reliable friends and relatives are advised to cater for a large wedding reception themselves.

You should be ruthless with pinning everyone down, so that you know where every quiche is coming from. Make careful lists of who is preparing what food and who is helping on the day and what jobs you have earmarked for them.

If you have gaps in your list of helpers, you might consider hiring waiters and waitresses to serve the food. Look in the Yellow Pages under catering firms. You should allow one waiter for every 15 guests, and make sure they are well briefed in advance with your requirements. Gratuities given before the party, rather than afterwards, can oil the wheels.

The food If you are providing a sit-down meal then everyone will be eating basically the same food, so it is wise not to saddle half your guests with something they don't like. Make sure there is something provided for vegetarians.

If you are doing the catering yourself, a buffet is usually more practical, but remember that dishes like risotto, a chicken mayonnaise or fish mousse take far less time to prepare than scores of little 'nibbles'. The test for food at a stand-up buffet is whether it can be eaten easily with a fork, so make sure that none of your choices are likely to fall to pieces or drip down the front of your guests' best clothes.

If you have to manage with very little help, then a midday or early evening drinks party with chicken drumsticks, sausages and cheese cubes on sticks or a paté and wine party might fit the bill. An alternative is a mid-afternoon reception with sandwiches and cakes, served with tea or coffee, with champagne only for the toasts.

The cake Cakes come in all shapes and sizes: round or square, with or without tiers and pillars, shaped as hearts, lovers' knots or lucky horseshoes. In Britain the traditional type is a rich fruit cake with white royal icing, though more and more brides are now choosing colours to tone in with the flowers in their bouquet or with the bridesmaids' dresses. Thick royal icing can be very hard, so it can be a good idea to have a cut made through the icing, ready for the bride and groom to insert the knife and cut the first slice. Make sure that the caterers know how much you will need to have kept in reserve, to send small slices to guests who were unable to accept your invitation, and whether or not you want to follow the tradition of saving a tier for the christening of a future first child.

The drinks The first drink offered at a reception is usually sherry, served to guests as soon as they pass down the receiving line. At a large wedding, where guests may have to wait for some time for their turn, the sherry (or wine if you prefer) may be served as they arrive, but it can mean that people are juggling handbags and glasses as they try to shake hands.

Champagne is, of course, the traditional wedding drink, but you do not have to serve it. In fact, you do not *have* to serve alcohol at all, and there should anyway be a good selection of non-alcoholic drinks for drivers, children and teetotallers. At a drinks party with light refreshments, champagne may be served all the way through or a sparkling wine might be substituted. These are less expensive and make a light, refreshing accompaniment to buffet food.

If still wine is served with a buffet, it is best to offer a choice of red or white. For a sit-down meal, the wine will be chosen according to the menu. For either style of reception, you should serve guests with a glass of sparkling wine for the toasts.

Calculate on the basis of at least half a bottle of wine to each guest (guests at sit-down meals always consume more than those at a buffet), with six glasses of champagne or sparkling wine to a bottle. If a hotel is providing the drinks, make sure that they charge only for the bottles actually opened.

At an evening party, or a midday reception in a public house, it is quite usual to have a 'cash bar' where you pay for the first couple of rounds and provide wine for the toasts but otherwise guests pay for their own drinks.

The flowers Flowers add an air of elegance and luxury to the reception venue. The colours should echo those in the dresses and bouquets of the bridal party and the flowers should be positioned where they will make the most impact.

The key position is usually near the entrance, where the bride and groom will be receiving their guests and, as everyone will be standing at this point, they must be at eye level. If you are holding the reception at home, a profusion of flowers in the porch, or garlands down the staircase with a matching arrangement below, makes a great impression. Marquees can be decorated with hanging baskets and flowers twined round the supporting poles.

Table decorations need a great deal of thought. At a buffet meal they tend to get in the way; tall arrangements in the corners of the room – or as a focal point on the mantelpiece in a private house – may be more suitable. At a sit-down meal, never place tall arrangements on the top table, as they obscure the bridal couple from view, but set a low arrangement along the front of the table, with flowers flowing over the edge. Any flower arrangements on the other tables should be low and spreading so that guests can see one another without craning their necks. When the cake stands on a separate table the bouquets are usually arranged round it.

INVITATIONS

When the wedding is planned with plenty of time to spare, invitations should be sent out six weeks before the date, to maximize the chances of guests being able to accept and to enable the caterers to have final numbers in good time. If the wedding is small and informal, or the time for organizing is strictly limited, then it may not be possible to allow nearly as long, but bear in mind that printing may take one to two weeks.

At formal weddings where the bride's parents are the hosts and the guests are invited to both the ceremony and the reception the wording of the invitation runs as follows.

Mr and Mrs Dylan Jones
request the pleasure of the company of

————————————————

at the marriage of their daughter
Olwen
with
Mr Winston Patterson
at
St Cuthbert's Church, Puckleton
on Saturday, 11th June
at 3 o'clock
and afterwards at the King's Mitre Hotel, Puckleton

R.S.V.P.   Satis House   Dickens Avenue   Puckleton

Often, when the wedding is at a registry office, only close family and friends will be present at the ceremony, so the invitations will refer to the reception only.

The cheaper and quicker alternative is to buy cards ready-printed from the stationers' and fill in all the details by hand.

Children are normally included on their parents' card though they should be invited separately if they are over 18. Invitations should be sent to the best man, bridesmaids and ushers, and even the groom's parents will want one as a souvenir.

PRESENTS

There is no need to feel that you are imposing on people by drawing up a present list; those who have their own idea of what they want to give will not ask for it, but the others will be pleased to know they can give you something that you need.

The problem is how to send it out. If you do one copy and ask people to cross out what they are going to buy and pass the list on, it might still be circulating when you are celebrating your tenth anniversary. But if you photocopy it and send out lots of copies, then you are more than likely to have some presents duplicated, or worse.

One way is to make two or three separate lists, perhaps one for close relatives who want to make a substantial gift, one for close friends and the rest of the family, and the third for more casual friends, listing smaller, cheaper items.

Some department stores have a special bride's service, so you can draw up a list from what they stock. The shop keeps your list and you simply direct people there; guests living out of town can order by phone.

Displaying the gifts Presents are sometimes displayed at the hotel or hall where the reception is held; alternatively they can be set out in a spare room at the bride's home and relatives and friends invited to see them on one or more evenings, a few days before the wedding. It is often convenient to add a line to thank-you notes, giving a date and time.

Many couples use the gift tags arriving with the presents to identify the senders, but a white card propped in front of each item, with the name of the sender and their relationship to the bride and groom, can look neater and is less confusing.

Any item too large for the display should be described on a card placed in a prominent position, for instance 'From Uncle Robert: a grand piano'. Cheques and other financial gifts should be treated in the same way: 'From Mrs Ethel Gold, the bride's grandmother: share certificates' or: 'Cheques received from: Uncle Bert and Aunt Florrie, and Uncle Clive'.

Thank-you letters Gifts should be acknowledged promptly, and only those arriving at the very last moment should wait until the return from the honeymoon. The best thank-you letters should give the senders a glow of pleasure, making them feel that the time and money spent on your gift were well worthwhile. Everyone knows that you are writing dozens of similar letters but each one should sound personal, as though you really mean what you say.

Of course, you may find yourselves thanking people for gifts you find neither useful nor decorative. In this case, try to see them through the eyes of the senders and comment on them accordingly: mention the unusual design or colour, the quality of the workmanship or the fact that it will last a lifetime!

THE PARTICIPANTS

The best man   The bridegroom will normally choose his closest friend as best man. If that friend is dependable, calm, quick-witted and with a good eye for detail, then he is an admirable choice; otherwise it is better to go for a friend you are not so close to than to have the worry of someone unreliable. If he has to make a speech, then remember this is a family occasion and avoid the man who is renowned for his *risqué* stories. He must also be someone who can be relied on not to imbibe too freely and end up making a far less suitable speech than was planned – or even no speech at all!

At Jewish weddings, the best man is traditionally the bridegroom's eldest brother; otherwise one of the bride's brothers. If neither partner has a brother, the best man is usually another close male relative.

The best man's chief duty on the wedding day is to keep the groom calm, smart and prompt. He should be the one producing a spare pair of shoelaces, a clothes brush or an extra clean handkerchief for the groom – not, as happens at some weddings, the other way round. Though he is not officially involved in the wedding preparations he should have a good working knowledge of the arrangements, so that he can discharge his duties properly, leaving the chief participants free to relax.

The best man is often involved in arranging the stag night, unless the groom prefers to handle this himself, and he should certainly make arrangements to see that the groom gets home safely. The day before the wedding, if a car has been booked to take the two men to the ceremony, he can help the groom by checking with the car hire firm that there is no hitch over transport arrangements. He should also make sure that the ushers are fully briefed.

The best man will need to collect morning dress for himself and the bridegroom, if this is being hired. He might also confirm with the florist that the orders for buttonholes are correct and that they will be delivered or collected on time. He should also collect the order of service sheets from the bride's mother.

The best man should arrive at the groom's home on the wedding day, with plenty of time to spare. Apart from helping the bridegroom to dress and making sure he has everything he needs, he will take charge of the wedding ring, putting it safely in a

---

THE PROCESSION TO THE ALTAR

1 Minister

2 Bride

3 Bridegroom

4 Bride's father

5 Best man

6 Chief bridesmaid

7 Bridesmaids

pocket where he keeps nothing else and also the various travel documents the couple will need for their honeymoon. The two men should arrive at church about twenty minutes before the ceremony is due to begin and move to their place facing the altar when the bridesmaids arrive; one of the ushers can be asked to give the signal when this happens. The best man's only part in the ceremony is to produce the ring, immediately after the couple have made their vows, and lay it on the open prayerbook offered by the minister. He escorts the chief bridesmaid to the vestry, where they will probably both be called upon to sign the register as witnesses.

At the reception the best man may be called upon to act as toastmaster, calling for order when the meal is over and calling on the first speaker to propose the toast to the bride and bridegroom. Later in the proceedings, he responds to the toast to the bridesmaids. He also reads out any telemessages, keeping them so that the couple can reply to them later. If the reception includes dancing, he should dance with the bride, both mothers and the bridesmaids.

When the couple leave the reception to change into their going-away clothes, he must see that the honeymoon luggage is ready and, if the couple are leaving in their own car, that it is securely locked into the boot. A good friend will see that merry guests are not able to do anything more serious than adorn the car with a little lipstick and a string of tin cans.

Once the couple have left, the best man collects the groom's wedding clothes; later he will return any hired finery. He should be among the last of the bridal party to leave, making a last-minute check to make sure that no toppers, umbrellas or gloves have been left behind and, if necessary, helping the bride's parents to remove wedding presents from the display and store them safely.

Ushers The ushers are the first people your guests meet when they arrive at the wedding, so they should be friendly but dignified. Their job is to greet each guest, asking if he or she is a friend of the bride or groom, then show them to their places for the service. The bride's relatives and friends sit in the pews on the left of the nave facing the altar, those of the groom sit in the pews on the right. The ushers should also make sure that each guest has an order of service leaflet or hymn sheet.

At a large, formal wedding they may have a list of guests, so that close family can be shown to the front pews, with relatives in the seats behind them and friends further back. The head usher should know the bride's mother by sight, so that he can escort her to the right seat.

The bridesmaids Most brides decide on two or four bridesmaids but numbers can range from one to eight. Traditionally, the bride chooses them first from her own sisters, then the sisters of the groom. In practice, many girls choose friends rather than the groom's sisters, who may be near-strangers.

Ideally, the chief bridesmaid should be someone who is good-natured enough to want to put the bride first on her special day and to care just a little more about the bride's appearance than her own. In the case of a buffet-style reception, it is an advantage if she is a good mixer. Bridesmaids are always single girls, so if your chief attendant is married, she is called a 'matron of honour'.

Child bridesmaids can look delightful but they do have a habit of running amok at the most awkward moments, so it is wise to have at least one adult bridesmaid who can keep an eye on them. If you cannot resist choosing an angelic-looking three-year-old as a flower-girl, make sure that her mother is sitting at the end of the nearest pew, so that she can be rescued if she suddenly bursts into tears as you reach the altar.

The chief bridesmaid often stays overnight with the bride, or arrives in good time on the wedding morning so that she can help the bride with hair, dress and makeup, unless the bride's mother prefers to fill this role. She can also help the bride's mother to iron out any last-minutes hitches in the arrangements, make sure that the right number of bouquets arrive in good time and help to dress child attendants.

The bridesmaids travel to the church ahead of the bride and wait for her there. The chief bridesmaid has the task of checking that nothing is amiss with the attendants' clothes and that they all have the right flowers. When the bride arrives, the chief bridesmaid will adjust her train and veil, paying particular attention to the view from the back and checking that all fastenings are secure. Then she arranges the attendants in order, ready for the procession up the aisle.

As the procession reaches the altar, the chief bridesmaid should be ready to take the bride's bouquet, prayerbook or whatever else she is carrying, so that her hands are free to receive the ring. If necessary, she will lift the bride's veil from her face and arrange it neatly, either before the minister begins the service or in time for the couple to take their vows. She must be sure to take the bouquet into the vestry when the couple go to sign the register, so that the bride can carry it in the procession down the aisle.

AT THE ALTAR

1 Minister
2 Groom
3 Best man
4 Bride's father
5 Bride
6 Chief bridesmaid
7 Bridesmaids

The bride's mother The bride's mother is chiefly concerned with planning and preparation, in conjunction with her daughter. It is traditionally her responsibility to deal with the wedding announcements, compile the guest list, send out the invitations, make the reception arrangements, and order flowers, cars and photographer. In practice, the chores will probably be shared by the bridal couple.

At the reception the bride's mother is hostess (unless the whole wedding has been organized by the bride and groom), so she will make sure that no one stands alone in a corner and that each guest has a few words with the bride and groom. Even if there is no receiving line, the bride's parents should greet everyone as they arrive.

After the wedding she may see that slices of wedding cake are boxed and sent to those unable to attend the wedding, as well as circulating wedding photographs to those who might wish to order prints.

The bride's father The bride's father may or may not be involved in the wedding preparations, though his role will depend to some extent on whether he is paying for all or part of the celebrations. On the day itself he will escort his daughter to church and lead the procession to the altar with the bride on his right arm.

When the minister asks, 'Who gives this woman to be married to this man?' he takes the bride's right hand and gives it to him.

DRESS

The bride A 'white' wedding is still the most popular among church brides but it is by no means obligatory. Day clothes are just as acceptable or, if you opt for a long dress, train and veil, they can be in other colours. The most important thing is to choose clothes that will feel right and match the style of your wedding.

The idea that white is for virgins only was jettisoned long ago and many a pregnant bride has been glad of the loose, flowing lines of a carefully chosen wedding dress. Older brides, or those marrying for a second time, are entitled to wear white if they wish, though cream is a more usual choice and there are many alternative colours – perhaps gold, rich blue, or russet colours for an autumn ceremony.

The bridegroom and best man All the men of the wedding party should dress with the same degree of formality. Strictly speaking, when the bride wears white the groom should wear morning dress, and this means that the best man, the two fathers and the ushers must follow suit. Morning suits consist of black or grey morning coat, grey pin-striped trousers, grey waistcoat, grey tie or a cravat, white shirt, black socks and shoes. Jewish bridegrooms wear a dinner jacket and black tie.

The bridesmaids When planning dresses for bridesmaids, keep in mind that on the day you will be seen as a group. The style of their clothes should follow the style of the wedding dress: frills and flounces on the bridesmaids would look quite wrong alongside a bride dressed with classic simplicity.

When bridesmaids are paying for their own dresses, they will want a say in what is chosen, and in any case, you should plan clothes that will take account of their individual looks, height and colouring. Pastel colours like pink, pale blue, lilac and peach are always popular, but darker ones like turquoise or deep red can look good on girls with the right colouring. Dresses for adult bridesmaids are normally the same length as that of the bride, but children's dresses can be long or short. It is usually wiser not to expect very small children to manage floor-length dresses.

The mothers Some mothers like to keep their wedding outfit a close secret, but there are pitfalls. If the mothers of both bride and groom turn up in similar colours, or one is far more formally dressed than the other, it can be embarrassing.

6

Weddings

ESSENTIAL EXTRAS

Flowers for the church   You may or may not have the opportunity of choosing flowers to decorate the church but, if you do, take the style of the church into account. The larger the church, the larger and more striking the arrangements will need to be; in a smaller church it might be better to concentrate the flowers in one place, perhaps alongside the altar, as this will be the focus of all eyes.

The photographs   Most couples look on the wedding photographs as a souvenir to treasure, so it is worth ensuring that the job is done well, and paying a professional rather than relying on amateurs. Methods of charging vary a good deal. Some firms charge for each print but not for the job itself; some set an overall charge for the day, including a set number of prints, in which case you need to know whether they select the prints or provide you with a contact sheet so that you can choose those you like the best. You may pay a smaller fee if you allow the photographer to circulate the contact sheets at the reception and take orders from the guests – and it can be interesting for guests to see the range of photos, especially if they are never likely to see your album.

You will need to tell the photographer whether you want colour or black and white and whether you want 'candid' pictures as well as the formal shots.

PHOTO SUBJECTS

The bride putting the finishing touches to her preparations
The bridesmaids, or the bride's mother, helping the bride to get ready
The bride and her father leaving the house
The groom and the best man arriving at the church
The bride's father helping her out of the car
The bridesmaids at the church door
The bride and her father approaching the church
The bride and her father going down the aisle
The bride and groom standing at the altar
The ceremony itself
The procession leaving the church or the bride and groom leaving the registry office
The bride and groom outside the church or registry office
The bride and groom, best man and bridesmaids
The bride and groom, attendants and both sets of parents
The bride and groom with all the family members
The bridal party with the guests (several groups if necessary)
The cake
The receiving line at the reception
The top table once the guests are seated
The toasts
Cutting the cake
The bride throwing her bouquet
The couple leaving the reception

Video recordings of weddings are becoming increasingly popular and make a delightful keepsake, particularly if the minister will allow you to include the ceremony, but they are best left to the experts.

Transport   There are various luxurious ways of travelling to your wedding – perhaps a white Rolls-Royce, a vintage car or a horse-drawn carriage. However, many families manage perfectly well with their own or borrowed cars, with or without white ribbons for the occasion.

The large cars hired from specialist wedding firms have the advantage of plenty of room to accommodate long flowing dresses. Two will normally be required: one to take the bride and her father to the church, the other for the bridesmaids and possibly the bride's mother. The first car will then take the bride and groom on to the reception; the second transports the attendants. The best man will usually drive the bridegroom to the ceremony in his own, or the groom's, car. Be sure not to forget that the bride's parents need transport to the reception, and should not be reduced to begging lifts outside the church.

LEAVING THE CHURCH

1 Bride's father
2 Groom's mother
3 Groom's father
4 Bridesmaids
5 Bride's mother
6 Best man
7 Chief bridesmaid
8 Groom
9 Bride

AT THE RECEPTION

The reception follows a simple order: the greeting of all the guests by the receiving line of parents, bride and groom, the meal (generally preceded by saying of grace), cutting the cake, speeches, and then the going-away. The food should be served soon after the last guests have arrived, as those who came first will probably be quite hungry by then, and the drink may be beginning to affect empty stomachs. It is customary to give the guests some time to mix after the cutting of the cake, especially if there has been a sit-down meal rather than a buffet; the bride and groom should circulate amongst them at this point, making sure that they have some words with everybody. Then they will retire to change into their going-away clothes, and come back for final goodbyes, which should be kept short.

You will be lucky to escape the tail of tin cans and old shoes on the back of the car and lipstick messages on the screen. It's all designed to let the whole world know that you have just got married, but why not? A wedding is a public statement, and its celebration is to be shared.

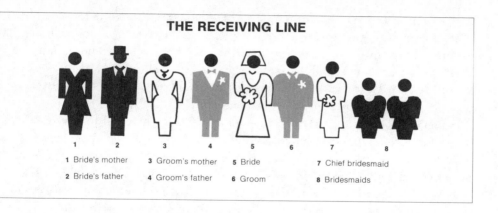

THE RECEIVING LINE

| 1 | 2 | 3 | 4 | 5 | 6 | 7 | 8 |

1 Bride's mother   3 Groom's mother   5 Bride   7 Chief bridesmaid

2 Bride's father   4 Groom's father   6 Groom   8 Bridesmaids

Funerals

The gathering after a funeral is one of the hardest events to organize. We scarcely associate such occasions with celebration, but on the other hand it is worth bearing in mind that some cultures do make a special effort to send off the departed in style. But even if we do not feel that we want the party mood of an Irish wake, the fact remains that after the departed has been consigned to ashes or the earth, there will be a lot of people to look after. Some of them will have come a long way to pay their last respects, and they are people the departed would have wanted to see well cared for.

There is a north-south divide here. In the north of England and Scotland the funeral director would expect to organize the catering for you. In the south, this is the moment when things are handed back to you and he bows out, though he would recommend catering firms if asked. Funerals are generally held from mid-morning to mid-afternoon, so the options range from coffee and biscuits through lunch to afternoon tea. That is unless you decide that what the deceased would have most wanted is for you all to go round the pub and drown your sorrows!

Some crematoria have catering facilities available. It is quite common for them to have a café which is ordinarily open to the public, but which you can hire for private functions. However, the space available is usually small. The people who run them will be well versed in what is required for such events.

For a large, well-attended funeral you can hire a hall, but best to make sure that it is suitably decorated – you might not like it to show signs of being prepared for a Hallowe'en party. If the funeral is in a church, then the church hall might be appropriate, though church halls are not always the most comfortable of places. However, the most popular venue is the home. Everybody is more likely to feel relaxed there; it is easy to lay on the food and drink; and it is the place the guests associate with the person they have come to honour.

CHOOSING THE REFRESHMENTS

Two things generally most worry the bereaved who are organizing the function. The first is what sort of refreshment is suitable. To some extent this is determined by the time of day – sandwiches and cakes for afternoon tea, a cold buffet for lunch, for example. Large sit-down meals are too formal for funerals. The amounts individuals will eat will vary fantastically, from those whose grief destroys all appetite, to others who have to drive back across the country and want to stock up. Assume everyone will want to eat at least a moderate amount.

A bigger problem is what to drink. You may feel it irreverent to have the booze flowing freely, but that does not mean that it should be excluded altogether. In fact, it could be argued that a little drink has a sedative effect! Unless the deceased was a principled teetotaller, some drink is more than acceptable. There are no rules as to what in particular, but a wide choice is not expected. Tea and/or coffee are essential throughout, both for those who want only them and for the drivers.

LOOKING AFTER THE GUESTS

The other question that tends to concern the organizers beforehand is how to look after people. Often this is associated with wondering what mood to strike. However, in practice this is usually not a problem. Most guests will happily talk and reminisce for an hour or so, usually not more than two, and then leave. The chances are that everybody will know at least some other people and will be busy catching up with old friends. The only real social obligation on the family of the deceased is to try to get round all the guests so as to exchange at least a few words with each of them.

For this reason it is important that the immediate family is not tied to serving the food and drink. Use outside caterers if you can afford them. As soon as you have a date for the funeral, find a suitable firm (again, the funeral director should be able to help with names, if he is not actually organizing the function for you). Tell them what you want and what you want to pay, and let them get on with it. If you decide to do the catering yourself, then prepare the food the previous day or in the morning, leaving it wrapped and cool to stay fresh.

Funerals are not, of course, planned well in advance, so you do not usually have the time to have invitations printed. The funeral director will offer to place a notice in the newspaper of your choice announcing the death, and this is likely to prompt many friends to get in touch to send their condolences. If they ring, you can tell them about the funeral arrangements then. Otherwise, most people send out a brief handwritten note to those close to the deceased, announcing the death, the place and time of the funeral, and where the reception will be held afterwards. Alternatively, you can ask those you want to come to the reception at the funeral itself; it is also polite to ask the officiating minister and the funeral director.

Finally, make sure everyone knows how to get there. Crematoria and cemeteries are usually well signposted; the location of a church may not be so obvious. Some of the guests may use public transport to get to the service, and will require lifts from there. If you are the deceased's spouse you may well not want to have to bother about these details. In which case depute them to a close relative or a friend.

Organizing the funeral and dealing with the other practicalities often keeps the bereaved going through the first days after the death. Be prepared for the full force of grief to hit you after everybody has left. It is best to arrange to spend some days with friends or family so as not to be alone.

Christenings

Even for parents who are not themselves regular churchgoers a christening marks the welcoming of a new child into the community in a heightened and festive way. Like the other major ceremonies of our lives, it combines three features: the acknowledgement of the sanctity of human life, rejoicing, and the public marking of one of the great milestones of life.

Christenings are usually planned to involve primarily the family and close friends, and naturally those chosen to be godparents, but also usually a few other special family friends. Whereas protocol determines that for weddings all branches of the family should be invited, including cousins who live the other side of the country and who have not been seen since the last big family celebration, this does not apply to christenings. Feelings are generally not hurt if you stick to the immediate family, or if you do not haul old but little seen friends from miles away.

Despite your knowing all the guests well, written invitations should be sent – printed ones, if you can possibly afford this. You will probably have to book the church several weeks ahead, so there is plenty of time to organize this and give everyone good notice.

For a long time christenings were traditionally held in the mid-afternoon, at a special service. Although this is still often the case in the Catholic Church, most Church of England parishes have now determined that christenings should take place during the regular Sunday morning family services. Some parents do not like this, but it helps to remember that children attend these services and that christenings are events that they can particularly relate to. The argument is that the new child is being welcomed into the body of the church and that this should be done when the congregation is present.

'Party' does not seem like the right word to describe the post-christening celebration. When the service was always in the afternoon it was known as the christening tea, and even when the celebration is held at lunchtime the concept of high tea still determines the nature of the food provided. A cake is as essential to the proceedings as it is at a wedding. And like a wedding cake, a christening cake is usually a rich fruit base with royal icing. Indeed, some people preserve one tier of their wedding cake for the christening of their first child. However, if the thought of such a rich cake is not appealing, a sponge cake is a perfectly acceptable alternative, providing that you do not intend to post pieces afterwards to people who did not attend – unless you want them to sink their teeth into bits of sweet cardboard!

FOOD AND DRINK

For the rest of the food most people elect to provide a buffet. Of course, the choice of venue will determine this: if you go for a large formal event you may want a sit-down lunch in a hired banqueting room or hall. For a smaller occasion, held after an afternoon christening, you may be able to book a local tea shop for the function, and then your only worry with the catering on the day is paying for it. However, most christenings are celebrated in the baby's home with a buffet meal. Savouries, in the form of open and closed sandwiches, cold chicken drumsticks, vol-au-vents, and so on, are needed to balance the sweet things. Almost inevitably some of the guests will already have young children of their own, so it is often a good idea to produce more sweet things (in addition to the cake) than you would for an adult party.

Another great advantage of providing cold food is that it can all be prepared in advance. The host and hostess are going to be involved with looking after the real star of the show during the tea and showing him or her off to the guests, so they are not going to have the time to think about getting food out of the oven. But even cold food has to be served, so line up helpers well in advance. There is usually no shortage of willing volunteers when a baby is involved, so you need not be bashful about asking.

If the function is at lunchtime, how much alcoholic drink you provide is purely a matter of taste, though bear in mind that there are both children to be catered for, and adults who do not want to drink or who have to drive. In the afternoon there should be both tea and some sparkling wine or champagne. The relative quantities provided of each and of any other drinks are then determined by your assessment of what people will want to drink and what you will want to provide. The champagne is for a toast to the new arrival, which is usually made by the godfather. If there are two of them, decide in advance which one to ask to do it.

Parents who are not themselves regular churchgoers sometimes leave christening until the child is old enough to decide for him- or herself. There is no need to be embarrassed about christening a five- or six-year-old, or an even older child. The celebration afterwards will be much as above, with the exception that a large occasion may well cause embarrassment. Anyway, it would not be appropriate, since you are scarcely introducing a new arrival to masses of friends for the first time. Inviting lots of children is not right either, as it can destroy the true spirit of the occasion by turning it into a children's party with attendant noise and games.

DISPLAY

Christening robes are beautifully made garments of cotton lawn with lace trimmings that have often seen many generations come into the world. Keeping the baby dressed in one after the service is impractical, but guests will still want to see it. The answer is to leave the robe out on display, in the hall or on an unused table, together with the christening presents and any other christening accessories.

Dinner Parties

The scene is familiar from films and television programmes: a beautiful dark-wood table, places elegantly laid with silver cutlery, three cut-glass wine glasses by each place, women in long gowns and men in dinner jackets, and at the end of the meal the ladies retiring for coffee while the men get out the port and cigars.

Such may be the popular view of what is implied by the words 'dinner party', but in reality it has come on a long way since the world of Bertie Wooster. Any occasion on which you invite friends round for an evening meal can be classified as a dinner party, even if it is without a hint of formality. Formality is merely one option. It is, though, an important one, in that it may not have any bearing on the food prepared, but it will affect the style of the event.

Who To Ask and How

If you invite a few people by phone at short notice, their assumption will be that the occasion is informal, and they will come casually dressed. If you want everybody to dress up it is essential to issue written invitations. These can be bought from stationers already printed with blank spaces to fill in. For those who want to be really formal and who do not mind the expense, you can get invitations printed.

The invitation has to state not only the date and venue of the dinner party, the hosts' names and those of the people it is sent to, but should also specify the type of dress required. 'Black tie' indicates that the men should wear dinner jackets and the women should come in evening dress. 'Lounge suits' means that the women should be smart but not formal and the men should wear suits. You may still issue invitations and yet plan a casual evening, in which case the invitations should say 'informal dress'. These words appear in the bottom right-hand or bottom left-hand corner of the invitation.

It is customary just to state the time at which you expect people to arrive. The practice of putting a certain time 'for' another, such as '8 for 8.30 pm' indicates that drinks will be served from the first time, and dinner from the second. Guests are therefore expected to arrive between the two. However, it also implies a large party at which people will mix over cocktails before being ushered into a grand dining room or hall. It's fine if that is what you really have in mind.

Those well versed in etiquette send out the invitations as from the hostess, using the husband's name prefaced by 'Mrs', as in the form 'Mrs Ernest Wrung-Wythers requests the pleasure of . . .'. Most people outside the county set regard this as stuffy nowadays.

> Mr and Mrs James Johnson
> request the pleasure of your company
> at dinner
> *RSVP* on Saturday 19 February
> 18 The High Street, at 8.00pm
> Chefton,
> Blankshire
> lounge suits

Numbers are simply a matter of preference and the space available. However, it is worth bearing in mind that with six people there is likely to be a single conversation around the table, but with eight or more there will be a plurality.

Much anguish has been known to go into finding 'suitable' partners for single people at informal occasions, with the only notable result being the embarrassment of the two guests concerned. The best advice is not to worry at all about asking the same numbers of men and women unless you are going for a black tie event.

Rather more thought has to go into choosing the actual guests. Inviting only people who are already good friends will guarantee an enjoyable evening for all, but removes the fun of making new acquaintances. However, to throw one alien couple into a bunch of well-established friends is not the answer as they may feel outsiders, however well intentioned everyone is. When looking at people who do not know each other, think of their backgrounds and find people who have something in common. You may consider a certain couple as your golf-club friends, but it could be that they have a passion for the theatre that you do not share but which should make them get on with another couple you had not initially thought of inviting.

THE MENU

Balancing the menu is as important a part of a successful evening as balancing the guests. Much of the time is going to be spent around the dinner table, so this is not then the best occasion to try out three courses that are completely new to you, unless you have nerves of steel and 100 per cent confidence in your culinary skill. On the other hand, this does not mean that you have to be timid. Trying one new dish may represent a challenge that you can rise to – and will ensure that you are cooking at least one thing which you have not given any of the guests before.

Plan your meal outwards. Think first of what you want to provide as a main course, and then settle on the starter and the dessert. Dishes which are your own favourites separately will not necessarily go together. For example, if you want to produce a steak tartare you should not precede it with a beef consommé, while a gigot of lamb *en croûte* is not best followed by an apple pie, even for pastry enthusiasts.

Look out, too, for hidden ingredients. Not only sweet dishes but a lot of savoury ones include cream. This does not mean that you have entirely to avoid having two or three dishes that have one such common ingredient, but you should consider how dominant it is in the taste or texture of the dishes planned.

Finally, think of the effects of variety. A change in itself can stimulate the appetite, and just because someone cannot manage any more fish pie does not mean they will not have room for your homemade strawberry ice cream. Visual variety is important, too, especially with the main course. Chicken, mashed potatoes and cauliflower taste fine together, but look unappealingly anaemic.

This is assuming three courses. It is easy to increase the number up to five by providing a salad after the main course and a cheese course after the dessert. Really to impress requires another cooked course, usually fish between the starter and the meat course. For those who want to go the whole hog there is the *entremet*, which is a light sweet, usually a sorbet, between the fish and the meat.

Finally, chocolates with coffee. This introduces a touch of luxury, though after-dinner mints are rather hackneyed now. Plain chocolates, liqueur chocolates, or the little pastries known as *petits fours* are just as delicious.

DRINKS

A conventional dinner party starts with aperitifs and ends with liqueurs, while the food itself is accompanied by wines. Offering guests something to drink when they arrive both breaks the ice and stimulates the appetite. If you do not have the means to offer a wide range of drinks, it is perfectly acceptable to offer a choice of two standards. A spirit and a wine-based drink make the best alternatives, typically sherry and gin and tonic. Alternatively, you can start guests with the wine, or a cocktail. Don't overdo the ice breaking, though; the intention is to get guests loosened up, not legless so that they cannot reach the table or face any further drinks.

At one time wine buffs used to lay down simple rules about what wines should be drunk with what food, but now that both the range of wines available and public appreciation have grown, things are not so rigid. 'White with fish and red with meat' is only a rough guideline: some red wines go well with some fish, and there are white wines which accompany some meats well, especially white meats like chicken. The simple principle is that the more full-bodied the food, the more robust the wine needs to be. Thus beef calls for a Burgundy-style wine, and a meaty fish like salmon will go with lighter red wine such as claret (red Bordeaux), while a more delicate one such as sole will go only with white wine.

Generally, within these guidelines it is best to serve wines that you like and feel you will enjoy with the food, with two provisos. The first is that sweet wines go only with dessert, and the other is to offer a choice of white and red to allow for people's preferences. White wine should always be chilled, and red wine brought to room temperature, apart from Beaujolais Nouveau which can be chilled.

Many a dinner party continues to the final departure happily with only wine bottles on the table, even long after the coffee has been drunk. But formal occasions call for port, spirits or liqueurs, or all of them, at the end of a meal. With spirits only the finer and, regrettably, the more expensive ones are appropriate – Cognac, or another refined brandy such as Armagnac, and malt whisky. Spirits and liqueurs can be drunk with coffee, but the flavour of port does not blend well with it; hence the old custom of port being drunk with cigars, while coffee was served separately for the ladies. Another outdated convention was that guests helped themselves to the port (the servants having left the scene), but in strict order, with the decanter always being passed to the person on your left.

Don't forget to serve non-alcoholic drinks for drivers and others who do not want to drink. The range of 'designer waters', non-alcoholic beers and non-alcoholic wines is now extensive.

TABLE SETTING

In France you would be likely to find that even for a grand meal you sit down to a single knife and fork, but the tradition in Britain is to lay out all the cutlery before the start. The principle is simple: dessert spoons and forks go at the top of the mat, the spoon above the fork, with handles to right and left respectively. All the other cutlery is put with forks to the left of the place mat and knives to the right in order of use, with the first to be used on the outside. Soup spoons go on the extreme right.

One of the advantages of this custom is that everyone can gauge how many courses are going to be provided, and then avoid filling themselves on extra helpings of soup and later running out of room with half the meal still to come.

Sometimes dinner plates are placed on the mat at the outset of the meal, and then removed before the first course is served – a custom now more observed in the United States. The reason behind this is not so that you can check that the china is clean, but to let you admire the pattern before it is covered up with food!

Napkins can either be placed on a side plate to the left of the last fork, in a neatly folded triangle or rectangle, or you can fold them into a shape such as the bishop's mitre, and put them on a place mat. A seating plan always needs a little thought in advance. Even if you are having a relaxing evening with good friends, it pays to direct guests to their places, if only because everyone will dither uncomfortably if you leave it to a free-for-all. Alternate the sexes, and separate married couples.

PLANNING

A successful dinner party requires careful planning. It is best not to leave the shopping to the day itself if any of the planned dishes call for an ingredient that might be hard to find. Go for at least one cold course, or one that simply needs warming up; otherwise you can find yourself tied to the kitchen for much of the evening.

If you have any doubts, write yourself a checklist of things to do, starting with when to do the shopping, and taking you through the cooking schedule, and including the accessories. Things that easily get forgotten but which can cause last-minute hitches include taking the butter out of the fridge to soften, preparing the salad dressing, bringing the cheese up to room temperature so that it 'breathes', making sure there are sufficient salt and pepper in the cruets, and deciding what you are going to wear yourself!

Children's Parties

There are three essential ingredients to successful children's party-giving, no matter what the age group – plenty to do, plenty to eat and plenty of help. Parents often worry about giving children's parties because they feel that a number of children brought together in one place will be difficult to control, but in practice with careful planning a children's party can be just as much fun for adults as for the children themselves. Also, children come to parties expecting to enjoy themselves, so parents can build on this basic good will.

There are various factors to take into account when preparing to give a children's party. These are: what kind of party; the venue; the date and time of day.

WHAT KIND OF PARTY?

This depends very much on the age of the children involved and the occasion you are celebrating. When thinking about parties you can divide children into three main age groups – five and under, six to ten and over ten. The youngest group are usually quite happy with a simple tea party with conventional party games and a traditional tea. The middle age group often appreciates the traditional party meal, but they have a lot of energy to expend, and your games may need to be much more sophisticated. This age group, too, likes a good entertainer, or can be taken out to sporting or creative activities. The over-tens are beginning to be a lot more grown up, and will probably expect dancing or a disco.

Children from seven upwards enjoy giving a party with a theme. This is easy if it is to mark a particular event like Hallowe'en or Saint Valentine's Day, but you can also vary a birthday celebration by having a pyjama party, or a colour party such as red, silver, or black and white. You can also make the theme something like animals or pirates, which doesn't have to involve full fancy dress. Many parents find fancy dress difficult if they don't have much money or aren't very creative, so if you do give a fancy dress party with a theme make sure it is relatively simple to do.

THE VENUE

Even the smallest home can usually accommodate six or eight under-fives at a tea party, and there are plenty of quiet games that they appreciate playing. Remember that toddlers and small children are often accompanied by an adult, who provides extra help. But as children grow older and more boisterous you may find that your home simply isn't big enough to cope with them. If the party is happening during the summer months and you have a garden, then it is a very good idea to organize activities outside, weather permitting (always have contingencies in case of rain). Otherwise you can hire a venue – such as a community hall or similar. You need somewhere with lots of room and kitchen facilities, and usually these can be found for hire for two or three hours quite inexpensively. The cost usually outweighs the worry of having 20 ten-year-olds disco-ing on your living room carpet!

Alternatively, you could arrange to meet the guests at a park, swimming pool or sports hall, where you can often hire the facilities for private use, and many places provide a celebratory meal as well. If this seems too costly, you can bring the children back to eat at your home. If you do decide to take the children out, make sure you have at least two other adults present to supervise both the activity and ferrying the children home afterwards.

DATE AND TIME

Traditional parties for young children happen in the afternoon and last for about two hours (one and a half hours is long enough for toddlers); 3.30–5.30 pm is an acceptable time. However, it is sometimes a good idea to give a party at lunchtime for a young child with older brothers and sisters at school, so that the older children do not dominate the little ones. If you are going to a sports hall, for instance, with older children you might find morning or mid-afternoon a better time for booking.

Older children feel more grown up if you let them have their disco starting in the early evening, and 12-year-olds might like to give a proper evening dinner party. Alternatively, if it's summer they might like a barbecue lunch in the garden.

It is important in all cases to make sure that the finishing time is clearly set out on the invitations as well as the starting time, so that parents know exactly when to collect their children. Send invitations out no less than two weeks beforehand, particularly if the party is to be at a weekend. If you are taking the children swimming or to the theatre ensure that this is made absolutely clear so that the children bring the necessary equipment.

GETTING HELP

Never attempt a children's party on your own. Even two parents find it hard to deal with organizing games, preparing and serving food, helping children go to the bathroom and dealing with the shy or aggressive child all at the same time. You have to keep in mind that children are often very excited by parties and it is easy for them to lose control. Grandparents or older friends can be a great help at younger children's parties, either in the kitchen or by providing a quiet refuge for children who are shy or overwhelmed by the occasion. Always make sure you've got at least one other adult around to help, and more if you're taking the children out anywhere.

ENTERTAINERS AND PROFESSIONAL PARTY ORGANIZERS

You can hire entertainers, mobile discos or even people who will run your whole party for you, including providing the food. They may not be particularly cheap but they can take all the fuss out of party-giving. Good entertainers get booked up a long time in advance, so you need to think ahead if this is your plan.

If you are going to book someone to come and help make sure you know exactly what you are paying for before the party, and if possible get a personal recommendation or take up references to avoid disappointment. If you're hiring equipment such as a bouncy castle, make sure there is adequate insurance.

CHILDREN'S PARTY FOOD

Children often do not eat very much at parties – they are usually too excited. The younger they are, the more likely this is and, while you occasionally may have a child who over-indulges, in practice it is a good idea to be prepared for quite a lot of waste.

Party meal tips
* Save on the washing up and your peace of mind by providing disposable plates and crockery, and paper napkins and tablecloths.
* If you have not got enough chairs, set the meal out on a cloth over a plastic sheet on the floor, with cushions all round (this is a good idea for outdoor parties).

* Provide savoury as well as sweet things, even for the youngest children.
* To make sandwiches look more appealing remove crusts and cut them into shapes with pastry cutters.
* Serve savoury items like sandwiches, cheese straws, cocktail sausages, cheese squares, crisps, etc before bringing on the sweet things.
* Always provide lots to to drink – while children enjoy the treat of fizzy drinks, they don't quench the thirst as well as juices or squash.

FOOD IDEAS FOR YOUNGER CHILDREN

Savoury	Sweet
Cocktail sausages	Slices of raw fresh fruit
Bite-sized sausage rolls	Jam tarts
Prawn crackers	Butterfly buns
Pitta bread fingers with taramasalata	Jellies in individual bowls
Crackers with pâté	Chocolate fingers
Halved hard-boiled eggs	Marshmallows
Slices of cucumber, tomato, raw carrot	Iced biscuits
Sprigs of mustard and cress	Chocolate buttons
	Ice cream cones

Food for older children's parties Once children reach eight or nine, they appreciate more sophisticated party fare, and also more substantial food, especially if the party has been pretty active. Many of the favourites for this age group can be barbecued: hamburgers, hot dogs, Chinese-style spare ribs, chicken drumsticks, kebabs. Cocktail sausages wrapped in bacon, mildly spicy samosas filled with vegetables or minced chicken or beef, and celery boats with cream cheese also go down well. For dessert banana splits, ice cream sundaes, toffee apples, meringues and fruit turnovers usually all find happy customers.

The party cake Most parties are given to celebrate birthdays, but even at other times and festivals it is a nice idea to have a cake as a centrepiece. You can make it yourself or have one prepared to order by a professional cake maker. If you decide to make one to fit a theme, you can hire specially shaped tins – this is a good idea for birthdays if you want the cake in the shape of the child's age.

CAKE DECORATION SHORT-CUTS

Chocolate buttons for tiles, eyes, buttons, etc
Liquorice bootlaces for whiskers, tails, edging
Liquorice sweets for windows, knobs, wheels
Chocolate squares for windows, keyboards, chimneys
Angelica for leaves
Dessicated coconut for snow, with green food colouring for grass
Marzipan shaped into animals, flowers and figures
Sugar-coated chocolate buttons or jelly sweets for roof tiles, paths, flowers, etc, or for simply picking out names or numbers if you don't want to pipe icing
Ice cream wafers for roof tiles, fans, etc (depending on shape)
Individual Swiss rolls for wheels, chimneys, etc.

Note that sponge cake is preferable to a heavy fruit cake, which most children find too rich. Don't expect the children to eat much cake at the time – ask one of your helpers to cut it up into sensible slices and wrap them in paper napkins to be taken home by the guests at the end of the party.

TIMETABLING

It is worth your while preparing a mental timetable for your child's party. This is of course essential if it involves an outside entertainer or taking the children to a particular activity. No party for children of seven or under should be for more than two hours – an hour and a half is quite enough for toddlers (see above). Older children might appreciate three hours if you've provided a disco or something similar.

Allow a quarter of an hour after the official start time for all the children to arrive and for presents to be opened and for everyone to settle down. Then have games or another activity for half to three-quarters of an hour, followed by the party meal. After the meal is a good time to schedule in the entertainment, or to have quiet pencil and paper games, for half to three quarters of an hour, then a few more games or dancing until the parents arrive.

PARTY GAME FAVOURITES FOR UNDER-SEVENS

Indoors	*Outdoors*
Musical chairs/statues/hats	Hopping race
Oranges and lemons	Somersault race
The farmer's in the den	Three-legged race
Here we go round the mulberry bush	Tag
Tail on the donkey	Egg and spoon race
Musical statues	
Squeak piggy squeak	
Blind man's buff	
Sleeping lions	

PARTY GAME FAVOURITES FOR OVER-SEVENS

Indoors	*Outdoors*
Charades	Slow bicycle race
My grandmother went to market	Apple bobbing
Memory games	Four-legged race
Consequences	Passing an orange from chin to chin
Pairs	Relay obstacle race
	Forfeits

Gardening 7

At the same time as gardens have tended to become smaller as the price of land has increased, so they have become in many ways more integral than ever before to family life. Houses, too, have become smaller and the garden has become more precious because it can provide additional space. It is a waste not to make use of it. The concept, much lauded in house and gardening magazines, that the garden is an extension of the home – an outdoor room – originated in a sense of constriction, in the growing feeling that the house no longer provided enough space for all the needs of the family.

That, in turn, has put pressure on the garden. It is no longer enough for a garden to provide vegetables and a few herbs for the kitchen, some flowers to look at and a bit of grass to sit on. Today it has to be – or, perhaps, should be – designed to be just as functional as the house. And, in addition, it has to combine in some sort of coherent design a variety of needs which were unknown to our parents and grandparents – perhaps to accommodate a bar (the drinks on the patio) and dining room (the built-in barbecue) as well as a playroom (the swing and climbing frame).

All this means that today's family is likely to spend more time in the garden, but enjoying it rather than working in it. Fortunately, though, gardens have never been so easy to manage as they are today. Much of the hard labour has been taken out of gardening. Modern surfaces provide maintenance-free sitting-out areas. Container-grown plants make it possible to bring almost instant colour to the garden. The work of the plant breeders and hybridizers has resulted in not only a seemingly infinite number of plant varieties to meet every conceivable need but has produced disease-free and pest-resistant strains that ensure that the modern gardener does not have to fight a constant battle to keep his plants healthy. (That is why there is no long section on Pests and Diseases in this chapter.) Hybrid vegetables and fruits crop more

199

heavily, take up less space and need less attention than ever before. Hybrid flowering plants can give almost any flower colour that can be imagined and almost any habit of growth to meet the garden designer's vision.

As the garden has become more important to family life, it has become easier and pleasanter to create and maintain it. Hopefully, the information you will find in this section will increase your enjoyment of your garden and help you to get greater use from it.

The Flower Garden

The flower garden will not also be a pleasure garden if it involves constant hard work and constant worry. The sensible amateur gardener aims at a labour-saving garden, which means choosing plants that will need the minimum of attention and that will be at home in the conditions existing in the garden. The most important of these conditions is the type of soil in the garden and the most important rule for the flower gardener is 'know your soil'.

VARIETIES OF SOIL

You can learn a lot about your soil simply by taking a handful in your hand. If you have a heavy clay soil, better suited to pottery making than to gardening, that will be immediately obvious. If the soil does not mould into a ball, however hard you compress it, then it is a sandy soil, a light soil. If it feels crumbly and looks rather grey, then you are gardening on chalk. Most soils fall into categories that are not as extreme as any of these types, but it is usually obvious towards which extreme they lean. Looking and feeling, though, will not tell you the thing you most need to know – whether your soil is alkaline or acid.

Gardeners distinguish between three different types of soil – acid, neutral and alkaline. Acid soils are mostly dark and light-textured, though some heavy clays are acid. If you have a neutral soil you are fortunate. Neutral soils normally have a reasonable level of humus and of plant nutrients, are fairly easily workable and are hospitable to most plants. Alkaline soils are often the most difficult to work, particularly when they consist of a thin layer of topsoil resting on a base of solid chalk.

Soil-test kits, available from garden centres and shops, enable you to measure the acidity/alkalinity level of your soil. The unit of measurement is pH, which stands for 'potential of hydrogen'. Soils with a pH of 7.0 are neutral; those with a pH lower than that are acid and those with a higher pH alkaline.

If you have an alkaline soil, some plants will never flourish, however much you coddle them. You will be wasting your time to try to grow camellias and rhododendrons, for example. If you feel that no flower garden is complete without them, grow them in containers. Lilac and viburnum, though, will be completely at home in alkaline soil. In acid soils, on the other hand, it would be optimistic to expect a philadelphus or tall-bearded irises to do well.

■ ASPECT AND SHADE ■

Factors other than the pH of the soil, of course, should also govern your choice of plants. Aspect is another important consideration. Consider which areas of the garden seem always to be damp in winter, those that are scorch-dry in summer, those so shaded by buildings and trees that the ground never glimpses the sun and those exposed to icy north-easterly winds or those in particularly draughty situations – perhaps where a narrow passageway funnels the winds.

Shady parts of the garden need not be dark and depressing. There are many plants that grow best in shade or semi-shade. But many of these plants prefer a dampish soil, which presents difficulties where the shade is created by a house wall – there the soil will probably always be dry. Here you must select a plant that is able to tolerate a certain amount of dryness and, even so, you should take especial care in planting it and watering it. Dense shade, too, will limit you more than dappled shade under, for example, spreading trees.

In moist shade you can grow irises, campanulas and primulae. In dry shade, try evergreen shrubs. In partial shade, primroses and many winter- and spring-flowering bulbs will naturalize themselves – try the wood anemone (*A. nemerosa*), the common snowdrop (*Galanthus nivalis*) and almost any of the narcissi. In deep shade few flowering plants will flourish. Play safe and stick to foliage plants. Variegated varieties will prevent a look of uniform greenness.

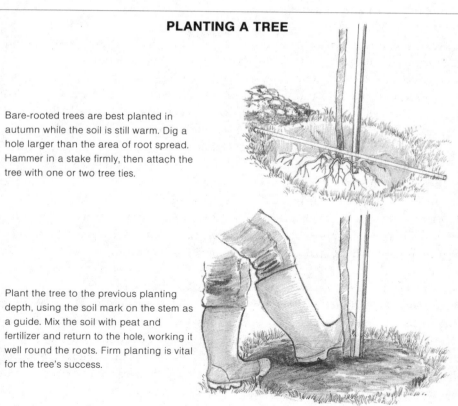

PLANTING A TREE

Bare-rooted trees are best planted in autumn while the soil is still warm. Dig a hole larger than the area of root spread. Hammer in a stake firmly, then attach the tree with one or two tree ties.

Plant the tree to the previous planting depth, using the soil mark on the stem as a guide. Mix the soil with peat and fertilizer and return to the hole, working it well round the roots. Firm planting is vital for the tree's success.

PLANTING

Most plants today are bought as container-grown plants. The great advantage of this system is that it permits plants to be bought and planted at almost any time of the year and so we can have an almost instant garden. A shrub seen in flower at the garden centre in the morning can be flourishing and flowering in your garden before dusk falls. Container-grown plants can also be left unplanted for a reasonable length of time without endangering them. If you cannot plant them out immediately, keep them well-watered and they will wait contentedly enough in the containers.

It is important, though, to prepare the planting hole adequately. Dig a hole of generous area and depth, loosen and fork over the soil beneath the hole and incorporate into it well-rotted manure or compost. If it is a shrub or small tree that you are planting, scatter a handful of bonemeal in the planting hole. Position the plant, being careful to maintain the same planting depth as in the container. Replace the soil, firming it well down as you go. Finally, water the new plant well in.

SHRUBS AND HERBACEOUS PLANTS

Many thousands of shrubs and herbaceous plants are available to today's gardener. The few recommended here are beautiful or interesting, readily purchasable and easy to manage. So are many more – but these the amateur gardener will discover for himself or herself as enthusiasm for flower-gardening grows.

Shrubs and climbers Shrubs are woody-stemmed plants that bush out either from one short main stem or from soil level. They may be either deciduous (they lose their leaves in autumn and are bare-branched throughout the winter) or evergreen (they replace their leaves gradually throughout the year and so are always in leaf). Garden shrubs vary greatly in height – from a few centimetres to 5 m/16 ft or so – and in spread. They can provide a great variety of leaf colour, size and shape and of flower colour, size, shape and season. Conifers (the name simply means 'cone-bearing') are among the most useful of shrubs. Most are evergreen, so they provide an all-year screen if used for hedging, and most, including the dwarf forms that are so well suited to the small garden, will grow in poor soil.

■ BERBERIS is an easy shrub, grown for its striking yellow flowers and blue-black berries. There are many species, some evergreen, some deciduous. Many of the deciduous species have striking autumn foliage. Of the evergreens one of the most popular is *B. darwinii*, whose leaves are as dark green and shiny as holly, and one of the most beautiful *B. linearifolia*, in the variety 'Orange King'.

■ BUDDLEIA (*B. davidii*) deserves a place in any garden for the butterflies it attracts as well as for its clusters of small, often fragrant, flowers. It likes a sunny position, but is happy in most soils as long as they are adequately fertile. There are several good varieties, differing in flower colour, among them 'Black Knight' (violet-blue), 'Empire Blue' (blue with orange centres), 'Harlequin' (purple), 'Peace' (white), 'Pink Pearl' and 'Royal Red'.

■ CAMELLIAS look rather tropical and exotic, but in fact they are generally

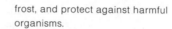

PRUNING CUTS

Where possible, all cuts should be made at an angle to the horizontal, so no water can remain on the bare wood to cause rot. All cuts should be cleaned up with a sharp pruning knife and, if large enough, painted with a proprietary sealing compound to help keep out damp and frost, and protect against harmful organisms.

1 This cut is too close to the bud.
2 This one is too far away from the bud.
3 A cut should not slope to a bud.
4 A correct pruning cut.

1   2   3   4

hardy and not at all difficult to grow. They insist, though, on lime-free soil. If your garden soil is alkaline you will have no alternative but to grow your camellias in containers filled with an ericaceous compost. The common camellia is *C. japonica*, of which there are now many named varieties giving all the colours from white to red and with both single and double flowers.

■ CLEMATIS climbs and twines by twisting its leaf stalks around the nearest support it finds. There are three groups of clematis which, between them, can produce flowers at any time of year between late winter and autumn. The three groups differ in habit and therefore require different approaches to pruning. *C. montana*, with its numerous named varieties, is in the early-flowering group. Many of the large-flowered hybrids – which include 'Barbara Dibley (white), 'Nelly Moser' (pinky mauve), 'The President' (purple-blue) and 'Vyvyan Pennell' (violet-blue) – flower next, in late spring and early summer and, often, again in autumn. These two groups are easy – they call for no regular pruning. Then, flowering later, come the clematis of the third group, which includes the *C. × jackmanii* hybrids, *C. orientalis* and *C. viticella* – 'Abundance' and 'Hagley Hybrid'. All these should be cut back hard in spring. All clematis prefer to have their roots in shade.

■ FORSYTHIA The yellow flowers of the forsythia open in early spring before the leaves appear. It needs to be positioned in full sun. *F. × intermedia* 'Beatrix Farrand' is erect and bushy and, like the larger-flowered 'Lynwood', suitable for hedging. *F. suspensa* is a gracefully arching species, of which 'Nymans' is a lovely variety.

■ FUCHSIAS are hardier than they look, although they will all succeed best in a warm, sheltered, sunny position and in a moisture-retentive, humus-rich soil. Hardiest of all is *F. magellanica*, but many of the large-flowered hybrids make no great demands on the amateur gardener – 'Alice Hoffman' (pink and white), 'Brilliant' (red and purple), 'Chillerton Beauty' (white and violet), 'Madame Cornelissen' (red and white) and many others.

■ MAHONIAS are valued for their glossy evergreen leaves and their racemes of yellow flowers. The most commonly grown is *M. aquifolium*, whose brightly coloured flowers are followed by clusters of blue-black berries. It grows to a height of about 1.5 m/5 ft, tolerates most soils and is one of those useful shrubs that will flourish in an exposed, windy spot. *M. japonica*, with paler, scented flowers, grows taller – to 2.5 m/ 8 ft – and so does perhaps the most splendid mahonia of all, the hybrid 'Charity'.

■ RODODENDRONS come in almost every size, from tiny shrubs to trees that, in their natural habitats, may tower to 18 m/60 ft. Some are evergreen, some semi-evergreen, some deciduous. Their flowers are of every colour of the rainbow. Among them are the azaleas, a group of usually smaller-leaved and smaller-flowered shrubs that flower mostly in late spring. Some 800 species of rhododendrons have been described and there are thousands of hybrids. The one thing that they all have in common is that they can stand no hint of lime in the soil. Many are unhappy in bright sunlight, preferring dappled shade, and almost all are very shallow-rooted, which means that they may need a lot of watering in dry weather. There is no point in recommending any species and varieties out of so many. The best way to make a selection is to visit one of the great azalea or rhododendron gardens and see these magnificent shrubs in flower.

■ ROSES It is hard to imagine a garden with no roses in it, but it has to be recognized that they are not the most trouble-free shrubs it is possible to find. They are prone to diseases such as rust, black spot and mildew (though modern breeders are breeding more and more resistant strains) and aphids attack new growth and ruin unopened buds. Again, there is little point in picking out species or varieties from the multitude. Among the climbing roses, though, it is still possible to select one outstanding performer. The white-flowered, scented *Rosa filipes* 'Kiftsgate' is the most vigorous of them all, capable of reaching up to a height of 6 m/20 ft or more and rambling all over the branches of a big, mature tree.

■ WEIGELAS are easy deciduous shrubs, usually trouble-free, that now come in a wide range of colours. Two particularly attractive varieties (of *W. florida*) are 'Foliis Purpureis' (rose-pink flowers and purple leaves) and 'Variegata' (pale pink flowers and cream-edged green leaves. There are many outstanding hybrids, for example the vigorous 'Koster Variegata', with green and gold leaves, and the compact, red-flowered 'Lucifer'.

Perennials Perennials are plants whose stems, leaves and flowers die down in autumn but whose roots survive the winter so that the plant puts out new growth in the spring. They are thus valuable plants for the flower garden.

■ ASTERS, or Michaelmas daisies, which produce their colourful flowers in autumn, need no special attention and no special soil. There are many named varieties, some of which grow tall and may have to be supported. The superb *A. novae-angliae* can reach 1.5 m/5 ft, but has some beautiful varieties, including 'Harrington's Pink' and 'September Ruby'. Some varieties of *A. novi-belgii* are less troublesome and more suited, perhaps, to a small garden because they grow no higher than 45 cm/18 in. Among these are 'Little Pink Beauty' and 'Royal Ruby'.

■ DELPHINIUMS The tall-growing delphiniums certainly need staking from early

PRUNING ROSES

Hybrid tea roses (**1** and **2**) are pruned hard back to encourage new shoots to grow from the base of the plant. Always cut the shoots back to outward-pointing buds, to ensure good circulation of air within the plant. Cut back only into wood produced the previous year which still has dormant buds.

Floribunda roses (**3** and **4**) are not pruned as severely as hybrid teas. Cut to outward pointing buds.

Standard roses (**5** and **6**) are pruned by cutting back shoots produced the previous year to outward pointing buds. Choose a mild spell in late February or early March.

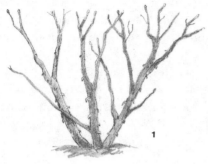

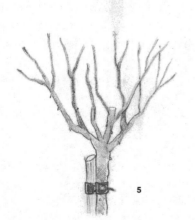

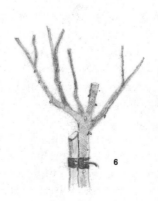

in the year. There are two main groups – the Pacific hybrids (which have rather short lives) and the Belladonna hybrids. Both will achieve heights of up to 1.5 m/5 ft. Pacifics include 'Astolat' (pink), 'Black Knight' (dark blue), 'Blue Jay' (mid-blue) and 'Sir Galahad' (white) and the Belladonnas 'Lamartine' (deep blue) and 'Pink Sensation'.

■ LUPINS Those of most interest to the amateur gardener are all hybrids, in reds, pinks, yellows, blues and white and in two-colour combinations. These may grow up to 1.2 m/4 ft high in good, acid soil. If the soil is too rich, though, lupins make softer stems and greater height and can collapse under the weight of their own blooms. Some of the many varieties available are 'The Chatelaine' (pink and white), 'Inverewe Red', 'Noble Maiden' (white and cream) and 'The Governor' (blue and white).

■ PEONIES The most attractive of the peonies are the showy double-flowered types, now available in many colours, which often also have leaves that add a rich autumn colour to the garden. Peonies are very long-lived. Plant them where they can carry on undisturbed for many years. Try 'Ballerina' (bluish pink), 'Baroness Schroeder' (creamy pink), 'Flamingo' (salmon pink) or 'President Poincaré' (crimson) if you can find them – all are superb.

■ PHLOX (*P. paniculata*) flowers in late summer. It grows to a height of some 90 cm/3 ft but, because of its strong woody stems, does not need staking. However, the strong, bare lower stems are not beautiful and are best hidden behind the more attractive foliage of other plants. Cultivated varieties are more colourful than the species – particularly, perhaps, 'Harlequin' (purple-red) and 'Amethyst' (violet). There is an Alpine phlox, *P. douglasii*, that grows only 5 cm/2 in to 10 cm/4 in high, and which produces lavender-coloured flowers in late summer. There is also a white variety, 'Snow Queen', that is pure delight.

Container and Patio Gardening

Given a few tubs and troughs even the smallest and most cramped of patios can be transformed into a colourful garden. If you wish, it can be a garden that is constantly changing. As long as you restrict yourself to small, easily handleable containers you can move plants around at your pleasure, give them turn and turn about in the sun, and even push out of sight those that have passed, or have not yet reached, their best. But, of course, you do not have to move your containers around. You can use a permanently sited container to grow a climbing plant in order to conceal an ugly wall or fence or, more positively, to grow a specimen plant such as a hardy palm that will make a focal point on the patio.

Gardening in containers is also pain-free. There is no heavy digging and even weeding is scarcely a chore. Apart from watering and feeding the plants, there is little to be done. Nor do you have to battle to keep 'difficult' plants alive. You choose the soil to suit the plant, filling some containers with acid soil for lime-haters such as camellias, rhododendrons and azaleas, and some with alkaline soils for plants such as fuchsias and clematis. And, within limits, you can choose a position to suit the plant, putting sun-lovers against a warm south-facing wall and shade-lovers in a tucked-away corner.

CHOOSING A CONTAINER

The range of containers that can be utilized is very large. Anything from a plastic yoghurt tub to half a beer barrel can be commandeered to provide a home for plants.

Containers are available, too, in several different kinds of material. The commonest today is plastic. This has the advantage that it is lightweight, cheap, easy to clean and long-lasting. It is also impermeable, so that the compost does not dry out as quickly as in clay pots. From it are made containers in an endless variety of shapes, sizes and textures. Some imitate classic stone garden urns, some mimic wooden boxes and some take advantage of being plastic by flaunting colours unobtainable in nature.

Glass-fibre containers are more expensive than plastic ones and, being more brittle, have to be handled with greater care. They are also more expensive. But they look less artificial than plastics and can ape classic and period-piece containers more convincingly.

Clay and terracotta pots, with their brick-red colour, are thought by many to complement plant colours in a natural-feeling way that plastic cannot equal. They tend, however, to be fragile and they are heavy to handle. Plants grown in terracotta pots need frequent watering, because the material is permeable, and their roots are not well protected from frost. Terracotta containers may themselves break if subjected to sharp frost.

Wooden containers also seem to be a more 'natural' accompaniment to plants, and wood is the only material from which the do-it-yourself gardener can create custom-made containers of a size and shape to fill an unusual need – a window-box to fit a non-standard window or a triangular box to fill a crooked corner. Wood, though, must be painted or treated with preservative, and even then will not last for ever.

PLANTING A TUB

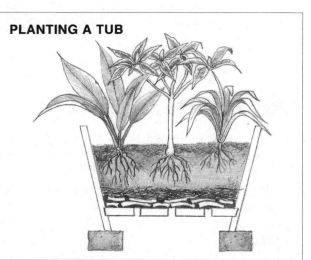

Place a layer of crocks at the base of the tub over the drainage holes, then add a layer of leaf mould if wished. Fill with compost or a mixture of soil and compost so that it comes to about 2 in/5 cm below the rim when filled.

Put in the dominant plants first, stake if necessary, then place soil over, firm the root area and water thoroughly.

For a really big container it is hard to beat half a wooden barrel. But remember that once filled with earth or compost it will be very heavy, so make sure that you have positioned it where you want it before you fill it. It will lose moisture almost as quickly as terracotta, so a wooden tub on a sunny patio may need watering once a day and perhaps more often still.

If you do manage to lay your hands on a secondhand half barrel or wooden tub, clean it very thoroughly before putting it into use – you cannot be sure where it has been or what it once contained. Use a scrubbing brush and lots of plain water and finally paint the inside with a solution of permanganate of potash and the outside with a preservative.

Varieties of container

Try to look out for receptacles never intended for the garden that will nonetheless make attractive containers for plants. Old copper kettles, saucepans, cauldrons and coal scuttles will do nicely, and so will china wash basins and chamber pots and stoneware jars. The only difficulty with containers such as these is that they will not have drainage holes and it is not easy – even if it is not an act of vandalism – to make holes in them. The solution is to give them an exceptionally deep bottom drainage layer of pebbles, crocks or gravel and to water carefully so that the plants never sit with their roots in waterlogged soil. Chimney pots, which can make interesting patio features, present the opposite problem – they are, of course, open-bottomed. It is probably best to treat them not as planters but as plant stands and to fit a plant pot inside the top of the chimney pot.

PLANTING A HANGING BASKET

Line the basket with damp moss and half fill with compost. Insert plants through the sides into the compost. Add more moss and compost to within 1 in/2.5 cm of the rim. Plant the top of the basket and water thoroughly.

CHOOSING THE RIGHT COMPOST

The best compost for all planters, window-boxes and hanging baskets is John Innes No 3 or, particularly where weight is a consideration, an equivalent peat-based compost. Alternatively, now that the conservation of peat has become an issue, mix vermiculite with the John Innes compost to lighten it. Always, if you can, fill containers with purpose-made compost rather than garden soil. Apart from having added fertilizer, it will be sterile and free of weed seeds, insect pests and harmful bacteria. If you have a large container to fill and have, for economy, to use some garden soil, put the soil on the bottom and top up with as much compost as you can lay your hands on. The nutrients added to the compost will then seep down to nourish the soil and any weed seeds in the soil will be less likely to germinate.

If you have used a good compost, container-grown plants will not need feeding for the first month or so. After that a fortnightly feed of a proprietary fertilizer should be enough. But for all container plants watering is more critical than feeding. During the summer you may have to water twice a day. If the pot has clear drainage holes and a layer of crocks in the bottom it is almost impossible to over-water.

PLANTS FOR CONTAINERS

The plants growing in their containers on your patio need not simply be ornamental. A surprising number of herbs can be grown in pots in a very small space and so can several salad crops. Strawberries may be grown in a proprietary strawberry tub or in a simple container of your choice – the small, alpine strawberry 'Baron Solemacher' is particularly easy to grow, pretty to look at and delicious to eat. You can even grow tree fruits on the patio – Ballerina apple trees planted in tubs or other containers will not only produce fruit but will look attractive too.

Of the purely ornamental plants that will flourish in containers there is an enormous range – far too many to list comprehensively here. Conifers in tubs can provide a permanent focus of interest. Many shrubs are very happy, and very easily looked after, in containers – hydrangeas, the smaller magnolias, azaleas and fuchsias, for example. Miniature and patio roses have been bred in a number of beautiful, disease-resistant and even scented varieties to flower over a long period and to provide compact, bushy plants ideally suited for growing in containers.

The selections recommended here are for generally smaller ornamental plants that fill particular needs. All are reasonably tolerant and none require unremitting attention.

Permanent plants

■ AUBRIETIA (*A. deltoidea*) is a hardy evergreen, undemanding and uncomplaining, that seems to thrive on neglect and so is a useful ground-cover plant for the window-box or other multi-planted container. Its flowers, ranging in colour from pink to purple according to variety, appear in spring to early summer. To maintain its shape, trim it ruthlessly after it has finished flowering.

■ CREEPING JENNY (*Lysimachia nummularia*), which bears yellow cup-shaped flowers in June and July, is another useful ground-cover plant. 'Aurea' will grow no higher than 5 cm/2 in.

■ LILY-OF-THE-VALLEY (*Convallaria*) has waxy white bell-like flowers that come in May or April or even earlier. It does well in partial shade and will grow in any type of soil. It spreads quickly and will need thinning out from time to time.

■ LONDON PRIDE (*Saxifraga × urbium*), an evergreen with leathery, spoon-shaped leaves, produces masses of tiny white, pink-flushed flowers during the early summer. It is another easy ground-cover plant. Look out for the variety 'Valerie Finnis', which has yellow flowers and which forms a compact cushion no more than 10 cm/4 in high.

Hardy annuals Because these are annuals, they will only last one summer. They are, though, hardy annuals, which means that they can be planted out earlier in the season than the half-hardy annuals that form the bulk of the bedding plants offered for sale in garden centres. Better still, they can easily be raised from seed. They can be sown in early spring in position in the planters where they are to grow – a quick sprinkle of seed, a light covering of compost and all that remains is to thin out the resultant seedlings. With luck even this will not be necessary in the second and future years – many will propagate themselves by self-sowing.

■ ALYSSUM produces tufts of tiny flowers and is a useful edging or carpeting plant because it will not grow higher than about 10 cm/4 in. *A. argenteum* has bright yellow flowers and blooms from June to August.

■ CORNFLOWERS (*Centaurea cyanus*) now come in white and shades of pink and scarlet as well as in the true cornflower blue. The dwarf variety 'Jubilee Gem', which is particularly suitable for planters, has, however, the traditional bright blue flowers.

■ PANSIES (*Viola × wittrockiana*) can give almost unequalled brightness and variety of colour to the container garden. Garden centres tend to stock the vividly coloured, large-flowered Pacific hybrids but, if you wish, it is easy enough to grow from seed the smaller-flowered, more subtly coloured varieties. So many strains are now available that it is pointless to advise on varieties. It is largely a matter of seeing what your favourite garden centre stocks and reading the seed packets.

■ POT MARIGOLD (*Calendula officinalis*) This plant, with its brightly coloured, daisy-like flowers, will grow up to 60 cm/2 ft high even in poor soil and will flower right through the summer until cut down by autumn frosts. 'Kelmscott Giant Orange' is a reliable variety. 'Gitana' has double flowers in colours ranging from cream to orange and will not grow to more than 30 cm/12 in high. Another useful dwarf variety is 'Baby Gold'.

Half-hardy annuals These are not quite so easy to grow from seed – they must be sown indoors or under glass and planted out later. But these are the bedding plants sold by garden centres in their many thousands in late spring and buying them ready-grown is the easiest way of obtaining them.

■ BEGONIAS (*B. semperflorens*) have stiff green or bronze leaves and pompom-like flowers that now come in many colours, from white through yellow to pinks and deep reds. They will bloom all through the summer until killed by the first autumn frosts. So many varieties have now been bred that no garden centre can stock more than a tiny fraction, but 'Frilly Pink', 'Frilly Red', 'Pink Avalanche' and 'Red Ascot' are all good varieties for planters, should you come across them.

■ LOBELIA (*L. erinus*) There are two sorts – upright and trailing. The trailing varieties can cover the fronts of window-boxes and the sides of tubs and are particularly suitable for use in hanging baskets. Lobelias now come with red and white flowers as well as the original blue. 'Blue Cascade', 'Light Blue Basket' and 'Red Cascade' are good choices for a hanging basket. So is 'Colour Cascade', which bears flowers in a mixture of colours from white through mauve to red. 'Cambridge Blue' and the red-flowered 'Rosamond', being more compact, are better suited to window-boxes and planters.

■ **PETUNIAS** (*P.* × *hybrida*) come in almost every colour under the sun, in three main forms (trailing, standard and dwarf) and in two main types (Grandiflora, with large flowers, and Multiflora, with smaller flowers borne in greater abundance). All sorts will, if persistently dead-headed, continue to flower right through the summer. A weakness of petunias has always been that the flowers are damaged by rain, and this is still true of many varieties. The Multifloras are more resistant to rain damage than the Grandifloras and, of the Multifloras, the Resisto strain is the most rain-resistant of all.

■ **SALVIAS,** too, come in a great variety of colours. The two species most commonly grown in containers are both, in fact, perennials, although they are treated as annuals by the gardener. *S. farinacea* is a vigorous species, of which there are several attractive varieties, among them the white-flowered 'Alba', the violet-blue 'Victoria' and the darker blue 'Blue Bedder'. *S. splendens* is shorter, growing only to about 30 cm/12 in high. Other colours have now been bred, but the original scarlet has been preserved and heightened in 'Blaze of Fire' and the even more dwarf 'Rodeo'.

■ **TOBACCO PLANT** (*Nicotiana*) This is grown as much for its fragrance as for its appearance, although its flowers are pretty enough, in white and yellow-green and shades of pink. They open (except in shade) only in the evening, and it is then that the scent is strongest. Tobacco plants grow to a height of about 1 m/3 ft and are therefore not suitable for small containers or for the fronts of large ones. Hybridists have now, however, produced dwarf plants whose flowers open in the daytime and these are eminently suited for container growing. Most of these newer varieties have lost much of their scent. The best exceptions are 'Lime Green', which grows to about 60 cm/2 ft, and the Nicki series of varieties, which have white, pink or red flowers and grow to only about 40 cm/15 in high.

The Kitchen Garden

MAKING THE BEST USE OF YOUR SPACE

Growing your own vegetables has many advantages over buying them from the supermarket shelves. Home-grown vegetables are tastier, because you can grow varieties chosen for their flavour not their marketing qualities, safer, because you control what sprays and chemicals are used on them, and, always, fresher. It is unlikely, though, that you have a kitchen garden large enough to provide all the vegetables and fruits your family needs. This means that you should be very selective in choosing which vegetables it is worth your while to grow and that you should try to get the heaviest crop you can from the space available. One way of achieving this is by planting crops closer together than old-fashioned gardening books used to recommend – spacing them so that when fully grown each plant's leaves will just touch those of its neighbours and planting not in straight lines distanced from one another but in zigzags or staggered rows. This system of 'optimum spacing' works best if the vegetable plot is divided into a number of small beds 1.2 m/4 ft or 1.5 m/5 ft

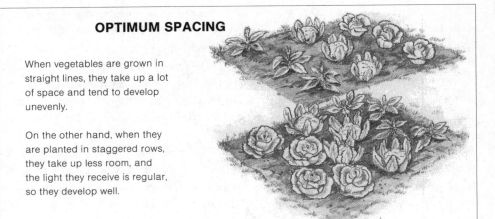

OPTIMUM SPACING

When vegetables are grown in straight lines, they take up a lot of space and tend to develop unevenly.

On the other hand, when they are planted in staggered rows, they take up less room, and the light they receive is regular, so they develop well.

wide, separated by narrow paths. All the plants can then be tended from the paths and it is never necessary to trample on the cultivated soil.

Another way of making the most of the available space is 'catch cropping', putting in a quick-growing crop – perhaps a salad crop such as radishes – in the space that becomes available after one crop has been harvested and before the next is sown or planted or when, as will happen even in the best-run vegetable gardens, a crop fails. 'Intercropping' is another way of maximizing soil use. Long-term crops, such as Brussels sprouts, occupy in the early part of their lives more ground than they need and between them can be sown or planted quick-growing crops that will be harvested or transplanted before the original crop grows big enough to demand all the space allotted to it. Still another space-saving technique is 'inter-sowing', mixing two types of seed in one sowing. One crop should be quick-germinating and quick-growing, so that it will be harvested before the other matures. Spring onions mixed with main-crop carrots is one possibility, radishes with parsnips another.

PREPARING THE SOIL

If you try in ways like these to get the utmost out of your vegetable plot, you must remember that you are taking a lot of goodness out of soil and that this must be replaced – preferably, in these ecologically conscious days, by non-chemical means. Good gardening begins with returning nutrients to the soil and with conditioning the soil to make it more workable and more capable of retaining water without becoming waterlogged. The best way of achieving this is by incorporating organic matter into the soil. Farmyard manure, stable manure, chicken manure, sewage sludge and seaweed are all excellent for this. Contrary to general belief, farmyard and stable manures are at their most nutritious when they are fresh and the straw has hardly begun to decompose. The trouble is that they can at this stage be fatal to a plant's roots and may also contain a host of unwelcome weed seeds. They also smell. For these reasons most gardeners, sensibly, wait until the manure is well rotted or fully decomposed. Then it is practically odourless, easy to dig in and in the best condition to improve the soil in the short term.

Compost Garden compost is a useful substitute for or, better, complement to manure. Fallen leaves, lawn mowings, soft clippings and vegetable waste from the kitchen can be composted down to form a valuable source of organic matter for the garden. Woody prunings from shrubs and long tough stems from herbaceous plants should not be incorporated unless you have an electric shredder or are prepared to chop them up very finely by hand. They will keep the compost too open. Lawn mowings may have the opposite effect. Too many of them will form a dense mass that will exclude air from the heap and prevent it from warming up and breaking down.

Compost heaps in the small garden need to be contained. A simple wooden framework supporting a wire-netting surround is adequate, though the compost may be slow to heat up, but a surround of planks, corrugated iron or bricks, with plenty of gaps so that air can reach the compost, is better. Proprietary compost bins can be bought and, although expensive, are best of all.

Some care should be taken in building up the heap – it is not simply a matter of tossing in whatever is to hand whenever it is to hand. The first layer, ideally of mixed vegetable waste, should be spread over the base and firmed to make a thickness of about 15 cm/6 in. Then a compost accelerator (a lime and nitrogen mixture available from garden centres and nurseries) should be sprinkled over the layer and well watered. Further layers of about the same thickness, interspersed with accelerator, should be built up until the heap is complete. A height of about 1.2 m/ 4 ft is the optimum.

Crop rotation Another important consideration for the vegetable gardener is crop rotation. Even on the smallest plot this should always be borne in mind, for two good reasons – different types of vegetables make different demands upon the soil, and so need different soil preparation, and growing the same crop on the same piece of land year after year encourages a build-up of the pests and diseases that such a crop particularly attracts. The three groups of crops that should be kept separate in the kitchen garden are root crops, brassicas (the cabbage family) and everything that is left – mainly peas and beans, onions and leeks. Dividing your plot into three sections to correspond with these groups enables you to practise a three-year rotation, never growing the crops of any one group in the same ground more often than every third year.

VEGETABLES

Because growing vegetable crops other than in the traditional rows has become so popular, spacings are given as the number of plants that will grow to maturity in the area of 1 sq m/1 sq yd. The figures should not be taken as mathematically precise. They are intended to give a rough idea of the sort of yield you might expect from the ground you have available. Similarly, the growing times described here cannot be exact, but they will give you a good idea of how long you will have to wait before you can harvest a crop for the table. Weather conditions, your geographical position and the micro-climate of your garden will all affect the growing time. Similarly, when sowing or planting times are given, they should be interpreted and adjusted

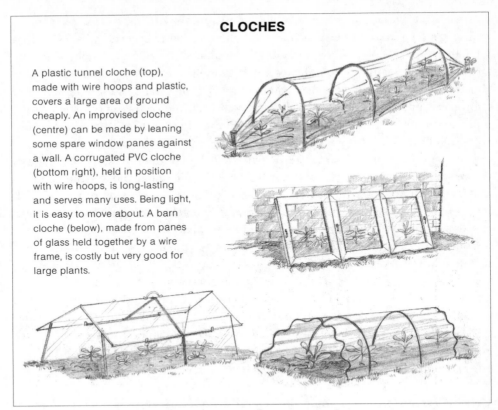

CLOCHES

A plastic tunnel cloche (top), made with wire hoops and plastic, covers a large area of ground cheaply. An improvised cloche (centre) can be made by leaning some spare window panes against a wall. A corrugated PVC cloche (bottom right), held in position with wire hoops, is long-lasting and serves many uses. Being light, it is easy to move about. A barn cloche (below), made from panes of glass held together by a wire frame, is costly but very good for large plants.

according to the conditions – in a cold, late spring it will be better to delay sowing into the ground for a week or two. It is assumed that seeds are sown into the open ground unless it is specified that they should be sown 'under glass' or 'indoors'.

Salad crops Even in the smallest garden there is always room for a few salad plants – a patch of radishes takes up almost no space at all and lettuces will grow happily among the flowers. Most salad crops, too, are quick-growing and may be grown as a catch crop between more permanent vegetables.

■ BEETROOT is a root crop that is happiest in light friable soil. Do not grow it in ground that has been manured within the last year or so – if you do it will produce forked rather than neatly globular roots. Sow the seeds from early April onward, at fortnightly intervals, if you want a succession of young, tender beetroots. Each 'seed' is in fact a pellet containing two or three seeds, so thin out the weaker seedlings as soon as they are handleable. Beetroots need careful watering – if the soil is too dry they will become tough and woody, if it is too wet they will split. The aim is to keep them evenly moist. Space: 32 per sq m/sq yd. Growing time: three to four months. Varieties: 'Boltardy', 'Crimson Globe' and the very deep red 'Detroit'.

■ CHINESE CABBAGE is a fairly recent addition to the ordinary gardener's repertoire. It can be used in salads and as a stir-fry vegetable. There are three main kinds – a short, thickish type rather like a cos lettuce, a slimmer sort known as Michihili, and Pak Choi, which has leaves with thick, juicy midribs. Chinese cabbage is very prone to bolting if it is sown too early or if it suffers drought, so do not sow before mid-June and keep the plants well watered. Space: 10 per sq m/sq yd. Growing time: three to four months. Varieties: 'cos' types 'Tip Top', 'Hopkin' and 'Kasumai'; Michihili 'Jade Pagoda'; Pak Choi 'Mei Quing Choi'.

■ CUCUMBERS can be grown successfully outdoors, but they demand a sunny site, sheltered from cold winds, and they will not flourish in a cool, wet summer. They used to be known as 'ridge' cucumbers, because they were grown on heaped ridges of farmyard manure. Nowadays, unless your soil is exceptionally deep, rich and well manured or well composted, make growing pockets by digging pits 30 cm/12 in square and at least as deep. Fill the pockets with manure or compost or a mixture of the two and finish off with a layer of topsoil to form a shallow mound. Sow seed in May, three seeds to each site, and cover each seed with a jam jar. When the seedlings have produced the first true leaves, remove the two weakest on each mound. When the plants have made five or six leaves, pinch out the growing tips to encourage the development of the side shoots on which the cucumbers will grow. The plants must then be continually supplied with water and, after the cucumbers start to swell, with liquid fertilizer. Growing time: 12 to 15 weeks. Varieties: 'Patio Pik' (a compact plant suitable for even the smallest plot), 'Burpee Hybrid' and 'Burpless Tasty Green' (trailing and needing more space), and the reliable 'King of the Ridge', which is still hard to beat.

■ LETTUCES do best in well-drained, fertile soils and demand plenty of water throughout their growing season. There are four main types: butterhead, with soft leaves; crisphead, with crisp, wrinkly leaves; cos, with long, upright, thick leaves; and loose-leaved, which do not heart up and whose leaves can be picked, like spinach, a few at a time. The only cultural difference between the four sorts is that butterhead and crisphead varieties – the two kinds of cabbage lettuce – are more tolerant of poorer, dryer soils. Sow every two weeks or so in succession where the plants are to grow. Space: nine or ten per sq m/sq yd, but this varies with the variety. Growing time: loose-leaved six to eight weeks; others eight to fourteen weeks. Varieties: butterhead 'Avondefiance' (stands hot summers without bolting) and 'Clarion' (tasty and disease-resistant); crisphead 'Saladin' (does not go to seed as quickly as other crisphead varieties); cos 'Little Gem' (the best-known and the best, it can be planted closely – 15 cm/6 in apart – and crops throughout the summer); loose-leaved 'Salad Bowl' (the easiest to grow and can be picked over a long period – only two sowings are needed to provide leaves through the summer and into the autumn) and 'Red Salad Bowl' (a more colourful variant).

■ RADISHES are small, quick-growing roots that come in different shapes – spherical or cylindrical – and different colours – red, white and yellow. They require a light, fertile soil. In summer they need a shady spot and to be kept constantly watered, otherwise they will bolt and go woody. Sow seeds successively, at weekly or fortnightly intervals, from the beginning of March to the end of May. Space: some 300 per sq m/sq yd, but the figure is largely meaningless because radishes are best treated as catch crops or intercrops. They need only to be thinned to leave the plants about 4 cm/1½ in apart. Growing time: three to five weeks. Varieties: 'Cherry Belle' (round and red-skinned), 'French Breakfast' (cylindrical, with white-tipped red skin) and 'Long White Icicle'.

■ SALAD, OR SPRING, ONIONS are slender, white-skinned, green-leaved onions picked for eating before their bulbs develop. Thinnings from the main onion bed can be used for salad onions, but for a regular, more assured supply sow the seeds in succession at fortnightly intervals from March to July. Space: 150 or more per sq m/ sq yd. Growing time: ten to fourteen weeks. Variety: 'White Lisbon'.

■ TOMATOES grown outdoors are always something of a gamble. In a dull summer the fruits refuse to ripen before winter cold kills the plants. A long, warm summer, though, makes the effort worthwhile – freshly picked sun-ripened outdoor tomatoes are unsurpassed in flavour. The seed must be sown indoors or under glass, from mid-March to early April. Prick out into pots or soil blocks as soon as the seedlings are big enough to handle. Harden the plants off gradually before planting in the garden when all risk of frost has passed and the soil has thoroughly warmed up. Alternatively, grow the plants in growing bags or large pots. Choose a sunny, sheltered spot – beside a south-facing wall is ideal. Bush varieties will need no support. Other, cordon, varieties should be supported by 1.5 m/5 ft stakes or canes. On these varieties it will be necessary to pinch out side shoots that appear in the angles between stem and leaves and to stop the plants by pinching out the growing point when four trusses have set fruit. It is most unlikely that any more than this will ripen. Water all varieties regularly and frequently and feed weekly with a proprietary liquid tomato fertilizer as soon as the first truss has set. Space: three per sq m/sq yd. Growing time: some five months. Varieties: 'Alfresco', 'Red Alert' and 'Sleaford Abundance' (modern hybrid bush varieties with modestly sized fruits), 'Ailsa Craig' and 'Alicante' (early, heavy-cropping bush varieties) and 'Gardeners Delight' (small, delicious fruits that can be eaten like sweets).

Vegetable growing It has to be admitted that vegetable growing does involve some work. It is not possible to avoid a certain amount of digging – the traditional autumn digging of the old-time gardener and the modern allotment-holder is still the best way of preparing the soil for the spring burst of sowing and planting. It buries annual weeds, breaks up and aerates the earth and provides the opportunity to incorporate organic matter into the soil. Neither black plastic sheets nor shredded-bark mulches are capable of achieving the same result. One advantage, though, of growing vegetables in small, manageable beds is that digging can be done in small doses and never seems a major chore.

You will not be able to grow all the vegetables, much less all the varieties, described here. Nor indeed would you wish to do so. But only you can choose which among them will give the greatest pleasure to your family in relation to the amount of work involved in their growing and the area of garden that will have to be devoted to them.

Brassicas, which include all members of the cabbage family – including broccoli, Brussels sprouts, cabbages themselves, cauliflowers, and swedes and turnips – all like the same soils and growing conditions. They prefer a fertile, deep, firm soil. They should – with only a few exceptions such as kale and Chinese cabbage – be raised in a seedbed and planted out in their growing positions when they have made three or four leaves, usually some five to seven weeks after sowing. Water the seedlings the day before transplanting so that they can be lifted easily without tearing their roots. Water, too, the plot that is to receive them. Make the planting hole with a dibber or trowel, fill it with water and wait until the water has drained away before planting the seedling and firming the soil around it with your hand. Keep the seedlings well watered until they are firmly established. Raising brassicas in a seedbed in this way saves space because their permanent plot can be used for other vegetables while the seedlings are growing. An alternative is to buy young brassicas ready to plant out. You may find, though, that only a limited number of varieties is available from garden centres and nurseries.

Brassicas are more vulnerable to pests and diseases than most other vegetables. Of the pests, caterpillars are the most common. The best way to deal with them is simply to search them out and pick them off by hand. Slugs, too, can be captured individually, but it may be necessary to take more general measures against them. Proprietary slug pellets are safe if used carefully. Pigeons, another of the brassica's enemies, are more difficult to deter; in extreme cases the only answer may be to net the plants against them. Cabbage root flies lay their eggs in the soil and the emerging grubs bore into the plant's stem at soil level. Proprietary pesticides against them are available or a protective collar of tarred paper or carpet underlay can be placed on the soil around the stem of each plant to prevent the flies laying their eggs. Finally, there is club root. This is a fungus disease that distorts the roots of brassicas and can kill the plants or, at best, severely restrict their growth. The disease is more prevalent in acid ground, so liming the soil discourages it, as does dipping the seedlings in a proprietary deterrent when they are transplanted. Club root, though, once in the soil is extremely difficult to eradicate and it is one of the most potent arguments for crop rotation. It is an absolute rule of vegetable gardening never to plant brassicas in the same ground more than once in at least every three years.

■ BROCCOLI, which produces flower spikes like small cauliflowers, is one of the more demanding brassicas to grow. More than most brassicas it requires that sometimes self-contradictory condition, well-drained, very firm soil. Sow in mid-April to May. Space: two per sq m/sq yd. Growing time: 10 months. Varieties: 'Purple Sprouting' and 'White Sprouting'. Both these come in early and late varieties. Earlies will be ready for harvesting in late February and March, lates in late March to April.

■ BRUSSELS SPROUTS take up a good deal of space and need a continually moist, fertile, firm soil if they are not simply to produce disappointing small, loose sprouts. Sow seeds in mid-March to April. Space: three per sq m/sq yd. Growing time: seven to nine months, depending on the variety. Varieties: the very early 'Peer Gynt', 'Mallard' and 'Fortress'. All these are medium to short varieties. Tall Brussels sprouts, unless they are very firmly rooted in very firm soil, tend to fall over and are therefore best avoided by the more casual gardener. If, however, you feel confident of your soil and your skill, try 'Roger', which, when well-grown, produces masses of big well-flavoured sprouts.

■ CABBAGE is the best known and most widely grown of all brassicas. Between them, spring, summer and autumn cabbages can produce crops for harvesting in almost every month of the year. The mid-summer period is the most difficult to cover, but at that time so many other vegetables are available that it is scarcely worth the bother to try to close the gap. Cabbages are reasonably easy to grow, giving a good account of themselves on less firm, less fertile soil than other brassicas. Summer cabbage should be sown in April or early May, winter cabbage about two weeks later and spring cabbage (that is, cabbage that will be ready to eat in the spring of the following year) in August. Space: spring cabbage (which can be cut as spring greens from March onward, leaving the remaining plants to heart up) 10 per sq m/sq yd; summer and winter cabbage five per sq m/sq yd. Growing time: spring cabbage eight months, summer four to six months, winter five to eight months. Varieties: 'Durham Early' for spring greens only. Then, for early summer, 'Hispi' and 'Spivoy', both of which have pointed heads, and 'Golden Cross', the earliest of the round-headed varieties. Follow these with 'Stonehead', which will stand in the garden for a long time without bolting or deteriorating, and then with 'Hawke', which matures in October. The January King hybrid 'Aquarius', whose small heads will stand for two or even three months, will then take you to Christmas and beyond. But there are numerous varieties of cabbage, every gardener has his favourites and it is always worth experimenting.

■ CAULIFLOWERS take up a good deal of time and space and are notoriously difficult to grow satisfactorily. You need a deep rich soil that will retain water without becoming waterlogged. If the soil is too dry or too poor you will grow only small, prematurely ripened, blowsy curds that are not worth harvesting. Sow mid-March to May. Space: two per sq m/sq yd. Growing time: five to nine months, depending on type. Varieties: for summer cauliflower 'All the Year Round' is as easy as any cauliflower can be and 'Snow Crown', an F1 hybrid, is worth trying. For autumn cauliflowers try 'Barrier Reef', 'Flora Blanca' or the vigorous 'Wallaby'. Of the winter cauliflowers (which are sown in spring, stand through the winter, and head up in the following spring) the earliest is 'Asmer Snowcap March', but it needs a mild, early spring if it is to succeed and its heads are rather loose and vulnerable to frost. The 'Walcheren Winter' selections, although they do not mature until April or May, are hardier and more reliable.

■ KALE is useful because it is very hardy and because it is ready to eat in winter, when not much else may be available in the vegetable garden. Sow in April and May for planting out from late June to early August. You may have to stake the plants or earth them up to the base of the lowest leaves to protect against wind rock, but otherwise they require little attention. Do not try to encourage growth by feeding them with a nitrogen-rich fertilizer; this will merely encourage tender growth that winter frosts will cut down. Space: four per sq m/sq yd. Growing time: seven to eight months. Varieties: 'Fribor', 'Pentland Brig' and 'Dwarf Green Curled', a shorter variety that may well not have to be staked.

■ KOHLRABI is a swollen-stemmed brassica that looks rather like a turnip growing above ground. It needs a fertile soil and plenty of water, because it has to grow quickly and without check if it is to remain tender. Sow seeds successively from early April onward at three-weekly intervals. Sow where the plants are to grow – they will not transplant. Harvest when the swollen stems are something between the sizes of a squash ball and a tennis ball. Space: 18 per sq m/sq yd. Growing time:

eight to ten weeks. Varieties: 'Green Vienna' for the early sowings, 'Purple Vienna' for later.

Broad beans are among the hardiest of beans and, picked young, are an ideal vegetable for home freezing. It is possible to get a very early crop by sowing seed in the autumn and allowing the young plants to over-winter, but it needs some luck and a mild, dryish winter. It is probably wiser to abandon hope of the very early crop you might get from an autumn sowing and to sow instead in early spring, from February to March. Broad beans are happy in any reasonably fertile soil. Taller varieties will almost certainly need support, most easily done by planting a stake at each of the four corners of the bean bed and surrounding the block of plants with twine. It is always advisable to pinch out the tips of the plants as soon as they are in flower. This reduces the damage done by black bean aphids, which suck the sap from the tender new growth. Do not water until the pods begin to swell, but then water consistently in dry weather. Space: five per sq m/sq yd. Growing time: three to four months. Varieties: 'Aquadulce Claudia' is very reliable and hardy – if you wish to sow in autumn for a very early crop in spring this is the variety to choose. 'Express' gives the earliest crop from the spring sowing, but 'Hylon' and 'Relon', although cropping later, give a greater yield.

Carrots, if left to themselves, would flower in their second year. Instead, we harvest them for their roots in their first year of life. They do best in light, reasonably rich soils, but like all root crops they dislike recently manured ground. In shallow soils it is best to grow only the short- or ball-rooted varieties, rather than to struggle unsuccessfully to get the older, longer varieties to grow satisfactorily. Sow in March to July, successionally, for tender carrots to be eaten young and in April to May for the later, bigger maincrop carrots that will stand through the winter. Keep the soil uniformly moist – the roots will split if, after a dry spell, they are suddenly watered. Carrot fly, whose maggots tunnel into the roots and make them rot, is a problem. Watering and firming the soil around the remaining carrots after thinning out helps to deter the fly. So does growing onions among the carrots and deferring sowing until after the end of May. Space: maincrop 80 per sq m/sq yd; for successional sowings to be eaten when immature up to 150 per sq m/sq yd. Growing time: 11 to 12 weeks for thinnings, five months for main crop. Varieties: earlies 'Nandor', 'Early Nantes', 'Amsterdam Forcing' and 'Paris Forcing'; ball-rooted 'Kundulus'; intermediate 'Chantenay Red-cored' and 'Autumn King'; long-rooted 'Scarlet Perfection' and 'St Valery'.

Courgettes are simply marrows harvested before they become mature. Because they grow vigorously they need a well-drained, rich soil. If in any doubt, dig planting holes and fill them with well-rotted manure or compost. Choose an open, sunny site. Sow seeds on site in May or June, when all danger of frost has passed. Water the plants copiously and, when the courgettes have begun to swell, liquid feed with a potash-rich fertilizer. Bush varieties need no training, but pinch out the growing points of the lateral branches of trailing varieties, both to keep them under control and to encourage them to fruit. Space: one per sq m/sq yd. Growing time: three to four months. Varieties: 'Aristocrat' is quick-growing and high-yielding; 'Ambassador' and 'Early Gem' are bush types that can be left to produce full-size marrows.

French beans are like smaller, usually rounder-podded, runner beans. Most people think they have a more subtle taste. Although there are tall, climbing varieties it is simpler to grow the dwarf, bushy sorts, which reach only to 45 cm/18 in high and need no staking. Make two or three sowings of the seeds *in situ*, at intervals of about three weeks, from May to July. French beans produce their pods over quite a short time and it is best to have a succession. Do not allow the pods to age on the plant – keep picking even if you have to give the pods away. Water generously, but only after the flowers have appeared. Space: nine per sq m/sq yd. Growing time: two to three months. Varieties: 'Masterpiece' (an early and prolific cropper), 'The Prince', 'Sprite' and 'Evergreen'.

Leeks are one of the most useful crops for the small garden because they produce a high yield from a small area and emerge unscathed from even the hardest winter. Sow in a seedbed in March or April and transplant into the growing position when the plants are pencil-thick and about 15 cm/6 in high. Choose the strongest seedlings. Make holes 20 cm/8 in deep, about 15 cm/6 in apart; drop one plant into each hole; fill the hole with water and leave well alone. The surrounding soil will gradually fall into the hole, effectively earthing up and blanching the leek's stems. To get a greater length of white stem, draw up the soil around the plants as they grow. Otherwise they need little or no attention – water only if there is a prolonged dry spell. Space: 18 per sq m/sq yd. Growing time: nine or ten months, but then they can be left in the ground until needed through the winter. Varieties: 'King Richard', 'Musselburgh' (an old reliable), 'Royal Favourite' and the very hardy 'Winter Crop'.

Onions may be grown either from seed or from the small immature bulbs called sets. Seed should be sown in March and sets planted out in April. The seeds are slow to germinate and seed-grown plants frequently perform less well, especially in poorer soil, than set-grown plants. Sets should be planted very firmly and with only the tips just showing above the soil surface, otherwise birds will pull them up. If they do, or if frost lifts the sets, replant them firmly. Onions need a rich soil, with a good organic content, but not one which has been recently manured. Because they are prey to some soil-borne problems, such as stem eelworm and white rot, they should be grown on a new site each year. Do not water except during a period of prolonged drought and even then stop when the bulbs begin to ripen. This will be in late August or September, when the leaves will begin to yellow and collapse. The process can be encouraged by bending over the ripening leaves and carefully scraping away the soil from the tops of the bulbs. About two weeks later the bulbs can be pulled up and left to dry in the sun for storing. Do not attempt to store any bulbs whose leaves remain standing after the others have toppled or whose bulb necks are swollen. These should be used at once because they will rot if kept in store. Space: 40 per sq m/sq yd. Growing time: from seed five to six months, from sets five months. Varieties: 'Ailsa Craig', 'Bedfordshire Champion' (both old, still-reliable favourites) and the newer 'Hygro'.

Parsnips, like carrots, are biennials that are harvested in their first year. Like carrots they dislike freshly manured soil. Sow in April to May on the site where they are to mature. Parsnips should be ready to harvest by about November, but they can safely be left in the ground until needed. They are subject to attack by canker, which causes the roots to rot. There is no specific cure. Preventive measures include growing parsnips on a fresh site each year and avoiding damage to the roots when hoeing. Space: 20 per sq m/sq yd. Growing time: eight to nine months. Varieties: 'Avonresister', bred for resistance to canker, is smaller than most varieties but has excellent flavour. 'White Gem' is also good.

Peas take up a considerable amount of space and demand some attention, both from the gardener and from the cook, but their taste is greatly superior to that of frozen peas from the supermarket. Should you decide to grow them, choose a dwarf variety, although even this will need some kind of support if the plants are not to drape themselves messily over the ground. The traditional way was to push bushy twigs into the ground beside the seedlings when they reached about 7.5 cm/3 in high, but it is now more usual to surround them with netting on a post and wire framework. It is probably sensible, too, to concentrate on the early varieties. Sow in rows in a V-shaped drill, or scattered in a 20 cm/8 in wide, 5 cm/2 in deep flat-bottomed drill, from the beginning of March until the end of April. Peas need a fertile soil, deeply dug, with plenty of organic material incorporated. Seeds, as well as newly emerged seedlings, are vulnerable to attack by birds. Protect them by putting a hoop-shaped netting over the rows immediately after sowing, or try a tangled network of black cotton supported on sticks just above the seed row. Space: 30 to 40 per sq m/sq yd. Growing time: three to four months. Varieties: 'Feltham First' and 'Kelvedon Wonder' (first earlies) and 'Onward' (second early). 'Hurst Beagle' produces smallish, tasty peas that are excellent for freezing. For mangetout peas 'Sugar Rae' is recommended.

Potatoes are grown from seed potatoes, which should always be bought afresh each year – never save seed from your own garden. Sprout them before planting by standing the tubers in shallow boxes, in a light, cool place, until green shoots about 2.5 cm/1 in long have grown from the uppermost eyes. If many shoots have grown, rub off all except three or four. Tubers set out to sprout in late February will be ready to plant out, about 30 cm/12 in to 45 cm/18 in apart, when all risk of frost has passed. As soon as the plants are some 23 cm/9 in to 25 cm/10 in high, draw the soil from the sides to earth up the plants. This is to prevent light reaching the tubers and greening them, which makes them slightly poisonous. An alternative is to plant potatoes through slits cut in black polythene sheeting – the plastic has the same light-excluding effect as does earthing up. Early potatoes are ready for lifting as soon as the flowers open. Then lift them as soon as possible, before potato blight has a chance to appear. Space: two to four per sq m/sq yd. Growing time: about three months. Varieties: earlies 'Arran Pilot', 'Epicure' and the high-yielding 'Estima' and 'Maris Bard'. The most reliable main-crop potatoes seem to be 'Desiree', 'Pentland Squire' and 'Pentland Javelin'. 'Maris Piper' crops heavily and has more flavour than most potatoes, but it does not stand drought very well and is reputed to be particularly attractive to slugs.

Runner beans grow vigorously and crop heavily, so they need lots of nourishment and water. They also need supports because, left to themselves, they climb to a height of 2.4 m/8 ft or more. The traditional system of support is that using

2.4 m/8 ft canes or sticks planted in the ground, crossed over and tied towards the top and held together by a horizontal pole slotted in the V-shape thus formed. One plant should be allotted to each pole, which should be about 20 cm/8 in from its neighbour. Sow one seed at the base of each pole, after all danger of frost has passed, which usually means around mid-May. Alternatively, raise seeds earlier under glass and plant out in late May. The traditional preparation for runner beans is very worthwhile – dig a trench in the autumn where the bean row is to be and fill it with well-rotted manure or compost before replacing the topsoil. Failing that, the trench can be left open until just before sowing or planting time and then filled with any compost, rotted or unrotted, or even newspaper (which will at least help to retain moisture). In dry summers water copiously when the plants are in flower or in crop. The beans will be produced until frost kills the plants; pick regularly to keep the plants in production. Space: nine per sq m/sq yd. Growing time: about three months. Varieties: 'Butler' is virtually stringless, as is 'Red Knight', which produces exceptionally long pods. Both of these are red-flowered. Of the white-flowered varieties (there is no difference in taste or culture, only in appearance) 'Desiree' is probably the most productive.

Spinach is a catch-all heading under which the gardener includes not only true spinach but New Zealand spinach and spinach beet or perpetual spinach. Spinach beet makes an excellent substitute for true spinach in the kitchen and is far easier to grow. It does not demand so rich a soil, does not bolt so readily, tolerates drought better and gives a heavier yield. Sow in April, and again in July to give an autumn crop, and thin the seedlings to about 24 cm/9 in apart. Space: 15 per sq m/sq yd. Growing time: three to four months. There are no named varieties – seed packets are labelled simply 'perpetual spinach' or 'spinach beet'.

Swedes belong to the brassica family, have the same likes and dislikes as regards soil as other brassicas and, like them, are susceptible to club root, but the practical gardener tends to look upon them not as brassicas but as root crops, so they are dealt with separately here. Sow *in situ* in April and thin in two or three stages to leave the seedlings about 23 cm/9 in apart. Keep the soil evenly moist or the swedes will become woody. Lift the roots as required from autumn onward. Swedes are hardy and may be left in the ground until wanted in the kitchen. Space: ten per sq m/sq yd. Growing time: five to six months. Varieties: 'Chignecto' and 'Marian' are both resistant to club root; 'Acme' is quicker-growing.

Turnips are also members of the brassica family. They are not quite as hardy as swedes and may not survive in the ground in a bitter winter. Increasingly they are being grown, not as a winter main crop, but as young, tender roots for summer eating. Sow seeds in March or April. Space: 15 per sq m/sq in. Growing time: six weeks (for earlies eaten young) to fourteen weeks (for main crop). Varieties: 'Purple Top Milan' for early, flat, tender roots; 'Golden Ball' for maincrop.

HERBS

Most of the herbs we grow in our gardens originated along the coasts of the Mediterranean, where they enjoyed hot, dry summers and mild winters. If they are

HERBS

to do well in the garden, we need to reproduce these conditions for them as closely as possible. Herbs thrive in a sunny position (though most will accept light shade for part of the day) and on well-drained soil. Apart from that all-important requirement, herbs are generally undemanding as to soil – often it seems that herbs grown in poor soil have more flavour. And herbs ask for very little attention. They are resistant to most pests and diseases, because their oils seem to act as repellants. The only attention a herb bed needs is routine weeding and even that can be cut down if you spread a mulch of chipped bark about 5 cm/2 in deep around the plants.

Most herbs can be bought ready growing in pots from garden centres, nurseries and even supermarkets, but almost all are very easy to propagate. Annual and biennial herbs, and most of the perennials, can be raised from seed, sown directly into the soil where they are to grow as soon as the soil has warmed up in spring. Only a few demand anything more than this.

PRICKING OUT SEEDLINGS

1 When the seedlings are large enough to handle, loosen the roots with a stick, and prick them out, holding by the leaf. **2** Fill new trays with John Innes potting compost No 1. and plant the seedlings up to their necks. **3** Water gently. Keep the seedlings out of direct sunlight for the next few days.

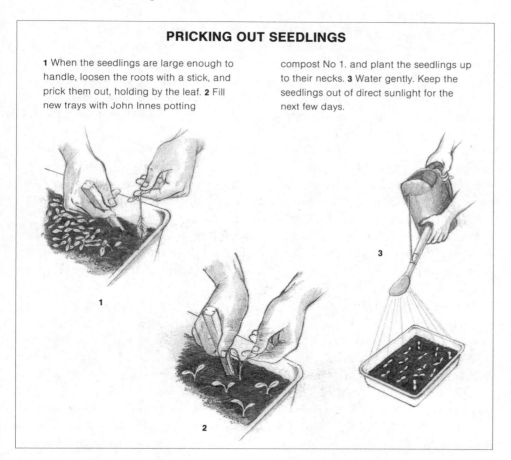

Basil (*Ocimum basilicum*) is a half-hardy annual whose leaves are used, either fresh or frozen, particularly to flavour tomato and egg dishes. It grows quickly and readily from seed, but must not be sown too early – the young seedlings are very tender and will damp off if they become wet and cold. Basil is excellent as a pot-grown herb; it will flourish on a well-lit windowsill.

Bay (*Laurus nobilis*) may eventually reach a height of 4.5 m/15 ft, but in spite of its size, and the tolerance with which it allows itself to be clipped back and trimmed into a variety of shapes, it is potentially fragile. It needs shelter from cold winds and is best grown in a large pot. Then its growth can be controlled and it can be brought indoors, or into a sheltered corner, during the worst of winter. If grown in a pot it will need very frequent watering and should be fed weekly during the growing season with a nitrogen-rich fertilizer. It is best propagated from cuttings, which root fairly readily.

Chives (*Allium schoenoprasum*), with their grass-like, mildly onion-flavoured leaves, will tolerate most conditions, but do best in semi-shade. Both the flowers and leaves may be used in salads. Chives can be grown from seed or propagated by division.

Mint comes in a number of different species. The ones most commonly grown in the garden are spearmint (*Mentha spicata*), the best known because it is used to make mint sauce, and apple mint (*M. rotundifolia*). Both are liable to become rampant and to take over the herb garden if their roots are not restrained. Plant them in a bottomless bucket or remove a paving slab from a path or patio and plant the mint there. It will be contained, handy to pick and deliciously scented if trodden on. Alternatively, it can be grown in a pot on a bright windowsill. Propagate by division – mints are difficult to grow from seed because they cross-pollinate easily and produce very variable seedlings.

Parsley (*Petroselinum crispum*), a biennial treated as an annual, is probably the most frequently used culinary herb. To be at its best it needs to be grown in deep, rich, well-dug soil. It can be grown from seed, but germination is often slow and unwilling. Wait until the soil has well warmed up before sowing outdoors. There is a theory that it helps to pour boiling water into the seed drill just before sowing.

Pot marjoram (*Origanum onites*) is used a great deal in Greek and Italian cooking. It should be planted in full sun in the most sheltered spot that can be found for it or grown in a container and brought indoors during the winter. It can be grown from seed.

Rosemary (*Rosmarinus officinalis*) is an evergreen perennial shrub that can grow to a height of 90 cm/3 ft or more. Its short, spiky leaves have a variety of culinary uses, most commonly as a flavouring for lamb and chicken. There are many attractive varieties, among them 'Benenden Blue', which has exceptionally aromatic leaves and dark blue flowers, 'Miss Jessup's Upright', which grows tall and erect, and the pink-flowered, trailing 'Majorca'. All rosemaries should be grown in sheltered corners, protected from winter winds, but in full sun. Propagation is from cuttings.

Sage (*Salvia officinalis*) is, like rosemary, an evergreen perennial. Its leaves are traditionally used in poultry stuffings. It does best in a light soil in bright sunlight. Left to itself it produces an abundance of blue, pink or white flowers and grows tall and straggly. The flowers should be pinched out to encourage leaf growth and the growing tips pinched out to encourage the plant to bush. Propagation is from cuttings.

Tarragon (*Artemisia dracunculus*) is an unimpressive-looking plant whose narrow, pale green leaves are an essential ingredient of *fines herbes*. It is a perennial that,

TAKING CUTTINGS OF SHRUBBY HERBS

1 Take a cutting of a semi-ripened shoot in summer. Neaten the end with a sharp diagonal cut. **2** Gently strip the leaves from the end. **3** Wet and dip in hormone rooting powder. **4** Fill pots with seed compost and insert the cuttings. **5** Firm them in with your fingers and water gently. **6** Cover with clear polythene and place on a warm windowsill.

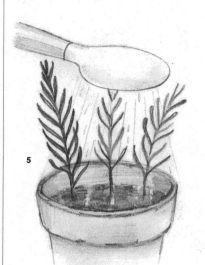

The Kitchen Garden

because it is sterile, cannot be grown from seed. The plants may be propagated by division or by cuttings taken in early summer, although these do not root readily – most commercial tarragon is grown by tissue culture.

Thyme (*Thymus vulgaris*) is a quick-spreading, strongly scented perennial whose leaves are used in stuffings for meats and vegetables. It needs frequent clipping if it is not to become straggly. It can be grown from seed, but stronger plants result from cuttings taken in early summer and planted out in late summer. It is an evergreen perennial, but normally needs to be replaced every three or four years because by then it will have become straggly in spite of conscientious trimming. There are several species of thyme, among them lemon thyme (*T. citriodorus*), which is similar in appearance to common thyme but whose leaves are strongly lemon-scented, and many varieties, of which 'Doone Valley', 'Creeping Lemon' and 'Wild Lemon' are also lemon-scented. 'Silver Posie' is a variegated thyme that is decorative as well as useful in the kitchen.

Communications **8**

One of the most striking features of modern life is the ease of communication. We talk to each other more than ever before. Even a hundred years ago it would have taken news of the most world-shattering event several days to get around the country, but now we can gossip with relatives on the other side of the globe about the most trivial of happenings.

New technologies, of which there has been a proliferation since the Second World War, do not replace old ones, they supplement them. This has created a choice of media that can, in fact, make communication more complex. For most of the time, for personal contacts between friends, this is not a problem, but there are times when formality or care is called for, and it is a good idea then to know both what method of communication is best, and what is the most appropriate style within that method. The telephone and the fax are handy for many messages and conversations, but there are times when they cannot replace pen and ink. Moreover, there are times when the best method might not necessarily be the most efficient. If you are wanting to make a business contact with a busy person who does not know you, it may seem that all you need to do is to pick up the phone. However, this may only result in your leaving a frustrating series of unanswered messages. In that case a letter would have got through much faster, and made your point succinctly and effectively.

The novelist and university teacher, E.M. Forster, summed up his advice to writers in the two words 'only connect'. Connections are also the key to both a successful business life and a happy social one. The benefits of following that advice are there for anyone with the confidence gained from knowing their way around modern communications media, and with the skills to use them to best advantage.

Writing Letters

There was a time in recent years when letter writing was predicted to become obsolete as the technology of telecommunications became more sophisticated. On the contrary, it is just as important as ever to be able to express yourself in writing whether through a letter sent by post or by fax. Word processors make it easy to keep copies of everything without cluttering up a filing cabinet, and as so much communication is done on the telephone, personal messages sent by letter are appreciated much more by friends and relations.

STARTING AND FINISHING

If a letter is to do its job properly, it must catch the reader's attention at first glance and give the impression that what you have to say will be worth reading. Your letter does not have to be a literary gem, but it should look neat to inspire confidence.

Use plain, unlined writing paper. White or cream is preferable for business letters, especially if typed. Pale blue can also be used for personal letters as it is easy on the eye. Personal letters are best handwritten in ink; typed personal letters used to be frowned on but are now more acceptable, and if your writing is difficult to read you will be doing everyone a favour. Typewritten letters should be single-spaced, but a very short letter looks better double spaced. Always keep copies of business letters, either as carbon copies or saved in your word processor.

If you know the person to whom you are writing well, whether the letter is for business or is personal, you can use the first name. However, a business letter should always have the full name and address typed in above the opening greeting as well (see below). If you don't know the person very well you should always start the letter 'Dear Mr (or Mrs, Miss or Ms) Lee'. Use 'Miss' or 'Mrs' if you know for sure the marital status of a female correspondent, otherwise use 'Ms'. Normally you should not start 'Dear Shelley Jones' if you know the sex of your correspondent, but if the name could be male or female and you do not know which, this form is acceptable.

If you do not know the name of the person to whom the letter is addressed (that is, it is simply to a company or manager) then always start it 'Dear Sir' or 'Dear Sir or Madam'. If the letter is a circular, for instance to club members or office workers, you can start it 'Dear Member' or 'Dear Colleague'.

Informal letters to close family and friends can be ended how you like – 'love from', 'best wishes', 'with our love', 'yours' or 'yours ever'. For more formal letters, when you have a name in the opening greeting, the ending is 'Yours sincerely', and 'Yours faithfully' for a letter beginning 'Dear Sir'.

SETTING OUT LETTERS

Personal letters usually have the address written at the top right-hand side of the sheet, with the date underneath or sometimes at the top left hand corner. Paragraphs can be indented or blocked as you prefer.

If you do not have headed writing paper with the address printed on it, business letters should always have your address typed in either centred across the top of the paper or on the top right-hand side. The name and address of the correspondent should be typed in on the left-hand side above the 'Dear . . .'. The usual style is single spacing, with paragraphs blocked without indents at the beginning, and with a line space between each paragraph. If you think you will not have enough space to sign off without going on to another sheet always make sure you have at least two lines of the final paragraph to take over to the next page. It is important to have enough space to sign the letter clearly and type your name and title (Mr, Mrs, Miss etc) under your signature. You can either centre the 'Yours sincerely' and your name or align them with the left-hand margin of the letter.

SCREW AND BRACKETT
157 Commercial Road Nailham Leeds LG4 7JE

Your ref . . .

12 September 19—

Mr Nicholas Nailer
Manager
Put-It-Up DIY Ltd
Ditchum Trading Estate
Sailbury
Essex
ES5 9TD

Dear Mr Nailer

Order number . . .

Thank you very much for your order, which will be dispatched promptly. I am sure you will find that the goods live up to our usual high standard.

I enclose a copy of our new catalogue for your information. I would like to draw your attention to the new range of kitchen shelving, which I think will be of special interest to you.

If you need any further details, please do not hesitate to contact me.

Yours sincerely

Derek D. Driller
Sales Director

Enc.

ADDRESSING ENVELOPES

Envelopes can be addressed to the full name or initial and surname of the correspondent. You can either put 'Mr Harold Snodgrass', 'Mr H. Snodgrass' or H. Snodgrass Esq., although Esq. is becoming much less common today. Some people address married women with the initial of their husbands – 'Mrs H. Snodgrass', but nowadays women are more often addressed in their own names – 'Mrs Maureen Snodgrass' or 'Mrs M. Snodgrass'. If you are writing jointly to a married couple, use the husband's initial – 'Mr and Mrs H. Snodgrass'. For women who are unmarried or whose marital status is unclear use 'Miss' or 'Ms' depending on what you have used in the letter itself.

If you are writing to a firm but you don't know which department, simply put the name by itself; otherwise address it to 'The Accounts Department', 'The Sales Director', 'The Personnel Manager' or whatever is appropriate.

The address is clearer if it is blocked, and lined up to the left-hand margin. However, sometimes handwritten letters may be easier to read if each line is staggered. Always include the post code as the last item of the address, unless the letter is going abroad, in which case the country of destination should be put last, in capital letters:

Mr Nick Nailer		Mr and Mrs H. Snodgrass
General Manager		27 rue Beaumarchais
Put-It-Up DIY Ltd	or	Beauregard-sur-Mer
Ditchum Trading Estate		Normandy 08975
Sailbury		FRANCE
Essex ES5 9TD		

PERSONAL CORRESPONDENCE

The golden rule for personal letters, whether thank-yous, congratulations, apologies or condolences, is that they should be sincere. Remember that letters are more permanent than telephone calls and can cause offence if dashed off without thought. A useful tip is to put yourself in the shoes of the recipient and imagine how you would feel receiving the letter you have written. You should always write and thank friends for presents sent to you or your children (if they are not old enough to write themselves they should be encouraged to as soon as they are able to write a few simple lines) and for overnight hospitality. It is not necessary always to write after lunch or dinner parties to which have been invited, but it would be much appreciated by your hosts, especially if you have had a particularly nice time or they have gone to a lot of trouble.

Letters of sympathy and condolence can be the most difficult of all to write, but they can also be very important in supporting and comforting someone who is suffering. Never hang back because you feel there is nothing useful to be said; you are letting people know you care about them, which can be extremely supportive in itself. Again, sincerity is all, so avoid clichés like 'sad demise', 'beloved wife' and 'happy release'.

Thanking an acquaintance for a wedding present

Dear Mr and Mrs Murgatroyd,

Ann and I were delighted with such a useful and practical wedding gift. In my bachelor flat the smell of burnt toast was a regular morning feature and now that will be a thing of the past!

Thank you very much for thinking of us on our special day.

Yours,
Nicholas Chan

Thanking a relative for money

Dear Uncle Cyril,

Thank you so much for the cheque; it really was very generous of you. I shall have lots of fun deciding how to spend it. At the moment I'm torn between a personal stereo or a new programme for my computer.

Believe it or not, I'm working quite hard at the moment, with the exams coming in a few weeks' time, so I will write a more newsy letter once they are over and look forward to seeing you in the holidays.

Love,
Darren

Thanking friends for a weekend's hospitality

Dear Ben and Beatrice,

Thank you so much for a really happy weekend. It was lovely to escape from the city and relax with you in such a lovely setting. We do appreciate the trouble you took to make us comfortable and feed us splendidly. It was good to see the children again and we specially enjoyed the Sunday ramble through the woods with them.

We shall look forward to your weekend with us in the summer and hope that we can make it as enjoyable as our stay with you.

Love,
Ed and Eileen

Apologizing to a neighbour

Dear Mr Household,

I must apologize for the behaviour of my son and his friends. I know how much time and trouble you take over the plants in your greenhouse and appreciate how infuriating it was when a carelessly kicked football crashed through the glass.

Believe me, I shall do my best to see that nothing like this ever happens again. In the meantime, please send me the bill for replacing the glass and for any plants that have been damaged.

Yours sincerely
Norman Nipper

Congratulating a friend on an engagement

Dear Fay,

I was very excited to hear your news. Congratulations to you both. I thought from the very beginning that this was something special and I'm chuffed to be proved right.

I think you'll make a terrific couple and I wish you lots and lots of happiness. I'll look forward to hearing all your wedding plans.

Love,
Jackie

Sending congratulations on a silver wedding

Dear Dick and Jean,

We had to write to wish you happiness on your silver wedding anniversary and send you many congratulations.

Twenty-five years is quite a score and it's hard to believe so much time has passed since that beautiful summer day when you married. We thought then that you would make a splendid couple and the years have proved us right.

Have a wonderful day.

Love,
Sylvia and Sam

Writing to a wife
whose husband is terminally ill

Dear June,

We have only just heard about Don's illness and it came as a terrible shock. The last time we met he seemed so fit and well.

You must be having a very hard time at the moment and we should like to help if possible. Please tell us if there is anything we can do.

Love,
Al and Annie

Responding to a letter of sympathy

Dear Jim and Jean,

I did appreciate your sympathetic letter. I told Gillian that I had heard from you and she sends her love. Some days she is quite alert and interested in what is going on around her, then other days she sleeps all the time.

It's kind of you to offer to help but at the moment we are coping reasonably well and the neighbours have been marvellous. However, if we do need a hand later on, I will certainly let you know.

Love
Arthur

Sending sympathy to a friend
on the death of his wife

Dear James,

I was so sorry to hear of Muriel's sudden death. It must have come as a terrible shock to you and we do feel for you at such a sad time. We shall always remember Muriel as a kind, loving person and the sort of friend you could always count on in a crisis. We shall miss her badly.

If there is anything we can do, or you feel like talking to someone, please give us a call.

Love,
Joan and Arthur

Replying to a friend's
letter of condolence

Dear Joan and Arthur

Thank you very much for your letter and your kind words. There's no way I can tell you how I feel about losing Muriel but it is a great comfort to know how many good friends she had. Letters and cards have been pouring in and I am really touched by the warmth of feeling in them.

Love,
James

Formal expression of condolence
from an acquaintance

Dear Anne,

I was very sorry to read in the paper of Tony's death and I am writing on behalf of all the members of the snooker team to express our deep sympathy.

I assure you that our thoughts are with you in this trying time.

Yours sincerely,
Percy Jones

Formal reply to a letter of condolence

Dear Mr Jones,

Thank you very much for your kind letter and expression of sympathy. It helps to know how many friends Tony had made through his work. He will be missed by so many people.

Yours sincerely,
Anne Soper

PRACTICAL MATTERS

Letters on practical matters need to be short and direct. The reader should be able to absorb them quickly and easily, maximizing the chances of your getting what you want. If you are booking or confirming an arrangement in writing, make sure you list all your requirements so that there is no doubt in the mind of the recipient what you want or what you are confirming. They will then be able to come back with any queries, and if there is a problem later you will have something in writing.

Booking a hotel

Dear Sir

I should like to book a double room for my wife and myself for seven nights from 9 September to 15 September inclusive. We would require a room with twin beds and sea view. Please let me know the price per person for dinner, bed and breakfast for this period.

Perhaps you could also let me know the names of any water sports firms in the area who could give tuition in wind surfing and water-skiing.

Your faithfully
Toby Trott

Writing to a tenant about overdue rent

Dear Mrs Felix

I write to remind you that the half yearly rent on 12 Rundle Road, payable on 1 March, is now overdue. No doubt this is due to an oversight on your part and I shall be pleased to receive your cheque as soon as possible.

Yours sincerely
Gary Grout

Proposing a new club member

Dear Mr Bunker

I wish to propose Mr Michael Brown for membership of Nobs Golf Club. Mrs Barbara Birdie seconds the nomination. We both know Mr Brown as a keen golfer who has recently moved into the area and will be a real asset to the club.

Yours sincerely
Peter Parr

Writing to a head teacher about bullying

Dear Mr Jolly,

Three times this week my son Patrick, who is in form 2A, has come home very hungry because his lunch money was extorted from him by older boys, with threats of beatings.

There seem to be several fourth years who regularly lie in wait for the younger boys at the side of the building, near the science laboratories, and force them to hand over their cash. I have talked to two of Patrick's friends and they tell the same story.

I am sure that you are as concerned as I am to have this behaviour stopped and that you will take the necessary measures to see that younger boys are no longer terrorized by these bullies.

Yours sincerely,
Pauline Pepper

Requesting an estimate for home improvements

Dear Sir

I would be grateful if you could give me an estimate for re-fitting a bathroom, including wall tiling, new bathroom suite and installation of an electric shower. I attach a list of fixtures and fittings to be included in the work.

Would it be possible for your representative to call on a weekday evening or a Saturday to assess the job in detail? Perhaps you could also give me a possible starting date. I would need the work completed some time within the next two months.

Yours faithfully
Horace Household

8

Communications

COMPLAINTS

If a letter of complaint is to be effective it must be calm, clear and firm. Even if you are furious at the treatment you have received your letter needs to be crisp and concise, and will be taken more seriously if it is. However justified your complaint, you will undermine your case if you are abusive or hysterical.

State your grievances clearly, giving any relevant dates, prices and names. State plainly what you are asking for: an apology, a refund, a replacement, compensation for loss or inconvenience, or action to ensure better standards in future. It is worth calling the organization concerned to find the name and department of the person who will be dealing with your complaint and address it directly. Always keep a copy of your letter, and if necessary send it recorded delivery to provide proof of receipt.

Letters of complaint are more businesslike if typed. If handwritten make sure the letter is clearly set out and legible. Be prepared to persist if you don't get results immediately, and threaten legal action if you get no reply after a specified time.

Claiming for faulty goods

Dear Mr Flack

On 13 October I bought a Super-Duper Iron, Model No . . . from your shop. Two days later I used it for the first time to press my daughter's dress. Though I used the lowest setting, it left a large scorch mark.

When I returned the iron on 17 October I spoke to your Mr Philpott. He tested it, decided that the temperature control was faulty and offered me a replacement. I felt that, in the circumstances, I must claim recompense for the ruined dress, which had only been worn once. Mr Philpott told me that I should approach you about this on your return from holiday.

The dress cost £30 when I bought it eight weeks ago and I consider that £20 would be a reasonable amout of compensation.

Yours sincerely
M. L. Shopper (Mrs)

Complaint to the council about rubbish collection

Dear Sirs

I wish to draw your attention to the deteriorating standard of rubbish collection in the district.

My dustbin has remained unemptied for three weeks out of the last six. Neighbours tell me that they have experienced the same problem. Sometimes the dustmen ignore two or three houses in a row, sometimes a single house is missed. Every visit by the dustmen means a trail of rubbish strewn over gardens and down the roadway. Bin lids are thrown carelessly on the ground to blow about in the wind.

Please let me know what action you propose to take to improve this service.

Yours faithfully
Arthur Houseman

HOME FINANCE

Brevity and clarity are essential for any letters dealing with financial matters. Keep your statements factual and make sure you leave no room for misunderstanding. Make a check list of all relevant facts, and quote your account number when corresponding with your bank, building society, insurance company, etc. If you have to send documents with the letter, get them photocopied and keep the originals.

If you get into difficulties over finance it is important to write promptly to your creditors, explaining the situation and asking for time to pay. Creditors will look more favourably on your problem if you let them know rather than simply letting things slide until the situation is desperate.

Requesting an overdraft

Dear Mr Thrift

Account number . . .

I have recently set up my own business as a management consultant and this has made my cash flow position difficult, on a purely temporary basis.

Would it be possible to arrange overdraft facilities for me up to a limit of £ . . . per month? I will probably need this facility for 12 months.

Please let me know whether there is a fee for this service and how much interest will be charged.

Yours sincerely
Toby Trott

Adding to all risks insurance

Dear Sir

Policy number . . .

Please add the following item to the specified items covered by my all risks policy:

1 XYZ computer, value £1,700

I attach a copy of the sales receipt. Please let me know if any additional premium is payable.

Yours faithfully
Christopher Crisp

Enc.

Notifying lenders about problems in keeping up payments

Dear Sir

Mortgage account number . . .

I am having great difficulty in meeting my mortgage payments at the moment. I have been out of work for the past four months, since the closure of Reckless and Quick Ltd.

If possible, I would like to arrange to pay interest only on my mortgage for a short period, say six months, in which time I hope to resolve my present difficulties.

As you know, new industries are moving into the area and should be recruiting in the autumn, so I have high hopes of new employment at that time.

Yours faithfully
Lawrence Luckless

Querying a telephone bill with telephone company

Dear Sir

Your ref . . .

I have received my telephone bill dated 3 July and find the amount of £130 inexplicably high.

The charges for previous quarters have been steady at between £60 and £75. During the latest quarter only my wife and I have had access to the telephone. We have made no more calls than usual and were away on holiday for three weeks during this period.

I would be grateful if you could check your records for possible mistakes and let me know the result.

Yours faithfully
Albert Anxious

Communications

It is worth taking trouble over a letter of application. This is the first contact you will have with a potential employer, and if he is unimpressed you may never have the chance to put yourself across in an interview. Care should be taken to set the letter out presentably and you should use good quality paper. Type your letter for clarity, unless the employer has specified handwritten letters of application, but even then if you are asked to provide a CV (Curriculum Vitae) this should be typed.

Curriculum vitae for a job as retail sales manager

CURRICULUM VITAE
DAVID DOE
The Falcons, Manor Road, Carberry CV4 9LS

Telephone: 456 6789 (home); 234 5678 (business)

Date of birth: 22 June 19—

EXPERIENCE
March 19— to date
Branch manager, Toogood Stores, Carberry High Street, Carberry
Responsible for the profitable operation of a 745 square metre retail shop and the recruitment, training and supervision of an assistant manager and 20 sales assistants.

January 19— to March 19—
Assistant manager, Toogood Stores, Portsend
Responsible to manager for day-to-day running of a 835 square metre retail shop, including performance of sales staff.

October 19— to January 19—
Departmental manager, lingerie department, Toogood Stores, Oxford Street, London

May 19— to October 19—
Section manager, beauty department, Toogood Stores, Oxford Street, London

January 19— to May 19—
Junior management trainee, Toogood Stores, Oxford Street, London
Job rotation training including distribution, dispatch, personnel and accounts as well as work on the shop floor.

September 19— to January 19—
Sales assistant, Toogood Stores, Oxford Street, London

EDUCATION
September 19— to July 19—
David Dalrymple Comprehensive School, Roundabout, London SW10

June 19— 4 GCE 'O' Levels:
English Language, English Literature, Mathematics, Home Economics

Your letter should be long enough to mention the main points of your suitability for the particular job on offer and no more. Compose it in rough form first, then copy it out neatly. Make sure that you do everything the advertisement asks. If it says 'state age', then do so even if you would rather conceal it. If you are asked to 'state salary required', use your best estimate, even though you would rather hear what they are offering first. Many firms discard letters that do not give all the facts requested.

You do not have to give your reasons for leaving your present job but if you do, never openly criticise your employer. The prospective employer will be looking for loyalty, and anyway may call upon your present employer for a reference. Refer instead to the extra scope and wider horizons offered by the new post.

Application for a job as a trainee VDU operator

Dear Sir

Trainee VDU operator

I wish to apply for the job advertised in today's Portsend Post.

I am 18 years old and have 'O' levels in English and Maths and CSEs in Technical Drawing, Computer Studies, Geography and Biology.

On leaving Alderman Carter Comprehensive in July 1988, I spent six months as a counter-hand at Henry's Hearty Hamburgers and since then I have been employed as an office junior with Bodge and Blowitt, Building Contractors.

Though this has given me a useful training in the basic working of a busy office, I am keen to find an opportunity to learn about computers.

I should be pleased to attend an interview at any time.

Yours faithfully
Holly Hopeful

Applying for a job as retail sales manager

Dear Mr Pushitt

Retail sales manager

I would like to apply for the position advertised in the Carberry Courier on 17 April.

As you will see from the enclosed curriculum vitae, I have worked for Toogood Stores for 12 years, progressing from sales assistant to branch manager. I now manage the Carberry High Street branch where I am responsible for recruiting and supervising 21 members of staff.

The store was acquired in the merger between Toogood Stores and Homeshops and when I took over as manager in 19—, my brief was to reorganize and revive a flagging business. Within the first year the volume of sales increased by 60 per cent and in the two years since my appointment has risen by 90 per cent.

At the moment I am looking for an opportunity to take on a new challenge, such as the post you advertise.

Yours sincerely
David Doe

Providing a reference for a school leaver

Dear Mr Pullon

Tracey Tripp has attended Canon Carr Comprehensive from September 1985 to July 1990 and during that time she has always been hardworking and determined to succeed in anything she attempted. Her attendance record is good and she has a pleasant personality.

In her year as a prefect she has shown that she is able to take responsibility and cope with situations on her own initiative.

Yours sincerely
Reginald Rule
Deputy Head Teacher

Accepting a job offer

Dear Mr Pushitt

Thank you for your letter dated 20 September.

I am very pleased to accept your offer of a post as secretary to the works manager. I have signed the contract of employment, which I return with this letter.

I look forward to working for you and shall be pleased to report to the Personnel Department at 9 am on 30 September.

Yours sincerely
Prunella Prim

Never try to put your full work history in a letter; instead put this in a separate CV. It should contain basic information such as your name, address, age, home and work telephone numbers, date of birth, educational and other qualifications. List your present job first and work backwards. Give a clear idea of what it involves, including your responsibilities, the field covered, and people who report to you.

Letters accepting or refusing a job offered, or resigning from a job, follow a particular pattern, but if you are asked to write a reference it is a bit more tricky. The convention is to be as encouraging as possible about former pupils or employees but never deliberately misleading. Employers are adept at reading between the lines. They know that someone described as 'accurate and trustworthy' may be a plodder, while 'capable of flashes of brilliance' means a clever but unreliable person.

Resigning after the offer of a new job

Dear Mr Murgatroyd

I have accepted a position as works foreman with Box and Cox Ltd and must therefore give four weeks' notice of my intention to leave the company on February 28.

As you will understand, this post is an important career step for me and I am looking forward to tackling new responsibilities.

However, I shall be sorry to leave Bell and Clapper. My three years here have been very happy and I am sure that the experience I have gained will stand me in good stead in the future.

Yours sincerely
Brian Bush

Requesting a salary review

Dear Mr Frost

As you know, over the past 12 months I have taken on additional responsibilities within the department but this has not been reflected in my salary.

I would be grateful if you would consider reviewing my salary to take account of the extra work now involved in my job.

Yours sincerely
Sue Gubbins

Telecommunications

What is hailed as a great technological breakthrough by one generation becomes accepted as a part of life by the next. Thus young people take faxes, modems and car phones for granted, while for many of their elders it still seems remarkable that you can talk to anywhere in the world from a car on Exmoor, or send documents instantaneously to Hong Kong from a flat in Manchester.

One of the advantages of the information revolution of recent years is that it is easier than ever before to run a business from home. You do not need to transport yourself to attend a meeting, show someone a sketch, or discuss the terms of a contract, but can do this without leaving your desk at home. We may not yet have the situation predicted where working from home is the norm – and indeed it may never come, as many people prefer to work with lots of others around them – but in many occupations it is already an option for those who want it.

But information technology is not just relevant to those who wish to run a business from home, as the communications systems appropriate to the office are also suitable for personal use. There has been a blurring of the lines between work machines and domestic machines. The personal computer that is capable of acting as a sophisticated word processor or can handle accounting spreadsheets may have been bought primarily to play games or for writing letters. All that is needed to change function is the right software. Answering machines can be bought very cheaply in a variety of high street shops. The humble telephone with a fixed ring and no other function is a thing of the past, and even cheap domestic models have memories that enable you to store commonly used numbers and dial them at a touch of a single button.

COST

The array of equipment available is itself bewildering. Just going to buy a telephone can be like diving into an Arab bazaar, and it is easy to be seduced by functions that you do not need but which sound glamorous. For example, is it necessary to have an answering machine that will enable you to phone in and take messages off it from an outside number? Do you need a model that can record an hour's conversation when the most you are likely to get is three or four brief messages on days you go out for lunch?

On the other hand, if you are running a business, it is worth getting the extra functions if you suspect they might be useful. Spending the extra pounds on the polling off facility on the answering machine (a device whereby you can ring into your own telephone and listen to your messages) could prove an excellent investment on the day you are called out unexpectedly but are awaiting an important phone call that you need to respond to at once. Likewise, where you have a lot of people you have to ring regularly, it can save many hours over a year in not having to look up their numbers all the time. It is worth bearing in mind that capital expenses are tax deductible for businesses and, if you have a healthy profit one year, buying useful equipment is a good and perfectly legitimate way of simultaneously investing for the future and reducing your tax liability.

With a fax you have to consider not only the cost of the machine, but the cost of the telephone line. Undoubtedly the most efficient way of running a fax is to have a separate line for it. You can then leave it to receive messages 24 hours a day without your having to adjust it. But the cost of having a line installed is high, and you then have to pay rental. The fax can be plugged into the same socket as your telephone, but you may have to switch it on every time you send or receive a message. To avoid this, buy a smart machine that incorporates a telephone and automatically decodes the incoming message to decide whether to receive it through the fax or the phone.

PERSONAL COMPUTERS

If it is easy to spend far more than you need on the humble telephone, the problem becomes much more acute when buying a personal computer. The range varies from a few hundred pounds to several thousand, the differences being determined by the complexity of the operations the machine is able to take on and its speed of operation.

While a computer has many uses, in this context it can be seen as a tool of communication. As a word processor this is obvious, and the machine is a boon for both skilled typists, who can exploit its speed, and for two-finger operators, who can correct all their mistakes. But the computer communicates by other ways: by copying material on to floppy disks to give to other users, and by direct exchange of information down telephone lines by means of a device known as a modem.

For the business user compatibility is an important factor in both respects. If you are likely to do either then you should get a model that is compatible with the type that is most widely used in your sort of business. Fortunately, this is not the problem that it was a few years ago as industry standards have now emerged. Most computers are 'IBM compatible', which means they can use the same software as IBM computers, the market leaders, and floppy disks can be swapped between the machines. Now even Apple and IBM, which were once deadliest of foes, are working closely together and it is much easier to transfer information between machines.

If you have clients who work on machines compatible with yours you can send each other documents through a modem so they are never printed out at all. Computer enthusiasts also use them to dial into what are known as bulletin boards where you can deposit messages for other computer users. Users have been known to conduct relationships with people for years whom they have never seen, spoken to or sent a letter to.

An important element that is often overlooked is the cost of a printer. Most computers are sold without them, which is a bit like getting a car without wheels. A printer, too, can be a very expensive item, costing as much as a small personal computer. So when you see a machine advertised for £500, bear in mind that you may be paying as much again for the means of getting your work out of it in a readable form. The rule with printers is that you get what you pay for. Laser printers give high-quality results and can print large quantities cheaply, quickly and silently. They are also expensive. Bubble-jet printers are much cheaper and also give good finished results, but they are slow and their working life is short. Daisy wheel printers print from moulded letter forms in principle rather like a typewriter, but are not flexible and are noisy. As a result they are now on the way out. Also less common than previously are dot matrix printers, which print letters out of a series of tiny dots. They are cheap, but slow and do not give printed-quality results. For business users, the best advice is to buy as good a printer as you can afford – it will certainly prove cheaper in the long run and will help present a good image.

CLOSING THE DOOR ON IT

The home office can be a great boon, and many people who work from home regard it as a definite improvement in their lifestyles. But you still need to get out and see people every so often. It is also vital to be able to turn your back on it. The office should have a door that you can close, so that you do not find that instead of having an office at home, you have turned your entire home into an office.

Money 9

Whatever stage of life you are at, managing your money efficiently can bring peace of mind and improve your lifestyle.

In the first instance it means doing a little homework – finding out where your income is going and where you might be able to make some savings. This may seem like a chore but it will repay you with handsome bonuses.

For most families, coping with ever-rising prices is a constant battle. Even when everyday expenses are under control, unexpected bills can send finances haywire.

Utility bills go up with heart-stopping regularity and all too often drop on to the doormat at just the moment when you are having to dig into your savings to pay for a major repair or replacement. Do you cut back on the insurance or the family holiday? Or is there another way out?

Paying by credit card or some other credit deal is one way of spreading the cost. 'Buy now, pay later' is one of the most seductive phrases ever devised.

While it can make good sense to use credit for some transactions, taking on too much can add up to a load of trouble. Even the most careful borrower can run into difficulties when interest rates rise or when income suddenly drops because of redundancy, the break-up of a marriage or some other unforeseen event.

Taking stock of your finances means planning for major events and allowing for emergencies. You might not be able to cover every contingency but you can iron out many difficulties if you are able to save regularly, make sure you have enough insurance cover, and have made full provision for retirement.

Insurance can seem like an expense you can do without – until you need it. Even if you are lucky enough never to make a claim – and you would be in a tiny minority – you will still have bought yourself peace of mind.

You cannot just fill in the annual tax return and put the subject out of your mind. If you don't know what allowances and relief you can be getting you may be robbing

241

yourself. Before you put your money into any savings or investment you should study the tax implications: some will be better for you than others.

For people of all ages, the great fear is debt. When you hit troubled times you may be tempted to put the bills behind the clock on the mantelpiece and hope that in some magical way the problem will sort itself out. It will not. The sooner you tell the people to whom you owe money about your problems the easier it will be to work out a solution.

Budgeting

It often takes a crisis to make us sit down and work out where the money is going and where economies can be made. But even if you have no money worries at the moment, it pays to check out your spending to see whether you could be doing better than you are.

First, you need to find out exactly what money is coming in and where it is going. If the idea of sitting down and drawing up columns of income and expenditure does not appeal, perhaps the thought that you might be able to save money without making any real sacrifices might make it seem more attractive. You may be able to save a significant sum, for instance, by buying in the sales and asking for a discount wherever possible.

Even the way you pay your bills can save – or lose – you money. It is easy to get into the habit of paying annual bills, such as those for insurance, automatically, without shopping round to see if you could get a better deal elsewhere.

GETTING ORGANIZED

If you do not already have a filing system, invest in three or four new or second-hand box-type filing cases, some files to go in them, clip-on label holders and a strip of labels. A cardboard concertina-type filing case is cheaper and will do as well provided it is going to be strong enough to hold all the papers you will be putting in. If you are really strapped for cash use large old envelopes and label them.

You might need files for: bank, car, credit cards, electricity, gas, guarantees, holidays, the community charge/council tax, home maintenance, insurance, investments, loans (HP payments, overdrafts and so on), mortgage, pension, receipts (for items that you may have to return if they go wrong), salary, savings, store accounts, tax, telephone, TV and/or video, and water rates. You may also need files for the garden, maintenance payments, pets, private health insurance, school fees, subscriptions (clubs, magazines, trade unions, etc). It is useful to have a miscellaneous file in which you can keep bits of information that you may need to get hold of quickly, such as your NHS or national insurance numbers.

Make a note of the serial numbers of valuables such as a camcorder, video or hi-fi, the chassis number of your car and your car key number . . . just in case. Keep them in a suitable file, such as that for 'insurance'.

Once the filing system is set up, put all bills and any letters referring to them in their appropriate files as soon as you have dealt with them. Keep useful telephone or reference numbers – including credit card numbers – in their file.

Make it a habit to check every item on a bill or bank or credit statement before it is filed. Mistakes can happen, or you might even be the victim of fraud. It is not unknown for additional items to find their way on to credit-card bills where the amount in the total column was not written in on the original.

While your filing system will help you monitor the major bills, they are only part of the picture. You also need to check out everyday spending on items such as food, fares and shoe repairs.

To find out where the day-to-day money goes, keep a tally of everything you spend over a four-week period at a time of year when spending is fairly typical – not at Christmas or holiday time. Have a notebook handy and put down every single item, no matter how small. Do not forget to include things you pay for by cheque or credit card.

With the major bills in the files and the day-to-day spending diary you should now have a complete picture of where the money is going.

To check the overall position draw up a simple balance sheet. Head one column Income and the other Expenses. Under Income write down all the money you received during the month in which you kept your spending diary. Include all earnings, extras such as tips or overtime payments, pensions, state allowances or building society income.

If you receive any other income during the year – such as investments that pay twice yearly – add those figures up, divide by 12 and include the sum in your Income column.

Under Expenses put down your total everyday spending for the month. From the bills in your files for electricity, gas, water, telephone, mortgage, community charge/council tax, car, insurance, loans, etc. work out how much each bill is costing you per month. You will get a more accurate figure if you have bills for a year which take account of the effects of the weather. Add them up and divide by 12.

Add on a suitable amount to cover occasional but heavy expenses such as Christmas, weddings, holidays, repairs to or replacement of domestic appliances, furniture, school uniforms or a new winter coat or suit. Work out how much these add up to over a year and divide by 12.

When you are sure you have included everything, add up the two totals.

You can now see whether you are managing your budget well or overspending. More importantly, you can see which items are the biggest drain on your income.

Keep in mind that inflation will push up next year's bills (and that you may not get an equivalent pay rise), and that you need savings for emergencies.

PAYING THE BILLS

If your regular bills tend to arrive at the same time, try to spread them out. Some organizations will let you choose a payment date that suits you.

Because the big bills can be a shock it is tempting to look at ways of spreading the cost by making regular payments towards them. Many people, especially the elderly who prefer to work on a monthly budget, find this provides peace of mind. It not only takes the edge off the bills but also means there is less chance of being cut off for nonpayment.

It's a good idea to pay the community charge/council tax and water rates this way, as otherwise you would pay out large sums in advance. For other bills you could be making better use of your money if you work out what you are likely to need to pay out in bills in the coming year (allowing for inflation), divide the total by 12 and transfer this amount each month into a special savings account that pays you interest. Then pay the bills from this account.

However, if you would still feel happier spreading the cost, there are various budget schemes run by banks, gas and electricity companies, etc. that can help.

> *Start budget account payments for fuel bills in the autumn and you will get what is in effect an interest-free loan during the winter months when you use most fuel.*

If your gas or electricity bill seems too high it could be because: there has been a price rise; it is an estimate; you have used more energy than you realized; you have recently bought a new appliance that uses more energy; you have had someone ill at home or visitors to stay and used more heating; the weather was unusually cold; your meter is faulty.

Before challenging an estimated bill, find out whether the price is about to go up. If it is you might be better off paying the inflated estimate at the lower price.

> *If you do not use a lot of water but your water rates are high, consider installing a meter. Most households are assessed for water rates on the value of the property. So someone living in a large house pays more than someone living in a smaller property regardless of how much water is used.*

PROBLEMS

If you have difficulty in paying the bill, communicate. The sooner the people you owe money to know you are in difficulty the easier it will be to come to some sort of arrangement to pay off the bill.

The gas and electricity industries both have a code of practice for domestic customers which now forms part of their licences. Under this you cannot be cut off if you agree to keep to a payment arrangement and pay off the debt by instalments within a reasonable period. The arrangement takes account of your circumstances and income. You can make an offer or the amount may be decided for you.

MAKING SAVINGS

The next step is to work out your priorities and see where savings might be made. Outgoings such as the mortgage or rent or the council tax have top priority and must be paid if you are to keep a roof over your head and the bailiffs out.

THE EFFECT OF INSULATION AND HEATING IMPROVEMENTS

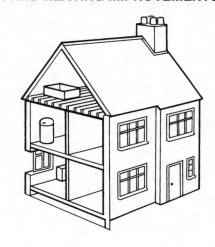

HOUSE A: UNINSULATED
No insulation
Boiler more than 10 years old
Time switch
No draught-proofing and single
glazing only

Total annual heating cost £497

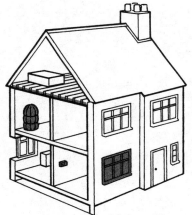

HOUSE B: TYPICAL
As house A except:
50 mm/2 in loft insulation
25 mm/1 in hot water cylinder
insulation
25% double glazing
Room thermostat

Total annual heating cost £426

HOUSE C: DESIRABLE
As house B except:
150 mm/6 in loft insulation
80 mm/3 in hot water cylinder
insulation and thermostat
100% double glazing
Condensing boiler
Thermostatic radiator valves
Wall insulation
Full draught-proofing
Floor insulation

Total annual heating cost £150

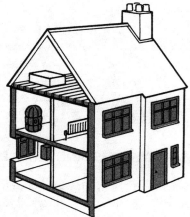

Note: These figures are based on an average semi-detached house with a total floor area of
80 sq m/870 sq ft with three occupants and whole house heating morning and evening to
achieve 21°C/70°F in the living room (1991 figures). Energy costs are for space heating and hot
water, based on a gas cost of 45.9 p/therm; the standing charge is not included.

Next look at the big utility bills – gas, electricity, water and telephone. Here you may be able to make significant savings.

* Put in as much insulation as you can possibly manage. Fit six inches of loft insulation.
* Insulate hot water pipes.
* Up to half the heat loss in a house can go through the walls. Effective cavity wall insulation can reduce this loss by up to two-thirds. Solid walls can also be insulated.
* Single-glazed windows can account for around 20% of the total heat loss from an uninsulated house. Double glazing can halve this loss.

Get *full* quotes from three or four contractors before going ahead. Choose a company that is a member of the Glass and Glazing Federation, which has a code of practice that should ensure that the work is done to industry-agreed standards. It is considerably cheaper to fit double or secondary glazing yourself, although you need to be an experienced DIY worker.

> *A recent development called low-emissivity glass can improve the effectiveness of any double glazing that you install still further. The glass goes on the inside of the outer pane and reflects heat into the room, reducing heat loss.*

Depending on how draughty your home is, draught-proofing can save up to 10% on your fuel bill. But make sure there is sufficient ventilation for air to circulate where there is a fuel-burning appliance in the room so that it can operate safely and efficiently. Putting insulation such as mineral wool mat or expanded polystyrene boards between the joists under the floorboards can save between £10–£25 a year on your fuel bill.

> *Low-income households may be eligible for a grant from their local authority towards the cost of draught proofing, loft, tank and pipe insulation, and sometimes other measures as well, such as cavity wall insulation.*
>
> *Grants are also available to low-income households for draught-proofing and for loft, tank and pipe insulation under the Department of the Environment's Home Energy Efficiency Scheme (HEES). For information about HEES contact: Energy Action Grants Agency, PO Box ING, Newcastle upon Tyne, NE99 1NG. Freephone 0800 181 667.*

HEATING SYSTEMS AND CONTROLS

If your fuel bills are sending your temperature soaring, it is time to take stock of your present heating system and controls. An old-fashioned, oversized central heating boiler is inefficient and could be wasting your money.

If you do not want to go the whole hog and replace the boiler yet, you may be able to make savings by putting in more efficient central heating controls, including a modern time-switch or programmer, a room thermostat and/or thermostatic radiator valves and a hot-water cylinder thermostat.

THREE WAYS TO HELP CUT YOUR HEATING COSTS

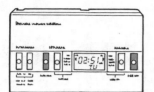

Room thermostat
This keeps the temperature of your home at the level you choose, turning the heat on and off automatically.

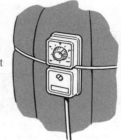

Programmer
A time switch that turns the heating and hot water on and off at times you set.

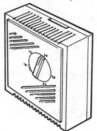

Hot water cylinder thermostat
A clamp-on thermostat helps you run your hot water system more economically.

HOT WATER

The biggest saving you can make is to put a thick jacket round your hot water tank. It should be at least three inches thick. Look for one made to British Standard 5615: 1985. Depending on size it will cost between £6 and £8 and should pay for itself in lower fuel bills in a matter of months.

If the jacket already on your tank is thin or worn you will save money by putting another on top. If the cyclinder needs replacing you can buy one which comes ready-fitted with a pre-formed foam insulation jacket. It is less bulky and will leave more room in the airing cupboard. If your hot water cylinder has a thermostat a setting of 60 °C or 140 °F or less (but not below 55 °C) should provide enough hot water for an average family.

APPLIANCES

With anything that runs off electricity, the price you pay for it in the shop is only part of the cost you have to consider. There is also the running cost. (An efficient appliance not only saves money on bills but is environmentally friendly. Because it uses less energy, it helps reduce the amount of carbon dioxide released into the atmosphere from power stations.)

Until recently it has not been easy to compare running costs. But many manufacturers' brochures and user leaflets now include this information and energy labels have started to appear on fridges and freezers sold by electricity companies. It is planned to extend the scheme to other products and outlets.

An electric bar fire, using full-price electricity, is an expensive way of providing warmth. Storage heaters using Economy 7 cheap-rate electricity are the cheapest form of electric heating – almost as cheap as gas.

HOW MUCH DOES IT COST TO KEEP WARM

The greater part of your fuel bill goes on heating and hot water.
It depends on:

* the fuel you use
* the sort of heating you have
* the standard of insulation in your home

heating   hot water   lights and appliances   cooking   standing charges

How your money goes on fuel

Your costs will also depend on the size of your rooms, the numbers in your household and the amount you use your heating. Shown below are the average costs of keeping warm.

| | MAINS GAS | | | ELECTRICITY | | SOLID FUELS | | | OTHER FUELS | |
	gas fire	gas wall heater	central heating	fan heaters and bar fires	off-peak (Economy 7)	open fire	open fire with back boiler	roomheater with back boiler	calor gas cabinet heater	paraffin heater
Living room only	£5.30	£3.80	£4.50	£13.50	£7.00	£11.10	£5.90	£5.10	£11.70	£7.30
1 bedroom flat	£6.20	£4.60	£5.70	£16.00	£7.70	£13.00	£7.80	£6.70	£13.60	£8.50
3 bedroom house	–	£8.80	£10.25	£30.30	£15.50			£14.40	£12.10	–

These costs are for an average winter week (1990 prices), and for all day heating. They do not include standing charges or maintenance costs. The fuel costs were calculated on the Energy Targeter computer program.

The difference between models that are energy guzzlers which will push up your bills and mean machines that will save you cash is surprising. Some models use less than half the electricity consumed by others of similar size and performance. They are not necessarily more expensive to buy. But if they are dearer you should get the extra cost back in lower bills within a year.

Fluorescent lights and compact energy-saving bulbs use a quarter of the electricity usually required by ordinary filament bulbs for the same amount of light. And they can last up to eight times as long. They are more expensive but you will recoup this with the energy they save.

TELEPHONE

The simplest way to keep your telephone bill down is to make calls in the cheap-rate period as far as possible; keep calls short; and avoid using premium rate services (they usually start with the figures 0898, 0836 or 0077).

Avoid using the operator if you can. Avoid using directory inquiries if possible (or phone up from a call box where the service is still free). You can get two numbers from directory inquiries for the price of one.

Do not invite people to make reverse charge calls. It is better for someone to make a brief call to you and then for you to ring them back.

If you are on a modern digital exchange you can ask for a call-barring facility. You will have to pay extra for it on your quarterly bill but it might be cheap at the price, especially if you have a household full of teenagers who seem to live on the phone as soon as your back is turned.

There are two types: one that bars all calls other than 999 ones and another that allows local calls but bars long-distance ones.

There is also a BT-approved call-barring panel that fits over any BT wall socket. Once the key is turned only outgoing 999 calls can be made.

People who make little use of their phone, such as pensioners who may have it mainly for incoming calls, can get 25% rebate off BT's rental charge under a low-user rental rebate scheme. Supportline, which works in a similar way, benefits people who use fewer than 120 units in a quarter. It will eventually replace the low-user rental rebate scheme.

Checking how much a call has cost by using the ADC (Advice, Duration and Charge) service is expensive. Similarly, personal calls, alarm calls, fixed time calls and calls to a cellular phone cost extra.

EVERYDAY SPENDING

The notebook in which you wrote down details of everyday spending over a month can help you make significant economies.

Work out separate totals for your average monthly spending on such items as: food and drink; fares; toiletries, cosmetics and hairdressing; clothes; meals out; outings to the pub, café, cinema or leisure centre; cleaning materials; laundry; shoe and other repairs; TV or video rental; pocket money; magazines and newspapers; credit cards; postage and stationery; garden; savings etc. You should get some idea of where you can cut down without hardship.

> *Leaving credit cards and chequebook at home and carrying less money on you is one way to resist buying nonessentials.*

* Do you look for fabrics that can be washed in the machine and do not require expensive dry cleaning?
* Could you reduce repair bills by DIY? It might be worth investing in local evening classes in car maintenance, plumbing, decorating or whatever you think you could do best.
* When there is a big service or repair job to be done on your home or car do you shop around? Cheapest is not always best but it is worth asking friends and neighbours to see if there is someone they could recommend.
* Do you buy too many things on credit and store card accounts?
* Do you always pay full price for everything? Do not be afraid to haggle for a discount, especially when you are paying cash.

> *Traders can charge two prices for the same item under dual-pricing laws. Pay cash if it is going to cost you more to pay by credit card.*

Shopping around for the weekly groceries is time-consuming and can be pretty unrewarding. Supermarkets generally have the cheapest prices for groceries because of their buying power. It does not make much difference which one you use.

But local greengrocers and markets are often cheaper for fresh fruit and vegetables; and although small local shops may find it difficult to compete with the big stores on price they often score by offering more individual advice, staying open longer, or by being situated within easy walking distance.

Preparing a shopping list before you set out and sticking to it will make you less likely to fritter money on nonessentials. But this does not mean that you need ignore all the special offers that supermarkets display to tempt you to part with your cash.

A 'two for the price of one' offer on something you regularly buy, for instance, is worth getting – as long as the normal price has not been increased and it is still a bargain.

Watch out for special offers and be ready to switch the menu you had in mind for the family meal if you can make a saving. A supermarket's own-label products are generally cheaper than equivalent brand-name products and are worth trying.

Buying in large quantities can pay off, although never take it for granted that bigger means cheaper. It is no saving either if you buy in bulk only to find you have not room to store the extra products at home or that they are past their best by the time you get around to using them all up. A sack of potatoes, for instance, can save you pounds, but only if you can eat them before they start sprouting and going soft.

> *Drive carefully to save fuel. If you are buying a new car, look for one where running and service costs are low. A diesel-engined car may cost a little more initially but is economical to run.*

Banks and Building Societies

Many people have no idea whether their money is in the best bank or building society account. That is hardly surprising, given the number and type of accounts available and their advantages and disadvantages. Even the experts find it difficult to pick their way through the fine print of the different deals.

All banks offer basic facilities such as a paying-in service, chequebooks, cheque guarantee cards, automatic cash machines (not always available in smaller branches) so you can draw money from your account or check your balance at any time of the day or night, credit cards, debit cards, regular statements, standing orders, direct debits, overdrafts and personal loans.

You can open a special account to pay large household bills, take out insurance, a pension, a Tessa (Tax-Exempt Special Savings Account), a mortgage, draw holiday money, make investments or get help to draw up your will or a trust for the benefit of your children when they grow up. Important documents or jewellery can be left in their safe. If you find it difficult to get to the bank during opening hours, they may have a telephone banking service which enables you to use the bank's services by picking up the phone and giving your account number and a special personal number.

Most of the big building societies and some finance houses offer some or all of the basic facilities but not all of the services. Most people need:

* An account into which wages or salary can be paid, which offers a chequebook, the usual cards and a full service. It should preferably also pay interest on your money.

* A high-interest account for any money you have over after everyday expenses have been met.

* A bank or building society branch that is close to your home or workplace, although this is not so necessary if you can use a home banking system.

You may be able to fulfil all these needs with one bank or building society. Or you could consider a bank account that gives you access to the extra services that a bank provides plus a building society account that pays interest when you are in credit and does not slap on charges when you are overdrawn.

It is convenient to pay regular bills by standing order or direct debit. With a standing order you tell the bank (or building society) how much is to be paid, to whom, and when. It is particularly useful for fixed amounts such as club subscriptions. This amount cannot be altered without your permission.

With a direct debit, the person receiving payment tells your branch how much is due and when. When you agree to pay by direct debit, you give permission for the other party to make changes to the amount that has to be paid. This is a useful way of paying bills where the amount is liable to change from time to time.

CHARGES

These can be hefty and are imposed when you are overdrawn without the bank's permission or when you use some of the special services. Charges vary from bank to bank and building society to building ·society. A study by the Consumers' Association magazine *Which?* (October 1991) found that the cost of going £500 overdrawn for just one week each quarter in one year ranged from less than £10 to over £100, depending on the account.

It is vital therefore to make sure that your account is always in credit. If you do accidentally slip into the red by a small amount for a few days, write to your bank manager as soon as possible explaining why it has happened and ask if he could overlook the error on this occasion. Bank managers have discretionary powers and can arrange a refund of the interest and charges if they think it was an uncharacteristic mistake on your part.

If you think you might on occasions become overdrawn, consider switching to an account where you can be overdrawn up to a set limit with the manager's agreement without incurring charges. If that is not available at your bank see if there is an account that charges you a fixed fee and allows you to be overdrawn up to an agreed limit without paying charges.

Otherwise, ask if you can have an overdraft. This gives you the right to be overdrawn up to a set limit. Although you may have to pay interest and fees they will cost you less than if you slipped into the red without permission.

> *Check bank or building society statements carefully. If there is an error the sooner you report it the better. Keep receipts for cash withdrawals. They can be useful evidence if a query arises.*

It is worth considering a building society account that does not charge you for being overdrawn and that pays a good rate of interest on your credit balance. Even if your account is not in deficit you can run up charges if you use one of the bank's special services.

> *If it is getting towards the end of the month and you are worried that your current account is getting low, use your credit card instead of writing a cheque.*
> *Even if you cannot pay off all that you owe on the card at the end of the month, the interest you pay will not be as high as bank charges.*

Credit

Most people need to borrow money at some time or other, whether it is to buy a house, a car, a domestic appliance, or to pay for a holiday.

If you use it wisely, credit can work to your advantage, enabling you to buy expensive items that would otherwise be out of reach, or to cope with emergencies, for example when funds are short and your old washing machine dies on you. But unfortunately credit can also be a temptation to overspend.

There are many types available and it is as important to shop around for credit as it is to shop around for anything else. Do not accept the first deal that is offered. If you are buying a video, for instance, the shop may offer to arrange credit for you. But you may be able to borrow the money more cheaply elsewhere.

The simplest rule-of-thumb guide to the best credit deal is to look out for the APR (Annual Percentage Rate of Charge) figure. This has to be worked out in a standard way so that customers can compare like with like. As a general guide, the lower the APR figure, the less you will have to pay.

> *To work out the APR the lender must add all the interest and other charges together. He must also take into account how and when payments are made. The longer a deal lasts the more it costs in interest charges.*
>
> *This is because the APR is worked out on the cost of credit over one year. On a deal that lasts two years the interest will cost twice as much. So a shorter deal with a higher APR can work out cheaper in the end.*

If the interest rate is variable the interest rates can go up or down. With a fixed interest loan you pay the same amount each month. This might suit you better if money is tight. If you are taking out a loan, ask for a written quotation that you can take home and study – you must be given one if you ask. It will tell you all you need to know and make it easier to compare one deal with another. If there is anything you do not understand, ask whoever is arranging the deal to explain it to you. If you are still not sure, get advice from your local Citizens' Advice Bureau or Money Advice Centre.

Some loan schemes provide insurance which will ensure that repayments continue if you are unable to keep on paying. Check the policy, because some do not cover self-employed or part-time workers or certain age groups such as pensioners. If you fall into any of these categories you could be wasting your money by having an insurance-included deal.

With certain loans, settling up early can be expensive. At best you may still have to pay some of the interest you would have paid if the loan had run for the full period. Think carefully before taking out a secured loan. You may lose your home if, for any reason, you cannot keep up repayments.

> *If you need a big loan, perhaps for a car, and you do not have time to shop around for the best deal, a credit broker may be able to help you. You will either have to pay him a fee on top of what you are paying for the loan, or he may get commission from the lender.*
>
> *If a fee has to be paid it must be included in the APR, which will then be higher than if no fee was involved. If the loan is for buying a house or for £15,000 or less, the broker can charge a fee of only £3 if you have not received your loan within six months.*

CREDIT CARDS

Credit cards are issued by banks and building societies under the MasterCard/ Access and Visa schemes. They are accepted in a wide range of outlets and can be used for withdrawing money over the counter or from cash-dispensing machines. You are given an individual credit limit and can spend up to that limit in any one month. If you think the limit is too low, write and ask the card issuer for it to be increased.

You can either pay off all that you owe each month or pay a minimum amount, which is usually either £5 or 5% of what you owe, whichever is the larger. All cards allow you up to 25 days after your statement date in which to pay your bill without incurring any interest charges. If you time your purchases and payments carefully and you pay it all off each month you should be able to get up to 56 days interest-free credit.

But if you miss the payment date you will have to pay interest for the whole period, not just from the time your payment goes overdue. Even if you pay the bill over the counter at the bank it still takes four working days for the payment to reach the card company. If you do not pay off all that you owe each month you are charged interest. You may also be charged from the date of your purchase, not from the statement date.

Many banks and building societies charge an annual fee. If you usually pay off your credit card in full each month you might want to switch to a card without an annual fee and a low APR – in case you occasionally need credit. If you do not always pay off what you owe in full, look for a card with a low interest rate and that charges from the statement date, not from the date when you made the transaction. Credit cards can be used at overseas banks to make cash withdrawals.

Some cards offer perks, such as discounts on travel and insurance, and purchase protection (which reimburses the cardholder if goods within a certain price range purchased anywhere in the world are stolen or broken within so many days of purchase).

You may be able to get an Affinity Credit Card that is linked to a particular charity or cause and pays an amount to that charity every time you use the card to make a purchase. The charity also gets a donation when the card is issued.

The Consumer Credit Act gives you additional protection if you buy something with your credit card and then run into problems when you try to claim from the business you are dealing with. Provided the purchases cost between £100 and £30,000 (and you have used less than £15,000 credit), you can claim from the credit card company. The company and the retailer have 'dual liability' if anything goes wrong. If, for instance, you buy a faulty video recorder from a shop that then goes bust, you can claim from the card company.

Always check your statement carefully and make sure nothing has been added on or that items do not appear twice. If you find an error, pay the card company but deduct the extra you have been charged and inform them why you have done so.

STORE CARDS

Many high street stores and retail chains offer customers their own credit card. There are various kinds. An option account works in much the same way as credit cards. If you pay off what you owe each month no interest is charged, or you can have extended credit and pay interest on the outstanding balance. A monthly account is similar but you are expected to pay your bill in full every month.

With a budget account you pay in so much every month and can borrow a multiple of this, perhaps 12 to 20 times the amount. Interest is charged on any outstanding balance. A budget account can be useful if you know you are going to do a lot of shopping in one store, or as a way of spreading the cost of Christmas. But if you do not normally spend a lot in that particular store, the amount you pay in each month will build up and *you* will not get the interest on it. Interest rates on store cards are generally higher than for many other forms of borrowing, but there are extras such as invitations to sales previews, special discounts, and free catalogues or magazines. Many cards also offer cardholders protection if the store goes bust.

CHARGE AND GOLD CARDS

American Express, Diners Club and Visa are the best known charge cards. For American Express and Diners Club you pay a fee to join and there is usually an annual fee. They are similar to credit cards but you must pay off what you owe each month. If you do not you could face late payment charges which are generally higher than credit card interest rates.

There is no spending limit, so they can be handy for someone who may occasionally want to borrow quite large sums at short notice. They offer perks such as purchase protection, free medical insurance if the card is used to purchase a flight or holiday, and cover for lost luggage and flight and baggage delays.

Gold cards are for high-earners – you usually have to earn at least £25,000 a year to qualify – and they offer extra perks such as 'free' travel insurance and large unsecured overdrafts at lower rates than those the banks charge. Fees are higher than for charge cards. Most do not offer the protection of the Consumer Credit Act if you run into problems with the retailer.

BANK OR BUILDING SOCIETY LOANS

A personal loan should be quick and simple to arrange. You can apply to your bank or you may be able to get one from a building society. You usually pay a fixed rate of interest based on the term of repayment. There may be an arrangement fee and you might also be charged a penalty if you decide to clear the debt early.

If you are faced with an emergency or you think your account might slip into the red in the coming years you can ask your bank or building society for an overdraft facility. You can have one for a limited time or arrange for it to run for a longer period. It enables you to write cheques for more money than is in your account. You pay interest on the amount that is overdrawn, not on the full overdraft limit. You may also have to pay a quarterly fee, but it is cheaper than letting your account slip into the red without getting permission first.

OTHER SOURCES

If you have a mortgage you may be able to raise extra cash by getting a further advance. Even if your mortgage is below the £30,000 tax relief limit, you will not get relief on the new loan.

Hire purchase You pay a deposit on something you want to buy and make weekly or monthly repayments. You can have the goods straight away. The agreement must show the cash price, the total hire purchase price and the amount of each repayment. You do not own the goods until you have made the last payment. If you fail to keep up payments the HP company can take the goods back, although if you have paid a third of the money owed they would need a court order.

Finance company loans Shops, car dealers and gas or electricity boards may offer to arrange a finance company loan if you are buying an expensive item. You may be able to get the money for less elsewhere, so shop around before signing up.

Check trading This is available only in some parts of the country. You buy checks of differing values which can be used in certain shops instead of cash. You repay the check trader in weekly instalments with interest. It may be convenient, but it is an expensive form of credit.

Mail order catalogues They save time and travelling and are becoming increasingly popular. You usually get at least 20 weeks of interest-free credit. Goods are sent on approval and weekly instalments are collected by the agent. You may have to pay interest if you want to pay over a longer period for more costly items.

Moneylenders This can be an expensive way to borrow. Because the risks are high, so are the rates of interest.

Insurance companies Many insurance companies will lend you money against the cash-in value of their own life insurance endowment policies. You will have to pay interest on the loan. You can either pay it off gradually or leave it until the policy pays out.

Credit unions These are money cooperatives where a group of people get together to save and lend to each other. They may work in the same place, attend the same church or belong to the same club. Members pay a small joining fee and then save a regular amount. They elect a committee to run their affairs. Members receive a low rate of interest on their savings but can borrow at extremely low rates – a maximum of 12.68%, which is the legal limit. Unions can lend up to £5000 to a member plus another £5000 if he has £5000 savings in the union.

They are an excellent way of saving and borrowing small amounts. Repayments are arranged to suit the borrower. To find a credit union in your area contact either:

The Association of Credit Unions Ltd.,   or   *National Federation of Credit Unions,*
48 Maddox Street,   *1–3 Fairfax Crescent,*
London W1R 9BB   *Bierley,*
                                                                      Bradford BD4 4BP.

Planning for Retirement

Good health and financial security are what most people hope for when they reach retirement age. On average, women can now expect to live to 79 and men to 73, so it is important to plan ahead.

Long before you collect your bus pass you should be thinking of:

* Checking out, while you are in your 50s, that you will get a full state pension. Your local DSS office will calculate how many years you have paid the full National Insurance stamp.

* Finding out what your occupational pension will be worth. If you have not received a statement recently, check with the pension scheme manager.

* Boosting your occupational pension by paying in as much as you can with Additional Voluntary Contributions. The sooner you start the better. You are allowed to put in up to 15% of your annual salary, on which you get full tax relief.

* If you are not in an occupational pension scheme or are self-employed, putting the most you can manage into a personal pension. If you are in your 50s you should be putting in at least 20% of gross earnings, increasing the percentage as you approach 60.

* Saving as much as possible in safe investments in case your company pension is not going to be enough or to give yourself a higher standard of living in retirement. Look for tax-efficient ways.

* Taking advantage of personal tax-free allowances. If one partner has no income or a low income you should be able to rearrange your affairs so that you make use of both your personal tax-free allowances.

* Chasing up any pensions that may be due to you from former employers. The Pensions Registry, P.O. Box 1NN, Newcastle-upon-Tyne, may be able to help you with pensions taken out since 1975 and possibly earlier if the information is available.

Ten years before retirement is not too soon to start planning for retirement; and even just a year before the great change comes is not too late to make important decisions which might lead to a long-lasting improvement in your financial circumstances.

If you are married or living with a partner, it is essential to do your financial planning together. One is going to outlive the other, and your plans should ensure that the survivor has as secure a future as possible.

In the run-up to retirement, you should be considering whether:

* You are going to take a lump sum from your pension and how best to invest it.

* One or both of you plans to carry on working.
* You are going to stay in the same home or move.
* Your home needs expensive repairs or alterations that should be done before retirement, when your income will drop.
* You should change your car to a more economical model.

As R-day approaches, you should work out what your outgoings are and what income you will have. Draw up a budget to see where the money is going, keeping in mind that there will be changes in how you spend your money. Fuel bills, for instance, will probably increase when you are spending more time at home. You may also use the telephone more.

Then look at your expected income. A pension is likely to be the most important element in your retirement income. Most people are entitled to the basic state pension. This is a flat-rate pension paid to men at 65 and women at 60. In addition, everyone who is employed, except those on very low earnings, will have a pension linked to their earnings.

It may be from: *SERPS (State Earnings Related Pension Scheme); a contracted-out company scheme; a personal pension.*

To qualify for the full state pension you must have paid or been credited with National Insurance contributions at the full rate for most of your working life. If you have not paid enough you will probably receive a reduced pension. The term 'working life' means the number of tax years in which you are expected to pay, or have been credited with, contributions. The period normally starts when you are 16 and ends with the tax year in which you are 59 if you are a woman or 64 for a man.

Every week when you are at work your employer makes contributions on your behalf. You are credited for any missed if you are registered unemployed, or you are receiving sickness or invalidity benefit, maternity or invalid care allowance.

Married women, widows or divorcees may be able to use their husband's or ex-husband's contributions to qualify for a pension.

If you qualify your pension may consist of:
* a basic pension;
* plus an additional pension if you worked after April 1978;
* and a graduated pension if you worked between April 1961 and April 1975.

Whether you are entitled to a state pension or not you may also be entitled to draw other benefits, such as income support and housing benefit.

If you go abroad for less than three months you can cash all your pension orders when you get back to this country. As a pension order cannot be cashed more than three months after it is date-stamped, tell the Social Security office well in advance if you are going to be abroad for a longer period. Arrangements can be made for your pension to be paid into a bank or other account while you are away.

If you do not draw your pension by a weekly order book you do not need to tell your local Social Security office unless you are going to be out of the country for more than six months.

If you are going to be out of the UK for more than three months or have decided to live abroad, you can receive the pension in the country where you are going to live. But you may not get any increase when the pension goes up unless you are going to live in a country in the EC or certain others where the government has agreed arrangements. Your local Security Office will give details, or you can write to: *DS, Overseas Branch, Newcastle-upon-Tyne, NE98 1YX.*

SERPS

All employees not in a company scheme automatically belong to the State Earnings Related Pension Scheme. This provides an additional amount, within the pension, for those who contributed towards it from the time it was introduced in 1978. If you contributed you may qualify for an additional pension, even if you are not entitled to the basic pension.

The majority of company pension schemes have contracted out of SERPS. They can do this if they offer equal or better terms and have satisfied the Occupational Pensions Board.

OCCUPATIONAL PENSIONS

A pension is generally the best way of saving for retirement because you get tax relief on your contributions up to 15% of your pensionable earnings. The kind of benefits and pension you get depend on the type of scheme. There are two main types: final salary schemes and money purchase schemes.

With a final salary scheme your pension is based on your final salary at retirement and on the number of years that you have been contributing to the scheme. It could be based on an average of the best three consecutive years' pay in the last five or ten, or some similar arrangement.

Some calculations are based on all your earnings, others only on basic earnings, without taking overtime or commission into account. Some schemes also deduct the first slice of your earnings because you are getting money from the state pension.

You receive a fraction – usually 1/60th or 1/80th – of your final salary for each year that you have been in the scheme. So if your scheme is based on 1/60ths and you have been a member for 20 years you will receive a pension of 20/60ths (or a third) of final pensionable salary. You normally pay in a percentage of your pre-tax earnings and your employer may also contribute.

With a money purchase scheme you and your employer pay contributions to your pension which are then invested. On retirement your share of the fund is used to buy an annuity which provides a pension for you and maybe your spouse for the rest of your life.

Although you know what you are putting in, what you will eventually get out will depend on how well the pension fund is invested and what annuity it can buy when you retire. You do well when interest rates are high, but may get a much lower pension if you retire when interest rates are low. Some employers' schemes offer a combination of final earnings and money purchase schemes.

If you want a better pension you can pay in extra money known as Additional Voluntary Contributions (AVCs). Alternatively, you can pay free-standing AVCs (FSAVCs) into a scheme of your choice run by a bank, building society or insurance company. Check first whether you will get more benefits by sticking with your employer's AVC scheme.

When you retire you can give up part of your pension in return for a lump sum which you can invest. The sum can be up to one and a half times your final annual salary. Your pension is reduced accordingly. If your pension is index-linked you should think carefully before reducing it by taking a lump sum.

Most schemes include life insurance, a dependant's pension (which may be half of the pension you would have received if you had not taken a lump sum), and allowance for early retirement due to ill health.

REDUNDANCY

If you have been employed by a company for at least two years and have worked more than 16 hours a week (or five years if you have worked between eight and 16 hours a week) you are generally entitled to redundancy money. But you are not entitled to payment: if you are self-employed or on a fixed-term contract; if you are over retirement age; if you are working abroad; or if you work in certain jobs, such as a merchant seaman or docker. Both men and women are entitled to redundancy up to the age of 65. But if a company has a nondiscriminatory retirement age, that becomes the age at which the employee's entitlement to redundancy ceases, not 65.

You may have to decide whether to take your pension early, in which case it is likely to be much less than if you had remained until retirement age, or whether to defer it – leave the pension in the scheme until you choose to retire.

Unemployment benefit is taxable and depends on having paid sufficient National Insurance contributions. It can be paid for up to 52 weeks. The amount you get will be reduced if you are over 55 and are receiving payment through an occupational scheme. To qualify, you have to be unemployed but be capable of and available for work. You may be disqualified from unemployment benefit for up to 26 weeks if you leave a job voluntarily without what is known as 'just cause'.

You may also be disqualified if you choose to accept early retirement: but this does not apply if you are made redundant.

EARLY RETIREMENT

This can seem tempting to someone who has put in 40 years' work, but it needs careful consideration. By retiring five years early you could reduce your pension by a third. But you may not lose out if you are retiring because of ill health or company economies.

Talk to your pension fund manager or whoever is in charge of your company's occupational pension scheme and find out the terms offered to early retirers. Once you have this information it might be worthwhile consulting an independent financial adviser who will look at your situation and suggest how to make the best use of your assets.

If you are retiring early because of ill health you could be entitled to sickness pay for the first 28 weeks and then to invalidity benefit. If your savings and income fall below a stated amount you may be able to claim income support and/or community charge/council tax benefit. To make sure you have paid enough contributions to receive a full pension when you reach pension age check your contribution record through your local Social Security office.

You will receive credits towards your pension if you are drawing a benefit such as unemployment or invalidity. If you are under 60 and seeking work it may be worth signing on as unemployed, even if you are not entitled to benefit, to receive the credits. You will be automatically credited if you are a man aged between 60 and 64, providing you are not abroad for more than a year.

Redundancy or unplanned early retirement leaves you with an unexpectedly depleted income. It may be tempting to use a lump sum payment to pay off the mortgage but this is not necessarily a good idea. You usually get tax relief only on the first £30,000 so you could pay off anything in excess of this. But because you get tax relief at the basic rate on your mortgage you would probably be better off investing the money.

If you have a repayment mortgage you could ask to pay interest only. That will reduce your payments and leave you with extra money to invest. With an endowment mortgage you are paying only interest anyway. Keeping the mortgage going also means that you could borrow on it in an emergency.

PERSONAL PENSIONS

Personal pensions offer an alternative to SERPs or a company pension scheme. They are really savings plans or policies run by an insurance company, friendly society, a bank, a building society or a unit trust scheme. They have to be officially approved if they are schemes which are contracted out of the state scheme.

In these schemes you pay regular premiums or lump sums which are invested. When you reach retirement age the sum built up is used to purchase an annuity from an insurance company. There may also be a tax-free lump sum available at retirement.

If you move from job to job you should be able to take your personal pension with you, so a pension can no longer tie you to a particular company.

You will not be able to tell in advance how much pension you will get, although someone who is trying to sell you a personal pension may suggest various probabilities. No one, however, can know in advance what the rate of return on invested money will be, or what will happen to interest rates or your earnings. The main factors that will influence what you get are the amounts that have been paid in – the more you pay in the more you will get out – the length of time during which you pay in and the rate of investment return on your personal pension plan.

The main difference between a personal pension and a company pension is that you decide how the money you pay in should be invested. There are many types of personal pensions. The main ones are:

* Deposit-based plans where your money is invested in secure investments such as bank and building society accounts;
* With-profit plans where the money goes into a wide range of investments such as

shares and government stock;

* Unit trust and unit-linked plans where your money is used to buy units in a fund.

Once money is invested in a plan it is usually impossible to withdraw it until retirement. Tax relief on contributions is limited to 17.5% of earnings up to the age of 35 and then on a sliding scale up to 35% from age 56 to 74.

If you decided to leave your employer's scheme and take out a personal pension, it is important to compare the alternative benefits carefully. The older you are the less likely it is that you will be able to get better terms by leaving the company scheme unless you make a very large investment. You will also have to sacrifice the contributions made by your employer into the pension fund.

Most company pension schemes provide quite generous benefits for dependants when a member dies and if you switch to a personal pension you may find the cover is much less, especially if you die before retirement.

While retirement age for people in company schemes can be anything between 50 and 65, personal pension schemes allow you to retire earlier still with a minimum retirement age of 50. But you must have paid enough into the pension kitty to benefit from this concession. (If you have one of the old 226 private pension plans it will be less flexible.)

The self-employed As anyone who is self-employed cannot be in SERPS, they should take out a personal pension so that they have something in addition to the basic state pension when they retire. The sooner a pension starts the greater the benefits are going to be.

CONTINUING TO WORK

If you carry on working after the official retirement age you no longer have to pay National Insurance contributions. You should receive a certificate of exemption from the DSS to give to your employer who will still have to pay contributions for you.

Since the abolition of the 'earnings rule', your state pension is no longer reduced if you decide to carry on working. You can defer taking the state pension for anything up to five years after you reach retirement age. It will be increased by about 7.5% a year for each year that you put off drawing it. If you are drawing the pension and then decide you would rather defer it and let it accumulate, you are allowed to do this but only once.

Men under 70 and women under 65 who have put off drawing the retirement pension and who continue to work, can claim unemployment or sickness benefit in the usual way.

RAISING EXTRA CASH

When you retire and weigh up your assets against likely outgoings you may be able to manage comfortably at first. But high inflation erodes the real value of your pension and savings, and with time you may have trouble making ends meet.

You can then consider the following options:

* Reassessing savings and investments to see if they could be bringing in more money;
* Taking a part-time job or working from home;
* Making capital from your home.

If you are creative you should be able to use your talent to raise extra money. A hobby such as gardening or needlework could become a money-earner.

HOME INCOME PLANS

Sometimes called 'mortgage annuity schemes', these are arrangements whereby older homeowners can obtain some income from the capital value of their home, while still retaining ownership of it.

Normally an interest-only loan is raised on a proportion of the value of the property, up to a maximum of £30,000. The proceeds are used to buy a 'purchased life annuity' which will give you a regular monthly income for life. The interest payable on the loan has to be deducted from the annuity and as a result many people find that the extra income is not as much as they hoped it would be.

It means that there will be less money for you to leave to your heirs. The original loan does not have to be repaid in your lifetime but must be paid off if you give up ownership of the home (perhaps to go into a nursing home) or on your death, or, in the case of a couple, on the death of the surviving partner. Problems can arise if someone with a home income plan wants to move. You must be at least 65 or sometimes 70 to qualify for a plan. The older you are the more income you are likely to be offered. But whatever your age, take advice before committing yourself.

HOME REVERSION SCHEME

This is also available only to older homeowners. It involves selling all or part of your home to the reversion company in return for a lump sum or, in some cases, an annuity income. How much you will get depends on your age and the value of the property.

You carry on living in the house rent-free or for a nominal monthly sum for the rest of your life. An administrative fee is charged which could be around 1.5% of the house value. In some cases the cash sum from the sale can be 35% or less of the house value and will rarely be more than 60% even for people over 80. Repairs and maintenance normally remain your responsibility.

Age Concern have a fact sheet on this and many other subjects affecting the elderly. For further information phone 081 679 8000.

Buying and Selling a Home

Buying a home is the biggest financial investment in most people's lives. It is an expensive business and it pays to know your way around.

First, you need to be sure that buying a property is the best course for you. Most people have to borrow long-term and must be reasonably confident that they will be able to keep up repayments. At one time, when employment was stable, this could be taken for granted, but such is no longer the case.

It may be tempting to view the purchase as a first step to making money on a future sale. But in the short term property values can go down as well as up. It is better to regard your purchase as a means of acquiring a home rather than as a potential money-maker.

How Much Can You Afford?

Work out how much you want to borrow and can afford to repay each month. Talk to building societies and banks to get an idea of the amount they might advance and the type of properties they are willing to lend on. Lenders differ in the amount they are willing to offer to the same borrower, and lending policies differ from time to time, so it is important to shop around. There is little point in choosing an £80,000 house only to discover that no one will lend you more than £40,000. Lenders will generally offer from two to three and a half times your gross annual income. With a couple who are both earning they will take both incomes into account. Some lenders take account of overtime, bonuses and commission, provided you can show that they are regular.

At this early stage you will only be asking for a loan 'in principle'. The actual amount will depend on the valuation of the property you hope to buy. Most lenders will advance only 70%–80% of the full purchase price.

Deciding how much you can afford is not a simple matter of adding the amount of the loan to the amount of your savings. There are other costs involved. Some are unavoidable; others can be cut by doing the work yourself.

If you are buying a home without already having a property to sell, you should allow for the following costs:

* Solicitor's fees. There is no fixed scale of charges for conveyancing, but reckon on $\frac{1}{2}\%$ to $\frac{3}{4}\%$ of the purchase price. 1% would be on the expensive side. Fees are liable for VAT.

* Valuation fee. You will have to pay for the lender's valuation before they offer you a loan and, even if you do not go ahead with the purchase, this cost will have to be met. Costs vary, so check in advance on the scales used by your lender and allow for VAT.

* Survey fee. If you commission a surveyor to do a full structural survey the charge will be high. It is much less expensive if you can arrange to combine the valuation and survey. Remember to add VAT.

* Land registry fees. These are payable each time a property is purchased. There is a sliding scale of charges according to the price of the property. VAT is not payable on land registry fees.

* Stamp duty. This is a government tax that must be paid (after 20 August 1992) on any house bought for over £30,000.

* Indemnity guarantee. If the loan exceeds a certain percentage of the purchase

price – usually 75% or 80% – the lender will probably require a guarantee for the extra from an insurance company. The lender and the insurance company agree on the premium which you then have to pay.

* Lender's legal fees. You also have to pay the lender's solicitor's fee. This will be lower in cases where the solicitor acts for both lender and borrower.

* Removal costs. Remember to include the cost of insurance for breakages in transit.

If you are selling a property at the same time you must also allow for a solicitor's fee, which is usually $\frac{1}{2}$% to 1% of the selling price; and an estate agent's fee, where the charges can be from 1% to 3% of the selling price, depending on the terms, and are subject to VAT.

MAKING AN OFFER

When you make an offer, confirm it in writing to the estate agent, but make sure you add the words 'subject to contract and survey'. You are then free to withdraw from the deal later if you change your mind for any reason.

If your offer is accepted you may be asked for a deposit, which is paid either to the agent or to the seller's solicitor. Before you pay your deposit to the agent make sure he belongs to one of the professional organizations with an indemnity scheme to protect clients from fraud.

You could decline to pay a deposit at this stage, as it is not a guarantee that you will go through with the purchase, or that the property is reserved for you. If the agent or seller want some show of good faith it should be enough to demonstrate that you are laying out money for valuation, survey, or searches by your solicitor.

A deposit is simply a token of good faith that can be refunded in full if either party withdraws later. If you do pay, make sure that you get a receipt saying that it is 'subject to contract and survey'.

If it is a private sale and not through an estate agent, confirm your offer to the seller, specifying anything that the price includes, such as carpets and curtains.

Any deposit must be made to the seller's solicitor along with a letter saying that it is paid to him as a 'stakeholder, subject to contract and survey.' Never send a cheque direct to the seller.

THE PURCHASE

Tell your solicitor, or whoever is handling the conveyancing for you, the address of the property, the name of the seller, and particulars of his estate agent and solicitor.

> *Conveyancing firms who will handle the transfer of property, often for less than solicitors charge, may be run by solicitors' ex-clerks who have had a good deal of practical experience but without the paper qualifications. Choose a firm that is a member of the Council of Licensed Conveyancers or the National Association of Conveyancers. Keep in mind that they may not have the expertise to cope if anything goes wrong and might have to call in solicitors anyway, with resulting higher bills. But solicitors will also charge extra for unravelling complications.*

THE MORTGAGE

The lenders have to be satisfied that the property offers sufficient security for the amount of the loan, so they will arrange for a valuation. You have to pay for this whether you go through with the purchase or not. The valuation is not a survey but many lenders offer a more thorough assessment for an extra fee.

If the valuer discovers major problems he may decide that the house is worth less than you are being asked to pay, so the loan may be refused. Alternatively, the lender may withhold part of the loan until things have been put right. If you do not have the ready cash this could involve you in extra expense in the form of a bridging loan.

Lenders will normally let you see the valuation report but this is a limited survey report and you should not rely on it to point out all the defects of the house. You may wish to commission your own valuation and survey. You could have either a full structural survey, which is expensive, or a cheaper housebuyer's report, which is a partial survey of the state of the property.

There are various types of mortgage.

Repayment mortgage This is the simplest type. Each monthly payment pays the interest on the loan and also repays some of the capital. The amount you pay will depend on the size of the loan, the length of the mortgage and the current rates of interest.

Level repayment mortgage Many building societies offer only this type of repayment mortgage, which is repaid with a level monthly sum throughout the term of the mortgage, assuming that the level of interest remains the same. In fact, interest rates vary and you should take this into account when calculating how much you can afford. In the early years most of the repayments go in interest. As you gradually pay back the capital, the interest decreases, so that towards the end of the loan period you are paying much less interest.

Deferred repayment mortgage Some banks and building societies offer this type of mortgage because it can help buyers who are stretching themselves to the limit to get on the housing ladder. You make lower repayments in the beginning and higher ones later on. Over the whole period of the mortgage you pay out more. The lender may insist that you take out a mortgage protection policy that would pay off the mortgage and protect your family home if you were to die before repayments had been completed.

Endowment mortgage With this type of mortgage you pay interest only on the loan. You also pay premiums on an endowment life insurance policy which, when it matures, pays off the loan and may leave you an additional nest-egg, although you cannot rely on this. Both your home and the insurance policy act as security against the loan. If you die before it is repaid the policy covers the mortgage.

Non-profit endowment policy There is not much to recommend this type of loan. The proceeds of the policy are just enough to pay off the loan.

With-profits endowment policy   The policy will pay off the loan and in addition you receive bonuses from the company. Because you are saving as well as paying off your mortgage, premiums are expensive.

Low-cost with-profits endowment mortgage   This costs much less than the full with-profits scheme because it does not *guarantee* to pay off the loan when it matures. But with the addition of bonuses over the years the insurance company works out that it should not only cover the loan but leave you with something over. If the proceeds of the policy with bonuses come to less than the size of the loan you would have to find the difference, but this is not likely to happen.

Low-cost low-start with-profits policy   This is basically the same as above but the premiums are lower for the first few years and increase substantially later. Low-start mortages will not necessarily save you money in the long run.

Unit-linked mortgages   These are riskier than other schemes. You pay interest on the loan, together with premiums that are used to buy units in funds.

Pension-plan mortgages   These are available to the self-employed and to those without occupational pension schemes, and are similar to endowment schemes. You pay interest only during the life of the loan but the mortgage is linked to a pension plan, so that on retirement a lump sum pays off the capital and provides you with a pension on the remainder.

Interest-only mortgages   You pay interest only on the loan and can decide how and when to repay it.

Fixed-rate mortgages   The interest rate is fixed for a certain number of years. After that you pay the standard rate.

CLINCHING THE DEAL

Once the lender has agreed to the mortgage you will receive a 'formal offer of advance' stating the amount of the loan, the period over which it must be repaid, and the rate of interest you will be charged. Once the searches and legal inquiries have been completed your conveyancer arranges the exchange of contracts. Both parties are now committed. Contracts cannot be exchanged until:
* The draft contract has been thoroughly checked and any necessary changes made.
* The legal title of the property has been checked.
* The preliminary inquiries have been answered.
* The local searches have been completed.
* The mortgage loan is confirmed and the deposit is available.

Traditionally the deposit has been 10% of the purchase price, but raising this amount of cash can be a problem: try to negotiate a reduction – perhaps 5% deposit or less. If you have already paid a deposit when making the offer this should be deducted from the amount you are expected to put down on exchange of contracts. Once contracts have been exchanged the buyer is responsible for the insurance on the property, even though the seller may still be living there.

Whether you arrange the insurance through your (mortgage) lender or independently, read the policy and make sure you know what is covered and what is excluded. Ask them to explain anything that is not clear.

On exchange of contracts the final completion date will be set. If you are selling as well as buying, try to ensure that both completions take place as closely as possible.

Completion is when the buyer's conveyancer hands over the cheque for the balance of the purchase price, the seller's solicitor hands over the documents transferring the title, and the legal ownership passes from seller to buyer. The date for completion will be in the contract. It usually takes place 28 days after exchange of contracts but it can be longer or shorter if it suits both parties.

PUTTING YOUR PROPERTY ON THE MARKET

To get some idea of the right selling price study local newspapers to see what is being asked for similar properties in similar situations. It may help if you view one or two that are up for sale. Ask several estate agents to give you some idea of what they think your property would bring.

Depending on the market and on how urgently you need to sell, you might like to set your price 2% higher than you expect to get: buyers like to feel they have knocked something off. But do not set it too high or you could frighten off serious buyers.

HOW TO SELL

You then have to decide whether to sell your home through an estate agent. You may be charged a percentage of the selling price in commission, perhaps 1%, and you may have to pay other costs, such as advertising, or you could be charged a fixed percentage of the selling price, such as 2%, which will cover everything. Alternatively, you could save yourself several thousand pounds by advertising the property yourself. Begin your advertisement with the location of the property and end with the price.

If you use an estate agent you can instruct as many as you like, or give sole selling rights to one – which can be a saving. It is important to get in writing the details of the fees to be charged and whether or not the agency is a sole agency.

An estate agent will:

* Advise on the selling price.
* Measure your home and draw up a list of particulars. You should let them know about any recent replacements or work done.
* Take photographs for publicity purposes.
* Put up a 'For Sale' board. If you do not want one, make this clear at the start.
* Produce typed details of the property to hand out to prospective buyers.
* Advertise your property in their windows and in newspapers. Check that there will not be an extra charge for advertising.

* Arrange for prospective buyers to view, and show them round the property. You can leave it to them or show people round yourself. If you leave a key with the agent, make sure he lets you know every time he proposes to show someone round.

* Negotiate the selling price. Some buyers may prefer to make their offer directly to you, and this has its advantages as you can negotiate on the spot. If you do not like the idea of bargaining, ask them to make their offer formally through the agent.

THE OFFER

Once you are negotiating seriously, find out as much as you can about the buyer's position. Do they have a house to sell? Do they have the promise of a mortgage 'in principle'? If they are in a chain, try to find out how long the chain is and what situation everyone has reached. If you are selling through an estate agent they will arrange confirmation of the offer and forward details to your solicitor. If you are selling privately, make sure the buyer confirms any verbal offer in writing and that you accept in writing, giving the name and address of the conveyancer who will proceed with the legal arrangements on your behalf.

Give your conveyancer your buyer's full name and address, work and home phone numbers, the name and address of his conveyancer and copies of the offer and of your letter of acceptance. Your conveyancer is now in a position to get on with the legal work.

Nothing is guaranteed until contracts are exchanged, so it is unwise to take your property off the market as soon as you get an offer. It is safer to keep showing it to home-hunters who are genuinely interested, in case the deal falls through.

Never accept a higher offer without giving the first buyer a chance to match it. If other buyers are interested at about the same price, tell them they will have first refusal if your deal falls through. Then set a time limit within which contracts must be exchanged.

Do not accept a contract subject to searches, survey or anything else. It will tie your hands while the buyer finds it easy to back out.

If you agree to do any remedial work before contracts are exchanged, get an indemnity from the buyer (ask your solicitor to prepare a suitable form of words) so that, if the sale falls through he will cover the costs.

Never let the buyer move in before completion. If they do not come up with the full purchase price you will have all the trouble of getting them out. If you have already moved out and you let them have the key, make sure they sign an undertaking that this is only for viewing purposes.

Insurance

With most things you buy there is something to see for your money. With insurance you are buying peace of mind. Insurance provides protection for some of life's major catastrophes as well as the minor ones.

As with most things that are sold, it makes sense to shop around to ensure you are getting the best value. The cheapest policy is not necessarily the best, but you could lose out year after year if you automatically renew policies as they become due.

Whether you are taking out a policy for the first time or coming up to a renewal date you should work out what cover you need, get quotes from several companies and make sure the policy you take out will pay out in all the circumstances you want covered. To do this you will have to read the policy document. It might be tedious, but it is a legal document and the company will pay up only in the circumstances described in it. Do not rely on the salesman's word for what it covers. Do not be swayed into signing for life insurance just to get rid of a persistent salesman. It can cost you heavily if you change your mind and try to end the policy early.

THE COVER

There are two main types of insurance. General insurance covers you against accidents or loss – damage to your home, a car crash, burglary, and so on. Life insurance is taken out on your life and pays up either at a specified date or when you die.

If you own or are buying a house or flat you need house and buildings insurance. Whether you own or rent your home you should insure your possessions against loss, damage and theft. If you own a car or a motorbike you are legally required to have it insured. If you go on holiday it is sensible to take out cover. If there is anyone who would suffer financial hardship because of your incapacity or death you need life cover.

If you already have all the insurance cover you need, make a note of when each policy is due for renewal. Some weeks ahead make sure it really covers everything you require, bearing in mind that there may have been a change in your circumstances.

Look out for discounts. Some companies offer special rates to people in certain jobs or in trade unions: to non-smokers; to people of a certain age, such as over-55s; or in the case of house contents insurance, where the company is satisfied that your home is specially secure against burglary.

You can shop around by ringing up half a dozen insurance companies and asking for a quote. If friends can recommend a company, so much the better. You can ask your bank manager for advice. If he can't help he can put you in touch with one of the bank's insurance experts, or you can use the service of a motoring organization for car insurance. Alternatively, you can ask a registered broker to help. You can find a broker through the Yellow Pages or by contacting the *British Insurance Brokers' Association, BIBA House, 14 Bevis Marks, London EC3A 7NT*. (Tel. 071-623 9043) who will send a list of members in your area.

Registered brokers look at the whole market and see what is best suited to your needs. They are bound by law to put clients' interests first and must be insured to protect clients against the possibility of their making a mistake. Brokers are also governed by a code of conduct. You do not usually pay them a fee. They get commission from the insurance company they introduce you to. Someone who calls himself a 'consultant' is unlikely to be a registered broker and may be selling insurance for one or more companies – and these may not be the best for you.

It is important when renewing a policy to tell the insurance company of any change in your circumstances during the year. It is equally important when taking out a new policy to tell the company about anything that might affect any claim you make in the future, especially about any criminal offence, however minor. Some of the biggest complaints from policy-holders have arisen because a company has refused to pay out on the grounds that the policy-holder failed to disclose all relevant facts about their circumstances. It is safest to tell them everything that might remotely affect any claim.

EXCLUSIONS

Generally, the more you pay in premiums the fewer exclusions there will be. If you find that a policy does not cover a particular situation you want covered, talk to the broker or insurance salesman about it. You may have to pay a little extra to get it included but there is no point in having insurance if it is not tailored to your needs.

INSURING YOUR HOME

You must have buildings insurance if you have a mortgage and it is essential even if you do not. Your home is probably the biggest investment you have and paying for repairs can cost a fortune. Property should be insured for what it would cost to rebuild it – not the market value. If you underinsure, the insurance company may not pay up, even if the claim is for something less than total rebuilding.

In addition to covering the structure most policies generally cover the permanent fixtures and fittings, such as sanitary fittings, a fitted kitchen, and bedroom cupboards and interior decorations. They usually also cover outbuildings such as garages, greenhouses and garden sheds, while limited cover should be included for boundary walls, fences, gates, paths, drives and swimming pools.

THE RISKS

Most policies cover damage to your home caused by fire, lightning, explosion, earthquake, thieves, riot and malicious persons, storm and flood, aircraft or things falling from them, subsidence, landslip and heave, falling trees, impact by vehicle or animal, breakage or collapse of radio and TV aerials, escape of water from tanks or pipes, or of oil from fixed heating installations.

If your home is so badly damaged by one of the risks above that you cannot continue to live in it until it has been repaired, your policy will help to meet the reasonable additional cost of alternative accommodation up to a certain limit, often 10% of the sum insured or maybe 20% on contents insurance.

Underground service pipes and cables for supplying gas, electricity, oil or water, as well as sewage pipes are insured against accidental damage but not wear and tear. Glass in doors, windows and skylights is covered against breakages, as are baths, washbasins and WCs. Most policies say that you will have to pay something towards the cost of some claims, such as for storm or flood damage or the escape of water from tanks or pipes – or for all claims. You will almost certainly have to pay an excess for damage caused by subsidence, landslip or heave. This is usually a specific amount, such as £500, but it may be a proportion of the rebuilding cost of your home.

Common exclusions include war risk, damage caused by storm or flood to gates or fences, or by frost or sonic bangs, or by contamination by radio-activity from nuclear fuel or nuclear waste.

WHAT IS IT WORTH?

You have to work out the cost of rebuilding your home, which is what you will insure it for. This is the maximum the insurer will pay in any circumstances. The rebuilding cost of your home should include an allowance for permanent fittings such as central heating, and additional charges which could be involved in rebuilding, such as demolition costs, professional fees and the requirements of local authorities.

You may need a surveyor or architect to make the valuation for you. You can get a general idea from the leaflet *Buildings Insurance for Home Owners*, which includes a chart prepared by the Building Cost Information Service of the Royal Institution of Chartered Surveyors. This is available from: the *Association of British Insurers, 51 Gresham Street, London EC2V 7HQ.*

Many insurers offer an index-linked policy by which the sum insured is changed automatically whenever there is a movement in the average cost of rebuilding houses. Even if you have an index-linked policy you should tell your insurance company if you make any home improvements, such as installing central heating or building an extension.

> *In an emergency, do what you can to prevent damage from getting any worse. Many policies cover the cost of temporary work. Some insurers operate Helplines which assist you in finding someone to do emergency repair work.*

INSURING YOUR POSSESSIONS

Whether you own your home or rent it you should have insurance protection for its contents. You can then claim for loss or repair if you are burgled or your possessions are damaged.

Most policies cover your family's furniture, furnishings, household goods, kitchen equipment and other appliances, food and drink, TVs, videos, computers and audio equipment, clothing, personal effects and valuables such as jewellery and personal money up to a stated limit: in fact, all the things in your home, garage and outbuildings that you would take with you if you moved. Boats, caravans and motor vehicles are normally insured separately.

THE RISKS

You are usually covered while in the home for loss or damage to your contents by fire, theft, lightning, escape of water from tanks or pipes, oil leaking from fixed heating systems, storm, flood, subsidence, heave or landslip, falling trees or aerials, riot or malicious acts, explosion, earthquake, or impact by aircraft, vehicles or animals.

Companies are specific about what they do and do not insure. For instance, they generally will not pay out on a theft claim if you have lent or let your home or part of it, unless there is a forced entry. They generally exclude damage caused by sonic bangs, contamination by radioactivity from nuclear fuel waste, and war risks.

They may put a limit on the value of any piece of jewellery or on any one work of art and maybe even on a video. There is generally an overall limit to all these valuables, but the company may raise it if you ask and give them details. Or you may be asked to bear the first part of any claim yourself.

LEGAL LIABILITIES

If as occupier of your home (but not as owner) you are responsible for injury to someone, or damage to their property, your policy will pay the damages for which you are legally liable, up to £1 million plus costs in many cases.

You and your family are usually covered up to the same amount arising in ordinary day-to-day life – for instance, as a pedestrian causing a road accident.

Many policies provide some cover for your liability as a tenant for damage to the building. They also include accidental breakage of mirrors, glass tops to furniture and fixed glass in furniture. Some policies include accidental damage to TVs, videos, home computers and audio equipment. Cover for accidental damage to all your contents may also be available as an extension of your standard contents cover. Standard home contents insurance does not cover every eventuality or risk and only limited cover applies to contents temporarily removed from the home.

You may be able to get a special extension of home contents cover to include valuable items which you take out of your home, such as jewellery, fur coats, cameras and sports equipment. This is often called 'All Risks' insurance. There are two types of cover available. The cheaper cover is 'indemnity insurance', where the company pays the cost of repairing damaged articles or of replacing what has been stolen or destroyed, less an amount for wear, tear and depreciation. Because it is relatively cheap it is attractive, but it is only the second-hand value that is covered and you could have to pay out quite a bit if you have to buy a new replacement. Replacement-as-new policies cover the full cost of repairing damaged articles, or the cost of replacing them with equivalent new articles if they are stolen or destroyed.

Furniture, carpets, domestic appliances, TVs, videos and audio equipment can normally be insured on a replacement-as-new basis, but not usually clothing and household linen. As the kind of property you can insure on this basis varies between insurers and as age limits sometimes apply, check your policy carefully.

Keep bills and valuations that you might need if you come to make a claim.

9

Money

MOTOR INSURANCE

There are three types of motor insurance.

Third party   This is the cheapest. It covers liability for: injuries to other people including passengers; damage to other people's property; and accidents arising from the use of a caravan or trailer, whilst this is attached to the car.

Third party, fire and theft   This costs between 10% and 20% more and, in addition to the above, covers fire or theft of your car. If your car is not normally kept in a garage at night theft cover may be excluded or subject to special conditions.

Comprehensive   This is the most expensive but it covers a lot more including: accidental damage to your own car even if the accident was not your fault; personal accident benefit in the event of death or of a specified permanent disablement of the policyholder (and sometimes of his/her spouse or family members); medical expenses necessarily incurred, up to a stated limit; and loss or damage to personal effects in the car, up to a stated limit. Some policies will pay out on extras, such as the cost of hiring another car while yours is being repaired. Two out of three owners have comprehensive cover.

> *Most policies cover the policyholder in person when he/she is driving a car belonging to somebody else. But cover is then limited to 'third party only', even with a comprehensive policy. So you would not be able to claim off your policy if you accidentally damaged a friend's car that you had borrowed. If you borrow a car, make sure that the owner has comprehensive insurance, which covers you as an alternative driver under the terms of his policy. Then if you damage his car he can claim off his insurance.*

If you have got an old banger worth only a few hundred pounds the extra cost of comprehensive cover can be almost as much as the car is worth. So you may be better off insuring it for 'third party, fire and theft', especially if the driver is under 25 and paying a high premium. If a car is not in a roadworthy condition the insurance company might not pay up on a claim.

Various factors are taken into account in deciding how much your insurance will cost, including the drivers, the type of car, where it is kept, and the uses to which it will be put, as well as the type of cover required.

Policyholders with a claim-free (not blame-free) record normally qualify for a discount on the premium. Scales vary, but usually range from 30% for one claim-free year to 60% or 65% after four or five years. No-claims discount protection is often available for motorists with maximum discount. For an extra premium a number of claims will be allowed without loss of discount – usually two claims – in a three- or five-year period.

TAKING YOUR CAR ABROAD

All UK policies automatically provide the minimum cover required by law in other EC countries. This does not include theft or damage to your car and may not completely cover your liability to other people. Your insurance company can extend your UK level of cover to most normal holiday destinations. They can also supply a Green Card, which is an internationally recognized document that is evidence that you have insurance cover.

LIFE INSURANCE

If you have dependants who would need money if you died you should have life insurance. It can also be a way of saving. Unfortunately, it is sometimes sold by fast-talking sales reps who are so eager to get you to sign up that they do not give you the full facts and you end up with a policy that is not best suited to your needs.

There are two main types of life insurance. Protection only, known as 'term insurance', pays out if you die within a set number of years. It is relatively cheap. You can choose a policy that pays out a lump sum to your dependants or one that pays them a regular tax-free income. You decide how long you want the policy to run – perhaps while the children are at school. You do not get anything back if you survive until the end of the agreed term. Investment-type insurance is a way of making long-term savings for the future that gives you some life cover in case you die. It pays out at the end of the agreed term or if you die beforehand.

> *If you are in an occupational pension scheme, check how much life insurance cover it provides before taking out separate life insurance. It may be enough.*

The main kinds of investment-type insurance are:

* With-profits endowment policies that guarantee the amount you will get when the policy matures: but you also get bonuses which depend on the success of the company's investments. These policies also pay out if you die.

* Low-cost endowment policies that are used mainly to repay mortgage loans. Bonuses are added so that by the time the policy matures there should be enough to pay off the mortgage and something over. The mortgage is paid off if you die.

* Unit-linked policies that buy units in investment funds. What you receive when you cash them in depends on the value of the units at the time. You get some life cover.

* Whole-life policies pay out an agreed sum on your death, whenever it is. It is a way of saving up for your dependants. It is not such a good deal for young people under 35 because it ties up money for a long time. But it can be useful for older people in case future health problems make it harder to get insurance.

> *If you cash in a life policy early you may not even get back the money you have paid in. If you need cash urgently you should be able to get a low-interest loan against the surrender value of the policy. If you cannot afford the premiums try to get the policy 'paid up'. You then pay no more premiums but your family will still have some cover, although not as much as if you had continued paying.*

Be wary of invitations to surrender an existing policy with one insurance company so that you can take out a policy with another. 'Switching' generally means you will lose money on the existing policy which, will either have to be surrendered or made 'paid-up'.

Under the Financial Services Act, 1986, information about surrender values has to be provided by the insurance company when a new policy is being taken out. The company has to give an estimate of the amount payable on surrender at the end of each of the first five years from the time the policy is issued.

HIV/AIDS

Having an HIV test will not necessarily prevent you from obtaining life insurance cover. If you are tested for routine purposes such as blood donations, prenatal screening, employment, or for personal reassurance, it will not prevent you from obtaining life insurance provided that the result was negative and that there are no risk factors present.

If an insurance company asks you to take an HIV test it can be done only after you have:

* been notified of the test procedure;
* given your written consent;
* nominated a doctor or clinic to receive the results if the test is positive;
* received counselling before the test.

All costs involved in the test and in obtaining any other medical evidence should be paid by the insurer. Life insurance is not given at present for anyone who has AIDS or who is HIV positive.

Savings

Financial planning usually takes two forms: savings and investments. The first is less risky than the second. You need to strike a balance between tucking your money away where it is safe but may not grow in line with inflation, and taking some risk in order to go for growth.

The important issues you need to consider are:

* Have you made provision for your retirement?
* Have you got adequate insurance?
* How much can you afford to save regularly?

Once you have worked out these priorities you can get down to the details. The kind of questions you should ask youself are:

* Is income or growth your main priority?
* Are you aiming for short-term or long-term growth?
* How regularly do you want payments to be made?
* What effect will your savings and investments have on your tax situation?

* Are the interest/dividends paid with tax deducted?
* What protection exists for your money?
* What risk are you prepared to take?

WAYS OF SAVING

First, you should have some 'rainy day' money in a safe account that you can draw on quickly. You can use it for such needs as paying heavy bills or for emergencies. How much you can afford to put into the account will depend on your circumstances, but aim for at least £500 or up to £3000. You may be able to build this up by regularly saving small amounts so that it does not hit your pocket too hard.

Your best home for this is a bank or building society account paying good interest but one that also lets you draw money out at relatively short notice. You can usually invest what you like when you like and some accounts let you start with small amounts. But you will often get better rates if you can put more in to start with. Remember that you will have to top up the account as you draw from it and to ensure that it keeps up with inflation. If you can save something on top of that, consider putting some of the money in safe havens such as the following.

Bank or building society high-interest accounts If you do not need to draw on the capital in the immediate future you will get a higher interest rate in an account where you have to give notice of anything from seven days to several months when you want to withdraw funds without losing interest.

If interest rates are moving, give notice as soon as you open the account so that you can switch your money quickly if you find it could be earning higher interest elsewhere. Postal accounts do not have the same administrative costs and can therefore pay higher interest rates to savers.

> *Be careful about investing in small, little-known banks that offer above-average rates. They are more vulnerable than the big high-street banks. If any bank authorized under the Banking Act, 1987, fails, the bank compensation fund will pay out only 75% of the first £20,000 of your investment in the UK (and none in the Isle of Man or Channel Islands). The building society deposit protection scheme pays out 90% of the first £20,000.*

Many bank and building society accounts will pay interest monthly and although it can fluctuate this can be a useful source of money for people who are retired or living off a limited income. However, the capital sum will be worth less each year because of inflation.

TESSAs (Tax-Exempt Special Savings Accounts). These are five-year savings accounts, available from banks and building societies, in which you can invest a lump sum or small amounts regularly. They are attractive to taxpayers, especially those paying at the higher rate because, providing the capital is left intact for five years, you do not pay tax on the interest so long as you keep to the rules.

You have to be aged 18 or over and can have only one TESSA at a time. There are limits on how much you can save each year with an overall total over the five years of £9000. You can usually withdraw interest after basic-rate tax has been deducted. Schemes vary and although some do not let you withdraw interest at all others pay you a monthly income. Interest rates are mostly variable but a few are fixed. It costs nothing to set up a scheme but you may be charged a fee or some other penalty if you want to transfer to another TESSA elsewhere.

National Savings schemes   These are super safe. There are several kinds.

■ ORDINARY ACCOUNT   Interest is low but the first £70 of interest is tax-free. You can withdraw up to £100 on demand and so it is handy for someone who does not have a bank account. You can invest from £5 to £10,000.

■ THE NS INVESTMENT ACCOUNT   The rate of interest varies and can be competitive. You have to give one month's notice if you want to withdraw your money. This is attractive for non-taxpayers because the interest is not deducted at source. You can invest between £5 and £25,000.

■ SAVING CERTIFICATES   Interest is added to the value of your certificates and they become more valuable the longer you hold them. You should keep them for the full five-year term. You can invest between £25 and £7500, plus £10,000 reinvested from matured certificates. There are also index-linked certificates which are a good buy when inflation is rising. You can invest between £25 and £10,000.

■ YEARLY PLAN   You save between £20 and £400 a month in units of £5 for a year and get tax-free interest. At the end of a year this is converted into a certificate. If you keep it going for a further four years the (tax-free) interest increases. Maximum monthly contribution: £400.

■ INCOME BONDS   They cost £1000 each and you must hold at least two (maximum: £50,000 per person, or £100,000 for joint account holders). They are suitable for retired people and others who need regular income. Interest is paid monthly to a bank or building society current account. Tax is not deducted but interest is taxable and should be declared.

■ SERIES D CAPITAL BONDS   Similar to savings certificates. You have to tie your money up for five years to make them worthwhile. Interest increases each year and is gross but taxpayers have to pay tax on the interest credited each year even though they do not get it until the fifth year. You can invest between £100 and £100,000 in total from Series B onwards.

Other savings schemes worth considering include the following.

Save As You Earn   Available through banks and building societies. You save a set amount monthly for five years, with the option to save for a further two years. Interest is tax free and there is a bonus at the end of the five years, with a bigger bonus if you keep your money in for the extra years. You can save from £1 to £20 a month.

Some companies run SAYE schemes linked to share options. Employees can buy shares in their company at a price fixed at the start of a five-year savings period. They invest a set amount each month and at the end of five years can either take the cash or use the money to buy shares in their company. This is also tax-free. They can also leave the money for a further two years to earn a bigger cash pay-out.

Children's bonus bond   Available from the Post Office. This is a fixed rate, tax-free investment which should be held for five years. There is a very large bonus on the fifth anniversary. Bonds can be bought only by people over 16. Maximum holding per child (for all issues) is £1000.

Guaranteed income bonds   Available from insurance companies. You invest a lump sum for a fixed period and get a fixed rate of return over a set period of years. It can be paid out annually, half yearly or sometimes monthly. Interest is paid net of tax and usually cannot be reclaimed by non-taxpayers. You must invest a minimum of between £1000 and £2000. Maximum holdings vary.

Guaranteed growth bond   These are similar, except that the interest accumulates. At the end of the term the insurance company pays the original investment plus the interest.

GETTING ADVICE

If you have come into an inheritance, taken a golden handshake or retired and commuted part of your pension you will suddenly be faced with a big decision on how best to invest it. You may want to do this for yourself or feel that you need the help of experts. There is no shortage of people willing to advise on investments. You can get help from your bank or building society, a financial adviser, an insurance company or broker, an accountant or a solicitor. Some stockbrokers and estate agents also provide an advice service.

Under the Financial Services Act, 1986, investment advisers are required to be either 'tied' – which means they promote the products of one company only – or 'independent'. Independent advisers can offer financial products from different companies.

Either way they must be regulated or authorized by an appropriate self-regulatory organization or a recognized professional body. They cannot trade legally without this authorization. If they do not belong, clients who let them handle their affairs will not be covered by the industry's compensation scheme. This is run by the Securities and Investments Board, the watchdog which supervises the regulation of financial services.

Advisers must tell you whether they are 'tied' or 'independent' and which regulatory body they or the company they represent belong to. All advisers get their income either by earning commission from the companies whose products they sell or by charging a fee to the client.

They must offer 'best advice' initially and then 'best execution' when the client decides to go ahead. That means they are legally obliged to offer the best product for your circumstances – not the deal that will earn them the most commission. Keep in mind, however, that the amount of commission varies from one product to another and this might influence your adviser.

Competent advisers will ask lots of questions about your circumstances, so that they have a good picture of your situation, needs and expectations. It is a good idea to shop around for advice as for anything else.

The main sources of advice are as follows.

Banks and building societies At one time the local manager would give advice on a range of products from various companies. But in recent years most banks and building societies have become 'tied' to one company and promote only their services. These may still offer a wide selection but you could be missing out on something more suitable that is available elsewhere. However, even if a bank or building society is tied it can refer you to someone who can give independent advice – but *only* if you request it.

Independent financial advisers They specialize in investment and insurance products from different companies, although they may be limited in which type of product they sell.

They must belong to FIMBRA (*The Financial Intermediaries' Managers' and Brokers' Regulatory Association*), *Hertsmere House, Hertsmere Road, London E14 4AB*. The initials should appear on any letter headings or advertisements.

Accountants and solicitors They are another traditional source of help and may be authorized to offer investment advice in the normal course of their business. They may have subsidiary companies which specialize in investments. Their respective professional bodies forbid them to be tied to one company, so their advice should be independent. Large accountancy firms, however, will probable be interested only if you have a lot of money to invest, and even with smaller firms you should check what fees they are likely to charge. You will be protected by their own compensation schemes if anything goes wrong. Accountants are regulated by the *Institute of Chartered Accountants, Gloucester House, 399 Silbury Boulevard, Central Milton Keynes, MK9 2HL*. Solicitors are regulated by the Law Society, Portland House, Stag Place, London SW1E 5BL.

Insurance brokers who give investment advice should be members of IBRC (*Insurance Brokers' Registration Council*), *15 St Helen's Place, London EC3A 6DS*.

Stockbrokers are regulated by the SFA *Securities and Futures Authority, Stock Exchange Buildings, Old Broad Street, London EC2N 1EQ*.

Insurance company representatives who may be self-employed or represent a company, are not directly regulated, but their companies are regulated by LAUTRO (*Life Assurance and Unit Trust Regulatory Organization*), *Canterbury House, 2–6 Sydenham Road, Croydon, CR0 9XE*.

Knowing Your Rights

When you buy something or pay for a service you expect to get value for money. Most of the time that is what happens. But when things go wrong it can be the start of a long battle to get them put right. Have you ever in a crisis called in a plumber who presents you with a bill that is so over the top that you feel like framing it? Have you ever bought a second-hand car that wasn't all it was claimed to be? Or gone on holiday hoping to relax from the worries of the world only to spend hours held up at the airport and then been put in a hotel that is nothing like the one you had booked?

Then there are those occasions when you think you are in the right but you can't be sure. What rights do you really have when you buy a video in the sales at a bargain price, only to find when you get it home that it won't work? Supposing you walk into a shop that displays a sign saying that no refunds are given on sales goods. It doesn't sound right, but is the shopkeeper entitled to make such a stipulation?

If you buy a new car and it breaks down because of a series of faults after a couple of months, you will probably think you are entitled to ask for your money back. But would you be within your rights? You might be surprised at the answer.

Someone somewhere every day is facing situations like these. There are seldom easy answers (although it is usually easier when you are dealing with a reputable trader). But knowing your rights and how to go about getting them is half the battle.

The Law

Criminal law discourages behaviour which is harmful to the community as a whole. In the consumer field this applies to areas such as deliberate fraud, false descriptions and dangerous acts such as selling bad food or electrically unsafe goods. Offenders are prosecuted either by Trading Standards/Consumer Protection officers or Environmental Health officers or by the police. In Scotland prosecutions in consumer cases are brought by the procurators-fiscal.

In England, Wales and Scotland courts can order compensation for those who have suffered personal injury, loss or damage as a result of someone's criminal activity. If, however, you have bought faulty goods your best hope of compensation lies with the civil law.

Civil law concerns your rights as an individual and the rights of other members of the community. When you buy goods from a shop the sale is governed by the civil law of contract. If the goods are faulty and the trader refuses to put the matter right you can choose to enforce your rights under civil law by suing in the courts.

Statutory law both criminal and civil law can be statutory, that is, contained in acts of Parliament. Examples include the Trade Descriptions Act (criminal) and the Sale of Goods Act (civil).

Common law is not contained in statutes but develops over the years from decisions made by judges in court cases.

Buying Goods

Whenever you buy something whether it is a pair of tights or a new car you are making a contract with the trader, even though nothing is written down. When you indicate that you would like to buy the article and the trader accepts your offer, a legally enforceable contract is made.

Under the Sale of Goods Act, 1979, goods must be:

* Of merchantable quality. This means they must be fault-free and reasonably fit for their normal purpose, bearing in mind the price paid, the nature of the goods and how they were described.
* Fit for any particular purpose you have explained to the seller. If you ask the sales assistant for a food processor powerful enough to knead bread dough, that is what you should get.
* As described. If a pair of shoes have 'made from real leather' on them, they should be made of leather, not plastic.

These conditions apply whether you are buying from a shop, a market stall, by mail order, at organized selling parties in private homes or from a door-to-door salesperson. If any of the conditions are not met the seller has broken his contract with you and you may be entitled to your money back or to compensation.

Legally, you are only entitled to ask for your money back, not for a replacement or a repair. But if the shop offers either of these alternatives you may be perfectly happy to accept. You are also entitled to ask for the loan of a similar item if the repair is likely to take a long time.

> *If you do accept a repair, write to the trader saying you reserve your rights under the Sale of Goods Act to reject the goods. You can then ask for a refund if you are not happy with the repair or if further faults occur.*

You should always complain to the seller, not to the manufacturer, as your contract is with him and he is legally responsible for the goods. You must complain immediately. You can lose the right to a refund and be left with only the right to damages (compensation) if you are considered to have 'accepted' the goods in the legal sense.

The law says this takes place when:

* The buyer intimates to the seller that he/she has accepted the goods (or signs something to that effect).
* The buyer does something in relation to the goods – such as altering them – which is inconsistent with the seller retaining the ownership.
* A reasonable time passes and the buyer retains the goods without rejecting them.

The phrase 'reasonable time' can mean a very short time indeed. In 1986 a court ruled that three and a half weeks was too late to get a full refund for faults in a new car. So if it takes a while for the fault to show up you might not get all your money back.

If you cannot claim a full refund because of the time factor, you are entitled to compensation, which is the difference between the price you paid and what the goods are worth now. This may be the cost of a repair. If the defect is very minor you may be entitled only to compensation for the reduced value of the goods or a repair.

Provided you have not 'accepted' the goods you do not have to accept a repair or replacement instead of cash compensation.

> *A trader does not have to sell you goods on display. He is inviting you to make an offer but he is not obliged to accept your offer. So you cannot insist that he takes something out of the window to sell you.*

SHOPPER'S RESPONSIBILITIES

You cannot claim a refund or compensation if:

* You were told about the fault by the trader, for example, if the goods were described as 'damaged'.
* You ignored the trader's advice on the suitability of the goods for any particular purpose you described to him. For instance, if he warned you that a food mixer might not be powerful enough to mix dough.
* You examined the goods when you bought them and should have seen the fault then. For instance, if you tried on a jacket where there were buttonholes but the buttons were missing, bought it and later complained because of its lack of buttons you would probably not have a case.
* If the trader had told you that he was not expert enough to advise you correctly

about your purchase. If, for example, he told you he did not know whether the glue you were buying would do the job you wanted – and you bought it anyway.

* The goods were received as a present. Only the buyer can claim.

* You changed your mind about wanting the article. Some shops will refund money or give credit notes in these circumstances but this is out of good will, not because of any legal obligation.

CREDIT NOTES

Be wary of accepting a credit note when you return faulty goods. If you cannot find anything else in the shop that you like, it could be very difficult to get your money back.

Sometimes the credit notes are valid for a limited period, such as six months. And, of course, once you have handed back the original goods you have lost the evidence that they were faulty.

THE SALES

You have the same rights when you buy something in a sale as at any other time. The goods should be of merchantable quality, fit for their purpose and as described. If you buy something marked 'seconds' or 'imperfect' or 'damaged' you cannot expect it to be of the same quality as something which is perfect. Examine it carefully. If you cannot see a fault ask the shop assistant or manager to point it out to you. It may be so slight that it is not really noticeable.

However, sales goods must still meet the three requirements of the Sale of Goods Act. Thus, if you buy a washing machine marked 'shop-soiled' which has scratches on the top you cannot later demand your money back. But if you find when you get it home and switch it on that the engine gives a grunt and then stops never to go again, you can ask for a refund on the grounds that the machine was not of merchantable quality.

Don't be put off by signs saying 'No money refunded' or 'No money refunded on sales goods'. A trader cannot wriggle out of his responsibilities if he sells you faulty goods. These signs are illegal. If you come across one report it to your local authority's Trading Standards/Consumer Protection department.

It is a criminal offence for a trader to mislead you about the price of goods and services. This applies however the price is indicated – whether it is in a television or press advertisement, in a catalogue or leaflet, on notices, on swing tickets, on shelf edge marking in stores or is given by word of mouth.

An official Code of Practice on Price Indications gives guidance to retailers to the effect that:

* The previous price should be the last price in the previous six months.

* The goods should have been available at that price for 28 consecutive days in the previous six months.

* The previous price should have applied for that period at the *same shop* where the reduced price is now offered.

If the price reductions do not comply with these conditions the trader should display an explanation such as 'These goods were on sale here at the higher price from 1 February until 26 February.'

The Price Marking Order, 1991, requires that:

* All prices indicated by traders to private consumers must include VAT as a legal requirement.
* In retail sales the selling price of virtually all goods must be shown. (This adds non-food items to existing requirements).
* If consumers have to purchase extras at the same time as the main item, then either the price has to be inclusive, or else indications for the extras must be given equal prominence.
* The price per unit of quantity has to be marked in the case of goods sold from bulk or prepacked in variable quantities.

You can be charged more if you pay by credit card instead of cash. Traders can legally give a discount to cash customers but they must make it clear if they intend to charge at two levels.

THE TRADE DESCRIPTIONS ACT, 1968

It is a criminal offence under the act for a trader to say or write something that is not true about the goods or services he is selling. Thus, if a car has 20,000 miles on the clock or a trader assures you that a pan has a non-stick coating the statements must be true. Special regulations apply to textile products to ensure that the fibre content is marked on them.

The local Trading Standards officer enforces the Trade Descriptions Act, which also gives him powers to enter premises, and to inspect and seize goods. If convicted, a trader can be fined or imprisoned. In England, Wales and Scotland the courts can award you compensation if you have suffered as a result of the offence.

BUYING SECONDHAND

When a trader sells something secondhand it will probably not be in perfect condition but it is still covered by the Sale of Goods Act. A secondhand cooker may have lost some of its sparkle but it should be of merchantable quality and fit for its purpose.

Your right to compensation will depend on many factors including the price paid, the age and how it was described. For example, if you bought a reconditioned vacuum cleaner which was said to be three years old and in excellent condition, but which did not work when you got it home you should be able to get a refund or the cost of the repairs needed.

GUARANTEES AND WARRANTIES

Any guarantee you get with something you buy is always offered in addition to your legal rights under the Sale of Goods Act and cannot take these away or affect them in any way. If the fault is fairly small you may decide it is quicker and easier to claim under the guarantee than to go back to the shop. (If the fault is so serious that you want to reject the goods and get your money back, you should claim against the shop. Manufacturers usually undertake only to repair or replace goods.)

The guarantee can also be useful if the shop where you bought the goods has closed down or where a defect does not show up until you have had a product for several months. Do not rely too much on long-term guarantees such as those offered for woodworm or damp treatment. Many firms go out of business long before the 20 years or so are up.

A number of shops in the radio, television and electrical business offer their own 12-month guarantee for parts and labour in addition to the manufacturer's guarantee. In this case it is probably simpler to take goods back to the shop if anything goes wrong in the first year.

When you buy a major appliance you may be invited to take out an extended warranty. You pay a one-off fee when you buy or soon after and the original manufacturer's guarantee is extended for anything from three to five years. Or you could be invited to take out a maintenance contract where you pay a certain amount each year which covers the appliance for free parts and labour and may also include a regular service.

Before committing yourself, read the contract carefully to see what it covers and consider whether it would not be cheaper to pay for repairs and servicing as and when needed.

DEPOSITS

Usually when you put down a deposit you are making a binding contract. So if you later change your mind about wanting goods (or a service) the trader can sue you for his losses. In the case of a shopkeeper it may be for the full price of the goods if he is unable to sell them to another customer.

If you want to reserve something in a shop while you think about it, ask the trader if he will agree to return your deposit provided you let him know within a short time, but get his agreement in writing.

MAIL ORDER SHOPPING

You are generally well protected when you buy from a catalogue published by one of the large mail order companies. They belong to the Mail Order Traders' Association which has a code of practice agreed with the Office of Fair Trading.

The code requires members to produce catalogues that are comprehensive and which accurately describe the goods. Delivery dates quoted should be met and if there is any undue delay you should be told. Refunds involving unwanted or faulty goods should be made promptly. If you have to pay any surcharges or there is restricted availability of goods this should be indicated. Goods normally requiring servicing should be offered on the basis that suitable facilities are available.

The Mail Order Traders' Association is at: *100 Old Hall Street, Liverpool L3 9DT.*

> *If mail order goods are lost in the post, legally speaking you have to bear the loss, provided the trader has entrusted the goods to a reputable carrier. In practice, many traders will themselves bear the loss as a matter of good will.*

BUYING FROM A NEWSPAPER OR MAGAZINE

There are various mail order protection schemes run by some publishers of newspapers and magazines. They are intended to protect readers who have no chance of receiving either the goods ordered or their money back because the trader has stopped trading.

Look out for short statements in the newspaper or magazine publicizing the schemes. They are usually headed 'Readers' Protection Scheme' or 'Mail Order Protection Scheme.'

> *If you receive goods through the post that you have not ordered and do not wish to keep you can write to the sender giving your name and address and say that the goods were 'unsolicited' and that you do not want them. The company then has 30 days in which to collect them – or they become your property. Alternatively, you can do nothing for six months. If they are not collected in that time they are yours to use, sell or give away. Whichever course of action you choose, keep the goods safely and do not use them. Ignore any letter demanding payment for unsolicited goods or take it to your local Trading Standards/Consumer Protection department.*

DOORSTEP SALES

Most salespersons who call at your door are reputable. They will identify themselves immediately and say what they are selling. If you tell them you are not interested they will go away, providing you are firm. However, some are rogues who will tell any tale to persuade you to open your door – and your purse – to buy something you do not need and cannot afford.

Do not be taken in by claims that you are being offered a special discount providing you buy immediately. Nor should you be taken in by a warning that prices are about to go up. These are intended to pressure you into buying. Never think of buying anything on the doorstep until you have checked the shops and compared prices. Never say 'yes' on the spot even if you are interested. Always ask the salesman to leave you information and literature. If he is genuine he will not mind calling back. Never pay in full before receiving the goods or services. If you pay a deposit insist on a receipt with the firm's name and address on it. Never sign anything until you have read it carefully and understand what it says.

If you want to sign a contract, but only on condition that the goods are delivered by a certain date, then make sure this is in writing. Salesmen are often paid on a commission basis and can make rash promises. If you do buy make sure you have the firm's name and address in case of problems later. Be sure you know the true costs involved when buying on credit and compare this with the cost of other types of credit.

The Glass and Glazing Federation, whose members sell double glazing, have a code of practice which is approved by the Office of Fair Trading. Copies of the code are obtainable from the Federation at: *44–48 Borough High Street, London SE1 1XB.*

YOUR RIGHTS TO CANCEL

You may be able to cancel a deal when you buy from a doorstep trader. Cancellation rights should be in writing. If not, don't sign.

When you agree to buy for cash anything costing more than £35 from a salesman who calls uninvited at your home you normally have seven days in which you can cancel. (You do not have this cooling-off period if you filled in and sent off a coupon or otherwise invited the salesman to call.)

When buying anything on credit costing more than £50 you can cancel whether you invited the salesman to call or not. You should be given a copy of the agreement that sets out your cancellation rights when you sign. You should also receive a second copy of your cancellation rights by post. You then have five days in which to cancel the whole deal.

You can cancel credit deals only if you have discussed them face to face with the trader and signed the forms away from their premises. You cannot cancel if you sign in their shops, offices or at temporary premises such as exhibition stands or if you negotiate the deal over the phone.

DIRECT MAIL

If you object to the amount of or type of advertising leaflets that are pushed through your letter box by the postman you can ask for your name to be taken off commercial mailing lists. You can also apply to receive more sales literature. Write to: *The Mailing Preference Service, Freepost 22, London W1E 7EZ.* They will send you a form to fill in.

If you opt to receive less mail your wishes will be passed on to those firms which support the Mailing Preference Service (this includes the majority of firms that do business by mail). It will not stop all 'junk mail'. For instance, smaller companies may not belong to the MPS and there may be stores and charities that send you leaflets as a customer or subscriber.

TELEPHONE SELLING

This is the latest and fastest-growing sales technique used to market a wide range of products from kitchens to life insurance. The Direct Marketing Association (UK) lays down guidelines for its members.

If you have any doubts whatsoever about the nature of the call ask if the caller is selling something. If you are not interested, say 'no thanks' and put the phone down. If you are interested give yourself plenty of time to think it over and compare prices.

PARTY PLAN SELLING

A great variety of products, ranging from underwear to kitchenware, are offered for sale at selling parties held in people's homes. On the whole the goods on display are of good quality but you should try to compare them with what is available in the shops.

Your rights with respect to faulty goods are precisely the same as when you buy them from a shop. If you have a complaint, tell the agent who organized the party. If he or she is unable to help, write to the Direct Selling Association, provided that the firm is a member. The address of the Association is: *29 Floral Street, London WC2E 9DP*.

Most companies organizing these parties are members of the Direct Selling Association and work to a code of practice which states that customers should have two weeks in which to change their minds about goods ordered and get their deposit refunded.

BUYING AT MARKETS

When you buy at a market you have the same rights as when you buy at a shop. You can usually rely on stallholders who have a regular pitch. If something is not up to standard they will generally give you your money back or else offer an exchange. If you cannot find the stallholder ask for the name and address of the company running the market or visit the market superintendent in the local council offices. Market traders have to be licensed by the local authority who keep a record of names and addresses.

ONE-DAY SALES

Some one-day sales held in halls, hotels or maybe pubs are genuine and some are mock auctions which are illegal and the cause of many complaints to Trading Standards officers.

They are often advertised at short notice, perhaps by fly-posting or through leaflets thrust into the hands of high-street shoppers. The aim is to make a quick killing – relying on the gullibility of the customers. The organizers then move on, leaving no trace or forwarding address.

The goods they are selling might be advertised as bankrupt stock but they are likely to be rubbish which no genuine trader would dream of selling. Some might even be dangerous.

If you attend one of these sales, check that the name and address of the organizer are on any advertising material. If you cannot see it, beware. Also, ask to examine the goods beforehand. Be suspicious if the organizer will not permit this.

Look out for the refund trick. Goods are offered at a price such as £10 and then a refund of £8 is offered if you buy. Only accomplices planted in the audience get the refund – not ordinary customers. If you do buy something try to get a receipt giving full details of the trader's name and address.

AUCTIONS

You need to be sure of what you are buying before you bid for something at an auction. You may have only a limited opportunity to check the item beforehand. An auction is not a 'consumer sale' in the normal sense of the phrase so you have virtually no rights if you end up with faulty goods. The conditions of sale usually state that neither the auctioneer nor the seller are responsible for the genuineness or the condition of the goods on sale. However, if you felt that it was unreasonable for an auctioneer to rely on a condition denying responsibility you could challenge this in court under the Unfair Contract Terms Act.

If you are thinking of buying at an auction try to get to the preview and examine any articles you like very carefully. Check the conditions of sale. Be prepared to pay cash or at least 25% by way of a deposit and the rest soon afterwards. Ask what the delivery charge is and what the time limit is for removing goods. The conditions may state that unless purchases are removed they can be resold. If you find that you have made a bid for the wrong lot and get it, tell the auctioneer's clerk as soon as you possibly can. You may be lucky and it will be re-offered but the auctioneer is under no obligation to do so.

BUYING PRIVATELY

When you buy something privately you have fewer rights if anything goes wrong than if you buy from a trader. Some traders try to cash in on this by advertising in small ad columns and pretending to be private sellers. This is illegal and publications often carry a warning notice pointing this out. If you buy something faulty and you suspect that the seller is a trader in disguise, tell your local Trading Standards/ Consumer Protection department.

When a private individual sells something it does not have to be of 'merchantable quality' or 'fit for its purpose.' The Sale of Goods Act states that goods bought privately merely have to match their descriptions. The only other legal requirement on private sellers is that they must not make false statements of fact.

If the goods are faulty you will probably have to rely on what was said or written for any remedy. It is therefore a good idea to take along a friend who is knowledgeable about the particular item and who could act as a witness when you buy something expensive.

Ask direct questions about whether the article works well and how long the owner has had it. If it is something mechanical ask the owner to give you a demonstration so that you can see it works.

Safety

Until a few years ago anyone who was injured or suffered damage from an unsafe product had to prove that the manufacturer had been negligent before they could successfully sue for damages. But the Consumer Protection Act, 1987, removed the need to prove negligence.

A buyer can already sue a supplier, without proof of negligence, under the Sale of Goods Act. Now anyone injured by a defective product has the right to sue the producer, importer or own-brand supplier.

If you have been harmed by a product seek advice from your Citizens' Advice Bureau or a solicitor. You will have to show that the product did have the defect that caused the damage. The manufacturers or the importer (or the supplier if neither can be identified) might contest the case and may try to show that you misused the product. But the burden of proof is on them. A 'defective product' is one that does not supply the standard of safety you are entitled to expect, bearing in mind its use and age.

There are also a large number of regulations made under Consumer Protection Acts which make it illegal to offer certain types of goods for sale unless they conform to statutory safety standards. Common household articles covered include: babies' dummies, carrycot stands, chemicals (packaging, warning labels), crash helmets, electric blankets, electrical equipment, fireguards on heaters, medicines, nightdresses (flame resistant material), oil heaters, pencils (lead content) and toys.

Look out for The British Standard safety mark, which can be found only on those goods which comply with the standards for safety laid down by the British Standards Institution. It is found mostly on gas appliances such as fires and cookers, and on some electric light fittings. Also look out for the BEAB label on any electrical product. A product carrying this label has been passed as safe by the British Electrotechnical Approvals Board. Many household articles such as food mixers, kettles and toasters carry it.

Electrical equipment with this sign on the rating plate or body of the appliance indicates double insulation which does not require an earth wire. It is found on articles such as television sets, electric lawnmowers, hair driers, electric drills and vacuum cleaners.

Gas work   The CORGI symbol is an indication of a firm's competence in terms of safety. The letters stand for 'Confederation for the Registration of Gas Installers', and mean that a firm has gained the necessary approval to carry out work on gas installations, complying with British standard codes of practice and government safety regulations.

Electrical work   On electrical work look for the sign of the National Inspection Council for Electrical Installation Contracting, which gives protection against unsafe or faulty workmanship. An electrical contractor who displays this sign has agreed to have work checked periodically by an NICEIC engineer to ensure that it complies with current regulations.

If you buy a product which you suspect is unsafe take it back to the trader who sold it to you. A dangerous product is not of merchantable quality and you are entitled to your money back. You should also tell your local Trading Standards/Consumer Protection department. Under the Consumer Protection Act it is a criminal offence to supply unsafe consumer goods in the United Kingdom.

If something you have bought injures you or damages your property you may be able to sue the supplier for breach of contract under the Sale of Goods Act, or for breach of statutory duty or for negligence.

If someone else is injured because the product you bought was unsafe, action should be taken against the manufacturer or importer, since the Sale of Goods Act covers only the contract between the trader and buyer (yourself).

> *You cannot usually tell whether a product is safe by looking at it, but with some items such as cheap children's toys a careful examination can sometimes reveal defects, such as sharp edges or parts that could easily come off and be swallowed by a child.*

In general you have more protection if you buy well-known brands, or from a major store or group because reputable manufacturers and retailers have stringent quality control checks and are keen to maintain their reputations. But even the most reputable firms can make mistakes. They usually advertise for the return to the shops of any goods which have been found to be defective.

Look out for the Kitemark label on goods. It means not only that the goods conform to British Standards but that samples of this particular product have been tested by the British Standards Institution.

Food

QUALITY

The Food Act, 1984, makes it a criminal offence to sell unfit food or to describe food falsely or to mislead people about its nature, substance or quality including the nutritional value. If you find something unnatural in your food such as a bandage in a loaf of bread or a piece of glass in a bottle of orange squash, report it to your local Trading Standards or Environmental Health department. Keep the food as evidence. Officers can take the trader to court if the offence warrants it but, if you want compensation you will have to take the matter up yourself with the manufacturer or retailer, or both.

Under the Food and Drugs (Control of Food Premises) Act, 1976, anyone who is convicted under the food hygiene regulations can have their premises closed down by a court order if these are found to be insanitary or in any way a danger to health.

LABELLING

Food must be clearly labelled so that you have some indication of what you are eating. Labels must include the name of the contents, a list of ingredients, in descending order of weight – so if the main ingredient is sugar that should be top of the list – the address of the labeller or packer, and any food additives used.

The ingredient list must show any additives that have been used as ingredients. They usually have an identifying 'E' number or they may be shown by their proper name. Unlike other additives, flavourings do not have to be individually identified by number or name. They are covered by the word 'flavourings'.

> *If something is called 'flavoured' the taste comes from the real thing. So bacon-flavoured crisps have been flavoured with bacon. But where the word 'flavour' is used the law says it does not have to contain any of the real ingredient.*

Buying Services

Whether you go on a package holiday, call in a repairman, have an extension built on your home or get your hair cut you are using a service. It covers almost every activity where you ask someone to do something for you. The chief protection when you pay for this service is under the Supply of Goods and Services Act, 1982. It mainly covers you when you make a contract for a 'pure' service, such as asking the dry cleaners to dry-clean your coat or the cobbler to repair your shoes. It also covers you in the case of a contract involving both work and materials, such as when builders, garages, plumbers or electricians supply some parts or materials as well as doing the work. It would cover, for example, bath taps fitted by a plumber or parts fitted by a garage or indeed a video camera hired to record a family wedding.

The Act states that goods supplied as part of a service, on hire or in part exchange must be of merchantable quality (the taps must not leak), fit for any particular purpose (a hired power drill must be strong enough for the kind of jobs you told the shop you wanted it for) and as described (if a car has plastic seats the trader must not describe them as leather).

If the goods fall short of any of the requirements you are entitled to claim some or all of your money back from the trader. The act also lays down the standard you should expect to receive from someone who does work or supplies a service, whether or not they supply the materials. The service should be carried out with reasonable care and skill. For instance, a builder who builds an extension to your house must do so to a proper standard of workmanship (the roof must not leak, the walls should be straight, etc.). Unless otherwise agreed, a person providing a service must do so within a reasonable time. For instance, a shop should not take three months to repair your television set.

You must expect to pay a reasonable charge. A garage that carries out a minor job on a car cannot expect to receive an excessive payment for it. But if a price is agreed in advance you cannot query it later.

The first right (about care and skill) applies even if nothing is said or written down at the start of your dealings with the supplier or if you have a written contract which does not mention it. The other two apply where nothing is said in the contract about time or charge. If a supplier does not observe these obligations he has broken his contract with you and you may be entitled to compensation.

ESTIMATES AND QUOTATIONS

Always get a 'quote' for the job beforehand and make sure you have it in writing. It is important to know the difference between an estimate and a quotation. An estimate is an indication – a good guess – of what the cost will be. A firm can charge you more for the job and you might not have strong grounds for complaint. Because many repairs are hard to assess in advance, some traders, such as builders, may give a basic figure and add a statement that this does not include anything else they might discover in the course of their work. If you accept an estimate like this make sure that the trader gets your permission before proceeding with more expensive work.

A quotation, on the other hand, is a firm price which, if accepted by the customer, is legally binding on the trader. In other words he cannot charge any more. Always make sure a quotation is marked with the word 'Quotation', so that there can be no confusion later.

If you want a job done by a certain date – for instance, a dress made in time for a wedding – make sure this is part of the contract. Try to get it put in writing if possible. Then if the firm does let you down you can cancel the contract and claim compensation for any loss you have suffered.

Ask friends and neighbours if they can recommend someone to do a job for you. If you cannot find anyone that way get quotations or estimates from several firms. Bear in mind, though, that the cheapest is not necessarily the best. Try to check on the firm and their standard of work. See if you can talk to some of their previous customers. If it is building work and you consult an architect or a surveyor they should be able to suggest a good firm.

PAYING IN ADVANCE

You may be asked to pay something in advance. To avoid problems later, do not pay any money in advance unless you have to. Sometimes it is unavoidable, as when you are booking a package holiday or ordering made-to-measure curtains. If you have to pay money in advance try to get the trader to accept a smaller sum. Never hand over money to a trader you know nothing about. If it is for something like building work you should decline and pay in stages as work is done satisfactorily. Retain some of the balance until you are happy with the job as a whole. If you do have to pay in advance, either pay by credit card (if what you have ordered costs more than £100 and you have a problem with the trader you may be able to claim your money back from the credit company), or else stick to companies belonging to trade associations that offer protection against lost deposits (called 'bonding' or 'indemnity' schemes). If you pay by cash insist on a receipt showing the trader's full name and address.

Before you place an order check out any special conditions. For instance, the contract may allow for the price to be increased. Make sure the contract gives full details of prices, cancellation rights and guarantees, and when the work will be started and finished. If it is building work, ask if any sub-contractors are to be used and who is liable if anything goes wrong.

THE BILL

If you do not agree with the bill, pay what you think is reasonable and explain why to the trader. It is then up to him to take further action if he wants. Sometimes a trader will not let you have your goods until you pay the bill in full. This might happen, for instance, with a garage that will not let you have your car back. In these circumstances you will have to make the payment but add the words 'without prejudice' to the account. This means that you have not accepted the bill as it stands and you can still take action.

If you are asked to sign a satisfaction note on completion and you have not had an opportunity to check or use anything, either don't sign or sign and add the words 'not tested yet' or 'subject to testing.'

If a firm makes false statements about the work done or the materials used it can be prosecuted. Claims such as '24 hour dry-cleaning' or 'while-you-wait repairs' or a tour operator's claim that a hotel is 'overlooking the sea' must be true. The Trade Descriptions Act applies to services just as much as to goods.

Some firms try to escape their responsibilities by using exclusion clauses or disclaimers on their premises, tickets, contracts or booking forms, such as, for example, 'Articles left at owner's risk'.

The Unfair Contract Terms Act, 1977, says that such disclaimers are not valid unless the firm can prove in court that the terms are fair and reasonable in the circumstances.

When you hire something whether it is a video or DIY tools read the contract carefully. In particular, see what it says about when you can end the agreement. Most contracts state that you must pay something if you pull out of the agreement early. With a few exceptions, the Consumer Credit Act states that you can give written notice to end a rental agreement after 18 months regardless of what the contract says.

REPAIRS

Any repair should be to a reasonable standard. In other words, if someone comes out to fix your washing machine you are entitled to expect that the appliance will then start working again. If you are not satisfied say so and, if necessary, telephone the repair firm and tell them that the fault is not properly fixed.

Try to choose a repair firm that has been recommended by friends and, for added protection, one that belongs to one of the trade organizations whose members work to an approved code of practice. In the electrical field these are: The Association of

Manufacturers of Domestic Electrical Appliances (AMDEA), Electricity Company shops and the Radio, Electrical and Television Retailers' Association (RETRA).

The first two deal with so-called 'white goods' – appliances such as washing machines, spin driers, refrigerators, toasters, electric cookers and freezers. RETRA deals with 'brown goods' – such as radios, television sets, stereo, videos and hi-fi equipment.

High call-out charges are a source of great concern. If you think the firm you have contacted are asking too much shop around. Charges vary greatly. Even if the repair does not go ahead – perhaps because the repairman says your appliance is not worth repairing – you still have to pay the call-out charge. It covers petrol, maintenance of the van, time (including travelling time), and time and expertise in diagnosing the fault and telling you about it.

Useful trade organizations include:

The Federation of Master Builders, Gordon Fisher House, 14/15 Great James Street, London WC1N 3DP. Runs a warranty scheme.

Building Employers' Confederation, 82 New Cavendish Street, London W1M 8AD. Runs a guarantee scheme aimed at driving out the cowboys.

National Inspection Council for Electrical Installation Contracting. Vintage House, 36–37 Albert Embankment, London SE1 7UJ. Registered electricians have passed an exam, and have their work inspected and equipment checked. They investigate complaints against members.

Institute of Plumbing, 64 Station Lane, Hornchurch, Essex RM12 6NB. Registered plumbers must be experienced and have proved their competence to the Institute. Their Business Directory of Registered Plumbers is held at many public libraries.

Association of Manufacturers of Domestic Electrical Appliances, Leicester House, 8 Leicester Street, London WC2H 7BN.

Radio, Electrical and Television Retailers' Association, RETRA House, 57–61 Newington Causeway, London SE1 6BE.

Confederation for the Registration of Gas Installers, St. Martin's House, 140 Tottenham Court Road, London W1P 9LN. Registered installers' work is inspected before they join and regularly monitored afterwards.

National Federation of Roofing Contractors, 24 Weymouth Street, London W1N 3FA. Members are all experienced contractors. They run an arbitration service.

The Heating and Ventilating Contractors' Association, ESCA House, 34 Palace Court, London W2 4JG.

Public Utilities

All the major utility companies have written standards of service, some of which are backed by guaranteed compensation schemes. Each industry has its own regulator who can set the terms of the utility's licence, impose limits on price increases, pursue consumer complaints where they think that the company has not dealt with them properly and enforce consumer rights. Complaints should be made in the first instance to the company.

ELECTRICITY

The regulatory body for the electricity industry is OFFER (Office of Electricity Regulation). It has 14 regional offices and the address of your local office is given on your electricity bill. There are also 14 regional consumers' committees, independent organizations representing consumers' interests.

> *Your meter belongs to the electricity company and they are responsible for the meter and the supply system up to that point. You are responsible for wiring on your side of the meter.*

The electricity companies have to pay compensation if they fail to meet certain standards. For instance, they must ensure that, if the fuse between your meter and the incoming cable fails and you call the company in office hours, someone should come round within four hours of your call. If there is a network power failure the company should restore your supply within 24 hours. And if they plan to interrupt the supply on a specific date you should be given at least two days' notice.

If the company fails to keep to these standards you are entitled to modest compensation. You can also be compensated if estimates for new supplies are not provided within ten working days to domestic customers. Queries relating to bills, voltage supply or possible meter faults must be responded to within ten days.

GAS

The regulatory body that oversees British Gas is OFGAS (Office of Gas Supply). There are also independent Gas Consumers' Councils in each region, who handle complaints locally. Their address is on the gas bill.

> *You have the right to be connected to the gas supply provided your property is within 25 yards of an existing gas main. You may have to pay. British Gas may be willing to connect you if you are beyond the limit but they are not obliged to. You are responsible for the pipes in your home on your side of the meter.*

Customers have no automatic right to receive stated sums of money as compensation from British Gas but in practice customer relations officers in each region have authority to award compensation for poor service.

BRITISH TELECOM

The regulatory body for the telephone service is OFTEL (Office of Telecommunications). There are also local telecommunication advisory committees which deal with complaints concerning local issues.

British Telecom has a code of practice which is printed at the back of the phone book. It has in addition operated a customer service guarantee scheme since 1989. This covers such situations as missed installation dates, failure to repair faults after one clear working day following the date the fault was reported, and missed appointments. Customers have four months from the date of the incident in which to register a claim.

> *You are responsible for the phones you own and any extension wiring in your home which was not installed by a BT engineer. If you call out an engineer and the fault is not their responsibility you face a stiff charge. If a phone is not working, unplug it and try another phone in the same socket.*

WATER

The regulatory body for the water industry is OFWAT (Office of Water Services), which is responsible for the privatized companies as well as for 24 smaller water supply companies which have always been privately owned. OFWAT has ten customer service committees whose addresses are not always printed on water bills but which may be available from your local library.

If the supply fails most water companies will try to restore it within 24 hours of being notified. After this they must arrange an emergency supply. If the water company expects to interrupt the supply you must be given reasonable written notice, usually at least 48 hours.

If the work is minor you may get less than 24 hours. You can claim nominal compensation if the supply is not restored within the time limit and for every 24 hours you remain cut off. The compensation scheme does not cover contamination of the water supply.

> *You are responsible for the water pipes up to the boundary of your property. If they leak you could be asked to repair them. If you fail to do this the water company can carry out the work and charge you for it. The water company is responsible for their stopcock, the meter and the rest of the supply system.*

POST OFFICE

The Post Office Corporation is made up of three separate businesses – Royal Mail, Parcelforce and Post Office Counters Ltd. Each has a code of practice produced with the help of the watchdog body POUNC (Post Office Users' National Council) and the Office of Fair Trading.

The code of practice states that all inquiries should be acknowledged as soon as possible and written inquiries within two working days of receipt. A full reply should be available within ten working days of receipt. If a claim involves lost, delayed, misdirected or damaged mail compensation may be payable by Royal Mail or Parcelforce.

Customers who are not satisfied with the response they are getting from the Post Office can contact their local Post Office Advisory Committee, an independent body that watches over local issues. Or they can contact POUNC at *Waterloo Bridge House, Waterloo Road, London SE1 8A*.

BRITISH RAIL

Under the Passenger's Charter travellers buying tickets on a daily basis must be paid compensation (in the form of free travel or discounts) if their train is more than one hour late. More complicated rules apply to season ticket holders. Some areas of the country are not covered by the charter.

Holidays

Booking a fortnight in Benidorm or a week in Torquay is not like buying a carpet or ordering a new kitchen. You cannot be sure beforehand what you will get. But you can take some steps to reduce the chances of your dream holiday becoming a nightmare by careful planning, by checking the small print and by knowing your rights and being prepared to use them.

Study the brochures carefully beforehand. Once you have decided where you want to go, see what is on offer. You could find that the same holiday on the same dates in the same hotel and with exactly the same food and accommodation can vary in cost by as much as £50 per person, depending on the tour operator offering the holiday.

Check on any extra charges. Find out what happens if your flight is delayed or your holiday is changed. Check on the amentities. How far from the beach is the hotel? How far are the local shops and public transport? Is the beach sand or shingle? If the brochure shows only an artist's impression of the hotel, ask if it has been completed?

The brochure must observe the requirements of the Trade Descriptions Act (all statements must be accurate and in no way mislead the customer), the Misrepresentation Act (this does not apply in Scotland) and the Civil Aviation Act, 1971. If you find that the facts in the brochure were not correct tell your local Trading Standards/Consumer Protection department.

> *If your holiday costs more than £100 and you have paid for it by credit card you may have extra protection if things go wrong. This is because you may be able to claim off the credit card company if you run into difficulties with the travel agent or tour operator.*

PROTECTION

New regulations, due to come into force in December 1992, lay down minimum standards for the way people on package holidays are to be treated by travel organizers and travel agents.

The legislation:
* Sets out the information to be included in brochures, and other information which must be supplied to the consumer before the start of the holiday.
* Defines the circumstances in which changes may or may not be made to the

particulars in the brochure.

* Lays down what must be included in the package contract.
* Regulates the circumstances in which surcharges can be made and provides that no price increases may be made within 30 days before departure.
* Places the liability for the package on the other party to the contract with the consumer (usually the organizer).

Apart from legal requirements you have additional protection if you book a package holiday with travel agents or tour operators that belong to either ABTA (Association of British Travel Agents) or AITO (Association of Independent Tour Operators).

You may also see the symbol of ATOL (Air Tour Organizer's Licence). All tour organizers using charter flights or making block bookings on scheduled flights must have this licence. If you see only the ATOL symbol you will not be protected if you are travelling on a scheduled flight. You will be protected, however, if it is a charter or part-charter flight. So always make a point of asking what type of flight you are booked on.

If an ABTA travel agent goes bust before you depart you are completely protected: you can either carry on with the arrangements you have made or obtain a full refund of all you have paid to the travel agent. If you are not on a package holiday, if you book a seat on a charter flight or get a part-charter booking, ABTA or ATOL protection will ensure you get your money back or are able to continue your holiday. If you want a scheduled flight, book with a travel agent who displays the symbol of IATA (International Air Transport Association) or who is a member of ABTA. Then your money is safe if the agent stops trading before you fly, provided a confirmed reservation has been made.

> *Cheap flights can be bought from bucket shops – agencies that resell spare tickets they have bought from airlines. They advertise in the holiday pages of newspapers and magazines. Do not hand over more than a deposit until you have seen your ticket. Ask for details of the flight and check with the airline that you are really booked on it before you pay the rest. When you reach your destination make sure you are booked on the return flight.*

INSURANCE

Holiday insurance is essential when taking a holiday abroad. It will provide cover if you have to cancel your holiday, or are taken ill or have an accident while away, or if you lose your belongings or have them stolen.

Most tour operators require you to take out insurance and some insist that you buy their own. If you object go to another operator. Ask to see the policy and study it for what it does not cover. If something important is left out get extra cover or choose a different policy.

Do not rely on the reciprocal medical health service arrangements within the countries of the EC. They will probably not cover the full cost and you will not be covered for any additional travel and accommodation expenses.

> *If something valuable is lost or stolen the insurance company will probably not pay out if they consider you have not taken care of the article. They might not reimburse you, for instance, if you left your handbag on the beach while you went for a swim and it was stolen.*

TIMESHARE

With a timeshare you pay an initial sum and have holiday accommodation for a regular week or weeks each year. You can also swap with another timeshare owner in another place or country. There are on-going expenses such as the cost of travel and annual maintenance charges, which need to be taken into consideration. You need to know that the building is up to standard, who is responsible for repairs and maintenance, who is responsible if services fail, who deals with complaints about standards, what you will have to pay on a continuing basis and the possibilities for resale and exchange.

These holiday homes are often sold at special presentations by high pressure sales methods.

If you are considering buying a timeshare:

* Never sign a contract on the spot.
* Do not take your credit cards to a presentation.
* Get proper legal advice and find out all you can about the timeshare company.

Finally do not look upon it as an investment that will make you money. There is little evidence that timeshare accommodation is likely to appreciate in value over the years.

How to Complain

It is irritating and frustrating when you spend money on goods or services that let you down. Many disgruntled customers never make a formal complaint because they do not think it is worth the trouble or because they do not expect to get satisfaction.

In fact it is nearly always worthwhile complaining. What is more, if people are not prepared to complain when they get poor service the standard will not get any better.

You are less likely to run into problems if you buy from reputable traders, ignore too-cheap-to-be-true offers or tempting discounts if you 'buy now', consider all aspects of a major purchase before committing yourself and do business with companies that belong to trade organizations with codes of practice offering a fair deal to customers.

Even the best traders can sometimes trip up but if you tell them quickly, take a receipt or other proof of purchase and ask to speak to the manager your problem should soon be solved. If it is a tricky problem it is better to write. Keep a copy of your letter and, to be on the safe side, send it recorded delivery.

Don't send guarantees, receipts or other proof of purchase – give reference numbers or send photocopies instead.

If you phone remember to first make a note of what you want to say, have receipts and useful facts handy, get the name of the person you are speaking to and jot down the date and time and what is said.

When you visit a shop ask for the manager or owner. It shows that you mean business. Try to keep calm and put your case clearly.

If you leave the goods behind, perhaps because you have accepted the offer of a free repair, ask for a receipt. If you have agreed to leave them for inspection only, then have this written on the receipt. If you get no satisfaction locally write to the managing director at the company's head office.

Don't be fobbed off with second best. If you are entitled to a refund and that is what you want, don't be pressured into accepting a replacement or a credit note.

If you still get no satisfaction you may be able to get help from your local authority's Trading Standards/Consumer Protection Department. They investigate false or misleading descriptions or prices, inaccurate weights and measures, the safety of goods, and problems with credit, selling methods and sharp practices. Alternatively, your local authority's Environmental Health Department may be able to assist. They deal with the law about health, hygiene, food, pollution, etc. Your local Citizens' Advice Bureau can advise on almost any problem from housing to faulty goods. Some bureaux have panels of solicitors, accountants, surveyors or other professionals who give free advice.

ARBITRATION

Various trade and professional bodies have their own low-cost arbitration schemes. Both sides put their case to an independent person – an arbitrator (or arbiter in Scotland). He considers the evidence and decides who is in the right, taking into account how the law applies to the facts put before him. Most of the code arbitration schemes are run by the Chartered Institute of Arbitrators. Both sides put in written evidence – you do not have to attend. Once you have agreed to arbitration you cannot change your mind and take the case to court. You have to pay a fee which is refunded if you win your case, together with any compensation the arbitrator awards. The decision is legally binding on both you and the trader.

Arbitration may also be offered as an alternative to court action by organizations that do not have an OFT-approved code.

OMBUDSMEN

Some industries have appointed Ombudsmen to investigate complaints by individuals. They are as follows:

Office of the Banking Ombudsman, Citadel House, 5–11 Fetter Lane, London EC4A 1BR.
Building Societies Ombudsman, 1st Floor, Grosvenor Gardens House, 35–37 Grosvenor Gardens, London SW1X 7AW.
Health Service Ombudsman, Church House, Great Smith Street, London SW1P 3BW.
Insurance Ombudsman Bureau, 31 Southampton Row, London WC1B 5HJ.

Office of the Legal Services Ombudsman, 22 Oxford Court, Oxford Street, Manchester M2 3WQ.
Pensions Ombudsman, 1st Floor, 11 Belgrave Road, London SW1V 1RB.
National newspapers also have their own ombudsman. Complaints should be sent to
the newspaper.

SMALL CLAIMS SYSTEM

This procedure in the county court is designed to provide a simple form of 'do-it-yourself' justice for anyone with a complaint involving a sum of £500 or less. There are no legal bills to pay if you lose the case. The procedure is simple, the atmosphere relaxed and the registrar who hears the case generally helpful. You or the trader can have a solicitor but if you employ one you must pay his fee, even if you win the case.

You give the court brief details of your complaint and fill in a 'request', which the court needs to prepare the summons that will be sent to the trader. You pay a fee which depends on the amount of your claim.

If the trader does not dispute your claim you can apply to the court for judgment in your favour. If he does dispute it the case will automatically be heard under informal arbitration procedures, except in special circumstances (for instance, if a complex question of law is involved.)

You and the trader are asked to attend a preliminary hearing where, if it is a very simple issue, the case may be decided there and then. Otherwise, you then attend the arbitration procedure carried out by the registrar. Both sides get an equal opportunity to present their cases. If it is a case of faulty workmanship the registrar may go along to see it for himself. The registrar's decision is binding.

Neighbours

Noise is probably the biggest cause of friction between neighbours. The main problems are caused by barking dogs, loud music or television, shouting and banging of doors or DIY activities.

In the first instance see if a quiet word will help: your neighbours may not realize how distressing the noise is to other people. If this has no result, write a note explaining the effect the noise is having on you and ask them if they would stop. Keep a copy of the letter and start keeping a diary of the dates and times of any noise nuisance – what it was and the effects it had on you. Keep a note, too, of any conversations you have had and what was said.

If the nuisance persists write to your local council's environmental health department. Under section 80 of the Environmental Protection Act, 1990, they can take action if they believe a statutory nuisance, such as noise or vibration, is occurring, or likely to occur or recur. The Act requires them to 'take all reasonable steps' to investigate your complaint. They may write informally to the neighbour, saying that a complaint has been made and asking them to do what they can to reduce the noise.

If it continues they may call round to see if, in their judgment, the noise amounts to a statutory nuisance. If it does they must issue a notice requiring the neighbour to stop causing the nuisance. If it continues the neighbour can be prosecuted.

With noises that occur only occasionally or where it is not possible for an environmental health officer to hear them, you can take action independently by complaining directly to the magistrates' court under section 82 of the Environmental Protection Act. This is a simple procedure and it should not be necessary to employ a solicitor.

Before applying to the court it is a good idea to write to the neighbour saying that if the nuisance is not abated by a certain date (such as two weeks), you will complain to the magistrates' court. The justice's clerk at the court will advise you on procedure.

You will have to prove to the magistrates beyond reasonable doubt that the noise you are complaining about amounts to a nuisance. Your diary would be useful evidence, so would evidence from other people who are similarly affected. If you prove your case the court will make an order for the nuisance to be abated and/or prohibit recurrence of the nuisance.

TREES

If your neighbour's trees overhang your garden you can cut off the branches that are on your side. You should then offer the pieces back to the owner. The same applies to fruit trees: you can cut them to the boundary but your neighbour is entitled to the fruit.

Many trees are the subject of tree preservation orders, so it might be as well to check before you get snip-happy. You can find out about this at the local council offices.

If your neighbour's trees or their roots damage your property he is responsible for the damage. You can sue him, although it might be simpler and cause fewer problems to claim on your insurance policy.

BONFIRES

If you are bothered by bonfire smoke approach your neighbour first and explain the problem. If this approach fails contact your local Environmental Health department. They may be able to take action on your behalf if they consider that the problem amounts to a nuisance. For a bonfire to be considered a nuisance it must be persistent – which can be difficult to prove. It will help if you have kept a diary and if other people can act as witnesses. If your local council are unwilling to act a private action may be taken in the magistrates' court.

Legal Affairs 11

Accidents and Personal Injuries

INTRODUCTION

In a case called Fowler v Lanning [1959] it was held that the victim of a shooting accident could not simply go to court and claim, 'the defendant shot me' and win his case. The court decided that as well as proving that he had been shot by the defendant he had also to prove that the 'defendant negligently shot me'. In other words, that the defendant had been careless. This is now a general principle of English civil law: that fault must be proved before any person, or their insurers, can be held liable for accidental injury caused to another person or property. (Criminal liability is different: strict liability may apply.)

Accidents are common, whether in the home, on the road, at work or even in hospital. Research has shown that most victims of minor accidents do not even seek legal advice, let along go to court to try to get compensation. Many people wrongly believe that because perhaps they were partly to blame they cannot claim. This is unfortunate because some injuries can turn out later to be more serious than at first thought and the amount of compensation can be substantial.

NEGLIGENCE AND DUTY OF CARE

What does fault or negligence mean? In legal terms it means that we all owe a duty of care to all those who it could be reasonably be foreseen might be injured in the event of an accident. But how careful do we have to be? That is the difficult question. Generally the standard of care varies with the activity. So motorists have to meet a common sense standard and medical doctors are expected to achieve the relevant professional standards at the time. The standard is an 'objective' one related to the group rather than a subjective one based on the individual.

A victim of an accident will have to show three things in order to claim from the person who caused the accident: that the person who caused the accident could have foreseen that the accident might happen; had failed to take reasonable care; and that the failure had caused injury, damage or financial loss.

COMPENSATION FOR PERSONAL INJURY

When someone causes harm to another or to their property the normal remedy which the law gives is an award of money, in law called 'damages'. The general principle in damages was stated in Livingstone v Rawyards Coal Co [1880]: 'where any injury is to be compensated by damages . . . you should as nearly as possible get at that sum which will put the person in the same position as they would have been had they not sustained the wrong'.

That principle works easily with damage to property, where the damaged item can be replaced, but it is difficult with personal injury or death. Lawyers will use the following checklist, grouped under two headings, General and Special damages, to try to arrive at a total compensation figure.

General damages (these cannot be given a precise value) are: pain and suffering, including nervous shock and distress; scars and disfigurement; physical and mental disablement; reductions in quality of life; loss of earning capacity; loss of expectation of life. Special damages (these cover those losses with a precise value) are: loss of earnings; damage to property including clothing; travel expenses; medical expenses.

The sums awarded for general damages have been steadily rising and lawyers work on case precedents which set the 'going rate' for different injuries. These can range from a few hundred pounds for a small scar to over a million for brain damage. Some examples of general damages are: death of 21-year-old, £150,000; quadriplegia at birth, £105,000; loss of sight, £25,000; broken wrist, £3000.

SPECIAL CASES

Criminal injuries Victims of crimes of violence may be able to claim money from the Criminal Injuries Compensation Scheme.

Uninsured drivers If the driver causing an accident is untraceable or uninsured, the Motor Insurers Bureau may meet claims from people who have been injured or who have had damage to property.

At work Employers are generally liable for accidents at work even if caused by the carelessness of fellow employees. This is based on the principle of 'vicarious liability'.

Defective pavements and roads Local authorities have a statutory duty to repair and maintain their public roads and pavements under the Highways Act,

1980. Many pedestrians injure themselves by falling over obstacles on the pavements or uneven paving stones. In Littler v Liverpool Corporation [1968] it was held: 'A length of pavement is only dangerous if, in the ordinary course of human affairs, danger may reasonably be anticipated from its common use by the public . . .' It has been accepted that a difference in level of at least three-quarters of an inch would be necessary before the local authority would be liable.

Premises   Under the Occupiers Liability Act, 1957, any occupier (owner, tenant, trader, etc) of premises has a statutory duty toward visitors to ensure that they will be reasonably safe in using the premises for the purposes of their visit. Occupiers of dangerous buildings or land also have to take care that uninvited visitors, including children and trespassers, are not injured.

Armed forces   The Crown can be sued for negligence causing injury or death to a member of the armed forces whilst on peace-time duties. This could arise, for example, during military training.

Medical accidents   It is not enough to claim that a doctor has made a mistake; but it is possible to claim substantial damages against health authorities where negligence is shown.

HELP FROM ALAS SCHEME

This is available under the Law Society's 'Accident Legal Advice Scheme', whereby solicitors who specialize in personal injury work offer a free initial interview.

Children and Parents

INTRODUCTION

The legal balance between parental rights and the interests of the child has shifted considerably since the last century when parents, particularly fathers, had extensive rights and powers of control over their children. The welfare of the child is now the decisive concern. This shift resulted in the Children Act, 1989, which came into force in October 1991 and was described by the lord chancellor as 'the most comprehensive and far-reaching reform of child law in living memory. It brings together the public and private law concerning the care, protection and upbringing of children and the provision of services to them and their families'. (Criminal law concerning children is not included.)

REGISTRATION OF A BIRTH AND CHANGING A NAME

Every birth must be registered within 42 days. This is normally done by the mother although the married father or other responsible adult may provide the necessary information to the local Registrar of Births and Deaths. If the parents are married both names must be registered but if not the father's name is optional.

A stillbirth must be registered within five days of birth and a certificate signed by the doctor or midwife is necessary. There is an old offence of 'concealment' which applies to any secret disposal of the dead body of a child. A parent can change the forename on the certificate within 12 months, but not the surname. The distinction between legitimate and illegitimate children and discrimination in maintenance and inheritance rights were abolished by the Family Law Reform Act, 1987.

ADOPTION

A single person or a married couple can adopt a child. Adoption orders can be made only by a court and give complete parental responsibility to the adoptive parents. The natural parents must consent to adoption but the court has the power to dispense with this in limited circumstances. The person to be adopted must be under 18 and have never been married.

Adopting children from other countries is complicated legally and quite difficult to achieve successfully. The law and practice are currently being reviewed but the principle will be that the interests of the child are paramount.

Since 1975 adopted adults have been able to apply for access to their original birth record but the Children Act, 1989, introduced a new confidential scheme, called the Adoption Contact Register, to enable contact between the adopted person and the natural parents, and other relatives, where this is what they both want.

PARENTAL RESPONSIBILITY

The Children Act, 1989, introduced the new legal concept of 'parental responsibility'. Instead of the concept of parents' rights we now have the concepts of duty and responsibility towards children. The mother of the child has parental responsibility regardless of her marital status but the father has this only if he is married to her, or if he applies to the court for an order, or if he enters into an agreement, recorded on an official form, with the mother that he shall have parental responsibility.

Parental responsibility covers things such as care and maintenance, residence, education, discipline, religion, property, litigation, medical treatment and emigration. Parental responsibility does not usually extend to holding the parent legally responsible for a child's negligence or criminal action.

COURT ORDERS

Five new orders were introduced by the Children Act, 1989, and replaced the old concepts of custody, legal custody, care and control, joint custody and access.

1. Residence Order specifies with whom the child should live and may say that the child should divide his or her time between the two parents.
2. Contact Order covers how much contact the child will have with a person,

normally the other parent, by letter, phone or in person.

3. Specific Issue Order allows the court to give directions on the important decisions such as education, medical treatment or abortions.
4. Prohibitive Steps Order is likely to be rarely made as it limits the power of the parent to take specific steps to fulfil their responsibility.
5. Family assistance order is a short-term provision which requires a social worker or probation officer to assist the family.

LOCAL AUTHORITY RESPONSIBILITY

Under the Children Act, 1989, local authorities have a responsibility to 'safeguard and promote the welfare of children' and to work with parents who, on the whole, know what is best for their children. Among other things the local authority is required to: maintain a register of disabled children; identify children in need; publish its services; take steps to prevent the need for care proceedings; and provide services to prevent children suffering abuse. The court has available several different child protection orders. The Child Assessment Order is applied where there is reasonable cause to suspect a child may be in danger. The Emergency Protection Order is used where the child is in danger or will be if not removed to Local Authority care. The Care Order is a longer-term measure where the local authority takes parental responsibility for the child because of neglect or harm, including sexual abuse and mental ill-treatment. In the case of the Supervision Order the child remains with the parents but the family is assisted by a social worker or probation officer to prevent neglect or harm. The Education Supervision Order is applied for by the education authority if the child is not being properly educated.

Crimes and the Police

INTRODUCTION

For many people 'the law' relates to crime, and that calls for the police: so in this section both are looked at together. However, first a few words about the general principles of criminal liability and the different kinds of criminal offences.

GENERAL PRINCIPLES OF CRIMINAL LIABILITY

The central principle of criminal liability is that a guilty act requires a guilty mind. The Latin maxim is 'actus non facit reus, nisi sit mens rea' – an act does not make a person legally guilty unless the mind is legally blameworthy. This has two parts:

1. The conduct of the accused that has to be proved – known as the *actus reus*. Conduct is usually a positive act but it can also be an omission, such as failing to blow into a breathalyzer when required. The circumstances are also relevant.
2. The state of mind of the accused (the *mens rea*) – which, in almost all offences, must

also be proved. This does not entail a notion of evil but rather a state of mind that the definition of the offence requires. Common ingredients are intention, recklessness and knowledge. In theft, for example, it must be proved that the accused 'intended' permanently to deprive the owner of what was taken.

Strict liability offences Occasionally Parliament decides that for reasons of public policy an offence can be proved without the need to show *mens rea*. These are called strict liability offences and a person can be convicted of these even if their conduct was accidental and blameless. Many offences under the Road Traffic Acts are in this category.

GENERAL DEFENCES

Most defences are based on arguing that the prosecution has not proved one of the essential ingredients of the particular criminal offence. However, there are some general defences based on the concept of 'incapacity':

Children At common law children under seven could not be guilty of an offence but the Children & Young Persons Act, 1963, raised this to the age of ten. Children between the ages of 10 and 14 are presumed to be incapable of committing an offence. However, this presumption can be rebutted, if it can be proved that the child knew that what was done was seriously wrong.

Insanity Sanity is presumed unless the contrary is proved. Medical insanity is not enough, but if the accused is legally insane then he or she has a defence – at a price. Legal insanity was considered by the House of Lords in the case of McNaghten [1843]. Three tests must be satisfied. At the time of the offence the accused: must (1) have been suffering from a disease of the mind (2) which caused a defect of reason resulting in the accused (3) not knowing what he was doing or that it was wrong.

   This defence was really useful only in the days of capital punishment because if insanity was proved the accused was liable to indefinite detention in a mental hospital, which may have been preferable to the gallows.

Automatism or involuntary conduct The general requirement of criminal liability is that the conduct must have been voluntary. An involuntary act will not usually be punishable. This may arise in cases of sleepwalking, spasms, fits, automatism resulting from insulin taken by a diabetic, or even as in Hill v Baxter [1958] where it was stated that a driver attacked by a swarm of bees could not even be said to be driving.

Intoxication by drink or drugs Intoxication, like ignorance of the law, is no defence, because it is generally voluntary. However, there are two situations where voluntary intoxication may be a defence. The first is where it causes a disease of the mind under the McNaghten Rules above. The second is where the offence requires specific intent and, because of the alcohol or drugs, the accused lacks that intent, such as the dishonest intent necessary for theft. Involuntary intoxication, for example where a victim has unknowingly been given a soft drink laced with drugs or spirits, allows the accused the defence that the necessary *mens rea* was absent.

Duress, necessity and coercion   These are very limited defences where the life of the accused or a third party is threatened or where a wife says she was coerced by her husband.

Provocation   This can be used only as a defence to murder. If successful it will convert the charge of murder to one of manslaughter.

WHO CAN BE CHARGED WITH AN OFFENCE?

As well as the person who carried out the offence, called the 'principal', there are others who can also be charged, in particular, an accomplice – any person who aids, abets, counsels or procures. The *actus reus* is basically assistance or encouragement and the *mens rea* is intention or knowledge. Vicarious liability is exceptional and much less common in criminal than in civil law. Examples include those under the Licensing Act, 1964, where the guilty knowledge of, say, an off-licence manager is imputed to the licensee, who is thus liable for the offences committed by the manager. Assisting those guilty of an arrestable offence is also an offence under the Criminal Law Act, 1967; but, unlike accomplices, the offender is not liable for the arrestable offence itself. Concealing offences is also an offence.

TYPES OF CRIMINAL OFFENCES AND POWERS OF ARREST

There are three categories of offences and police powers vary with each:

Serious arrestable offences   Some offences, such as murder and rape, are always 'serious arrestable offences'; others are ordinary arrestable offences which the police officer judges as serious because of the likely results. The following are always serious arrestable offences: treason, murder, manslaughter, kidnapping and hostage taking, rape, incest or intercourse with a girl under 13, buggery with a male under 16 or any person who has not consented, gross indecency, highjacking, serious firearms offences, and serious offences under the Prevention of Terrorism Act.

As well as their general powers relating to all arrestable offences, described below, the police have additional powers under the Police and Criminal Evidence Act, 1984 (called 'PACE'), in dealing with serious arrestable offences. They are entitled to: search and seize material for use in evidence; take intimate and other body samples; carry out road checks; hold the suspect in custody for beyond 24 hours before charging; delay the suspect's access to a solicitor or to friends and relatives.

Arrestable offences   Arrestable offences, as opposed to serious arrestable offences, are namely: those with a sentence fixed by law; those carrying a sentence of at least five years' imprisonment; certain other offences, e.g. indecent assault and drink driving; and offences under Customs & Excise and Official Secrets Acts.

The police can arrest a suspect at any time without a warrant for either arrestable or serious arrestable offences.

Other offences These offences are the more minor ones not falling into the previous category. Generally, the police have no power of arrest for these other offences and can only issue a summons for the person to appear in court. This category includes most motoring offences.

However, the police can arrest for other offences if serving a summons is inappropriate or impracticable, for example when the suspect has given a false name or address, or to prevent other offences such as unlawful obstruction of the highway, or to protect a child or other vulnerable person.

Citizen's arrest The arrest powers of the police are additional to the ordinary citizen's power of arrest set out in the PACE Act, 1984. Members of the public can, using reasonable force, arrest someone who is actually found committing, or is reasonably suspected of being in the act of committing, an arrestable offence.

One difference between the citizen's powers and the police powers of arrest is that the law allows the police to arrest when the situation is much less clear, that is, where there is only suspicion that an arrestable offence has been or will be committed.

POLICE POWERS IN THE HOME

The police have powers to enter a home, search and seize goods or evidence. However, there is no general right of entry to private premises. The PACE Act, 1984, contains some of the statutory rules although there are many other statutes with their own particular powers and under that act five separate codes of practice have been issued. Police officers who break the code are liable to disciplinary proceedings, and evidence wrongly obtained may be rejected by the court.

Entry without a warrant Under Section 17 of the PACE Act police may enter without a warrant if: the occupier consents; they are entering to arrest someone; they believe on reasonable grounds that inside an arrested person's property there is evidence related to the crime; they need to enter to save life or limb; or they are in pursuit of an escaped prisoner.

Entry and search with a warrant A police officer may apply to a magistrate for a warrant to enter and search premises. This can be granted under Section 8 of the PACE Act or under other statutory rules, such as searching for stolen goods, (Theft Act 1968) or drugs. (Misuse of Drugs Act, 1971). Under Section 8 the magistrate must be satisfied that there are reasonable grounds for believing all the following: that an arrestable offence has been committed; that there is material on the premises likely to be of substantial value for the investigation; and that the evidence is likely to be admissible and not excluded by legal privilege. The PACE Act also gives police officers powers to stop and search people or vehicles in the street.

RIGHTS OF DETAINED SUSPECTS

'Helping police with enquiries' is an ambiguous expression which can cover those voluntarily attending the police station or those who have been arrested but not charged. The detention code says that suspects should be given a written notice setting out their rights, including the right to have someone informed of their arrest, the right to consult privately with a solicitor, the fact that free legal advice is available through the duty solicitor scheme run by the Legal Aid Board, and the right to consult the codes of practice.

Cautions   The code prescribes that in three situations suspects should be cautioned with the words: 'You do not have to say anything unless you wish to do so but what you say may be given in evidence'. The three situations are: at the stage of reasonable grounds for belief that a person who has not been arrested has committed an offence, however trivial; on the arrest of a person; after arrest and before further questioning or investigation.

Detention before charge   As soon as the suspect arrives at the police station the custody officer must decide if there is sufficient evidence for him or her to be charged. If there is not the suspect should be released unless there are reasonable grounds for believing that detention without charge is necessary to obtain evidence through questioning.

How long the suspect may be detained without charge depends upon the nature of the alleged offence: 24 hours in the case of ordinary arrestable offences, 36 hours in the case of serious arrestable offences, or up to 96 hours with a magistrate's warrant.

The code lays down detailed detention procedures, particularly with regard to 'reviews', which are designed to ensure that suspects are not forgotten about. One of the most important of suspects' rights is to consult a solicitor; and there is a statutory right to consult the 24-hour duty solicitor (if there is a local scheme in operation), although a breach of this does not necessarily justify exclusion of evidence.

Detention after charge   Further built-in safeguards apply after a suspect has been charged. They cover the conditions in which charged suspects are interviewed, the tape-recording of interviews, the presence of parents or adults where juveniles or other persons at risk have been charged, the provision of interpreters, strip searches, fingerprinting, body samples and photographs. In general, a charged suspect who has asked for legal advice should not be interviewed until it has been provided, although there are important exceptions.

CRIMINAL RECORD

The Rehabilitation of Offenders Act, 1974, sets out to make life easier for many people convicted of a criminal offence in civilian life, or in the services, in Great Britain or abroad, and who have since kept on the right side of the law for a specified length of time called the 'rehabilitation period'. Such convictions are 'spent' and for most people the slate is wiped clean. Some convictions can never become spent and must always be declared. This happens when the person has had a prison sentence of $2\frac{1}{2}$ years for a particular conviction. And some types of employment, such as certain professions, health services, social services, administration of justice and national security, are exempt from the benefits of this act.

The main advantage when a conviction becomes spent is that for most purposes it does not have to be declared to an employer. However, it may still be mentioned in any later criminal proceedings and may be brought up in civil proceedings if necessary for justice.

The rehabilitation period varies with the sentence:

Length of sentence	Length of rehabilitation period	
	if over 17 when convicted	if under 17 when convicted
Fine or community service:	5 years	$2\frac{1}{2}$ years
6 months or less:	7 years	$3\frac{1}{2}$ years
6 months – $2\frac{1}{2}$ years:	10 years	5 years

VICTIMS' RIGHTS AND COMPENSATION

Victims of violence may be able to claim compensation under the government's Criminal Injuries Compensation Scheme (CICB). Those who have suffered only financial loss, such as through theft or criminal damage, cannot use the CICB scheme and must either attempt to get a magistrate or a crown court to make a compensation order against the offender or sue in the civil courts.

COMPLAINTS ABOUT POLICE CONDUCT

The police must make a formal investigation of every complaint unless: the complainant agrees to an informal resolution, suitable for minor matters such as bad language; the complaint is withdrawn; or the Police Complaints Authority give the police permission not to investigate because the complaint is anonymous or vexatious or that it is not practicable to investigate. The Police Complaints Authority sometimes supervises the police in their investigation and must do so in more serious cases.

Home and Property

INTRODUCTION

Housing is one of the most important areas of the law. It is also one of the most complicated and untidy. The key to making sense of housing law is to understand the four different categories of 'occupation' or 'tenure' as it is called in law. The following comments cover some of the most important legal rights and responsibilities associated with each type of tenure as well as some of the special cases.

OWNER OCCUPATION

Although this type of occupation is one of the most common and refers to people living in a home that they 'own', it covers quite a variety of 'ownership', in particular both freehold and leasehold interests. Freehold ownership, without any mortgage, brings the most complete legal ownership and the least interference and restriction. Leasehold, on the other hand, is much more limited, since the leaseholder has only the legal right to occupy the property for the period of the lease, which may be long or short. Leaseholders should be regarded legally as tenants but are commonly thought of as owner-occupiers. This is partly because the 'ground rent' paid to the freeholder is often fairly low and the lease itself can be sold, sometimes for large sums. In large cities it is quite usual for building societies to give mortgages on leaseholds with at least 30 years left to run. The 'ownership' in leasehold refers to the value of the lease. New rights are being given to long leaseholders under the 'commonhold' scheme currently being introduced, whereby some leaseholders will in effect share the freehold.

Checking ownership The law has relatively recently been changed to allow simple checks on who owns land and property. There is public access, for a fee, to the Land Registry, which keeps up-to-date records on freehold and leasehold ownership, along with details of mortgages and other charges on the property.

Couples If two (or more) people buy a home together there are normally two kinds of housing law relationship that they can choose between: 'joint tenancy' or 'tenancy in common' (tenancy is the legal term even though they are owner occupiers!). In a joint tenancy neither can sell without the agreement of the other and if one dies the survivor automatically inherits the other's share. A tenant in common, on the other hand, can dispose of his or her interest as they wish and on death their share forms part of their estate, to be distributed according to the will or the intestacy rules.

Unmarried couples may have different legal rights to the home. In the absence of joint ownership, unless there are children, the partner who owns the home will be able to ask the other person to leave, as they will normally only be a licensee. However, if they have contributed money or time to building up the home, they may have what is called a 'beneficial interest', which can be protected.

Mortgage When a bank, building society or other lender makes a loan to a home owner a contract is entered into for the repayment of that loan, usually in the form of monthly instalments and often together with some insurance policy. Part of the contract involves the lender having a charge on the property which gives the lender the right to sell the property if the instalments are not kept up and also prevents the home-owner from selling the property without the consent of the lender. The general name given to these loan arrangements is 'mortgage'.

Bankruptcy and mortgage possession   Bankruptcy is a legal procedure which is forced upon someone who is unable to pay their debts: all the bankrupt's available property is sold and the money distributed fairly between the creditors. Sometimes this procedure is chosen by individuals as it may result in debts being written off. Bankruptcy cases are handled by the Official Receiver or an insolvency practitioner, who may require the bankrupt's home to be sold, although there are safeguards to protect the bankrupt's family. In such a case the home cannot be sold without a court order, which may be for a delayed sale.

In mortgage possession cases the lender, normally a building society, will in the last resort ask the court to grant a possession order which enables the home to be sold. The lender is under a duty to get the best price and any surplus is paid to the borrower. If the person defaulting on their mortgage has tenants or licensees living in the home those people will probably not have any protection against eviction because the home will have to be sold. One exception may arise if the lender actually knew that the tenants or licensees were living there.

Mobile homes and houseboats   Many people live, sometimes for long periods, in mobile homes or houseboats and with the benefit of some legal protection. Under the Mobile Homes Act, 1983, the site owner must provide a written statement which covers the contract details, names of parties, dates, descriptions, charges for rent services and so on. In addition there are statutory rights covering termination of the agreement and the mobile home owner's right to sell up. It is a criminal offence for the site owner to harass the mobile home owner or family.

RENTING OR TENANCY

This second type of tenure is also very common and in law simply means that a person occupies property owned by another, called a landlord, under a contract whereby rent, normally money, is paid in return. Tenancies are generally of two types, periodic or fixed term. Periodic means, for example, from month to month, and generally runs on until the landlord or tenant brings it to an end. Fixed term, on the other hand means for a specified duration, say six months or a year. Subject to the tenancy agreement, which may provide for reasonable access for maintenance and so on, tenants have the right to exclude the landlord from the property. Tenants also have important legal rights covering repairs and protection from eviction, although the Housing Act, 1988, removed much of the regulation of private lettings.

There are in law many different types of tenancy, depending on who the landlord is and when the tenancy began.

Secure tenancy   Generally, public sector tenants living in accommodation which is their only home are 'secure tenants'. This applies to tenants of councils and of most registered housing associations. As the name indicates, they have 'security of tenure', which means that they cannot be evicted unless the local authority goes to court and proves one of the various legal grounds for possession. These grounds are set out in the Housing Act, 1985, grouped into three.

Group A: rent arrears; causing nuisance; other breaches of tenancy agreement; tenancy obtained by false statement; tenancy obtained by sale; tenancy tied to a job; temporary tenancy.

Group B: illegal overcrowding; demolition or major works required.

Group C: property needed for a new worker; property adapted for the disabled; group property for special needs; the tenant 'inherited' a property which is too large.

The court will grant possession on the above grounds only if the following additional grounds are also proved:

Group A + reasonableness, i.e. the court has a discretion not to order eviction.

Group B + suitable alternative accommodation, i.e. reasonably suited to the tenant's needs.

Group C + reasonableness and suitable alternative accommodation, i.e. both the additional grounds

Other important statutory rights include the right to pass on the tenancy, to exchange, to carry out repairs, even to opt out of the council sector through the so-called 'pick a landlord' scheme and the right to buy, described below.

Unlike private sector tenancies there are no rent controls in the public sector, where rents are fixed by local authorities, subject only to general financial control by the government.

Assured tenancy The Housing Act, 1988, introduced two new types of tenancies: 'assured' and 'assured shorthold' (considered below). They have less security of tenure than enjoyed by the previous 'protected tenancies' covered by the Rent Act, 1977, and little regulation by law of the rent that can be charged. Subject to certain exceptions, since 15 January 1989 all new private sector tenancies must be one of these two and no new Rent Act protected tenancies can be created.

A number of tenancy agreements are excluded from the legislation. Some of the most important exclusions are: resident landlord; college letting; business use; property at a very low rent; very high-value property; genuine holiday lets.

These tenancies are unprotected although a court order will still be necessary for eviction.

Assured tenancies are lettings at market rents with some security of tenure, although the grounds for possession are more widely drafted than in the case of protected tenancies (described below).

If the court find any of the grounds in Group A it must give the landlord possession of property provided that the correct procedures regarding notices to quit and so on have been followed.

Group A: returning owner occupier; mortgagee, i.e. bank or building society, requires sale; holiday lets up to eight months; college property let out of term; residences for clergy; demolition or reconstruction planned; death of tenant, unless spouse takes over; three months' rent arrears.

In Group B the court has a discretion whether or not to make a possession order in favour of the tenant.

Group B: suitable alternative accommodation available; rent arrears; persistent delay in paying rent; other breaches of tenancy agreement; making a nuisance; immoral use of property; accommodation tied to job which has ended.

There is no statutory rent control over the initial rent that a landlord may charge at the start of an assured tenancy. However, the legislation does provide a mechanism whereby a tenant can complain to a rent assessment committee about subsequent increases in rent.

Assured shorthold tenancy   This is another new type of tenancy which arises if it began after 15 January 1989 and the landlord gave a special notice to the tenant and the tenancy was initially granted for six months or more (hence the name 'shorthold'). For an assured shorthold tenancy to arise four conditions must be met: the tenancy must be for a fixed term of six months or more; the tenancy must not contain any conditions allowing earlier termination; notice in the prescribed form must have been served on the tenant prior to the beginning of the tenancy; the tenancy would otherwise have been an assured tenancy.

The security of an assured shorthold tenant is very limited. At any time after the end of the fixed term the landlord has the right to obtain possession through a court order provided the tenant has been given two months' notice. In addition, during the period of the shorthold the landlord may be able to apply for possession on other grounds, for example where there is three months' rent arrears.

The legislation provides greater rent control over assured shorthold tenancies. A tenant who has just taken up an assured shorthold can complain to a rent assessment committee about the level of the initial rent.

Protected or regulated tenancies   These are tenancies created before 15 January 1989 and governed by the Rent Act, 1977. The protected tenant has more extensive rights than do assured tenants under the new 'deregulated' scheme.

The two main advantages of a protected tenancy over other tenancies are as follows:

* a 'fair rent' can be set by the rent officer, following a formula which does not take into account the means of the tenant and any scarcity value.
* greater security of tenure with much more limited grounds of possession, such as the return of the landlord as owner-occupier, or, subject to the court's discretion, a breach of tenancy agreement.

Unprotected public sector tenancies and licences   A small number of tenants are not protected by the statutory rules above, for example, people in some tied accommodation such as caretakers or police officers. Nevertheless, a court order for possession must be granted and harassment of any tenant is a criminal offence under the Protection from Eviction Act, 1977.

Excluded occupiers   This category is important because these occupiers can be evicted by a landlord without going to court, although violence or harassment must not be used. Excluded occupiers include, generally, those living with the landlord, some hostel occupiers and some holiday lettings.

Right to buy Some secure tenants of public sector landlords have a legal 'right to buy' their home at a discount if they have occupied it for two years or more as their main home. There are also cash grants available under Section 129 of the Housing Act, 1988, to enable local authority and housing association tenants to buy or lease a home in the private sector.

LICENSEES

Licences can look like tenancies but the difference is that a tenancy brings a legal interest in the property whereas a licence is only a right to use the premises. Licence simply means permission to do something which would otherwise be unlawful; in housing, it means permission to occupy property which would otherwise be a trespass. Licences can usually be ended by the giving of 'reasonable notice'.

Although licensees do not enjoy the same rights as tenants there are some legal safeguards under the Protection from Eviction Act, 1977, such as the right to four week's notice to quit and protection from harassment and unlawful eviction.

In 1985 the House of Lords in Street v Mountford considered the question of how to tell the difference between a tenancy and a licence. The Lords held that to be a tenant the occupier had to be granted exclusive possession or occupation for a periodic or fixed term.

TRESPASSERS AND SQUATTERS

A trespasser has no permission to occupy property and has the fewest legal rights. The term 'squatter', like 'owner-occupier', covers more than one situation in law. Many occupiers of short-life property (often publicly owned or managed) do so with the permission of the owners but are seen as 'squatters'. In law these are licensees. On the other hand, those that occupy without any permission are trespassers and are subject to the criminal law set out below.

Entering premises Some kinds of forcible entry by squatters can be dealt with as general offences under the Criminal Damage Act, 1971, or if violence is used there is a separate offence under Section 6 of the Criminal Law Act, 1977. This, however, does not apply if the person using violence to enter is a 'displaced residential occupier' who was lawfully occupying the property as their home immediately before the squatters moved in. In theory this would protect a home owner or tenant returning from holiday to find squatters occupying his home.

Eviction There is a special procedure available to obtain a court order for possession against squatters, called the 'adverse occupation procedure', and there are specific criminal offences covering false statements, failing to leave and obstructing court officers.

REPAIRS

The legal rights of tenants, including leaseholders, to have the home properly maintained and repaired are, like the rules on security of tenure and rent, complicated and untidy.

There are three main kinds of right to repair:

Contract The tenancy agreement or lease should specify what the repairing obligations are but the law also implies certain repairing terms such as fitness for human habitation and quiet enjoyment. There will be implied terms which also require the tenant to look after the property.

Tort It is possible that an owner-occupier may be able to sue the builder for negligence in the case of a badly built home, or for a breach of the Building Regulations, or under the Defective Premises Act, 1972.

Statute Several statutes are relevant:

The Housing Act, 1985, is designed to ensure that homes which are unfit for habitation are either repaired or closed. The Environmental Protection Act, 1990, gives tenants important rights to take action against landlords where they think that their housing conditions are affecting their health. These laws give local authorities stronger powers and allow action to be taken very quickly. Examples of disrepair covered by the law are: dry rot, burst pipes, condensation, mould growth, leaking roof, dampness, dangerous wiring, or dust, smoke, or noise pollution. If the landlord does not deal with the health hazard the local authority may carry out the repairs and the landlord may be prosecuted as well as charged for the work.

The Landlord and Tenant Act, 1985, and the Housing Act, 1988, set out some of the obligations on all landlords to keep in repair the structure and exterior of their buildings, plus any services and heating installations. Help for owner occupiers is available from a new system of home improvements grants.

HOMELESSNESS

Under the Housing Act, 1985, local authorities have a duty to make accommodation available for certain categories of homeless people who are in what is called 'priority need' where:
* there are dependent children
* a member of the household is pregnant or vulnerable, e.g. because of old age
* there has been fire, flood or comparable emergency

There is a code of guidance which also covers other factors, such as whether the person was 'intentionally homeless' or if there is a 'local connection'.

'Homelessness' in law, means that a person or family is either actually roofless, with nowhere to stay or, under Section 58(2A) of the Housing Act, 1985, the family has accommodation which it would not be reasonable for them to continue to occupy.

Marriage and Divorce

INTRODUCTION

Although it has become common for many couples to live together, and to have children, without being legally, married there are still very many important legal differences between cohabitation and marriage. This section considers the legal requirements and consequences of marriage and divorce.

GETTING MARRIED

Who can marry? The legal requirements for marriage are simple. People can marry each other unless: they are already married; either is aged under 16; they are of the same sex; they are closely related.

Young people under 18 cannot marry unless there is parental consent (or consent from the guardian or local authority). If consent is unreasonably refused the couple may apply to the court for permission. In some cases the prohibition against marriage between close relatives may be lifted subject to conditions.

How to marry In general, getting engaged is just a custom rather than a legally binding act. It is many years since suitors could be sued for breach of promise.

Couples can only marry in:

* a registry office
* an authorized church, synagogue or other religious building
* a Friends' meeting house if the couple are Quakers
* at home, in hospital or in prison if unable to leave

Couples can choose between a civil ceremony in the local registry office, or a religious ceremony. A civil ceremony can be either with or without a licence. In both cases a prior visit is required by the man and the woman to their own local registry office to formally notify the registrar, who will later give authority for the marriage.

The main difference between these two types of civil marriage is the length of notice required. To marry without a licence the couple must have lived in the district for at least seven days before they give notice to the superintendent registrar of their intention to marry, and the marriage can then take place after 28 days from the notice. Marrying with a licence can be quicker. In that case notice need be given to the registrar only in the district where the couple intend to marry, subject to the condition that either person must have lived in that district for 15 days. If a licence is granted the couple can marry after only one clear day.

When a religious ceremony is chosen, since the Churches of England and Wales are the official churches of the state, they can both conduct the ceremony and register the marriage. Other churches and religions can perform the ceremony but can only register the marriage if the superintendent registrar has provided a licence or certificate. Some couples decide to have separate religious and civil ceremonies.

The procedure with a religious ceremony is different from a civil ceremony. In the Church of England, for example, 'banns' must be read in the church of both the man and the woman on three Sundays prior to the ceremony. There are different procedures for Jews, Quakers, Muslims, Hindus, Sikhs, etc.

A religious ceremony performed before a wedding at a registry office is not legally binding. A marriage in a country outside the United Kingdom will have to meet the requirements of that country. It will be valid in the United Kingdom provided it was valid according to the laws of that country and that the couple were free to marry.

Bigamy   If a person marries in the United Kingdom when they are already married the marriage will be void. Bigamy was created as a criminal offence by Section 57 of the Offences against the Person Act, 1861 (subject to certain defences); and the Perjury Act, 1911, also makes it an offence to make a false statement in order to procure a marriage.

LEGAL CONSEQUENCES

When a man and woman marry they make a legal agreement to live together and maintain each other. By implication they are also agreeing to many other obligations.

Names   Many women choose to continue using their existing surname for all or some purposes. A married woman is not obliged to take her husband's surname.

Living together   Although the fact that the couple have lived apart may be grounds for divorce there is no legally enforceable obligation to live together.

Sex   Nonconsummation would be grounds for annulment and the law implies consent to sexual intercourse within marriage. Unreasonable demands for sex, or refusal to have any, may be grounds for divorce. The previous common law principle that a husband could not legally rape his wife is no longer accepted and husbands can now be charged with and convicted of rape within marriage.

Children   The law presumes that the husband is the father of children born to his wife within their marriage. A legal presumption can be rebutted or disproved by evidence to the contrary.

Housing   Both husband and wife have the legal right to live in the matrimonial home unless excluded by a court order. The law gives greater housing and property rights to married couples than to those who only live together.

Maintenance   Both husband and wife have an equal duty to maintain each other, although they can agree that they will not do so. However, this will not affect the statutory duty under the social security rules, whereby it is an offence for a husband or wife to wilfully neglect to maintain the other. Similarly, both husband and wife have a duty to maintain their children, a duty which is to be strictly enforced by the new Child Support Agency. Under the Child Support Act, 1990, which comes into force in April 1993 both parents are each responsible for the maintenance of their children, whether or not they live with them. The amount of the maintenance is worked out using a formula which takes into account social security rates and the income of the parent but is certain to mean higher payments than before.

Savings   In general, savings and other property owned by either partner before marriage do not become joint property unless agreed. Money and property inherited or acquired after the marriage are likely to be considered jointly owned, but much depends on the facts. So-called prenuptial agreements, whereby the man and woman agree who gets what in event of the marriage breaking down, may not be legally binding.

Debts   In general, a husband and wife are not responsible for each other's debts unless jointly entered into or one has guaranteed that the debt will be paid.

Civil   It may appear a hostile act but it is not uncommon for a husband or wife to sue each other in court on a 'friendly' basis. This commonly occurs in insurance claims arising from road accidents.

DIVORCE

There are strict preliminary conditions for a divorce: the couple must have been married for at least one year; and one of the couple must be resident or have been living in England or Wales for one year before proceedings are begun.

'Grounds'   Under the modern divorce laws there is now only one ground on which a divorce can be granted – irretrievable breakdown. Irretrievable breakdown can be demonstrated by one or more of the following five 'facts':
* Adultery and other intolerable conduct – adultery is defined as voluntary sexual intercourse.
* Unreasonable behaviour – the test for this is that the one partner cannot be expected to live with the other any longer.
* Desertion – where one partner has left the other against his or her will and has been away for two years.
* Living apart for two years – after two years apart the couple can apply for a divorce by consent.
* Living apart for five years – consent is not necessary if the couple have been apart for five years.

Undefended and defended divorce   If neither partner objects to the divorce it is called 'undefended' and is dealt with by a special, simple procedure. Unless there are children or complications there will be no need to attend court. On the other hand, if one party does not agree it is called 'defended' and lawyers will be involved.

The court will deal first with the central question of the divorce and then separately with 'ancillary matters' concerning children, money and property. In some areas conciliation schemes are in operation and there is also a national family mediation scheme which is relevant where reconciliation is not likely.

Motoring

INTRODUCTION

There is a complex variety of laws regulating motoring on the highway, covering who may drive what vehicles and in what condition, what may be carried or towed, insurance, the standards of driving, and what happens if things go wrong.

DRIVING LICENCES

A driving licence from the Department of Transport is required by people who wish to drive on public roads. Vehicles covered range from cars to milk floats and tractors. The very few vehicles for which a driving licence is not needed are bicycles, horse-drawn carts, and electrically assisted bicycles with not more than 0.2 kw of output and maximum driven speeds of 15 mph.

Fitness to drive A person is required by law to disclose to the DVLA (the Driver and Vehicle Licensing Authority) any health problems except those likely to last only three months or less. The DVLA may contact the person's doctor.

From 1 June 1990 drivers disqualified for some drink driving offences have had to provide medical information that they are fit to drive. Depending on the assessment by the DVLA, the person may be either granted a full licence, or a licence with certain restrictions, or refused a licence. If the person is not satisfied they can appeal to a magistrate's court against the DVLA's decision.

Age restrictions There are different minimum ages at which drivers may legally operate different types of vehicle:
* 14 years: electrically assisted bicycle
* 16 years: mopeds, invalid cars, small tractors
* 17 years: motorcycles, cars, vans and lorries up to 3.5 tons, large tractors
* 18 years: vans and lorries up to 7.5 tons
* 21 years: all other vehicles, including buses and heavy goods vehicles.

Provisional licence A provisional or 'learner driver's' licence has restrictions including:
Motorcycles: motorcycles only up to 125cc; compulsory motorcycle training course; no passengers on the motorcycle; L-plates to be displayed front and back; no motorway driving permitted.

Cars: learner drivers must be supervised; the supervisor must sit in front passenger seat, must be aged 21 or over, and must have held a full licence for three years or more; L-plates to be displayed front and back; no motorway driving.

Note that the supervisor is legally in charge of the vehicle.

VEHICLE REGISTRATION

All mechanically propelled vehicles must be registered. The registration document, sometimes called a 'log book', contains the following information: keeper's name and address; number of previous keepers; make and model; registration number; engine number; colour; engine capacity; fuel type. The registration document does not prove ownership. Information about ownership, whether the vehicle has been written off and whether the vehicle is subject to any hire purchase or lease can be obtained from H.P. Information plc (part of the Infolink Group).

ROAD TAX

All vehicles used or parked on public roads must display a current tax disc unless exemption has been obtained on grounds of disability.

MOT CERTIFICATE

All vehicles over three years old need an MOT certificate and some other vehicles, such as buses, taxis and ambulances, after one year. An MOT certificate is not proof of roadworthiness. The police can carry out a roadside test at any time on any vehicle. Visiting car drivers to the United Kingdom are not subject to registration and MOT testing of their vehicles for 12 months.

SEAT BELTS

Cars first registered after 31 December 1984 must have front seat belts and those first registered after 1 April 1987 must have rear seat belts fitted.

A driver and front passenger must wear a seatbelt. Since 1 July 1991 a rear passenger must wear a seat belt if one is fitted. There are limited exceptions covering reversing, taxis, milk floats and medical exemptions.

TRAFFIC ACCIDENTS

Accidents involving a motor vehicle are regulated by the Road Traffic Act, 1972. A driver involved in an accident must:

* stop, whether the accident was their fault or not
* provide their/the owner's name and address to interested parties or
* to the police within 24 hours
* if anyone is injured, insurance details must be produced and the police notified.

There is a standard charge, currently £19.30, for any casualty treatment arising from road accidents. This is charged to the driver of the vehicle, regardless of fault.

DRINK DRIVING

Driving or attempting to drive under the influence of alcohol or refusing a specimen are serious offences, carrying a penalty of a £2000 fine plus six months' imprisonment and an automatic one-year disqualification. Slightly lower penalties apply to the offence of being 'in charge', which covers both sitting behind the wheel, supervising a learner driver and even, in one case, standing three metres away from the car.

The maximum permitted alcohol levels are:

Blood : 80 mg of alcohol in 100 ml of blood
Urine : 107 mg of alcohol in 100 ml of urine
Breath : 35 μg of alcohol in 100 ml of breath

If the breathalyzer readout is 50 μg or less the driver is entitled to ask for a blood or urine test.

FIXED PENALTY SYSTEM

Under the Transport Act, 1982, an extended fixed penalty system came into force on 1 October 1986. This provides for fixed penalties of £12 for nonendorsable and £24 for endorsable offences. Failure to pay will result in an enhanced penalty of 50% unless the driver successfully pleads not guilty at trial. Each endorsable offence generally attracts three penalty points and disqualification arises when 12 penalty points have been accumulated on the driver's licence.

WHEELCLAMPING

The police have statutory powers to remove or wheelclamp vehicles which are illegally parked. In addition to this official wheelclamping there is a growing practice of 'private wheelclamping' of vehicles parked on private ground. The RAC and AA have successfully helped victims of private wheelclamping sue for the return of the release fee. The legal argument in those cases is based on the common law of 'trespass', although at the time of writing the law is still unclear.

Work and Employment

INTRODUCTION

Employment law, like many areas of law is a mixture of the old, judge-made, common law and the newer, parliament-made, statutory laws. This part covers some of the most important rights and responsibilities at work as well as the key distinction between employees and the self-employed.

EMPLOYEE OR SELF-EMPLOYED

With the exception of the sex and race discrimination laws, and the restrictions on pay deductions, all the following rights are available only to employees and not to the genuinely self-employed. The distinction is also important because of income tax. Perhaps surprisingly, the view of the Inland Revenue is not conclusive in employment law.

In Lee v Chung & Shun Shing Construction Ltd [1990] the Privy Council of the House of Lords (which hears a few cases from the Commonwealth) considered the question of the test for employee status.

'Although there is no single conclusive test . . . it has never been put better than, is the person who has engaged himself to perform those services performing them as a person in business on his own account? In determining that question consideration will have to be given to control but that is not the sole determining factor. Other matters include whether the worker provides his own equipment, whether he hires his own helpers, what degree of responsibility he has for the investment and management and whether he has the opportunity to profit from sound management in the performance of his task.'

There will still be jobs where status is not clear, such as homeworkers, agency staff and those paid on commission only. Note that the label that the parties put on the job is not conclusive. The advantages of self-employment are more generous tax rules on expenses and less red tape for the 'employer'. The disadvantage is that if something goes wrong, such as an accident or dismissal, the 'employee' may be unprotected.

ACCESS TO EMPLOYMENT

In the area of discrimination and human rights, there are antidiscrimination laws affecting access to employment.

It is unlawful under the Race Relations Act, 1976, and the Sex Discrimination Act, 1975, to discriminate directly or indirectly against a person in recruitment (and afterwards) on grounds of their race or sex. In Price v Civil Service the government was told by the court that it had to raise its age limits, at the time 28, on certain jobs because they indirectly discriminated against women who were more likely than men to be caring for a family at that period of their life. However, apart from cases of indirect discrimination there are no laws preventing an employer from discriminating against older applicants.

There are also rules which are intended to make it easier for people with disabilities and those with spent criminal convictions to get jobs, although these are much weaker than sex and race discrimination laws.

CONTRACTS AND JOB OFFERS

The job contract can be an informal verbal agreement or a written document drafted by lawyers. The heart of the contract is the employee's agreement to be willing to work and the employer's agreeing to pay for that willingness. Unless the contract says 'if there is no work then no pay' the employee should get paid even if there is no work available, because the employee has kept his or her part of the bargain. Sometimes the employer withdraws a job offer after it has been accepted by the applicant for the job. Generally this will be a breach of contract. Depending on the terms of the offer, which will ideally be in writing, the job applicant will be able to sue for at least the notice period.

INITIAL STATUTORY RIGHTS

The initial rights listed below are available to all employees (subject to very limited exceptions) regardless of how long they have been working for the employer. Most employee rights are provided for by the Employment Protection Consolidation Act, 1978, the 'EPCA'. The contract may provide for better rights, such as notice or maternity leave, but it cannot provide for less. The EPCA and the other employment protection laws lay down a minimum statutory floor. Under Section 140 of the EPCA any 'contracting-out' term where the employee signs away these rights is void (except in a few cases such as fixed-term contracts and redundancy pay).

1. When wages are paid, a written pay statement showing any deductions must be provided.
2. Reasonable amounts of unpaid time off for public duties must be permitted.
3. There must be no discrimination, including dismissal, on grounds of race or sex.
4. There must be no dismissal or other action for union membership or activities.
5. Employers must comply with all health and safety rules.
6. Men and women must be paid equal pay for like work or equal value jobs.
7. There must be no deductions from pay unless authorized in writing.

This last right, introduced by the Wages Act, 1986, is an important safeguard against the unlawful imposition of fines, deductions and the withholding of pay by employers. Note that there is no statutory right to annual holidays or public holidays. Those rights, if any, are governed by contracts.

LATER STATUTORY RIGHTS

Later rights depend upon how long the employee has worked for the employer. There are different periods of 'continuous employment' for these later rights.

Employees normally working at least 16 hours a week qualify at the periods set out below. Part-timers working under 16 hours but not less than eight hours a week have to have worked for the employer for five years to qualify for any of these later rights. Those normally working under eight hours a week never qualify.

Notice (after one month) After one month of employment the employee has a statutory right to one week's notice or pay in lieu. This rises after two years to two weeks, after three years to three weeks and so on to a maximum of 12 weeks. The employee has a right to be paid for this notice if it is not worked because of sickness or holiday, or because there is no work to do.

The employee has a statutory obligation to give one week's notice but this does not increase over time. However these notice rights are only the minimum.

Written statement of contract terms   (within three months) The law does not specify any particular form of the contract but it does require the employer to provide the employee with a written summary of the main terms of the contract within the first three months, called the 'written statement'.

Written reasons for dismissal   (after two years) If requested, the employer must provide written reasons for dismissal within 14 days of the request.

Protection from unfair dismissal   (after two years) An employee who has been dismissed after at least two years of employment has the right to complain to an industrial tribunal of unfair dismissal. The tribunal has to decide two main questions under Section 57 of the EPCA. First, has the employer been dismissed for one of the five statutory fair reasons: on grounds of conduct, capability, illegality, redundancy, or some other substantial reason justifying dismissal? (Subject to limited exceptions, such as the woman's health, it is automatically unfair for an employer to dismiss for pregnancy. A woman with less than the necessary two years of service may also be able to claim direct sex discrimination if she was dismissed for pregnancy. Webb v EMO Air Cargo [1991].) Second, was it reasonable for that employer, having regard to the company's size and administrative resources, to have dismissed that employee, for that reason, and in the way that it did?

In cases of dismissal on grounds of conduct, it has been held in British Home Stores v Burchell [1978] that the tribunal has to ask (1) if the employer had an honest belief that the employee was to blame, (2) whether this belief was based on evidence, obtained (3) after a sufficient investigation.

This illustrates a salient feature of unfair dismissal law: it is not enough for the employee to prove that they were not to blame; rather, some fault on the part of the employer has to be shown. If the tribunal decides it was unfair dismissal it can order the employer to take the employee back or make a payment in compensation.

Maternity rights   (after two years) If an expectant mother gives the necessary formal notice to her employer that she is leaving to have a baby and wishes to return to work afterwards she has a statutory right to have her old job back. She may also have a contractual right to return, although she cannot exercise both rights. An expectant mother also has the right to statutory maternity pay, and time off for antenatal care.

Redundancy payment   (after two years) Redundancy situations include those where the employer has ceased business, or moved, or where the requirements for employees to do work of a particular kind have diminished or are expected to. Some business reorganizations are borderline redundancy cases.

Some employees are excluded from a redundancy payment if, for example, they have been on strike, or have been dismissed for misconduct, or have unreasonably refused an offer of alternative work.

BREACH OF CONTRACT

Generally the parties can agree what terms they like and, subject to a few exceptions, the employer or employee can sue for any breach of contract. Generally the courts will award damages, although, exceptionally, injunctions may be granted.

Some terms may be unenforceable, such as restrictive covenants which are unreasonably wide, and some contracts may be totally unenforceable if there is a clear tax fraud.

CHANGE OF EMPLOYER

The later rights mentioned above require a specified period of 'continuous employment' with the one employer. However, in the following situations 'continuity' is preserved if there is a change of employer: transfers of businesses, whether commercial or not; the employee is taken on by another company in a group; change in the partners of a business; death of the employer.

Under the Transfer of Undertakings Regulations, 1981, it is unfair to dismiss employees because of the transfer; and the buyer of the business is generally liable for the actions of the seller.

INSOLVENCY

Some debts are guaranteed by the state Redundancy Fund if the employees are owed money because of the employers' insolvency. They include: statutory redundancy pay; statutory maternity pay; statutory notice pay; six weeks' holiday pay; eight weeks' arrears of pay.

REFERENCES

There is no statutory right to a reference but any referee is under a duty to take care to provide a fair and accurate reference.

Animals

PROPERTY RIGHTS IN ANIMALS

Generally, 'property rights' exist only in domesticated animals and not in wildlife. This means that the owner of a domesticated animal can be compensated for the loss of the animal but generally there is no compensation for the loss of wildlife.

KEEPING ANIMALS AS PETS

The Animals Act, 1971, distinguishes between dangerous and non-dangerous animals. Dangerous animals are generally those not commonly domesticated in the

British Isles, including some that are kept as pets, such as monkeys and snakes. The owners of dangerous animals must obtain a licence from their local authority and are strictly liable for any damage caused. This means that, unlike the general rule on accidents, the victim does not need to show that the owner was at fault.

Dog licences are no longer required by law (except in Northern Ireland). However, dog owners are still subject to many legal responsibilities including the following: they may be fined if dogs foul pavements or parks; the court may order dangerous dogs to be controlled or destroyed; civil and criminal penalties apply if dogs attack livestock; cruelty to dogs is a criminal offence; keeping 'fighting dogs' is illegal without an exemption certificate.

FIGHTING DOGS

The Dangerous Dogs Act, 1991, introduced special restrictions on so-called 'fighting dogs', specifically the American pit bull terrier, Japanese Toza, Dogo Argentino and Filo Braziliera. The act also made it an offence to allow any breed of dog to be dangerously out of control in a public place. Ownership of a fighting dog is illegal unless the owner has registered and obtained an exemption certificate. Exemption is granted only subject to strict conditions including neutering, implanting a microchip and insurance.

PROTECTION OF WILDLIFE

The Wildlife and Countryside Act, 1981, gives protection to some wildlife, including specified animals, insects, fish, birds and plants. Certain animals such as bats, badgers, deer and seals are protected by their own specific legislation.

The general effect of the legislation is that killing protected animals, damaging habitat, selling and trapping are all criminal activities unless a licence has been obtained. Some offences, such as badger baiting, are punishable by imprisonment and the destruction of the dog involved.

The law has been further tightened up in the Wildlife and Countryside Amendment Act, 1991, by the creation of a new offence of knowingly allowing someone else to commit any of the offences above.

CRUELTY TO ANIMALS

In addition to the specific provisions above, cruelty to animals is a criminal offence. Cruelty includes causing unnecessary suffering, neglect, and abandoning. The RSPCA generally carry out the investigation and police are responsible for the prosecution. Animal experiments are strictly regulated and require Home Office licensing. By law all animals for slaughter must first be stunned, although exemptions are made for certain religious groups. Circus animals are also protected and some performances, such as rodeos, are banned. Legislation now protects animals in markets by covering the conditions in which they are brought to market and how they are treated there.

Index

Page numbers in *italic* refer to the illustrations

Index